Dun & Bradstreet's Guide to Doing Business Around the World

Terri Morrison • Wayne A. Conaway • Joseph J. Douress

PRENTICE HALL
Englewood Cliffs, New Jersey 07632

Library of Congress Cataloging in Publication Data

Morrison, Teresa C.
    Dun & Bradstreet's guide to doing business around the world /
Teresa C. Morrison, Wayne A. Conaway, Joseph J. Douress.
        p. cm.
    Includes bibliographical references and index.
    ISBN 0-13-531484-4
        1. Export marketing--Cross-cultural studies--Handbooks, manuals, etc.
    2. International trade--Cross-cultural studies--Handbooks, manuals etc.
    3. International business enterprises--Cross-cultural studies--Handbooks,
    manuals, etc. 4. Intercultural communication--Handbooks, manuals, etc.
    I. Conaway, Wayne A. II. Douress, Joseph J. III. Title.
    HF1416.M78 1997
    658.8'48--dc21   96-40929
                                                            CIP

Printed in the United States of America

10 9 8 7 6 5 4 3 2 1

ISBN 0-13-531484-4

PRENTICE HALL
Career & Personal Development
Englewood Cliffs, NJ 07632
A Simon & Schuster Company

On the World Wide Web at http://www.phdirect.com

Prentice Hall International (UK) Limited, London
Prentice Hall of Australia Pty. Limited, Sydney
Prentice Hall Canada, Inc., Toronto
Prentice Hall Hispanoamericana, S.A., Mexico
Prentice Hall of India Private Limited, New Delhi
Prentice Hall of Japan, Inc., Tokyo
Simon & Schuster Asia Pte. Ltd., Singapore
Editora Prentice Hall do Brasil, Ltda., Rio de Janeiro

Dedication

To *Jeff, Monica Clarissa* and *Alexandra Lelia*
Who love to rock the boat.

Terri Morrison

To my *parents*
I hope I was a good long-term investment.

Wayne A. Conaway

To *Maureen, Joseph, Megan,* and *Amanda*
My most important sources—for inspiration, patience, and love.

Joseph J. Douress

No culture can live if it attempts to be exclusive.

—**Mahatma Gandhi**

Foreword

Globalization has become the watchword of American industry. In many areas, the United States of America has become a mature market. If American industry wants to grow, it needs to find foreign markets for its products and services. But 90% of foreign exports are executed by the largest 1,000 U.S. firms. Small and medium-sized companies have scarcely begun to enter the global market. These firms want and need to take advantage of the export boom. Unfortunately, too many of them do not know how.

Dun & Bradstreet's Guide to Doing Business Around the World is designed to be their globalization guidebook.

Businesspeople are not the only ones who will find this book valuable. Anyone who travels internationally or works with foreigners has use for this book. The data on how to communicate and negotiate with culturally diverse populations is useful whether one is in a foreign country or here at home. So, also, is the information on how foreign politics, religions, and societies influence decision making.

Change is a fact of life in international relations. Within a span of three years, the Mexican economy boomed, collapsed, and began to rebuild. Recognizing the volatility of their information, the authors have included a unique feature which will insure this book's value for years to come. Much of the time sensitive data in *Dun & Bradstreet's Guide to Doing Business Around the World* can be updated online. This insures that this book will be an invaluable resource, both now and in the times to come.

The judicious combination of cultural, political, and trade data in this excellent book makes it an effective tool for everyone, from the Fortune 500 to the individual entrepreneur.

Hans H. B. Koehler
Director, Wharton Export Network

Introduction

Great Britain reigned supreme in the 19th Century. Once Napoleon was defeated, the Pax Britannica made the world safe for British trade and commerce until the First World War began in 1914. A businessman (virtually all traders were male in those days) could make a good living without going outside the boundaries of the British Empire.

The 20th Century is often called the American Century. The United States of America turned the tide in two World Wars, and emerged from the Cold War as the last Superpower. By mid-century, any businessman who restricted his trade to the British Empire found himself without an Empire to trade with.

Now the millennium approaches. What will the 21st Century bring? Will this be the Pacific Century? If power shifts to the world's most homogeneous and forward-looking nation, it will be the Japanese Century. Or it may go to the world's most populous nation, and give birth to the Chinese Century.

No one can say with certainty.

However, one *can* predict that globalization offers businesspeople their best chance to participate in the economy of the 21st Century. None of us wants to be like that British businessman who found himself without an Empire to trade with. Successful executives of the 21st Century will compete on a global scale.

This book, *Dun & Bradstreet's Guide to Doing Business Around the World*, is designed to help you enter that global market. This expansive volume includes vital data and guidelines for conducting business with the top 40 trade partners of the U.S.A.

The information in *Dun & Bradstreet's Guide to Doing Business Around the World* is organized for ease of use by both new and experienced exporters. Each chapter is crammed with data on every topic which impacts on exporting. This plethora of information is carefully broken down into category and type so as to remain accessible. If (for example) your only interest was whether or not each country is a member of the Berne Convention for the Protection of Intellectual Property Rights, this information is easily found (in this example, under "Comparative Data").

Of particular note is a section near the beginning of each chapter listed as "5 CULTURAL TIPS." Not all businesspeople have the time to read *Dun & Bradstreet's Guide to Doing Business Around the World* in its entirety. But even if you are too busy to read anything else, knowing these top five need-to-know precepts can double your chances of success in these 40 target countries.

In selecting these "5 CULTURAL TIPS," the focus is on information which is *vital* to effective business relationships. Failure to heed these guidelines is guaranteed to damage your prospects. Many of these tips cover the protocols for initial business contacts—which, like any first impression, can be difficult to overcome. A single cultural gaffe in an initial contact can eliminate the possibility of a second contact. In effect, a bad first impression can ruin any chance of a business deal. Some topics covered in the CULTURAL TIPS include:

- Techniques for selling to Australians (and why high-pressure sales won't work).
- Eye contact among Mexicans, and what it reveals about relationships.
- Why a Dutch executive may be preparing a complete dossier on you.
- How foreigners can run afoul of the Indonesian precept of *"asal bapak senang"* (which translates as *"keeping father happy"*).
- How many kisses on the cheek a woman should expect in Brazil.
- Why a disregard for history will cause you problems in Poland.
- What to expect when you are invited to a South African *braaivleis*.
- Who a *mudang* is, and why this person can spoil your deal with South Koreans.
- In what everyday environment do the normally-smiling Thais lose their smiles.
- Why handshakes among the French are brief, and how to keep the French from considering you to be dull.

Failure to respond correctly to *any* of these cultural idiosyncrasies can result in the ruination of a deal. But forewarned is forearmed. These tips alone can be worth the price of this volume.

Each of the USA's 40 top trading partners is given a separate chapter. Each chapter begins with vital demographic data. Population figures are important, but less-commonly-provided data such as age breakdowns are equally important. If you're marketing in-line roller skates, you need to know the number of young people in a country—not just the overall population. For example, both Costa Rica and Ireland have roughly equal populations. But some 70% of Costa Ricans are under 29 years old, compared to only 48.5% of the Irish. Other factors being equal, Costa Rica looks like a much better market.

Of course, there are many other factors to be considered. Once the size of a market has been determined, you will need to know the per capita income. Can the people in your target country afford to buy your product? Is their economy growing or shrinking? *Dun & Bradstreet's Guide to Doing Business Around the World* will provide this data.

What about cultural factors? Will your product encounter opposition on political or religious grounds? Can such opposition be overcome? Opposition from religious leaders won't stop your product from selling in Sweden . . . but it may stop it in Saudi Arabia. Each chapter includes an evaluation of the religious and societal influences on business. And the religious breakdown of each nation is included, detailing what percentage of the population adheres to which religion.

Each chapter also has a general overview of a country's history and politics. Nothing is more insulting to natives of any country than being confused with natives of someplace else. These general overviews will enable you to pin down each nation's global identity. In addition, that country's relationship to the United States is noted. Is their government friendly and cooperative? By its nature, international trade is subject to the whims of governments. While the numbers may say that trade is worthwhile, a difficult government may make an otherwise-profitable deal more trouble than it is worth.

Dun & Bradstreet is well known for its ratings of stocks and companies. This book includes comparative data ratings for each country. On a scale of one through five, the country is judged as to the following:

- Gross Domestic Product Growth
- Per Capita Income
- Trade Flows with the U.S.A.
- Risk Factors
- Monetary Policies
- Trade Policy
- Protection of Intellectual Property Rights
- Foreign Investment Climate

As with the Cultural Tips, this section alone is worth the price of the book.

Following these ratings, the exact dollar figures are detailed as to the country's imports and exports with the USA. The growth rate of these imports and exports are also listed, as are the country's GDP, rate of growth, and per capita income.

In addition, we list the top US exports to each country, as well as *the top prospects for export in the future.*

Ratings are useful only if what they are measuring is clear. The third section of each chapter (following the demographic and comparative data sections) explains in detail what is being measured in the following areas:

- Country Risk
- Monetary Policy
- Trade Policy, including Tariffs, Import Licensing, and Import Taxes
- Protection of Intellectual Property Rights
- Foreign Investment Climate

The next section in each chapter lists the major political leaders (elected or otherwise) of each country. This highly dynamic, valuable data is provided through the International Academy at Santa Barbara, which produces the *Current World Leaders Almanac. CWL* is continually updated; you can contact them via their website (listed next to their data).

Since trade does not take place in a vacuum, there is a section covering the political influences on business. Once you have decided whom to contact (and whom to avoid), a list of contact addresses and phone numbers is included.

To facilitate your trips to these countries, we have also listed the passport and visa requirements.

Finally, in the hope that we can all profit by learning by our mistakes, many chapters contain a business error or gaffe. Listed under the title *faux pas*, these range from simple mistranslations to serious breaches of cultural etiquette. Each of these errors resulted in serious costs to the businesspeople involved. The first businesspeople to make these errors had an excuse: *they didn't know any better*. You won't have that excuse. But you won't have to suffer their consequences either.

From the first conception of a deal to the final consummation, we have endeavored to include all the information you might need. Whether you are a one-man or one-woman trading concern or an integral part of a vast trading empire, *Dun and Bradstreet's Guide to Doing Business Around the World* should have the answers you need.

As if the above was not enough, we have supplemented this book with two appendices. They are:

Appendix 1. Samples of the trade forms required for export. We include the actual forms currently used for:

- Bill of Lading
- Air Waybill (a.k.a. Air Consignment Notice)
- Certificate of Origin (including two different examples)
- Commercial Invoice (a.k.a. Customs Invoice; including three different examples)
- Dock Receipt
- Shippers Export Declaration
- Packaging List
- Pro-Forma Invoice

In addition to the actual samples of the trade documents, we include relevant information on these forms. Time is money, and you don't want your shipment held up because you didn't know if your Bill of Lading should have been *straight*, a *Shipper's Order*, or a *To Order Bill*.

Appendix 2. Useful websites on international trade.

While the data in *Dun & Bradstreet's Guide to Doing Business Around the World* contains valuable statistics, trends, facts, commerce and culture, it is clearly a snapshot in time. It is a template of important information to be used over and over, as well as dynamic data to be updated as time goes by. Of course, much of the information in this book (ranging from attitudes towards time to the cultural notes) will remain as useful decades from now as it is today.

We wanted to make *Dun & Bradstreet's Guide to Doing Business Around the World* a truly invaluable resource of current and future information for business travelers, researchers, educators, and tourists. That is why we also direct readers to online web sites where more cultural, political, and trade data can be found online.

Armed with the information in *Dun & Bradstreet's Guide to Doing Business Around the World*, you will be prepared to profit from the challenges of the new millennium. And, unlike that proverbial British businessman who found himself without a British Empire to trade in, you will always find new markets for your trade.

The authors welcome your input to our book, and can be contacted at 74774.1206@compuserve.com; telephone (610) 353-9894; fax: (610) 353-6994; or mailing address: Box 136, Newtown Square, PA 19073. You are also welcome to visit our website at www.getcustoms.com.

Table of Contents

Appendices

Index   475

Argentina

Official Name:	Argentine Republic (República Argentina)
Official Language:	Spanish
Government System:	Federal Republic
Population:	34.6 million (1995 est.)
Population Growth:	1.1% (1995 est.)
Area:	2,766,890 sq. km. (1.1 million sq. mi.); about the size of the U.S.A. east of the Mississippi River
Natural Resources:	fertile plains of the pampas, lead, zinc, tin, copper, iron ore, manganese, crude oil, uranium
Major Cities:	Buenos Aires (capital), Cordoba, Rosario, La Plata, Mendoza

---

Cultural Note: After a decade of stable politics and economic growth, Argentina's leadership seems to have finally adopted workable economic policies. In years past, Argentines said that their country was "blessed by resources but cursed by politics." The land's abundant natural resources should have made it one of the world's wealthiest nations, but poor leadership kept Argentina in turmoil for decades.

Age Breakdown

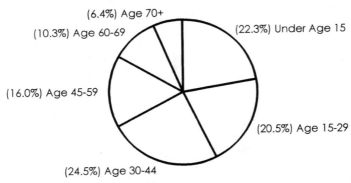

(6.4%) Age 70+
(10.3%) Age 60-69
(22.3%) Under Age 15
(16.0%) Age 45-59
(20.5%) Age 15-29
(24.5%) Age 30-44

Life Expectancy: 68 years male; 74 years female (1991)

 ## Time

North American executives are expected to be punctual to business appointments, but do not be surprised if your Argentine counterpart is late.

Everyone, even North Americans, is expected to be thirty to sixty minutes late for dinner or parties. It would be considered impolite to show up on time.

If you are confused about whether or not to be on time, ask "*¿En punto?*" ("*On the dot?*")

Argentina is three hours behind Greenwich Mean Time (G.M.T. − 3), which is two hours ahead of U.S. Eastern Standard Time (E.S.T. + 2).

 ## Holidays

(Update: Getting Through Customs *http://www.getcustoms.com*)

This list is a working guide. Dates should be corroborated before final travel plans are made. In cases where holidays fall on Saturday or Sunday, commercial establishments may be closed the preceding Friday or following Monday.

New Year's Day	1 January
Labor Day	1 May
Independence Day	25 May
(Anniversary of the 1810 Revolution)	

Sovereignty Day	10 June
Flag Day	20 June
National Independence Day (1816)	9 July
Anniversary of the Death of General José de San Martín, the liberator of Argentina	17 August
Discovery of America (Columbus Day)	12 October

Argentina has two Independence Days; each one celebrates a different historical event.

Work Week

- Argentine executives may put in a very long day, often lasting until 10:00 P.M. An 8:00 P.M. business meeting is not at all unusual.

Religious/Societal Influences on Business

Roman Catholicism is the official religion of Argentina, and about 92% of Argentines belong to this religion. However, freedom of religion is guaranteed, and Argentina has citizens of virtually every belief.

Argentina remains a male-dominant culture. The Argentine dance called the *tango* is seen by many as the ultimate expression of indigenous popular culture. Certainly, the tango reflected male-female roles in Argentina: in its original form, the tango was a dance of complete male dominance over the female, with the woman clutching onto her partner as he drags her around. Putting lyrics to tango music broadened its popularity while it diminished its eroticism. The heyday of the tango has passed, but many Argentines remain fanatic admirers of it.

All Argentines must deal with the repercussions of the military dictatorship, the six years of the so-called "Dirty War." Some nine thousand Argentines were missing and are presumed dead. Few officials have been punished for the kidnapping, tortures, and executions. Complicity with the dictatorship was widespread, even in the Church (some Catholic clergy offered council to torturers disturbed by their jobs). Most Argentines seem to want to forget those days. Notably, the group known as the Argentine Forensic Anthropology Team (which unearths the mass graves of anonymous victims of the Dirty War) is funded from outside Argentina. The *junta* was disgraced by Argentina's defeat in the 1982 Falkland Islands War (remember, the Argentines call them the Malvinas Islands); which led to the return of a civilian government in 1983.

5 Cultural Tips

1. Success in business in Argentina requires first establishing successful social relationships. Business meetings will begin *and* end with polite small talk. Don't expect to get down to business right away. Be aware that you can insult Argentine executives by rushing off without chatting at the end of a meeting.

2. Compared to other South Americans, Argentines, especially those from Buenos Aires, have a reputation for seriousness and melancholy. To call someone or something "not serious" is one of the most damning accusations an Argentine can make. A formal, sober manner (with a firm handshake and good eye contact) is called for in Argentina.

3. On the other hand, when the somber Argentines become humorous, you will know that they have become comfortable with you. Argentine banter is full of put-downs, from comments about your wardrobe to your weight. Don't be offended. You may respond in kind, but do not comment on Argentine institutions or traditions in an unfavorable manner, even in jest.

4. Expect long days in Argentina. Argentine executives work extended hours, sometimes lasting until 10:00 P.M., so business meetings as late as 8:00 P.M. are not at all unusual. Argentines do not eat dinner until 10:00 P.M. (at the earliest), so they break for tea or coffee and pastries between 4:00 and 6:00 P.M. If you are in a meeting during that time, you will be offered something. Accept something to drink, even if you don't want it.

5. North Americans in Argentina note two deficiencies in the local cuisine: Milk or cream is rarely available for coffee, since Argentines drink their coffee and tea with sugar only; and vegetarians have a hard time in Argentina, where the diet is heavily slanted toward meat. Argentina is a major cattle producer, and beef is served with most meals.

Economic Overview

Argentina, rich in natural resources, benefits also from a highly literate population, an export-oriented agricultural sector, and a diversified industrial base. Nevertheless, following decades of mismanagement and protectionist policies, the economy in the late 1980s was plagued with huge external debts and recurring bouts with hyperinflation.

Elected in 1989, President Carlos Saul Menem has implemented a comprehensive economic restructuring program that shows signs of putting Argentina on a path of stable, sustainable growth.

The economy registered an impressive 6% advance in 1994, fueled largely by inflows of foreign capital and strong domestic consumption spending. At the start of 1995, however, the government had to deal with the spillover from international financial movements associated with the devaluation of the Mexican peso. In addition, unemployment had become a serious issue for the government. Despite average annual 7% growth from 1991–94, unemployment surprisingly has doubled, due mostly to layoffs in government bureaus and in privatized industrial firms and utilities. Many U.S. and other foreign firms have continued substantial direct investment and demonstrated continued interest in taking advantage of opportunities in Argentina as part of a Mercosur market.

Argentine exports in 1995 were expected to be about 25% higher than in 1994. Sales were bolstered by record harvests of some agricultural products, good international prices for livestock, oilseeds, cotton, wheat, wool and dairy products, and devaluation of the U.S. dollar to which the Argentine peso is tied. Much remains to be done in the 1990s in dismantling the old statist barriers to growth, extending the recent economic gains, and bringing down the rate of unemployment.

Comparative Data

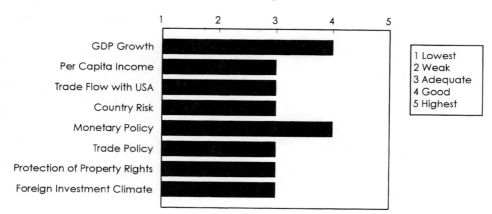

Overall Rating: 3.25

GDP Growth
Per Capita Income
Trade Flow with USA
Country Risk
Monetary Policy
Trade Policy
Protection of Property Rights
Foreign Investment Climate

1 Lowest
2 Weak
3 Adequate
4 Good
5 Highest

Country Risk Rating

Gross Domestic Product: $279 billion (1994)

GDP Growth: 6.5% (1994)

Per Capita Income: $8,200

Trade Flows with the U.S.A.

Rank as Export Market for U.S.A. Goods & Services: 26th

U.S.A. Exports to Argentina: $4.2 billion (1995)

Growth Rate of Exports: −6%

U.S.A. Imports from Argentina: $1.9 billion

Growth Rate of Imports: 10%

Rank as a Supplier of Imports into the U.S.A.:   43rd

Top U.S.A. Exports to Argentina: Machinery; electrical components; medical and optical equipment; motor vehicles; plastics; organic chemicals; aircraft and parts; mineral fuel; aluminum; paper.

Top U.S.A. Prospects for Export to Argentina: Electric power generation and transmission equipment; telecommunications equipment; oil and gas field machinery; computers and peripherals; medical equipment; computer software; airport and ground support equipment; franchising services; pollution control equipment; plastics processing machinery.

Country Risk

Dun & Bradstreet rates Argentina as having sufficient capacity to meet outstanding payment liabilities.

Letters of credit are recommended for initial transactions, along with credit checks on individual firms. When open account terms are used, 30 to 60 day terms are the norm.

Monetary Policy

The annual increase in Argentina's consumer price index during 1994, 3.9%, was the lowest recorded in 40 years. The forecast for 1995 and 1996 was for inflation to average less than 3% per annum. *Monetary Unit:* peso.

Trade Policy

TARIFFS: Tariff rates have been reduced. Argentina now has a tiered tariff schedule with a maximum rate of 20% *ad valorem* and an average rate of 10%. On January 1, 1995, Argentina partially implemented a common external tariff (CET) with other members of the Southern Common Market (*Mercosur*). The other Mercosur members are Brazil, Paraguay, and Uruguay.

The structure of tariffs is as follows: 10% on almost all capital goods; 2–14% on agricultural products; 2–16% on most industrial inputs and raw materials; 20% on consumer goods.

IMPORT LICENSING:　Import licenses are not required for any import, except autos which are subject to a special regime.

Permanent quotas remain on goods such as automobiles. Temporary quotas exist on paper, pulp, and a few other items. Other goods such as pharmaceuticals, foodstuffs, defense materials, and other particular items require the approval of the related government department.

IMPORT TAXES:　A 3% statistics fee is charged on all imports except capital goods. A 21% value-added tax (VAT) is levied on all imports.

Protection of Intellectual Property Rights

Argentina officially adheres to most treaties and international agreements on intellectual property protection and belongs to the World Intellectual Property Organization. However, the U.S. Trade Representative placed Argentina on its priority watch list in 1993 because of the lack of patent protection for pharmaceuticals.

Argentina's patent law, enacted in 1864, is the weakest component of the country's intellectual property rights regime. It excludes pharmaceutical compositions from patent protection. The law allows for a maximum patent term of just 15 years. Under Argentine law, patents of invention may be granted for a term of 5, 10, or 15 years by the Patent Office, according to merit of the invention and the wish of the applicant. Foreign patents may be ratified for a maximum of 10 years, but not to exceed the term of the original foreign patent registered by the Patent Office.

Argentina's present copyright law is adequate by international standards. Recent amendments provided protection to computer software and extended the term of protection for motion pictures from 30 to 50 years. Copyright piracy has become a serious problem for U.S. industries.

Trademark laws and regulations in Argentina are generally good. The key problem is a slow registration process.

Foreign Investment Climate

Foreign direct investment is an essential element of Argentina's economic growth. Argentina's climate for foreign investment is one of the most favorable in Latin America. The Menem administration has encouraged foreign investment through national treatment under a free foreign exchange and capital movement regime.

Decree 1853 of September 8, 1993, governs foreign investment in Argentina. Foreign companies may invest in Argentina without registration or prior government approval on the same terms as investors domiciled in Argentina. A U.S.-Argentina agreement for reciprocal promotion and protection of investments entered into force in October 1994.

Investors are free to enter Argentina via the most convenient vehicle, merger, acquisition, or joint venture. Foreign firms are among the most prominent participants in Argentina's ambitious privatization program, which includes gas, oil, electric power, telecommunications, transportation, water, and sewer sectors.

There are very few sectors in which Argentina reserves the right to maintain exceptions to national treatment for U.S. investors: real estate in border areas, air transportation, shipbuilding, nuclear energy, uranium mining, insurance, and fishing. Foreign firms can enter the fishing and insurance industries by purchasing an interest in existing firms. U.S. direct investment in Argentina has grown from $2.7 billion in 1991 to $6.3 billion in 1994.

 # Current Leaders & Political Parties

(Update: International Academy at Santa Barbara
http://www.iasb.org/cwl)

Pres.: Carlos Saul Menem
Vice Pres.: vacant

Cabinet Ministers:

Economics: Roque Fernandez
Interior: Gustavo Beliz
Foreign Affairs: Guido Di Tella
Education and Justice: Jorge Alberto Rodriguez
Defense: Vacant
Labor and Social Security: Enrique O. Rodriguez
Public Health and Welfare: Julio Cesar Araoz

Other Officials:

Pres. of the Senate: Eduardo Menem
Pres. of the Chamber of Deputies: Alberto R. Pierri
Pres. of the Supreme Court: Ricardo E. Levene
Ambassador to U.S.: Raúl Granillo Ocampo
Perm. Rep. to U.N.: Jorge Cardenas

Political Parties:

Justicialista (Peronist), Radical Civic Union, Union of the Democratic Center,
Communist Party, Democratic Progressives

Political Influences on Business

The Menem Administration has strongly encouraged private initiative through its privatization of state firms, deregulation of the economy, and encouragement of foreign direct investment, which it sees as a necessity to the country's continued growth. Foreign investors are welcome in virtually every economic sector.

The highly favorable investment climate notwithstanding, businesses continue to face occasional inconsistencies associated with governmental actions. A variety of cases exist in which U.S. companies which have invested in or traded with Argentina have been unfairly affected by what they consider to be the federal government's arbitrary and capricious enforcement of laws. Some cases endure from the old days of statist intervention by military juntas; others have occurred in the present environment, in which companies are buffeted by the sheer profusion of change. Although much has been achieved in such areas as deregulation and market opening, the government has been less successful in guaranteeing juridical security (*seguridad juridica*, or the rule of law). The government itself recognizes that the administration of justice could be improved as well, to speed up court cases; the U.S. government is providing assistance to promote the change.

Social stability is also a potential issue of the future. Despite the outward measures of success, a rate of economic growth second only to China's in the last three years, problems have cropped up in the model, such as a record-high, serious unemployment rate, regional disparities in economic development, and the lack of adequate social services. All these issues could erode popular support for the program and force the government to slow the pace of change or even roll back some reforms. On the other hand, the public's memory of decades of increasing economic chaos, which culminated in the hyperinflationary episodes of 1989–90, is still very fresh and was the key factor to Menem's reelection.

Contacts in the U.S.A. & in Argentina

THE EMBASSY OF THE ARGENTINE REPUBLIC
1600 New Hampshire Avenue, N.W.
Washington, D.C. 20009
Tel.: (202) 939-6400
Fax: (202) 332-3171

U.S. DEPARTMENT OF STATE BUREAU OF
CONSULAR AFFAIRS
Tel: (202) 647-5225
Country Desk Officer, Argentina
Tel.: (202) 647-2401

U.S. DEPARTMENT OF COMMERCE
Argentina Desk Officer
Tel.: (202) 482-1548
Fax: (202) 482-2218

ASSOCIATION OF AMERICAN CHAMBERS OF
COMMERCE IN LATIN AMERICA
1615 H Street, N.W.
Washington, D.C. 20062
Tel.: (202) 463-5485
Telex: 248302 CCUS UR

TOURISM OFFICE
Argentina National Tourist Council
12 W. 56th Street
New York, N.Y. 10019
Tel.: (212) 603-0443

THE EMBASSY OF THE UNITED STATES
4300 Colombia
1425 Buenos Aires
Argentina
APO AA 34034
Tel.: [54] (1) 774-7611/8811/9911
Telex: 18156 AMEMBAR
Fax: [54] (1) 775-4205

THE AMERICAN CHAMBER OF COMMERCE IN
ARGENTINA
Avenida Leandro N. Alem 1110, Piso 13
1001 Buenos Aires, Argentina
Tel.: [54] (1) 331-5420/5126
Fax: [54] (1) 331-9076

DUN & BRADSTREET S.A.
Postal Address: Casilla de Correo 954,
1000 Buenos Aires, Argentina
Street Address: Av. L.N. Alem 928-Piso
1o, 1001 Buenos Aires, Argentina
Tel: [54] (1) 318-3100
      [54] (1) 313-0223
Fax: [54] (1) 318-3199
      [54] (1) 313-2517

PRESIDENT CARLOS SAUL MENEM
Office of the President
Balcarce 50
1064 Buenos Aires, Argentina

 Passport/Visa Requirements

Visa Information Tel: (202) 663-1225

Entry Requirements: A passport is required. U.S. citizens do not need a visa for a three-month tourist stay. For current information concerning entry and customs requirements for Argentina, travelers can contact the Argentine Embassy.

Cultural Note: Argentina's natural wealth has attracted immigrants from all over the world. Rags-to-riches stories were common, and the phrase "wealthy as an Argentine" entered the world's vocabulary late in the 1800s. Immigrants arrived from England, Ireland, Germany, Poland, and Russia. The parents of Argentine President Carlos Menem came from Syria. Aside from Spain, the major country of origin for Argentines was Italy. As a result, the Spanish spoken in Argentina is heavily influenced by Italian. While it is comprehensible to most Spanish-speakers, it is quite unlike the Spanish spoken elsewhere.

Australia

Official Name:	Commonwealth of Australia
Official Language:	English
Government System:	Democratic, federal-state system recognizing Queen Elizabeth II as Monarch
Population:	18 million
Population Growth:	1.1%
Area:	7,686,844 sq. km. (2.96 million sq. mi.); about the size of the continental U.S.
Natural Resources:	bauxite, coal, iron ore, alumina, gold, copper, tin, silver, uranium, nickel, tungsten, mineral sands, lead, zinc, diamonds, natural gas, crude oil
Major Cities:	Canberra (capital), Sydney, Melbourne, Brisbane, Perth, Adelaide

Cultural Note: Australians call themselves *Aussies* while New Zealanders refer to themselves as *Kiwis* (after the Kiwi, their national bird). While there are many similarities between the two peoples, there are differences as well. Do not mistake an Aussie for a Kiwi, or vice versa.

Age Breakdown

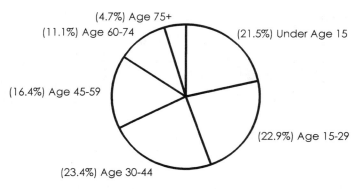

(4.7%) Age 75+

(11.1%) Age 60-74

(21.5%) Under Age 15

(16.4%) Age 45-59

(22.9%) Age 15-29

(23.4%) Age 30-44

Life Expectancy: 74 years male; 80 years female (1991)

 Time

Australian executives expect promptness from other executives. Tardiness, especially to business meetings, is seen as indicative of carelessness.

Australia spans three time zones. They are:

- *Western Australia* (including the city of Perth) is eight hours ahead of Greenwich Mean Time (G.M.T. + 8). This is the part of Australia furthest away from the United States, and it is thirteen hours ahead of U.S. Eastern Standard Time (E.S.T. + 13). Singapore and Hong Kong are also in this time zone.
- *The Northern Territories* (including Darwin) *and South Australia* (including Adelaide) are nine and a half hours ahead of Greenwich Mean Time (G.M.T. + 9 and 1/2). This is the middle section of Australia, and it is fourteen and a half hours ahead of U.S. Eastern Standard Time (E.S.T. + 14 and 1/2).
- *Eastern Australia*, which encompasses New South Wales (including Sydney and the capital territory, Canberra), Victoria (including Melbourne), Tasmania (including Hobart) and Queensland (including Brisbane), is ten hours ahead of Greenwich Mean Time (G.M.T. + 10). This is the part of Australia closest to the United States, and it is fifteen hours ahead of U.S. Eastern Standard Time (E.S.T. + 15).

When traveling to Australia from the Americas, remember that one crosses the International Date Line. When flying westward (U.S.A. to Australia), one loses a day. Flying eastward (Australia to the U.S.A.), one gains a day.

Holidays

(Update: Getting Through Customs *http://www.getcustoms.com*)

This list is a working guide. Dates should be corroborated before final travel plans are made. In cases where holidays fall on Saturday or Sunday, commercial establishments may be closed the preceding Friday or following Monday.

New Year's Day	1 January
Australia Day	26 January
ANZAC Day	25 April
Queen's Birthday	13 June
Boxing Day	26 December
New Year's Eve	31 December

Confirm your appointments with local representatives to avoid conflicts with regional festivities.

- The best time to visit is from March through November, since the peak tourist season is December through February. Christmas and Easter are especially hectic; many executives will be on vacation.

Work Week

- Business hours are 9:00 A.M. to 5:00 P.M., Monday through Friday; 9:00 A.M. to noon, Saturday. Banks are open 9:30 A.M. to 4:00 P.M., Monday through Thursday; 9:30 A.M. to 5:00 P.M. on Fridays.

Religious/Societal Influences on Business

Australia has no official religion. Most religions are represented in Australia, and almost 13% of the population professes to follow no religion. Roman Catholics, with 27.3%, constitute the largest group, with Anglicans close behind at 23.8%.

5 Cultural Tips

1. As a general rule, Australians are friendly, informal, and easy to get to know. They exhibit little of the British reserve of their ancestors. Unlike England, it is perfectly acceptable for foreigners to introduce themselves in social situations.

2. Meat is generally eaten at every meal. While Australians love to exercise and are health conscious, vegetarianism has not caught on as it has in the U.S.A. One very popular meat dish in Australia is originally from England: Toad-in-the-Hole. This is basically a chicken or roast beef casserole with a flour mixture on top.

3. *Less is more* in Australian business. Australians are fairly laconic; they consider brevity admirable. Keep your business presentation to the point; do not digress or go into too much detail.

4. High-pressure sales and hype are counterproductive down under. Australians prefer honesty and directness, and tend to fiercely resist pressure tactics. Present your case in a forthright manner, articulating both the good and the bad. Also, make the initial price realistic since the final price agreed upon will probably be close.

5. Argument is considered entertainment in Australia. People down under are very direct and love to banter, epecially in social situations. If you are teased, take it in stride. You are welcome to tease back. Never get angry or hurt.

 Economic Overview

The Australian economy is enjoying a period of sustained, moderate growth. In 1994, real gross domestic product (GDP) grew 5.1%, due primarily to a rebound in business investment. For the 1994–95 financial year, business investment is estimated to have grown by 18%, with plant and equipment investment up 23% on the year before.

Australia is well-positioned for continued solid economic growth, with very little in the way of unfavorable indicators. With increasing links to the dynamic economies in the Asian region, and a continuation of economic reform, Australia's trade and investment climate will be attractive for the foreseeable future.

Australia commenced a basic reorientation of its economy more than 10 years ago, and has transformed itself from an inward-looking, import substitution country to an internationally competitive, export-oriented one. The government's economic development strategy focuses on continued economic reform to encourage expansion of value-added production in the minerals and agricultural sectors; manufacturing in high-technology products; and expansion of the services sector. Manufacturing production has continued to outpace other sectors in the economy, growing almost 11% in 1994.

Trade is important for Australia. Merchandise exports in 1994 totaled $47.7 billion, about one-fifth of the nation's GDP. Australia imported $50.1 billion in merchandise in 1994. The United States is Australia's second largest trading partner, behind Japan only. The U.S. is Australia's largest source of merchandise imports ($10.9 billion in 1994).

Geographically, Australia is similar in size to the United States. Despite its small population and vast land mass, the country has well-developed, nationwide air, road, port, and telecommunications infrastructure networks comparable to those in other industrialized countries.

Cultural Note: Australians feel a strong impetus to deflate people who put on airs. Referred to as "cutting down the tall poppy," this habit is thought to have grown out of Australia's origin as a British penal colony. Naturally, the Australian prisoners hated their high-class British overseers, and wished to insult them whenever possible. Furthermore, many Australian convicts were Irish, a people already looked down upon by the British at that time. This feeling is still so ingrained that many Australian politicians decline an offer of a British knighthood for fear of alienating their constituents.

Downplay your expertise/knowledge/skills. Try to let your accomplishments speak for themselves. More than one Australian has complained that eager young U.S. executives "sound like walking resumes," since they are so quick to list their accomplishments and qualifications.

Comparative Data

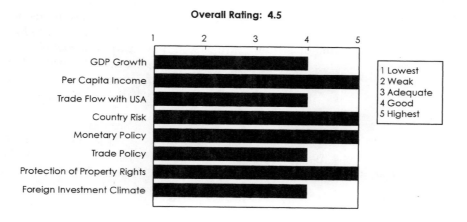

Overall Rating: 4.5

1	2	3	4	5

GDP Growth
Per Capita Income
Trade Flow with USA
Country Risk
Monetary Policy
Trade Policy
Protection of Property Rights
Foreign Investment Climate

1 Lowest
2 Weak
3 Adequate
4 Good
5 Highest

Country Risk Rating

Gross Domestic Product: $300 billion
GDP Growth: 5.1%
Per Capita Income: $17,000

Trade Flows with the U.S.A.

Rank as Export Market for U.S.A. Goods & Services: 15th

U.S.A. Exports to Australia: $10.8 billion

Growth Rate of Exports: 10%

U.S.A. Imports from Australia: $3.3 billion

Growth Rate of Imports: 3%

Rank as a Supplier of Imports into the U.S.A. :   32nd

Top U.S.A. Exports to Australia: Machinery; electrical components; motor vehicles; medical and optical equipment; plastics and resins; organic chemicals; books and newspapers; paper/paperboard; fertilizer; miscellaneous food.

Top U.S.A. Prospects for Export to Australia: Computer software; computers and peripherals; medical equipment; automotive parts; telecommunications equipment; telecommunications services; defense equipment; security equipment; aircraft and parts; laboratory and scientific equipment.

Country Risk

Dun & Bradstreet rates Australia as having excellent capacity to meet outstanding payment liabilities.

Generally, all common terms of payment are in use, but open account predominates. More secure terms are recommended for new customers. Credit terms of 30 to 60 days are the norm.

Monetary Policy

Inflation is predicted to remain relatively low, with only moderate upward pressure from wages and the effect of a weaker currency. Dun & Bradstreet forecasts that inflation will be under 3.5% in 1996 and 1997. *Monetary Unit*: Australian dollar.

Trade Policy

TARIFFS: On a trade-weighted basis, Australian duties on manufactured goods averaged about 4% in 1994 and were projected to average 2.8% in 1996/97. The government has pledged that, except for textiles, clothing, and footwear (TCF) and certain automotive products, all other tariffs will be reduced in stages to 5% by 1996. By 2000, apparel and certain finished textile tariffs will be reduced to 25%; footwear, sheeting, and certain other fabrics to 15%; and existing nonquota TCF products to 10%.

Tariff rates do affect competitive pricing of imported goods.

IMPORT LICENSING: Australia has phased out its import licensing requirements. Effective March 1993, import quotas were ended, except for cheese and curd.

Restricted imports include drugs, steroids, weapons/firearms, heritage items, and cordless telephones and CB radios (unless approved by the Department of Communications and the Arts), food, plants, animals and protected wildlife.

IMPORT TAXES: There are no import taxes in Australia. The Australian government does, however, impose a tax on the sale of both domestically manufactured and imported goods. The general rate of this tax is 21% of the sale value. There are a large number of exempt goods set out in a schedule to the Sales Tax Act. There are also categories of goods subject to tax at 11% (household goods) and 31% (luxury goods).

Protection of Intellectual Property Rights

Copyrights, patents, trademarks, industrial designs, and integrated circuits are protected under Australian law. Australia is a member of World Intellectual Property Organization, the Paris Convention for the Protection of Industrial Property, the Berne Convention for the Protection of Literary and Artistic Works, the Universal Copyright Convention, and the Patent Cooperation Treaty.

Patents are available for inventions in all fields of technology. They are protected by the Patents Act of 1990 which offers coverage for 16 years subject to renewal. Patents for pharmaceutical substances may have the term of protection extended to 20 years. Trade names and trademarks may be protected for seven years and renewed at will by registration under the Trademark Act of 1955. Once used, trade names and trademarks may also, without registration, be protected by common law.

Copyrights are protected under the Copyright Act of 1968 for the life of the author, plus 50 years.

Foreign Investment Climate

The Australian government welcomes foreign investment, and the United States is the country's largest source of foreign capital. Total U.S. investment in Australia, including both direct and portfolio investment, exceeds $54 billion. The federal and state governments vigorously encourage investment by offering incentives to multinational companies to set up regional headquarters for financial and other services, and manufacturing operations. The government touts the benefits of Australia's safe, stable business environment, skilled work force, and lower facility, site, and operating costs in comparison to other regional centers such as Singapore, Hong Kong, and Taiwan.

Takeovers of domestic firms by foreign investors generally are not interfered with. They are treated under the same guidelines as any other foreign investment.

The Federal Treasury regulates foreign investment with the assistance of the Foreign Investment Review Board (FIRB). The Board screens investment proposals for conformity with Australian law and policy. Foreign investment in three sectors is severely limited: media, civil aviation, and urban real estate.

 # Current Leaders & Political Parties

(Update: International Academy at Santa Barbara
http://www.iasb.org/cwl)

State, Government, and Political Party Leaders:
  Queen of Australia: Queen Elizabeth II
  Head of State, Gov. Gen.: William Deane

Cabinet Ministers:
  Prime Min.: John Howard
  Dep. Prime Min. and Min. of Trade: Tim Fischer
  Foreign Affairs: Alexander Downer
  Finance: John Fahey
  Defense: Ian McLachlan
  Treasury: Peter Costello
  Transport and Regional Dev.: John Sharp
  Industry, Science, Tourism.: John Moore
  Immigration and Multicultural Affairs: Philip Ruddock
  Employment, Education, Training, and Youth Affairs: Sen. Amanda Vanstone
  Primary Industries and Energy: John Anderson
  Social Security: Sen. Jocelyn Newman
  Science and Technology: Peter McGauran
  Industrial Relations: Peter Reith
  Attorney Gen. and Min. for Justice: Daryl Williams
  Communication and the Arts: Sen. Richard Alston
  Environment: Sen. Robert Hill
  Health and Family Services: Dr. Michael Wooldridge

Other Officials:
  Chief Justice of the High Court: Sir Anthony Mason
  Speaker of the House of Representatives: Stephen Martin
  Pres. of the Senate: Sen. Kerry Sibraa
  Leader of the Opposition: Kim Beazley

Ambassador to U.S.: John McCarthy

Perm. Rep. to U.N.: Richard Butler

Political Parties:

Australian Labor Party (ALP), Liberal Party (LP), Natl. Party (NP), Australian Democrats

 ## Political Influences on Business

The United States and Australia have been close allies for over 50 years, during which time Australia has been the southern link in the structure of Asia-Pacific strategic alliances. The Australian government contributes to mutual security and regional stability by hosting key joint defense facilities and ship visits, participating in a range of exercises and exchanges with U.S. forces, and fostering regional security dialogue. In addition, the two governments cooperate in worldwide nonproliferation, arms control, and peacekeeping efforts.

Like the U.S.A., Australia is a leading advocate of trade and investment liberalization. Because of common interests and convictions, the two countries work together on many global issues (e.g., U.N. reform, promoting democracy and human rights, protecting the environment, and enhancing the multilateral trading system and the new World Trade Organization).

In recent years, U.S.A. export subsidies for wheat and other agricultural commodities have generated periodic friction. But these concerns are being attenuated because of agreement during GATT's Uruguay Round on substantial worldwide reductions in agricultural-export subsidies.

There are no major political issues that detract from the business climate or the stability of the bilateral trading relationship with the United States. All of Australia's major political parties seek to promote growth and encourage investment, including investment from abroad. Although there are differences in approach, both leading parties strongly support Australia's internal economic restructuring to transform the country into a globally competitive trading nation.

Other policy directions that attract equally universal support include Australia's desire to define itself as a part of the dynamic Asia-Pacific region, as well as efforts to upgrade its mix of exports in order to reduce reliance on basic commodities and increase sales of value-added products. There is also broad political approval for federal and state government programs to privatize public services so as to reach world quality standards, and for labor and workforce reforms.

Australia has a federal system of government, and a long history as a multiparty parliamentary democracy. There is no written Bill of Rights, but fundamental rights are ensured by law and respected in practice. Voting has been compulsory since 1924, although many Australians feel that mandatory voting is no longer necessary.

The Commonwealth (federal) government and the six state governments operate under written constitutions that draw on the British tradition of a Cabinet Government, led by a Prime Minister, which is responsible to a majority in Parliament's lower house. The Federal Constitution, however, also contains some elements that resemble American practice (including a Senate, in which each state has equal representation). The Head of State is Queen Elizabeth II, the reigning British monarch, but she exercises her functions through personal representatives who live in Australia (i.e., Australian citizens who serve as the Governor-General of Australia, and the Governors of the six states). Australians are debating whether their country should become a republic, give up ties with the Queen, revise the constitution, and adopt a new flag.

Members of the Federal House of Representatives are elected for three years, and national elections were last held in March 1996. Members of the Senate are elected for six years. All major parties support the U.S.-Australia alliance and stress the importance of close relations between Australia and the United States. Thus, this longstanding and stable pattern is essentially unaffected by the outcome of national elections.

 # Contacts in the U.S.A. & in Australia

Contacts in the United States:

EMBASSY OF AUSTRALIA
1601 Massachusetts Ave., N.W.
Washington, D.C. 20036
Tel: (202) 797-3000
Fax: (202) 797-3168

U.S. DEPARTMENT OF STATE
Bureau of Consular Affairs
Tel: (202) 647-5225
Country Desk Officer
Tel: (202) 647-9691

U.S. DEPARTMENT OF COMMERCE
Australia Desk
Int'l Trade Admin.
Tel: (202) 482-4958

TOURISM OFFICE
Australian Tourist Commission
489 5th Avenue
New York, N.Y. 10017
Tel: (212) 687-6300

Contacts in Australia:

U.S. EMBASSY
Moonah Place
Canberra
A.C.T 2600, Australia
Mailing Address:
APO AP 96549
Tel: [61] (6) 270-5000
Fax: [61] (6) 270-5970
Telex: 62104 USAEMB

THE AMERICAN CHAMBER OF COMMERCE IN AUSTRALIA
Level 2, 41 Lower Street
Sydney, N.S.W. 2000, Australia
Tel: [61] (2) 241-1907
Fax: [61] (2) 251-5220

DUN & BRADSTREET (AUSTRALIA) PTY. LTD.
Postal Address: P.O. Box 7405, St. Kilda Road, Melbourne, Vic. 3004, Australia
Street Address: 479 St. Kilda Road,

Melbourne, Vic. 3004, Australia
Telephone: [61] (3) 9828-3333
Fax: [61] (3) 9828-3300 (General)
    [61] (3) 9828-3162 (Head Office)

PRIME MINISTER JOHN HOWARD
Office of the Prime Minister
Parliament House
Canberra ACT 2600, Australia

Passport/Visa Requirements

Visa Information   Tel: (202) 663-1225

Entry Requirements: Passport required. Persons traveling to Australia who are not holders of Australian or New Zealand passports require visas.

Visa Application Procedure: Applicants must forward or bring in the following to the appropriate Australian Consular Office; visa office hours vary from office to office.

1. Application Form 48 must be completed and signed by the applicant. A separate application form is required for each passport holder. For a visitor visa application form, please write to the nearest Australian Embassy or Consulate, requesting number of forms needed and enclose a self-addressed, stamped envelope for return of the forms.

2. Valid passport of the applicant. The visa will be placed in the passport. (Applicants must make certain that their passport has two free pages facing each other for this purpose.)

3. A business visitor must provide a company letter giving a description of proposed activities while in Australia and expected length of stay.

4. A child or children under the age of 18 years traveling to Australia without one or both parents or legal guardians, must submit, with the visa application, a birth certificate and notarized written consent of the nontraveling parent or legal guardian of the child or children.

5. With regard to fees, Australian visas and application forms for a stay of less than three months are issued free of charge. For a stay longer than three months and up to six months, or if a multiple entry visa with a validity of greater than twelve months is required, a fee of U.S. $24.00 is charged.

Important Note: Persons who travel to Australia as visitors are not permitted to engage in employment or formal studies. Those interested in entering Australia for either purpose should check Australian Consular offices to determine requirements and eligibility.

Departure Tax: Australian travelers and overseas visitors departing (Australia) for overseas destinations must purchase an A$25.00 departure tax stamp.

Three Ways in which Australia Is Different from New Zealand

1. The European colonization of Australia began as a penal colony. New Zealand was never a penal colony.

2. New Zealand declared itself a *Nuclear Free Zone*, and prohibits ships from entering its ports which carry nuclear arms. Since the U.S.A. would not confirm which ships carried nuclear weapons, this resulted in a de facto ban on virtually all U.S.A. military vessels in New Zealand waters, which suspended the ANZUS (Australia/New Zealand/United States) mutual defense treaty.

3. The indigenous people of New Zealand, the Maoris, have not been as marginalized as the Aborigines of Australia. Maoris still occupy a substantial amount of the country's arable land, and Maori words are in common use. In part, this is because the Maori make up a larger proportion of New Zealand's population. About 10% of New Zealanders are Maori, while only about 1.5% of Australians are Aborigines. (Australia will soon have more Asians than Aborigines.)

Belgium

Official Name:	Kingdom of Belgium
	Koninkrijk België (Dutch)
	Royaume de Belgique (French)
Official Languages:	Dutch*, French, German
	* The Belgian dialect of Dutch is also known as Flemish
Government System:	Parliamentary democracy under a constitutional monarch
Population:	10.1 million (1995 est.)
Population Growth:	3.5% (1994 est.)
Area:	30,518 sq. km. (11,780 sq. mi.); about the size of Maryland
Natural Resources:	coal, natural gas
Major Cities:	Brussels (capital), Antwerp, Ghent, Charleroi, Liege, Bruges

Cultural Note: Belgium may be small, but it nevertheless encompasses separate cultural and linguistic traditions which have threatened to divide the country into even smaller units. The majority (57%) of Belgians speak Dutch. They are known as the *Flemish*. (The term *Flemish* is also used to identify their Dutch dialect.) Most of the remainder (42%) speak French. French-speaking Belgians are known as Walloons. (Their language is French, not Walloon; linguistically, Walloon refers to a specific French dialect, which is now almost extinct.) Finally, a small minority (1%) speaks German.

Age Breakdown

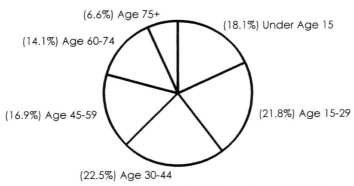

Life Expectancy: 73 years male; 80 years female (1992)

 Time

Most Belgians expect punctuality in all business and social engagements. This is especially true among Dutch and German-speaking Belgians. French-speaking Belgians tend to be a little more relaxed about punctuality, especially with regard to social events.

Belgium is one hour ahead of Greenwich Mean Time (G.M.T. + 1), which is six hours ahead of U.S. Eastern Standard Time (E.S.T. + 6).

 Holidays

(Update: Getting Through Customs *http://www.getcustoms.com*)

This list is a working guide. Dates should be corroborated before final travel plans are made. In cases where holidays fall on Saturday or Sunday, commercial establishments may be closed the preceding Friday or following Monday.

The following holidays should be confirmed by local contacts; regional observations of these and other festivals may vary.

New Year's Day	1 January
Labor Day	1 May
National Independence Day	21 July
Armistice or Veteran's Day	11 November
New Year's Eve	31 December

- Most Belgians take a one-month vacation per year.

Work Week

- At 35.8 hours, the Belgian work week is one of the shortest in the world.
- Businesses open at 8:30 A.M. and close at 5:30 P.M. for most of the week, although some stay open until 9:00 P.M. on Fridays.

Religious/Societal Influences on Business

Most Belgians, Dutch and French-speakers alike, are members of the Roman Catholic Church. There are small numbers of Protestants and Muslims.

Since they share the same religion, divisions in Belgian society run along linguistic lines. There are serious conflicts between the Dutch-speaking Flemish in the north and the French-speaking Walloons in the South. Political parties calling for the division of Belgium along linguistic lines have a small but significant representation in the Belgian parliament. Class differences contribute to the conflict, since French had become the language of the ruling and upper classes. The Second World War exacerbated these differences. Dutch-speakers hoped that Nazi rule would free them from their French-speaking overlords. (Despite Nazi collaboration by both Flemish and Walloons, the Belgian resistance helped half of Belgium's Jews flee the country.)

Attempts to mollify both sides have led to a complex patchwork of legislation. Belgium is divided into three regions, three cultural communes, and four linguistic areas. Numerous laws deal with the use of language in different locales.

Brussels, the Belgian capital, is officially considered a multilingual area, although French-speakers predominate. The political importance of Brussels is a point of pride for the Belgians. As the seat of the European Council of Ministers, Brussels is the de facto capital of the European Union. Belgium is also the central headquarters for NATO; the NATO Council meets in Brussels.

Belgium is a kingdom, although the king has only ceremonial duties. The royal family is generally popular and is seen as a unifying force.

5 Cultural Tips

1. Belgium has three recognized cultural groups including a small minority of German-speaking people, so it is important to know who you are dealing with. The Flemish (Dutch-speakers) have different traditions from the Walloons (French-speakers). And, since the two groups often do not get along, it is important not to mistake a Flemish executive for a Walloon, or vice versa.

2. Formerly a major industrial nation, Belgium has been shifting to a service economy. English is widely spoken and many Belgian executives have experience dealing with foreigners. However, your promotional materials should be translated into the main language of your Belgian counterpart, either Dutch or French.

3. The Belgians (especially the Flemish and German-speakers) place a high value on privacy. Doors are kept closed, both at home and in the office. Always knock before entering a room, even in an office after a secretary has told you that your Belgian counterpart is ready for you.

4. Flemish executives are generally very linear, and place great importance on planning. This contrasts strongly with the Walloons who tend to be more flexible and improvisational. Not surprisingly, the management styles of the two groups do not mesh well.

5. Some knowledge of Belgium's impressive artistic and cultural history will be appreciated by Belgians. This includes such world-famous artists as Peter Bruegel (the Elder), Jan van Eyck, Peter Paul Rubens, and the Surrealist painter René Magritte.

 Economic Overview

Belgium is the ninth largest trading nation in the world. It is highly outward-looking due to its long history of reliance on international trade. Because of this history and the lack of natural resources, Belgian business both imports and exports. Imports and exports are equivalent to nearly 70% of GDP, making Belgium one of the highest per capita exporters in the world. Belgium imports many basic or intermediate goods, adds value, and then exports final products. About 75% of Belgium's foreign trade is with other EU countries, pointing to the country's importance as a commercial axis in Western Europe.

Belgium and the United States have strong reciprocal trade relations. Belgium is the 12th largest market in the world for U.S. products and took $10.9 billion in American exports in 1994. The Belgian market has great depth and diversity in its import mix, with many excellent growth sectors.

Due to its history and location, Belgium is a true cultural microcosm of Europe with three linguistic communities: French, Dutch, and German. This diversity, combined with its small, manageable size, makes Belgium an excellent test market and subsequent launching pad for European operations of U.S. businesses.

Overall, government leaders at all levels are very supportive of open trade and investment.

Comparative Data

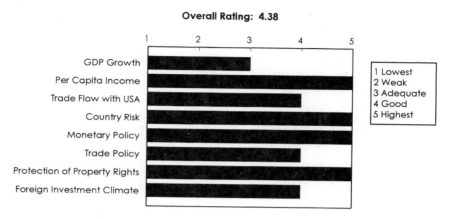

Overall Rating: 4.38

Country Risk Rating

Gross Domestic Product: $228 billion

GDP Growth: 2.2%

Per Capita Income: $22,860

Trade Flows with the U.S.A.

Rank as Export Market for U.S.A. Goods & Services: 12th

U.S.A. Exports to Belgium: $12.5 billion

Growth Rate of Exports: 15%

U.S.A. Imports from Belgium: $6.0 billion

Growth Rate of Imports: −4%

Rank as a Supplier of Imports into the U.S.A. :   23rd

Top U.S.A. Exports to Belgium: Tobacco; machinery; organic chemicals; precious stones; plastics and resins; motor vehicles; optical and medical equipment; electrical components; mineral fuel/oil; aircraft/spacecraft.

Top U.S.A. Prospects for Export to Belgium: Telecommunication services; computer software; aircraft and parts; automotive parts; computers and peripherals; telecommunication equipment; computer services; pollution control equipment; printing and graphic art equipment; plastic materials and resins.

Country Risk

Dun & Bradstreet rates Belgium as having excellent capacity to meet outstanding payment liabilities. It carries the lowest degree of risk when compared to other countries.

All types of payment terms are in use, including open account and letter of credit. Generally speaking, buyers show a preference for payment by cash against documents. The most common payment terms are net 30 days.

Monetary Policy

Inflation remains firmly in check at 2.4% in 1994 and under 2% in 1995. Dun & Bradstreet forecasts inflation at 2.5% in 1996 and 2.7% in 1997. *Monetary Unit:* Belgian franc.

Trade Policy

TARIFFS: As a member of the European Union, Belgium applies the EU common external tariff to goods imported from non-EU countries. There is a single duty among all EU members toward products coming from non-EU members. For goods imported into Belgium from other EU countries, no customs duties apply unless goods contain components imported from outside the EU upon which customs duties have not been paid in another EU country.

IMPORT LICENSING: Many products may be imported without any prior license, but products from certain countries and certain listed products are subject to an import license. Strategic goods are also subject to an import and/or quota license.

IMPORT TAXES: Goods imported into Belgium or made in Belgium are normally subject to a value-added tax (VAT) payable upon importation if Belgium is the destination of the goods being shipped into the EU. One of three rates will apply: 6% for daily necessities, foodstuffs, and so on; 12% for tobacco, fuel, and so on; 20.5% for the majority of commercial goods.

VAT is applied after all customs duties are added to the price of the goods. Since EU products do not pay customs duties, while those from the U.S. do, the effective VAT rate for non-EU goods is actually higher than the rates cited above.

Protection of Intellectual Property Rights

Belgium is a member of the World Intellectual Property Organization and the European Patent Convention. A single European patent, valid throughout the European Union (EU), does not exist, since the community patent convention has not yet come into force. In the meantime, the patent applicant can choose between a national and a multicountry patent. In the latter case, a single application to the European Patent Office in Munich, Germany, is required for obtaining patents valid in a number of countries within the EU. A patent thus granted will not be valid unless a copy of the grant in one of Belgium's three national languages is filed with the Belgian Office of Industrial Property.

To obtain a national patent in Belgium, the inventor or his assignee must file a request with the Office of Industrial Property in the Ministry of Economic Affairs. National patents are valid for 20 years if a search has occurred. If not, validity is reduced to six years.

The EU Trademark Office still needs to be established in Spain and the first EU trademark registrations were not expected until mid-1996. In the meantime, trademark registration is handled on a national basis. Trademarks in Belgium are regulated by the Uniform Benelux Law of 1962, which offers protection in Belgium, the Netherlands, and Luxembourg. An application for trademark can be filed either with the Belgian National Office in the Ministry of Economic Affairs or with the Benelux Trade Mark Bureau located in the Netherlands. If granted, trademark protection lasts for 10 years from the date of application and can be renewed for further periods of 10 years each. Trademarks must generally be used within three years of registration.

Belgium is a member of the Berne Convention and the Universal Copyright Convention. Belgium accords automatic copyright protection when registered with this organization. Protection exists for the life of the author, plus 50 years after his death.

Foreign Investment Climate

Belgium has traditionally maintained an open economy, highly dependent on imported inputs and international trade for its well-being. Since World War II, foreign investment has played a vital part in the Belgian economy, providing much technology and employment. Given the importance of trade and investment, Belgium generally discourages protectionism. The government actively encourages foreign investment on a national treatment basis. Foreign corporations in Belgium account for about one-third of the top 3,100 corporations.

With a U.S. direct investment position of $11.6 billion at the end of 1993 and a 40% share of total foreign investment, more than 1,300 U.S. companies are present, ranging from offices with one person to firms with thousands of employees. U.S. companies give employment to some 5% of the active population, and other foreign firms another 4%. According to statistics from the Ministry of Economic Affairs, foreign investment is concentrated mostly in manufacturing (45%), oil (21%), and chemicals (13%). Foreign companies investing in Belgium are generally eligible for the same tax-related investment incentives and subject to the same accounting requirements as domestic investors.

Any foreign company wishing to engage in trade or manufacture in Belgium can set up a subsidiary or branch. Belgian nationals are not required to own part of the equity of the enterprise, and the repatriation of capital and profits is unrestricted.

Certain restrictive rules do apply to investors. Belgian and foreign investors must obtain special permission to open department stores, provide transportation, produce and sell certain food items, cut and polish diamonds, and sell firearms and ammunition. Foreign interests may enter into joint ventures and partnerships on the same basis as domestic parties, except for certain professions such as doctors, lawyers, and architects.

Current Leaders & Political Parties

(Update: International Academy at Santa Barbara *http://www.iasb.org/cwl*)

King Albert II

Ministers:

Prime Min.: Jean-Luc Dehaene

Dep. Prime Min. and Min. of Interior: John Vande lanotte

Dep. Prime Min. and Min. of Economy and Communications: Elio Di Rupo

Dep. Prime Min. and Min. of the Budget: Herman Van Rompuy

Dep. Prime Min. and Min. of Finances and Foreign Trade: Philippe Maystadt

Natl. Defense: Jean-Pol Poncelet

Employment, Labor, and Equal Opportunities Between Men and Women: Miet Smet

Justice: Stefaan De Clerck

Social Affairs: Magda De Galan

Agriculture: Karel Pinxten

Transportation: Michel Daerden

Foreign Affairs: Erik Derycke

Sciences: Yvan Ylieff

Pensions and Health: Marcel Colla

Civil Service: André Flahaut

Other Officials:

Pres. of the Senate: Frank Swaelen

Pres. of the House of Representatives: Raymond Langendries

Ambassador to U.S.: André Adam

Perm. Rep. to U.N.: Alexandre Reyn

Political Parties:

Flemish Christian Party (CVP), Francophone Social Christian Party (PSC), Francophone Socialist Party (PS), Flemish Socialist Party (SP), Francophone Brussels Party (FDF), Flemish People's Party (VU), Flemish Liberal Party (PVV), Francophone Liberal Party (PRL), Brussels Francophone Party (PLDP), Walloon Union (RW), Flemish Ecologists (AGALEV), Francophone Ecologists (ECOLO), Communist Party (PCB)

Political Influences on Business

Belgium has been a constitutional monarchy since 1930. Albert II was invested as King in August 1993, after the death of his brother Baudouin. The King, Prime Minister, and Cabinet represent the executive branch of the federal government, with the newly formed 71-member Senate and 150-member Chamber of Deputies representing the legislative branch.

The Cabinet must retain the support of a majority in the Chamber of Deputies to remain in power. Federal parliamentary elections are held every four years (or before that if the government loses the support of a majority in the Chamber and no alternative coalition can be formed). There is universal suffrage, with compulsory voting and proportional representation. Governments are always coalitions comprising two or three of the traditional parties, the Christian Democrats (center), the Socialists (left wing), and Liberals (right wing). Elections were last held in May 1995, with no party gaining an absolute majority of votes in either of Belgium's two linguistic regions.

The government formed in June 1995 is a coalition of Christian Democrats and Socialists, led once again by Prime Minister Jean-Luc Dehaene. The central plank of its platform is reform of the social welfare system, both to stimulate job creation and to help Belgium meet Maastricht budget norms (which will allow Belgium to be one of the first countries to join the European Monetary Union). Along with espousing early entry into EMU, the platform also proposed an active role by Belgium during the 1996 EU Intergovernmental Conference, with emphasis on deepening European integration.

The most significant long-term factor in Belgian politics is the gradual devolution of powers from the central authority to the regions. In the new federal structure, approved in July 1993, sovereignty is spread over three authorities: the central state, the regions, and the language communities. There is no hierarchy between these policy levels. Each of the three levels has its own exclusive powers and is not allowed to interfere in matters that are under the jurisdiction of the others.

The regions are Flanders (the northern, Dutch-speaking part of Belgium), Wallonia (the southern, French-speaking area), and Brussels (the capital regions, limited to 19 bilingual communes). Each region is responsible for a wide range of socioeconomic matters for its own territory.

Elected regional assemblies for Flanders, Wallonia, and Brussels exercise legislative powers within their own regions and elect executive authorities. Under the evolving federal system, the responsibility for areas of interest to U.S. business, such as foreign trade, environment and investment regimes and incentives, will increasingly become the responsibility for the regional governments. This devolution means that U.S. executives wishing to do business in Belgium will eventually have more contact with regional officials than in the past.

Contacts in the U.S.A. & in Belgium

Contacts in the United States:

EMBASSY OF THE KINGDOM OF BELGIUM
3330 Garfield St., N.W.
Washington, D.C. 20008
Tel: (202) 333-6900
Fax: (202) 333-3079

U.S. DEPARTMENT OF STATE
Bureau of Consular Affairs
Tel: (202) 647-5225
Country Desk Officer, Belgium
Tel: (202) 647-6071
Fax: (202) 647-3507

U.S. DEPARTMENT OF COMMERCE
Belgium Desk
Int'l Trade Admin.
Tel: (202) 482-5401
Fax: (202) 482-2897

BELGIAN TOURIST OFFICE
745 Fifth Ave.
New York, N.Y. 10151
Tel: (212) 758-8130
Fax: (212) 355-7675

Contacts in Belgium:

U.S. EMBASSY
27 Boulevard du Regent
B-1000
Brussels, Belgium
Mailing Address:
APO AE 09724
Tel: [32] (2) 513-3830
Fax: [32] (2) 511-2725

THE AMERICAN CHAMBER OF COMMERCE IN
BELGIUM
Avenue des Arts 50
Boite 5, B-1040
Brussels
Tel: [32] (2) 513-6770
Telex: 64913 AMCHAM B

DUN & BRADSTREET - EURINFORM S.A.- N.V.
Postal Address: Avenue des Pleiades 73,
Plejadenlaan 73, B-1200
Bruxelles - Brussels, Belgium
Street Address: Avenue des Pleiades 73,
Plejadenlaan 73, B-1200
Bruxelles - Brussels, Belgium
Telephone: [32] (2) 778-7211
Fax: [32] (2) 778-7272

KING ALBERT II
Palais Royal
B-1000 Brussels, Kingdom of Belgium

PRIME MINISTER JEAN-LUC DEHAENE
Office of the Prime Minister
16 rue de la Loi
1000 Brussels, Kingdom of Belgium

Passport/Visa Requirements

Visa Information   (202) 663-1225

Entry Requirements: Passport is required. U.S. citizens do not require a visa for a temporary visit not exceeding three months. For a stay exceeding three months, U.S. citizens should apply for a visa of provisional sojourn before their departure.

Cultural Note: Multicultural Brussels has become a favorite locale for test marketing. There are few European cultures more different than the Dutch and the French, and both are represented in Brussels. A product which can appeal to both is likely to be a winner.

Brazil

Official Name:	Federative Republic of Brazil (República Federativa do Brasil)
Official Language:	Portuguese
Government System:	Multiparty federal republic
Population:	165.3 million (1995)
Population Growth:	2.0%
Area:	8,511,965 sq. km. (3,286,473 sq. mi.); about the size of the U.S.A. excluding Texas and Louisiana
Natural Resources:	iron ore, manganese, bauxite, nickel, uranium, phosphates, tin, hydropower, gold, platinum, crude oil, timber
Major Cities:	Brasilia (capital), São Paulo, Rio de Janeiro, Belo Horizonte, Recife, Porto Alegre, Salvador, Manaus

---

Cultural Note: A normal conversation between two Brazilians generally takes place somewhere between 6″ and 12″ apart. This seems either an intimate or hostile distance to most executives from the U.S.A., and can be stressful if they are not prepared for such close encounters. However, if you are going to conduct business in Brazil, it is advisable to practice interacting with co-workers at close proximity before your trip. It is insulting to continually back away from your Brazilian counterpart, since they feel uncomfortable at the normal U.S. range of 2′ or more.

Age Breakdown

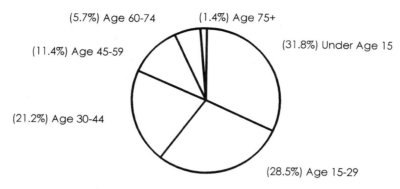

(5.7%) Age 60-74

(1.4%) Age 75+

(11.4%) Age 45-59

(31.8%) Under Age 15

(21.2%) Age 30-44

(28.5%) Age 15-29

Life Expectancy: 62 years male; 68 years female (1990)

Time

Punctuality often seems to be an alien concept to Brazil. In fact, prompt Brazilians are said to keep *tempo británico* (British time).

Brazil is large enough to have two time zones. Most of Brazil is 3 hours behind Greenwich Mean Time (G.M.T. − 3), which is two hours ahead of U.S. Eastern Standard Time (E.S.T. + 2). Western Brazil is four hours behind Greenwich Mean Time (G.M.T. − 4), which is one hour ahead of U.S. Eastern Standard Time (E.S.T. + 1).

Holidays

(Update: Getting Through Customs *http://www.getcustoms.com*)

This list is a working guide. Dates should be corroborated before final travel plans are made. In cases where holidays fall on Saturday or Sunday, commercial establishments may be closed the preceding Friday or following Monday.

New Year's Day	1 January
Tiradentes' Day	21 April
Independence Day	7 September
Nossa Senhora Aparecida (Our Lady Appeared)	12 October
Proclamation of the Republic	15 November
New Year's Eve	31 December

There are many additional regional holidays, and business may be particularly difficult to conduct around Carneval (which always precedes Ash Wednesday, the beginning of Lent), Easter, and Christmas.

Work Week

- Business hours are generally advertised as 8:30 A.M to 5:30 P.M., but decision makers usually begin work later in the morning and stay later in the evening. Try making appointments from 10:00 A.M. to noon, and 3:00 P.M. to 5:00 P.M. If your business runs into lunch, be prepared to spend at least two hours.
- The lack of punctuality is a fact of life in Brazil. Become accustomed to waiting for your Brazilian counterpart.

Religious/Societal Influences on Business

Brazil has no official church. About 70% of Brazilians are Roman Catholics. Protestant Churches, especially Evangelistic Sects, have experienced tremendous growth in Brazil in the past two decades. Virtually all religions are represented in Brazil, including Islam, Judaism, and Buddhism.

Religious beliefs in Brazil are not exclusive. People can hold seemingly contradictory beliefs. Brazilian Marxists can believe in Spiritualism; Catholic Bishops can preach Socialist Revolution.

A substantial number of Brazilians also follow the informal Afro-Brazilian beliefs known as *Umbanda*. When African slaves were brought to Brazil and forced to become Catholics, they transposed their native beliefs onto Christian ones. The sword-wielding African war god Ogum was disguised as the Christian Saint George; the sea goddess Yemanjá became the Virgin Mary. Such syncretic beliefs display the Brazilian ability to both absorb and adapt new cultures. Umbanda beliefs are pervasive enough to support the growth of anti-Umbanda churches, where former Umbanda clergy specialize in exorcising the various Umbanda deities.

Family and its related responsibilities exerts tremendous influence on Brazilians. The family is the most important institution.

5 Cultural Tips

1. There are two Brazilian professionals you will probably need to hire to conduct business in Brazil. A Brazilian contact (called a *despechante* in Portuguese) is invaluable for making introductions. Once the negotiation stage is reached, your

contracts will need to be reviewed by a specialist called a *notario* (there is no direct equivalent in English, but notarios are somewhat similar to lawyers).

2. Brazilians are a physically active people, and their greetings can be effusive. Even a first encounter will involve extended handshakes. As the relationship deepens, this will advance to embraces and back-thumping between men; women may kiss each other on alternating cheeks. (Married women kiss twice, but single women kiss three times; that third kiss invokes good luck towards finding a spouse.) Shake hands with everyone present, both upon arrival and upon departure.

3. While Brazil is one of the most informal of countries, people still tend to address each other by their last names. Most people will be addressed as *Senhor* (Mr.) or *Senhora* (Mrs.) plus their surname. People with titles should be addressed as such. Note that some Brazilians sometimes introduce themselves using their titles and their first names (i.e., Doctor John).

4. The "hard sell" does not work well in Brazil. Brazilians do business with people they like, and must get to know potential business partners first. This takes time. And Brazilians do not proceed in a linear fashion. During the course of negotiations, they are likely to go back and reexamine the entire deal several times.

5. Brazil has a very open culture, capable of absorbing disparate trends into Brazilian society at large. Both fact and fiction are absorbed and can be interpreted as evidence, based upon their feelings for the people or issues involved. This is especially true when it appears on television. Much of Brazil's large illiterate population watches television (more homes in tropical Brazil have television sets than have refrigerators), and they often believe what they see.

Economic Overview

With the largest economy in Latin America, Brazil is a country with immense export opportunities. U.S. exports grew 35% in 1994 to $8.1 billion. Increased demand for imports is being fueled in part by Brazil's best economic growth in almost a decade.

In addition, the stabilization plan introduced in mid-1994 successfully restrained Brazil's chronically high inflation. The plan, which included the introduction of a new currency, the *Real*, has proven to be the most successful stabilization plan the past 15 years.

The Real has also created more buying power for many Brazilian consumers. Salaried workers realized a 15% to 30% increase in actual purchasing power after the Real was introduced. The Cardoso government has pursued a comprehensive economic liberalization agenda. The government is emphasizing increased economic opportunities for the private sector through privatization, deregulation, and the removal of impediments to competition. The engine of Brazilian economic growth is more and more the private sector.

U.S. exporters are now able to expand and participate in new business opportunities that will make Brazil one of the strongest commercial partners of the United States. Nevertheless, the complexities of the Brazilian business environment still create formidable challenges for U.S. exporters. Doing business in Brazil is not easy and requires knowledge of local regulations and procedures. The U.S. and Brazil have historically had close and cordial relations. This relationship encompasses a broad range of political and economic agenda on both a bilateral and multilateral basis. Commercial and trade issues occupy a significant position on this agenda. Two-way trade exceeds $20 billion. Economic stabilization is the major political issue affecting the business climate.

Comparative Data

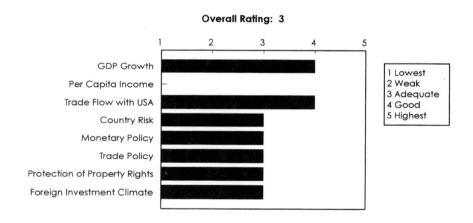

Country Risk Rating

Gross Domestic Product: $550 billion
GDP Growth: 5.7%
Per Capita Income: $3,452

Trade Flows with the U.S.A.

Rank as Export Market for U.S.A. Goods & Services: 14th
U.S.A. Exports to Brazil: $11.4 billion
Growth Rate of Exports: 40%
U.S.A. Imports from Brazil: $8.8 billion
Growth Rate of Imports: 0%
Rank as a Supplier of Imports into the U.S.A.:   16th

Top U.S.A. Exports to Brazil: Machinery; electrical components; organic chemicals; motor vehicles; medical and optical equipment; aircraft and parts; mineral fuel and oil; plastics and resins; beverages; fertilizers.

Top U.S.A. Prospects for Export to Brazil: Telecommunications; computer software; oil and gasfield machinery and services; security and safety equipment; pollution control equipment; industrial chemicals; medical equipment and supplies; automotive parts and service equipment; electrical power systems; machine tools and metalworking equipment.

Country Risk

Dun & Bradstreet rates Brazil as having sufficient capacity to meet outstanding payment liabilities.

A letter of credit is advised, although more liberal terms are often used for repeat business with the same customer. When open account terms are extended, 30 to 60 day terms are the norm.

Monetary Policy

A stabilization plan introduced in mid-1994 has reduced monthly inflation from 50% in June 1994, to between 1% and 3% in 1995. Annual inflation is forecast at 19% in 1996 and 18% in 1997. *Monetary Unit:* real.

Trade Policy

TARIFFS: Tariffs, in general, are the primary instrument in Brazil for regulating imports. The average tariff in late 1994 was about 11%. By contrast, the average tariff in 1990 was 32%. Brazilian import duties for most products range from zero to 20%.

Brazil signed and ratified the Treaty of Asuncion establishing the Southern Common Market (MERCOSUL) in 1991. Brazil and its MERCOSUL partners, Argentina, Uruguay and Paraguay, concluded negotiations in August 1994 for a common external tariff (CET) which went into effect on January 1, 1995.

IMPORT LICENSING: The import permit, known as the Guia de Importacao, is the single most important document required for importing goods into Brazil. An import permit must be obtained by the importer for all but a very limited list of products. Import permit requests must be accompanied by the foreign manufacturer's catalogs or price lists covering the goods to be imported. Import licensing is now automatic within five days of requesting a license, with a few exceptions.

The Brazilian government has eliminated most import prohibitions. However, it places special controls on certain imports. Importation of used machinery, automobiles, clothing, and many consumer goods continue to be restricted severely.

IMPORT TAXES: Brazil levies numerous import taxes in addition to import duties. These include an Industrial Products Tax which ranges from zero to 15% depending on the product, and the Merchandise Circulation Tax, a state government value-added tax, with the predominant rate of 17%.

Other import taxes include a 2.2% union fee; a brokerage fee equal to 1% of the value of the import; a warehouse fee equal to 1% of the value of the import, a $50 administration commission, and an additional port tax which equal 3% of the value of the import.

Protection of Intellectual Property Rights

A major concern of foreign companies trading with Brazil is that protection of intellectual property rights is often inadequate and uncertain.

Brazil is a member of the World Intellectual Property Organization (WIPO) and a signatory of the Berne Convention and the Paris Convention on protection of intellectual property. Many of the country's statutes on intellectual property are consistent with Western standards. However, serious deficiencies exist regarding protection for patents, trademarks, and trade secrets. Enforcement in these areas, and in copyright protection, is often lax. Legal cases can drag on for years. Brazil currently does not provide either product or process patent protection for chemical compounds, foodstuffs, or chemical/pharmaceutical substances. Product protection is not available for metal alloys, or for new uses of products, including species of microorganisms. The pending Industrial Property Bill would recognize the first four of these categories and extend the term for product patents from 15 to 20 years.

All licensing and technical assistance agreements, including trademark licenses and franchising, must be registered with the National Institute of Industrial Property. Without such registration, a trademark is subject to cancellation for nonuse. The pending Industrial Property Bill includes significant trademark revisions which will improve trademark protection. While Brazil's copyright law generally conforms to world-class standards, the 25-year term of protection for computer software falls short of the Berne Convention standard of life of the author plus 50 years. A bill designed to improve protection for computer software programs was submitted to Congress in early 1995. The bill would extend the term of protection to 50 years. Enforcement of copyright laws has also been lax.

Foreign Investment Climate

Brazil welcomes foreign investment with some restrictions. A wide-ranging reform effort, which includes constitutional reform, is currently underway to broaden the private sector, including foreign investors, and participation in a number of areas previously reserved for the state. The Cardoso administration has introduced constitutional amendments to eliminate the distinction between foreign and national capital, allow foreign private capital participation in the state petroleum and telecommunications monopolies, and private capital participation in those sectors, allow foreign companies to engage in marine transport between Brazilian ports, and to distribute natural gas. All these reforms were under consideration by the Brazilian Congress in 1995.

All foreign investment must be registered with the Central Bank.

Brazil has a privatization program in which foreigners have been allowed to participate, but are limited to 40% of the voting shares for sale.

Foreign and domestic private entities may establish, own, and dispose of business enterprises.

 # Current Leaders & Political Parties

(Update: International Academy at Santa Barbara *http://www.iasb.org/cwl*)

State, Government, and Political Party Leaders:
    Pres.: Fernando Henrique Cardoso
    Vice Pres.: Marco Antonio de Oliveira Maciel

Ministers:
    External Relations: Luiz Felipe Lampreia
    Justice: Nelson Jobim
    Navy: Mauro Cesar Rodrigues Pereira
    Army: Gen. Zemildo Zoroastro De Lucena
    Air Force: Brig. Mauro José Gandra
    Finance: Pedro Sampaio Malan
    Planning: José Serra
    Mines and Energy: Raimundo Britto
    Communications: Sergio Vieira Da Mota
    Agriculture and Land Reform: José Eduardo Andrade Vieira
    Education: Paulo Renato De Souza
    Industry, Commerce, and Tourism: Dorothea Werneck
    Labor: Paulo Paiva
    Health: Adib Jatene
    Social Security and Welfare: Reinhold Stephanes
    Science and Technology: José Israel Vargas
    Culture: Francisco Correa Weffort
    Sports: Edson Arantes Do Nascimento (Pelé)

Environment: Gustavo Krause
Transportation: Odacir Klein
Min. Chief of the Govt.: Clovis De Barros Carvalho
Sec. for Strategic Matters: Ronaldo Mota Sardenberg
Fed. Admin. Sec.: Luiz Carlos Bresser Pereira
Natl. Communications Sec.: Roberto Muylaert

Other Officials:

Pres. of the Fed. Senate: José Sarney
Pres. of the Chamber of Deputies: Luis Eduardo Magalhães
Head of the Armed Forces Gen. Staff: Gen. Alberto Mendes Cardoso
Pres. of the Natl. Economic and Social Dev. Bank: Luis Carlos Mendonça de Barros
Pres. of the Fed. Supreme Court: Octávio Galotti
Pres. of the Central Bank: Gustavo Loyola
Sec. Gen. of the Office of the Pres.: Eduardo Jorge Caldas Pereira
Ambassador to U.S.: Paulo Tarso Flecha De Lima
Perm. Rep. to U.N.: Celso Luiz Nunes Amorim

Political Parties:

Natl. Reconstruction Party (PRN), Social Democratic Party (PDS), Party of the Brazilian Democratic Mov. (PMDB), Democratic Workers' Party (PDT), Workers' Party (PT), Brazilian Labor Party (PTB), Liberal Front Party (PFL), Popular Socialist Party, Brazilian Social Democratic Party (PSDB), Liberal Party (PL)

 ## Political Influences On Business

Brazil and the United States have historically had close and cordial relations. Brazil has suffered from chronic inflation throughout much of its recent history. The initial success of the stabilization plan developed by Fernando Henrique Cardoso (when he was Finance Minister) was a significant factor in his election to the Presidency in October 1994. The Congress, though it approved the plan, did not at that time approve the constitutional amendments required to allow implementation of the structural reforms necessary for long-term stabilization.

Brazil is a federal republic with 26 states and a federal district. The federal government is comprised of the executive, legislative, and judicial branches. The system is governed by the 1988 Constitution, which grants broad powers to the federal government. The President holds office for four years and appoints his own cabinet. There are 81 Senators (three for each state and the federal district) and 513 Deputies. Senate terms are for eight years (with elections staggered so that two-thirds of the upper house is up for election at one time and one-third four years later). Chamber terms are for four years. Chamber elections are based on a complex system of proportional representation. Each state is eligible for a minimum of 8 seats; the largest state delegation (Sao Paulo's) is capped at 70 seats. The net result is a system heavily weighted in favor of geographically large, but sparsely populated states.

In addition to geographic imbalance, Congress is characterized by a large number of political parties, nearly 20 in all. President Cardoso won election supported by an alliance of his center-left Social Democratic Party, the PSDB, and two center-right parties, the Liberal Front Party (PFL) and the Brazilian Labor Party (PTB). Brazil's largest party, the centrist Brazilian Democratic Movement Party (PMDB), joined Cardoso's governing coalition after the election. The coalition is a fragile one, though Cardoso has been successful so far in holding members to their commitment to support Constitutional reform. The left-of-center Workers Party (PT) is Brazil's principal opposition party.

States are organized like the federal government, with three branches of government. Because of mandatory revenue allocation to states and municipalities provided for in the 1988 Constitution, Brazilian governors and mayors have exercised considerable power since 1989. The next national elections are scheduled for 1998.

Contacts in the U.S.A. & in Brazil

In the United States:

THE EMBASSY OF THE FEDERATIVE REPUBLIC OF BRAZIL
3006 Massachusetts Avenue, N.W.
Washington, D.C. 20008
Tel: (202) 745-2700
Fax: (202) 745-2827

U.S. DEPARTMENT OF STATE
Bureau of Consular Affairs
Telephone: (202) 647-5225
Country Desk Officer, Brazil
Tel: (202) 647-9407

U.S. DEPARTMENT OF COMMERCE
Country Desk Officer, Brazil
Tel: (202) 482-3871

BRAZILIAN TOURISM OFFICE
551 5th Avenue #-590
New York, N.Y. 10176
Tel: (212) 286-9600
Fax: (212) 490-9294

Contacts in Brazil:

U.S. EMBASSY
Avenida das Nacoes, Lote 3;
Brasilia, Brazil
APO AA Miami 34030, Unit 3500
Tel: [55] 61-321-7272
Telex: 061-1091
Fax: [55] 61-225-9136

AMERICAN CHAMBER OF COMMERCE FOR
BRAZIL-RIO DE JANEIRO
Praca Pio X-15
5th Floor
Caixa Postal 916
20.040 Rio de Janeiro, RJ Brazil
Tel: [55] 21-203-2477
Fax: [55] 21-263-4477
Telex: (391) 2134084 AMCH BR

DUN & BRADSTREET DO BRASIL LTDA.
Postal Address: Caixa Postal 2188,
01060-970 Sao Paulo - SP, Brazil
Street Address: Av. Dr. Chucri Zaidan,
80 -1o ander, Morumbi - Sao Paulo - SP,
04583-110 Brazil
Tel: [55] (11) 532-8800
Fax: [55] (11) 532-8900

PRESIDENT FERNANDO HENRIQUE CARDOSO
Office of the President
Palacio de Planalto
Praca dos Tres Poderes
70150 Brasilia, DF, Federative Republic
of Brazil

 Passport/Visa Requirements

Visa Information   Tel: (202) 647-1225

Entry Requirements: A passport and visa are required.

For current information concerning entry and customs requirements for Brazil, travelers can contact the Brazilian Embassy, or the nearest Brazilian Consulate.

Cultural Note: Brazilians do business through personal connections and expect to have long-term relationships with individuals (not corporations). Your business relationship will need to be reaffirmed each time your Brazilian representative changes.

Be prepared to commit long-term resources of time and money to establishing strong relationships in Brazil. Without such commitments, there is no point in attempting to do business there at all.

Official Name:	Canada
Official Language:	English and French
Government System:	Federal multiparty parliamentary democracy
Population:	29.5 million
Population Growth:	1.3%
Area:	9,970,610 sq. km. (3.8 million sq. mi.); second largest country in the world
Natural Resources:	nickel, zinc, copper, gold, lead, molybdenum, potash, silver, fish, timber, wildlife, coal, crude oil, natural gas, hydroelectric power
Major Cities:	Ottawa (capital), Toronto, Montreal, Quebec, Vancouver, Edmonton

Cultural Note: Canada has never invaded the United States of America. However, the U.S.A. has invaded Canada (unsuccessfully) several times. Every schoolchild learns about Canada's brave resistance to unprovoked U.S. aggression. Today, Canadians no longer fear a military invasion, but the U.S. economic and cultural influence continues to grow. The loss of Canadian culture and tradition remains a grave concern, although there is little unanimity as to what that culture actually is.

Age Breakdown

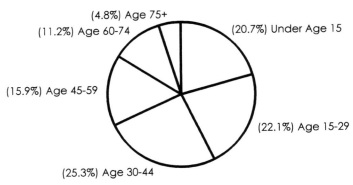

(4.8%) Age 75+
(11.2%) Age 60-74
(20.7%) Under Age 15
(15.9%) Age 45-59
(22.1%) Age 15-29
(25.3%) Age 30-44

Life Expectancy: 75 years male; 82 years female (1992)

 Time

Canada's different cultures take different attitudes toward time. In general, English-speaking Canada follows U.S. patterns toward punctuality: be on time to all business appointments, but be slightly late to social engagements.

French-speaking Canada follows the more polychronic French conception of time. Punctuality is expected from foreign business executives, but is not always practiced by French-speaking Canadians.

Canada is large enough to span six time zones. The following four correspond to the identically named time zones in the contiguous forty-eight United States:

- Most of Quebec and Ontario are on Eastern Standard Time, which is five hours behind Greenwich Mean Time (G.M.T. − 5).
- Western Ontario, Manitoba, and eastern Saskatchewan (including Regina) are on Central Standard Time, which is six hours behind Greenwich Mean Time (G.M.T. − 6).
- Western Saskatchewan, Alberta, and easternmost British Columbia are on Mountain Standard Time, which is seven hours behind Greenwich Mean Time (G.M.T. − 7).
- Most of British Columbia is on Pacific Standard Time, which is eight hours behind Greenwich Mean Time (G.M.T. − 8).

The remaining two Canadian time zones do not correspond to time zones in the contiguous United States:

- Atlantic Standard Time is one hour ahead of Eastern Standard Time, making it four hours behind Greenwich Mean Time (G.M.T. – 4). All the Maritime Provinces are on Atlantic Standard Time except Newfoundland Island, that follows.
- Newfoundland Island, which reminds the world of its separate identity by maintaining a separate time zone called Newfoundland Standard Time, is *thirty minutes* ahead of Atlantic Time, making it three-and-a-half hours behind Greenwich Mean Time (G.M.T. – 3 1/2). Note that this thirty-minute difference applies only to Newfoundland Island; Labrador, which is the mainland part of Newfoundland Province, is on Atlantic Standard Time. *Note:* Newfoundland is pronounced "new-fin-land," not "new-found-land."

Holidays

(Update: Getting Through Customs *http://www.getcustoms.com*)

This list is a working guide. Dates should be corroborated before final travel plans are made. In cases where holidays fall on Saturday or Sunday, commercial establishments may be closed the preceding Friday or following Monday.

New Year's Holidays	1–2 January
New Year's (Quebec only)	3 January
Family Day (Alberta only)	20 February
Victoria Day	20 May
St. Jean Baptiste Day (Quebec only)	26 June
Canada Day	1 July
Civic Holiday (most provinces)	7 August
Labor Day	4 September
Thanksgiving Day	14 October
Remembrance Day	11 November
Boxing Day	26 December

Note that while the United States and Canada share many holidays, the Canadian Thanksgiving comes over a month before the U.S. Thanksgiving.

Work Week

- Business hours are generally 9:00 A.M. to 5:00 P.M., Monday through Friday.
- Banking hours are generally:
  10:00 A.M. to 3:00 P.M., Monday through Thursday and 10:00 A.M. to 6:00 P.M. on Fridays. Some banks have later hours and/or Saturday hours.

- Shop hours are generally 10:00 A.M. to 6:00 P.M., Monday through Saturday, but many shops are open to 9:00 P.M.

Religious/Societal Influences on Business

Canada has become a truly multiethnic nation. Its citizens exhibit traditions of many backgrounds. This includes not just British and French, but Inuit, Indian, and Métis (a mixture of French and Indian) as well. Large numbers of immigrants came from Germany, Italy, China, Ukraine, and the Netherlands. The most recent influx comes from Hong Kong, and is concentrated in British Columbia. Many well-off Chinese have acquired Canadian citizenship in anticipation of Beijing's 1997 takeover of Hong Kong.

Most religions are represented in Canada. The largest group consists of Roman Catholics (45.7% of the population). Various Protestant denominations make up the next largest group (36.3%). Other religions include Eastern Orthodoxy, Judaism, Islam, Buddhism and Hinduism. This diversity is acknowledged in the phrase the Canadian *mosaic* (as opposed to the United States *melting pot*).

With such diversity, it is difficult to generalize about Canadians. Dividing Canadians into the two largest groups, English- and French-speakers, allows some characteristics to be noted.

English-speaking Canadians tend toward British manners and reserve. Public displays of emotion are frowned upon. On the other hand, they are capable of great exuberance in sport and revelry (as befits a people living in an often-harsh, low-population environment). The influence of the United States is seen in several areas, including a preference for U.S. terminology over British terms. However, Canadian spelling tends to follow British guidelines. English-speaking Canadians are usually Protestant or Roman Catholic, but religion does not tend to have great influence on everyday life.

French-speaking Canadians exhibit the language and traditions of France. Most (but not all) live in the province of Quebec. The majority are Roman Catholic, and probably were educated in a church-run school. The Church exerts a greater influence in everyday Quebec life than it does in France.

Since the future of united Canada is in doubt, Canadians of all ethnicities live with insecurity about their futures. Quebec separatists continue to push for an independent nation. Indians demand the return of vast areas of territory. The Western Provinces resent rule from Ottawa, and find more commonality with the Northwest United States.

Canadians are, and expect others to be, relatively honest and open. Canada's low population sometimes requires services to be paid for "on the honor system." Services which would have attendants to enforce payment (such as parking lots) in the United States often just have a box, in which users are trusted to deposit payment.

5 Cultural Tips

1. Although many Canadians are quick to move to a first name basis, it is best to wait for your Canadian counterpart to suggest doing so.

2. Gestures in Canada are similar to those in the U.S. However, note that the "V-for-Victory" sign is done with the palm facing out. It can be taken as an insult when done with the palm inward.

3. Respect the Canadian desire for "Canadian identity," even if the differences between Canadian and U.S. culture escape you. One difference is in how the two countries view the settlement of their Western regions. U.S. legend glorifies "taming the West," while Canadians celebrate *unifying* their country via their transcontinental railroad. (Of course, Canada is a much less violent country than the U.S.A.)

4. Many Canadians characterize U.S. businesspeople as purveyors of self-promotion and "hype." Avoid this image by sticking to the facts. Canadians expect to hear the truth.

5. Business gifts should be modest; ostentation is frowned upon by most Canadians. Gifts are usually given after the close of a deal. Wrapped gifts are usually unwrapped immediately and shown to all assembled. It is also customary to bring a gift of flowers, candy, or alcohol when visiting a Canadian home.

Economic Overview

The U.S.-Canada trading relationship is the largest in the world, with well over $300 billion in two-way trade taking place each year. Merchandise exports from the United States account for approximately 70% of the Canadian import market, and the U.S. remains by far Canada's largest export market. Despite a recent softening of the Canadian economy, the Canadian import market (already the most favorable for U.S. goods and services of any in the world) should see annual growth of at least 5% in real terms in 1996.

Since implementation of the North American Free Trade Agreement (NAFTA) in 1994, U.S. exports to Canada have increased by more than 20%. Despite some well-publicized trade disputes, overall market conditions are unlikely to experience any significant changes, and U.S. companies will continue to find Canada an extremely attractive and easily accessible place to do business.

The Canadian economy grew by 4.6% in 1994, the best performance in six years. Growth was fueled by exports, which reaped the benefits of a lower Canadian dollar and a strong U.S. economy. Canada is the world's seventh largest market economy. Production and services are predominantly privately owned and operated. With a population of about one-tenth of that of the United States, the Canadian economy mirrors that of the U.S.A. in approximately the same ratio, and has developed in many ways along similar lines. This has made Canada an ideal export and investment destination for many U.S. companies, who have found an environment and marketplace very similar to that of the domestic U.S. It also offers an ideal first stop for U.S. businesses seeking to begin export marketing, with business practices, attitudes, conditions, and environments here more similar to those found in the United States than any other country in the world. Notwithstanding these similarities, however, significant cultural and linguistic differences, which vary across each of Canada's four distinctive regional markets, allow first-time U.S. exporters to develop an appreciation of the complexities of overseas marketing.

Business opportunities in Canada fall within the full spectrum of industry sectors, and in virtually every business activity. Geographic proximity, cultural and historical ties, and strong awareness of business and other developments in the U.S. are key accelerators for the sale of U.S. goods and services in the Canadian market. Third-country competition tends to be far less prevalent in Canada than in most other international markets.

Cultural Note: As a general rule, Canadian businesspeople (especially English-speakers) respond well to direct eye contact and an open, friendly, honest manner.

Comparative Data

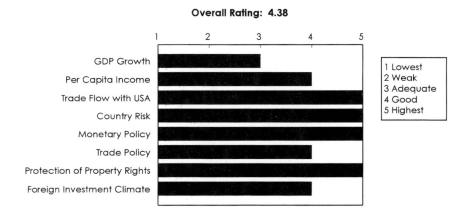

Overall Rating: 4.38

GDP Growth
Per Capita Income
Trade Flow with USA
Country Risk
Monetary Policy
Trade Policy
Protection of Property Rights
Foreign Investment Climate

1 Lowest
2 Weak
3 Adequate
4 Good
5 Highest

Country Risk Rating

Gross Domestic Product: $437 billion

GDP Growth: 4.6%

Per Capita Income: $12,696

Trade Flows with the U.S.A.

Rank as Export Market for U.S.A. Goods & Services: 1st
U.S.A. Exports to Canada: $127 billion
Growth Rate of Exports: 11%
U.S.A. Imports from Canada: $145 billion
Growth Rate of Imports: 12%
Rank as a Supplier of Imports into the U.S.A.:   1st

Top U.S.A. Exports to Canada: Motor vehicles; machinery; electrical components; plastics and resins; medical and optical equipment; iron or steel products; paper/paperboard; furniture and bedding; books and newspaper; rubber products.

Top U.S.A. Prospects for Export to Canada: Computer software; computers and peripherals; telecommunications equipment; pollution control equipment; automotive aftermarket parts; furniture; medical equipment; electronic components; sporting goods; machine tools and metalworking equipment.

Country Risk

Dun & Bradstreet rates Canada as having excellent capacity to meet outstanding payment liabilities. Open account terms are generally common. Normal credit terms are 30 to 60 days.

Monetary Policy

Subdued growth prospects, pulling capacity utilization downward, together with moderate wage growth is likely to keep a lid on price pressures. Inflation, which was 2.4% in 1995, is expected to reach 2.6% in 1996 and forecast to fall to 2.4% in 1997. *Monetary Unit:* Canadian dollar.

Trade Policy

TARIFFS: As a result of the 1988 U.S.-Canada Free Trade Agreement (FTA), many Canadian tariffs on U.S. products have been, or will soon be eliminated. NAFTA removes some remaining barriers and expands specific provisions of the FTA. The remaining tariffs, mostly agricultural products, textile and apparel products, will continue to be phased out by 10% annually to reach zero on January 1, 1998.

IMPORT LICENSING: There are no general licenses required for importing goods into Canada. There are, however, provisions related to a variety of prohibited, controlled, and restricted goods. The majority of U.S. products shipped to Canada enter the market free from any import restrictions. However, under the provisions of the Canadian

Customs Tariff regulations, certain commodities cannot be imported such as oleo-margarine, reprints of Canadian copyrighted work, and some game birds.

Other goods are controlled, regulated, or prohibited under legislation falling within the jurisdiction of other government departments. Examples of regulated goods include food products, clothing, drug and medical devices, hazardous products, some offensive weapons and firearms, endangered species, and motor vehicles.

IMPORT TAXES: Canada implemented a 7% goods and services tax in 1991. The tax does not apply to basic groceries, prescribed drugs, and medical devices, most agricultural and fish products, most educational services, most financial services, health and dental care services, and a variety of other services.

A separate excise tax of 10% applies to certain products such as watches or jewelry, when duty paid value exceeds C$50. Other excise taxes are applied to tobacco, cigarettes, liquor, and wines.

Protection of Intellectual Property Rights

Canada is a member of the World Intellectual Property Organization, the Berne Convention for the Protection of Literary and Artistic Works, the Universal Copyright Convention, and the Patent Cooperation Treaty.

Patent terms are 20 years from the filing date. The patent law generally provides for a 7- to 10-year period of exclusive use after the product obtains marketing approval.

Trademarks are good for 15 years and are renewable for like periods. A trademark not used for three consecutive years can be canceled.

Canadian copyright provides protection for 50 years after the author's death.

Foreign Investment Climate

Canada has long been considered a stable and remunerative environment for foreign investment, and its economic progress has been made possible to a large extent by a sustained inflow of foreign capital. Since 1985, foreign investment policy in Canada has been guided by the Investment Canada Act which replaced the more restrictive Foreign Investment Review Act. With few exceptions, Canada offers foreign investors full national treatment within the context of a developed open market economy operating with democratic principles and institutions. Canada is, however, one of the few OECD countries that still has a formal investment review process, and foreign investment is prohibited or restricted in several sectors of the economy.

While the Investment Canada Act provides the basic legal framework for foreign investment in Canada, foreign investment in specific sectors may be covered by special legislation. For example, foreign investment in the financial sector is governed by laws administered by the federal Department of Finance, and the Broadcast Act governs foreign investment in radio and TV broadcasting. Under provisions of Canada's new Telecommunications Act, foreign ownership of transmission facilities is limited to 20%, while in the case of holding companies that wish to invest in Canadian carriers, two-thirds of the holding company's equity must be owned and controlled by

Canadians. Canada's federal system of government subjects investment to provincial as well as national jurisdiction. Provincial restrictions on foreign investment differ by province, but are confined largely to the purchase of land and to certain types of provincially regulated financial services.

Since the beginning of 1994, investment relations between the United States and Canada have been governed by the NAFTA negotiated by the U.S., Canada, and Mexico. The U.S.-Canada Free Trade Agreement (FTA), which entered into force at the beginning of 1989, has been suspended as long as the two countries remain parties to the NAFTA. The NAFTA builds on the investment relationship created in the FTA.

In the FTA, the U.S. and Canada agreed on important foreign investment principles, including right of establishment and national treatment. The FTA recognized that a hospitable and secure investment climate was indispensable if the two countries were to achieve the full benefits of reducing barriers to trade in goods and services.

The FTA established a mutually beneficial framework of investment principles sensitive to the national interests of both countries, with the objective of assuring that investment flowed freely between the two countries and that investors were treated in a fair and predictable manner.

The FTA provided higher review thresholds for U.S. investment in Canada than for other foreign investors, but it did not exempt all U.S. investment from review nor did it override specific foreign investment prohibitions, notably in the cultural area. The NAFTA incorporates the gains made in the FTA, expands the coverage of the Investment Chapter to several new areas and broadens the definition of investors with rights under the agreement, and creates the right to binding investor-State dispute settlement arbitration under limited circumstances.

Current Leaders & Political Parties

(Update: International Academy at Santa Barbara *http://www.iasb.org/cwl*)

State, Government, and Political Party Leaders:

    Head of State: Queen Elizabeth II

    Gov. Gen.: Romeo LeBlanc

Cabinet Ministers:

    Prime Min.: Jean Chrétien

    Solicitor Gen. and Leader of the Govt. in the House of Commons: Herbert Gray

    Foreign Affairs: Lloyd Axworthy

    Human Resources Dev. and Western Economic Diversification: Doug Young

    Natl. Defense and Veteran's Affairs: David Michael Collenette

    Intnatl. Trade: Art Eggleton

    Natl. Revenue: Jane Stewart

    Agriculture: Ralph E. Goodale

Public Works and Govt. Services: Diane Marleall

Indian Affairs and Northern Dev.: Ron Irwin

Fisheries and Oceans: Fred Mifflin

Leader of the Govt. in the Senate: Joyce Fairbairn

Dep. Prime Min. and Min. of Heritage: Vacant

Citizenship and Immigration: Lucienne Robillard

Industry: John Manley

Health: David Dingwall

Finance and Responsible for the Fed. Office of Regional Dev.: Paul Martin

Transport: David Anderson

Pres. of the Treasury Board: Marcel Masse

Pres. of the Privy Cncl. and Min. of Intergovernmental Affairs and Public Service Renewal: Stephanie Dion

Natural Resources: Anne McLellan

Justice and Attorney Gen.: Allan Rock

Other Officials:

Speaker of the House of Commons: Gilbert Parent

Chief Justice of the Supreme Court: Antonio Lamer

Ambassador to U.S.: Raymond A. J. Chrétien

Perm. Rep. to U.N.: Robert Fowler

Political Parties:

Progressive Conservative Party, Liberal Party, New Democratic Party, Reform Party, Bloc Quebecois

 # Political Influences on Business

The United States and Canada share a range of fundamental values, such as a commitment to democracy, tolerance, and respect for human rights. It is no wonder that the two countries are close friends and allies. Both also have dynamic market economies with sophisticated industrial, agricultural, resource, and service sectors, and a commitment to high-living standards for their citizens. These factors complement the obvious geographic facts and have combined to make each the other's best customer. Despite occasional frictions, the relationship—probably the most intensive and complex in the world—between the U.S. and Canada is positive and cooperative.

The Parti Quebecois (PQ), which advocates withdrawing Quebec from Canada, controls the provincial government after having won election in September 1994.

In the meantime, the federal and provincial governments face debts accumulated over the last several years of recession with concomitant low levels of revenue. The

Federal government has acted to cut spending, but many economists are still concerned that Canada is facing a debt crisis with very grave potential consequences. Per capita debt ratios are among the highest in the world, and with taxes already at very high levels, the government's margin of manoeuver is constrained severely. Governments at all levels are struggling to contain costs while maintaining as much as possible of the social welfare programs Canadians value. A major effort to revamp such programs, including unemployment insurance, is underway but moving slowly. If successful, it could well reallocate premiums and benefits.

Canada is a parliamentary democracy and a federal state composed of ten provinces and two territories. The current federal government was elected on October 25, 1993, when the Liberal Party won 178 of the 295 seats in the House of Commons. A government is elected for a period not to exceed five years, but normally calls elections before that date.

Provincial elections were held in Quebec in September 1994, in Manitoba in April 1995, and in Ontario and Saskatchewan in June 1995. Elections must be held in British Columbia by fall 1996.

Contacts in the U.S.A. & in Canada

Contacts in the United States:

Embassy of Canada
501 Pennsylvania Avenue, N.W.
Washington, D.C. 20001
Tel: (202) 682-1740
Fax: (202) 682-7726

U.S. Department of State
Bureau of Consular Affairs
Tel: (202) 647-5225
Canada Desk
Tel: (202) 647-3135

U.S. Department of Commerce
Canada Desk
Tel: (202) 482-3101

Canadian Office of Tourism
1251 Ave. of the Americas
Room 1035
New York, N.Y. 10020
Tel: (212) 757-3583

Contacts in Canada:

The Embassy of the United States
100 Wellington St.
Ottawa, Ontario, Canada K1P 5T1;
P.O. Box 5000
Ogdensburg, N.Y. 13669-0430
Tel: (613) 238-5335 or 4470
Fax: (613) 233-5720
(Ottawa, Ontario)

Dun & Bradstreet Canada
Postal Address: P.O. Box 6200, Station A, Mississauga, Ontario, Canada L5A 4G4
Street Address: 5770 Hurontario Street, Mississauga, Ontario, Canada L5R 3G5
Tel: (905) 568-6000
Fax: (905) 568-5794

PRIME MINISTER JEAN CHRÉTIEN
OFFICE OF THE PRIME MINISTER
Langevin Blk.
Ottawa, Ontario K1A OA2, Canada

Passport/Visa Requirements

Visa Information   Tel: (202) 663-1225

Entry Requirements: Proof of U.S. citizenship and photo identification are required for travel to Canada. Visas are not required for U.S. citizens and permanent residents entering from the United States for stays up to 180 days.

Some Notes on French-Speaking Canadians

1. If English-speaking Canadians can be said to exhibit a traditional British reserve, French-speaking Canadians display French characteristics. Their gestures tend to be expansive, they may stand closer than the English when talking, and they are more likely to touch during a conversation.
2. French Canadian businessmen shake hands more often than English-speaking Canadians. Both groups shake hands upon greeting, but French Canadian men also shake hands at introductions and departures, even if the person has been greeted earlier that day. Women may decide whether or not to shake hands. In general, the French handshake is briefer and less hearty than the English handshake.
3. Only good friends and family members will be greeted with an embrace, and (sometimes) a series of kisses on the cheeks. French Canadians do not end an embrace by thumping each other on the back.
4. A French Canadian house is divided into "public" rooms (which visitors may enter) and "private" rooms (which one may only enter when asked). Be aware that the kitchen is often one of the private rooms.
5. Address French Canadians by their title and surname until invited to do otherwise. While they often use first names over the telephone, French Canadians usually revert to using surnames in person.
6. Of course, when dealing with French Canadians, it is important to have all material written in French as well as English.

Chile

Official Name:	Republic of Chile (República de Chile)
Official Language:	Spanish
Government System:	Unitary multiparty republic
Population:	14.1 million
Population Growth:	1.5%
Area:	756,626 sq. km. (292,058 sq. mi.); nearly twice the size of California
Natural Resources:	copper, timber, iron ore, nitrates, precious metals, molybdenum
Major Cities:	Santiago (capital), Viña del Mar, Valparaíso, Concepción, Temuco

Cultural Note: Chile is isolated. During the days of the Spanish Empire, it was the most remote colony on this continent. The Andes cut Chile off from the rest of South America. Isolation is a fact of life even within Chile itself; the deserts of Northern Chile are a long way from the rainy hills of Southern Chile. From a marketing point of view, Central Chile is the most important region to focus upon. Approximately 90% of the population resides in Chile's Central Valley.

Age Breakdown

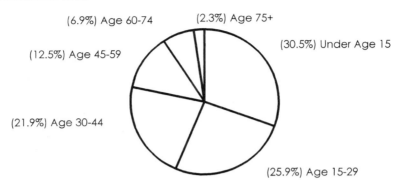

(6.9%) Age 60-74
(2.3%) Age 75+
(12.5%) Age 45-59
(30.5%) Under Age 15
(21.9%) Age 30-44
(25.9%) Age 15-29

Life Expectancy: 68 years male; 75 years female (1990)

 ## Time

For business appointments, punctuality is expected from foreigners. However, do not be surprised if your Chilean counterpart is late.

Everyone, foreigners included, is supposed to be late to social functions. For a meal at a Chilean home, arrive about fifteen minutes late. Be at least a half hour late to a party.

Chile is four hours behind Greenwich Mean Time (G.M.T. − 4), which is one hour ahead of U.S. Eastern Standard Time (E.S.T. + 1).

 ## Holidays

(Update: Getting Through Customs *http://www.getcustoms.com*)

New Year's Day	1 January
Labor Day	1 May
Commemoration of the Battle of Iquique	21 May
Saints Peter and Paul	29 June
Official Holiday	11 September
Independence Day	18 September
Day of the Army	19 September
Columbus Day	12 October

Work Week

- Business hours are 9:00 A.M. to 5:00 P.M., Monday through Friday. A two-hour lunch is usually eaten at 12:00. Government offices are open 9:00 A.M. to 4:30 P.M., Monday through Friday, and bank hours are 9:00 A.M. to 2:00 P.M..

- The best times to make appointments are from 10:00 A.M. to 12:00 and 2:30 to 5:00 P.M. Following-up a late morning appointment with a business lunch is also popular.

Religious/Societal Influences on Business

The majority of Chileans (over 75%) are Roman Catholic. However, Chile has no official religion, and the Chilean Catholic Church has never achieved the degree of political influence that the Church has in some other Latin American nations. Protestantism is growing rapidly, and now counts 13% of Chileans among its followers.

Chile's traditional values center around the family. As a corollary, Chileans prefer to do business with their relatives. Nepotism does not generate any controversy in Chile. Chile remains a male-dominated society, and machismo is still strong.

In their isolation from the rest of the world, Chileans developed a sophisticated body of art and literature. Pablo Neruda is one of the best known poets of the 20th century. The first Nobel Prize in Literature awarded to a Latin American went to Chile's Gabriela Mistral in 1945. Novelist Isabel Allende is the daughter of Chilean President Salvador Allende, the Marxist who was overthrown and slain in a C.I.A.-supported coup in 1973. Chileans are also proud of their world-class wines. In Chile's isolation, its vineyards escaped the phylloxera mite which has periodically devastated the world's vineyards since the 1870s.

5 Cultural Tips

1. Be wary about drawing parallels between Chile and other "Southern Cone" nations. Chile's relations with its neighbors are not always cordial. Chile and Argentina have had several border disputes, especially over the oil resources of Tierra del Fuego. To the north, Chile won the War of the Pacific in 1879 against Peru and Bolivia, after which Chile annexed the nitrate-rich Atacama desert. Peru and Bolivia still want this land back. Additionally, Chile lays claim to a large section of Antarctica, land also claimed by Argentina and the United Kingdom.

2. Although Chile won the War of the Pacific, it lost the first sea battle of the war. At the Battle of Iquique, two small Chilean ships fought a huge Peruvian warship off of the port city of Iquique. Badly outclassed, Chilean Captain Arturo Prat rammed the Peruvian ship and tried to board it. He and his men died in the attempt, but their never-say-die attitude inspired all of Chile. Chileans are very patriotic.

3. Chile is a conservative country in several respects. The Spanish spoken in Chile is fairly "pure," quite unlike the Italian-influenced Spanish of Argentina. Introductions are formal and business dress is conservative. Executives of both sexes generally wear blue or gray suits, without jewelry.

4. Chile is a major wine-drinking and wine-producing country. Wine makes a good topic of conversation. However, there are several traditions about pouring wine in Chile, so it is safer for a foreigner to avoid pouring wine rather than inadvertently cause offense. (For example, it is insulting to pour wine with the left hand, or so that the wine splashes against the far inside surface of a wineglass.)

5. When they're not drinking wine, Chileans are enjoying several other indigenous alcoholic drinks. *Chicha* is made from grape juice which has not yet fully fermented into wine. The powerful, colorless liquor called *pisco* is made only in Chile and Peru; it is often mixed into a pisco sour. And another strong liquor is *Aguardiente*, used in a traditional Christmastime coffee drink. Legend has it that the eleven letters in the word Aguardiente gave the name for the daily Chilean snack, *las once*. Belying its name, las once is not served at 11 A.M., but in the late afternoon like a British tea.

 Economic Overview

Chile's economy has expanded for the last 12 years, averaging over 6% growth per year. This growth has been led by a boom in exports, which are concentrated in primary and processed natural resources, principally copper, fresh fruit, and forestry and fishery products.

Chile has a prosperous, essentially free market economy, with the degree of government intervention varying according to the philosophy of the different regimes.

Copper remains vital to the health of the economy; Chile is the world's largest producer and exporter of copper. Success in meeting the government's goal of sustained annual growth of 5% depends on world copper prices, the level of confidence of foreign investors and creditors, and the government's own ability to maintain a conservative fiscal stance.

Since the return to democratic rule in 1990, Chilean-U.S. relations have flourished. The U.S. government has welcomed Chile's successful effort to regain its place in the international arena after years of political isolation, and views Chile's successful program of sustained economic reform and its peaceful transition to democracy as models for other countries.

Cultural Note: Although Chile's capital, Santiago, was founded in 1541, the Chileans did not settle their Southern frontier until the 1880s, around the same time the United States was settling its Western frontier. As in the U.S.A., Chile's Southern region had been the domain of formidable Indian tribes. These Araucanian Indians had defended their fjords and rain-drenched mountains from the Chileans in a war lasting 350 years!

Comparative Data

Overall Rating: 2.88

GDP Growth
Per Capita Income
Trade Flow with USA
Country Risk
Monetary Policy
Trade Policy
Protection of Property Rights
Foreign Investment Climate

1 Lowest
2 Weak
3 Adequate
4 Good
5 Highest

Country Risk Rating

Gross Domestic Product: $52 billion
GDP Growth: 4.2%
Per Capita Income: $3,700

Trade Flows with the U.S.A.

Rank as Export Market for U.S.A. Goods & Services: 28th
U.S.A. Exports to Chile: $3.6 billion
Growth Rate of Exports: 28%
U.S.A. Imports from Chile: $1.9 billion
Growth Rate of Imports: 2%
Rank as a Supplier of Imports into the U.S.A.:   39th

Top U.S.A. Exports to Chile: Machinery; motor vehicles; electrical components; plastics; medical and optical equipment; aircraft and parts; mineral fuel; paper; fertilizers; organic chemicals.

Top U.S.A. Prospects to Chile: Energy production equipment; franchising; pollution control equipment; telecommunications equipment; sporting goods/recreational equipment; computers and peripherals; mining equipment; medical equipment; port equipment; grains.

Country Risk

Dun & Bradstreet rates Chile as having good capacity to meet outstanding payment liabilities.

Liberal credit terms now predominate on sales to Chile. Letters of credit now account for only about 15% of shipments, but are still advised for initial transactions. Open account terms of 30 to 60 days is the norm.

Monetary Policy

Helped by an appreciating peso, inflation has declined gradually since 1990, reaching 7.4% in mid-1995. GDP growth in 1995 was expected to reach 6%, and inflation was expected to end the year at or below 9%. *Monetary Unit:* Chilean peso.

Trade Policy

TARIFFS: The Chilean tariff rate is currently 11% on nearly all products from most countries, although many products from Latin American countries with which Chile has trade arrangements enter with lower duties.

Chile maintains a price band system for wheat, wheat flour, edible oils, and sugar. This variable tariff system is designed to maintain domestic prices for these commodities within a predetermined band, which shields Chilean producers from price fluctuations in international market prices.

IMPORT LICENSING: Import licenses are granted as a routine procedure. Licenses are required for weapons and pharmaceuticals. Licensing requirements are maintained largely as a statistical gathering mechanism, not as a control or barrier.

The importation of used passenger and cargo transportation vehicles is prohibited, except in the following cases: used ambulances, armored cars, mobile homes, prison vans, street highway cleaning vehicles, and cement-making vehicles.

IMPORT TAXES: Imports are subject to the same 18% value-added tax (VAT) as are domestic goods.

Imported automobiles are subject to luxury taxes based on value and engine size. Other imported luxury goods such as yachts, some types of jewelry, and others are also subject to luxury taxes.

Protection of Intellectual Property Rights

Chile belongs to the World Intellectual Property Organization, and patents, trademarks, industrial designs, models, and copyrights are protected in Chile by the provisions of the International Convention for the Protection of Industrial Property (Paris Convention).

Chile's intellectual property regime is generally compatible with international norms, with a few exceptions. Industrial designs and models are protected for a nonrenewable period of 10 years. The registration of trademarks is also valid for 10 years.

The Industrial Property Law promulgated in 1991 substantially improved Chile's protection of industrial patents, but falls short of international standards. The law provides a patent term of 15 years from the date of grant. This will have to be changed to 20 years by the year 2000 as a result of the GATT Uruguay Round agreements.

In 1992, the Chilean Congress approved legislation that extends the term of copyright protection from 30 to 50 years.

A trademark should be registered as soon as the exporter/investor has any intention of doing business in Chile. Ownership of the trademark is not prejudiced by lack of use in cases where the registered party makes use of the mark in other countries, and trademarks may be registered perpetually in periods of 10 years at a time.

Foreign Investment Climate

In 1994, the United States was the largest foreign investor in Chile, adding $979 million to the overall U.S. portfolio of more than $3 billion in the market. The mining sector was the principal recipient of foreign investment, adding a total of $1.8 billion in 1994. The services sector received $314 million and the industrial sector received $321 million.

A key feature of Chile's development strategy is a welcoming attitude toward foreign investors, which is embodied in the country's foreign investment law, known as D.L. 600.

D.L. 600 was promulgated in 1974 and has frequently been liberalized. Since 1991, nearly all foreign direct investment in Chile has taken place through D.L. 600. Under this law, foreign investment must be approved by the government's Foreign Investment Committee, but approval procedures are expeditious and not burdensome. Typically, applications are approved within a matter of days, and almost always within a month.

Under D.L. 600, investors sign standardized contracts giving them the rights to: receive nondiscriminatory treatment; participate in any form of investment; hold assets indefinitely; remit or reinvest earnings immediately and remit capital after one year; opt for either national tax treatment or a guaranteed rate for the first 10 years of an investment; and acquire foreign currency at the inter-bank rate of exchange.

Chile's welcoming attitude to foreign investment, along with the country's wealth of natural resources, has led to approximately $16 billion of foreign investment in the 1986–1994 period.

Despite Chile's generally positive attitude toward foreign capital, certain negative treatment of foreign capital persists. Profits may be repatriated immediately, but capital may not be repatriated until after one year.

Businesses in Chile are predominantly owned and controlled by private interests. Although the military and democratic governments of the last 20 years have privatized many state corporations, the state retains holdings in several industries. The most important public corporation is CODELCO, the world's largest copper company, which the government has said it will not sell.

Current Leaders & Political Parties

(Update: International Academy at Santa Barbara *http://www.iasb.org/cwl*)

State, Government, and Political Party Leaders:

Pres.: Eduardo Frei Ruiz-Tagle

Cabinet Ministers:

Interior: vacant
Foreign Affairs: Carlos Figueroa
Defense: Edmundo Perez
Finance: Eduardo Aninat
Economy: Alvaro Garcia
Education: Ernesto Schiefelbein
Justice: Soledad Alvear
Mining: Benjamin Teplizky
Agriculture: Emiliano Ortega
Natl. Resources: Adriana Delpiano
Public Works: Ricardo Lagos
Health: Carlos Massad
Labor: Jorge Arrate
Transportation and Telecommunications: Narciso Irureta
Housing: Edmundo Hermosilla
Planning: Luis Maira
Natl. Service for Women: Josefina Bilbao

Sec. Gen. of the Govt.: Víctor Manuel Rebolledo
Sec. Gen. of the Pres.: Genaro Arriagada
Corporation for the Enhancement of Production: Felipe Sandoval
Natl. Energy Comn.: Alejandro Jadresic

Other Officials:

Pres. of the Senate: Gabriel Valdes
Pres. of the Chamber of Deputies: Jorge Schaulsohn
Pres. of the Supreme Court: Marcos Aburto
Ambassador to U.S.: Patricio Silva
Perm. Rep. to U.N.: Juan Somava

Political Parties:

Christian Democratic Party (PDC), Social Democratic Party, Socialist Party, Pro-Democracy Party (PPD), Centrist Alliance Party, Natl. Renewal Party (RN), Independent Democratic Union (UDI), Natl. Party, Radical Party (RP), Humane Party (PH)

 Political Influences on Business

Chilean politics is marked by broad consensus among the major parties about the importance of a democratic political system and a free-market economic system. Key differences between the governing coalition and the rightist opposition involve strategies for, and the role of government in, addressing issues such as poverty eradication, health care, infrastructure, and education, as well as the degree to which the political system should be reformed to eliminate power-sharing arrangements created under the former military government which protect the interests of the armed services and the political right at the expense of those of the elected majority.

President Eduardo Frei, a Christian Democrat leading a coalition of four center-left parties, won an overwhelming victory in December 1993 elections and began his six-year term on March 11, 1994, when he succeeded Patricio Aylwin (also a Christian Democrat). An engineer by training, Frei was a successful businessman before entering politics in the 1980s. Many of his closest advisors are U.S.-trained and share his commitment to Chile's successful free market economic model.

Frei heads Chile's powerful executive branch, and his center-left coalition has a majority of the elected seats in both the lower and upper houses of Congress (the Chamber of Deputies and the Senate). Nonetheless, under constitutional provisions promulgated during the period of military rule (1973–1990), the balance of power in the upper house is held by the eight living "institutional" senators appointed near the end of the Pinochet era. Thus, the government must negotiate with the conservative opposition to pass any of its legislative program.

For much of this century, Chilean politics have been marked by a three-way division between the political right, center, and left, with each holding roughly one-third of the vote. This division persists today with the important modification that, since the transition to democracy, the political center (including the center right and center left) has gained strength at the expense of the extremes.

Congressional elections (for all Deputies and half the elected Senators) are scheduled for December of 1997. In addition, barring constitutional reform to eliminate appointed Senators, new "institutional" Senators will also be named. The next Presidental election is scheduled for December of 1999.

Contacts in the U.S.A. & in Chile

Contacts in the United States:

EMBASSY OF THE REPUBLIC OF CHILE
1732 Massachusetts Ave., N.W.
Washington, D.C. 20036
Tel: (202) 785-1746
Fax: (202) 887-5579

U.S. DEPARTMENT OF STATE
Bureau of Consular Affairs
Tel: (202) 647-5225
Country Desk Officer, Chile
Tel: (202) 647-2575

U.S. DEPARTMENT OF COMMERCE
Chile Desk
Int'l Trade Admin.
Tel: (202) 482-1495

Contacts in Chile:

U.S. EMBASSY
Codina Bldg.
1343 Agustinas
Santiago
Mailing Address:
APO AA 34033
Tel: [56] (2) 232-2600
Telex: 240062-USA-CL
Fax: [56] (2) 330-3710

CHILEAN-AMERICAN CHAMBER OF COMMERCE
Av. Americo Vespucio Sur 80
9 Piso
4131 Correo Central

Santiago, Chile
Tel: [56] 2-208-4140
Fax: [56] 2-206-0911
Telex: (392) 340260 PBVTR CL

DUN & BRADSTREET LTDA.
Postal Address: Casilla 19096 Vitacura,
Santiago, Chile
Street Address: Av. El Bosque Norte
0177, Oficina 901, Santiago, Chile
Tel: [56] (2) 332-0800
Fax: [56] (2) 332-0810

PRESIDENT EDUARDO FREI RUIZ-TAGLE
Palacio De La Moneda
Santiago, Republic of Chile

Passport/Visa Requirements

Visa Information   Tel: (202) 663-1225

Entry Requirements: Passport is required. No visa is required for U.S. citizens for a three-month stay. Those considering scientific, technical, or mountaineering activities in areas classified as frontier areas are required to obtain authorization from the Chilean government. Requests for authorization must be presented to Chilean authorities at least 90 days prior to the beginning of the expedition. Upon request, a round-trip ticket or a ticket to any boundary country must be shown.

For current information concerning entry and customs requirements for Chile, travelers can contact the Chilean Embassy or the nearest consulate.

Faux Pas: A U.S. executive went to Chile for a final negotiating round with the owner of a major Chilean corporation. Unfortunately, the gentleman from the U.S.A. wore a heavy gold ring with a diamond, plus a gold watch. The Chileans interpreted this jewelry as proof that the American was in business to amass personal wealth, and furthermore had the poor taste to display it. The Chilean contract went to an Italian firm.

China

Official Name:	People's Republic of China (Chung-hua Jen-min Kung-ho-kuo)
Official Language:	Mandarin (Standard) Chinese
Government System:	Communist
Population:	1.2 billion
Population Growth:	1.1%
Area:	9.6 million sq. km. (3.7 million sq. mi.); U.S. is 9.3 million sq. km.
Natural Resources:	coal, iron ore, crude oil, mercury, tin, tungsten, antimony, manganese, molybdenum, vanadium, magnetite, aluminum, lead, zinc, uranium, hydropower
Major Cities:	Beijing (capital), Shanghai, Tianjin, Guangzhou, Shenyang, Wuhan, Chong Qing

Cultural Note: China is the most populous nation on Earth. One in every fifth person in the world lives in the People's Republic of China. A strict one-child-per-couple policy (enforced more in the cities than in the countryside, and more among ethnic Chinese than among China's minorities) has reduced the growth rate to 1.1%, where it is expected to stay in the foreseeable future.

Age Breakdown

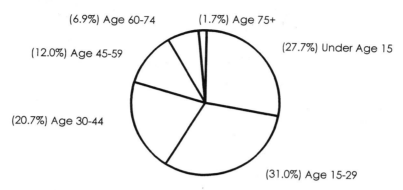

(6.9%) Age 60-74   (1.7%) Age 75+

(12.0%) Age 45-59   (27.7%) Under Age 15

(20.7%) Age 30-44

(31.0%) Age 15-29

Life Expectancy: 68 years male; 72 years female (1993)

 ## Time

Foreigners are expected to be prompt to all business and social appointments. Making someone wait or cancelling an appointment involves a loss of face and is a serious affront.

Despite its huge size, all of China is in the same time zone, eight hours ahead of Greenwich Mean Time (G.M.T. + 8), which is thirteen hours ahead of U.S. Eastern Standard Time (E.S.T. + 13).

 ## Holidays

(Update: Getting Through Customs *http://www.getcustoms.com*)

This list is a working guide. Dates should be corroborated before final travel plans are made. In cases where holidays fall on Saturday or Sunday, commercial establishments may be closed the preceding Friday or the following Monday.

Do not plan business trips during the Chinese Lunar New Year since many businesses close for a week before and after the festival. The date of the New Year varies according to the Lunar Calendar.

Spring Festival	19–20 February
Labor Day	1 May
National Day, celebrating the founding of the People's Republic of China in 1949	1–2 October
New Year's Day	Jan. 1

There are many local holidays which are celebrated in different regions. Check with your contact to insure your appointments will not conflict with these festivities.

Work Week

- The best times to schedule a business trip are from April to June or September to October.
- Business and government hours: 8:00 A.M. to 5:00 P.M., Monday to Friday.
- Banking hours: 10:00 A.M. to 6:00 P.M., Monday to Saturday.
- Shop hours: 9:00 A.M to 7:00 P.M., daily. Most stores in the major cities stay open until 10:00 P.M.

Religious/Societal Influences on Business

Foreigners often refer to the People's Republic of China as Mainland China, Communist China, or Red China. In the presence of Chinese, only the term People's Republic of China or the abbreviation PRC is acceptable. The national language of the PRC is Mandarin Chinese, a northern dialect of Chinese. (Note that most Chinese-Americans speak Cantonese, a southern dialect. The two dialects are not mutually intelligible.) Never confuse the PRC with the Republic of China (Taiwan), which the PRC considers a rogue province temporarily out of its sovereignty.

The Chinese are proud of their history and lineage. Historically, China (formerly known as the Middle Kingdom) has been a country ruled by strong dynasties. The first recorded dynasty was founded around 2200 B.C., and the last dynasty, the Ching (Manchu), ended in 1911. During this time, China produced some of the most important innovations in the history of the world, including the compass, papermaking, gunpowder, and movable-type printing.

While the PRC is nominally a Communist country (and still ruled tightly by its Communist government), capitalism is on the rise.

Harmony is prized by the Chinese. Every person is entitled to respect, which is spoken of in English as having face. Showing respect for someone causes them to gain face. Embarrassing them in public causes a loss of face, a very serious breach of etiquette. Criticizing or upbraiding someone in front of others causes that person to lose face. A person who loses his or her temper in public has shamefully lost face, and causes loss of face to the person at which the anger is directed.

Another important aspect of Chinese culture is *guanxi* (gwon-shee). Guanxi cannot merely be translated as "relationships," but an approximation would be "relationships that involve obligations." The people you know, your connection to them, involves responsibilities that are crucial for conducting business. Guanxi is the way a Chinese executive performs his duty for his associates, and maintains their obligations to him as well. These relationships are the way issues are resolved and deals consummated.

China's humiliation by foreign powers in the 19th and early 20th centuries is an embarrassing memory. All Chinese (Communists and capitalists alike) are adamant that it must never happen again. This is one reason that the PRC is so deaf to foreign demands over human rights; such demands are seen as foreign interference in China's sovereignty. Foreign executives should always be aware of the Chinese determination to oppose all aggressors.

Since the average Westerner is physically bigger than the average Chinese, Westerners need to be cautious not to intimidate the Chinese. (It is difficult to establish trust with someone who looms over you.) Tall people should take every opportunity to minimize the height differential. Sit rather than stand. When you must stand, try to stand on a lower level, such as a lower step on a staircase.

5 Cultural Tips

1. Always carry plenty of business cards; a foreigner without a business card in China is a nonperson. One side of your card should be in English, and the other side should have a translation in Mandarin Chinese. Gold ink is the most prestigious color for the Chinese side. Although red is considered a lucky color in China, do not print your name in red ink. (Some Buddhists only print the names of the deceased in red.) Accept cards graciously and treat them with respect. Do not put a business card in your wallet if you keep your wallet in your back pocket.

2. China is a hierarchical society. Confucianism gives a ranking to every individual in society. Deference to those of higher rank is expected. Status is acquired through age, job, marriage, and wealth. When entering a business meeting, the highest ranking member of your group should lead the way. The senior members of a delegation do all the talking, junior members do not interrupt, and only speak when spoken to. The guest of honor at a banquet is the last to arrive and the first to leave.

3. Conducting business in China takes time. If you deal with the government, expect the bulk of your first meeting to be taken up with a ritual introductory speech. A PRC official will usually detail the most general information about China and the state of your industry. (Typically the speech is so general that it would be useful only to a foreign amnesiac who inexplicably found himself in China.)

4. Despite official disapproval from the Communist government, traditional Chinese beliefs are still followed. This includes not only Confucianism but folk beliefs (such as astrology and geomancy) as well. Many Chinese will consult the stars for an auspicious day and hour before concluding a business deal.

5. Above all else, patience is required to do business in China. U.S. executives have a reputation for impatience, and the Chinese will typically drag out negotiations well beyond your deadlines just to gain an advantage. They may try to renegotiate everything on the final day of your visit! If possible, never let them know your departure date.

 ## Economic Overview

The People's Republic of China has in recent years boasted one of the fastest growing economies in the world. Its gross domestic product increased 11.8% in 1994 and was projected to grow at 9–10% during 1995 and 8% in 1996.

Certain regions in China (especially those along the coast) are booming, and many people are becoming more prosperous. Rapid economic growth, bold reform measures, and massive infrastructure plans point to enormous market potential in China. Chinese leaders project spending at least $100 billion per year on imports from now until the year 2000.

After a 20-year hiatus, trade between the United States and China resumed in 1972 and developed rapidly after normalization of diplomatic relations in 1979. Two-way trade increased from $2.3 billion in 1979 to $48.1 billion in 1994. However, U.S. trade with China has been in deficit since 1983, reaching an historic high at nearly $30 billion in 1994, second only to the U.S.-Japan trade deficit.

Foreign investment continues to pour into China. According to Chinese statistics for 1994, contracted direct foreign investment (which measures the commitment of private foreign funds to Chinese projects and joint ventures) amounted to roughly U.S. $69 billion, down from 1993's U.S. $111 billion. The United States (which had a total contracted investment for 1994 of U.S. $2.5 billion) overtook Taiwan to become China's second largest investor, following Hong Kong. By the end of 1994, more than 220,000 foreign-invested enterprises had registered in China, an increase from 1993 of more than 30,000.

China's political leadership, characterized by group consensus rather than strong leadership by a single individual, generally supports foreign trade and business investment in China, and agrees on the need for continued economic reforms and for political stability. In February 1995, the U.S. and China signed a major agreement on protection of intellectual property which improved the atmosphere for bilateral economic relations. China, however, sharply criticized the U.S. for allowing Taiwan's Lee Tung-Hui to make an unofficial visit in June, 1995, and disagreement over human rights, weapons proliferation, and trade issues could continue to affect bilateral relations.

Apart from macro factors affecting doing business in China, China's current state-controlled economic structure continues to erect roadblocks to doing business in China. These include:

- limitations on the right of foreign companies to directly access China's retail market
- foreign exchange controls
- an inefficient banking system
- insufficient enforcement of intellectual property laws
- very restricted access for foreign services
- an inadequate system for dispute resolution.

After more than 15 years of reform and opening, the government's role in the economy remains strong, and will be for the foreseeable future. The central government, however, continues to lack sufficient resources to carry out its programs. At times, the government appears to be more willing to use traditional tools of a planned economy rather than pushing forward with deeper reforms. This more cautious attitude toward market-oriented economic reform is apparent in the stronger emphasis on state planning in industrial policy. It is likely to persist for some time.

U.S. licensing requirements for most exports to China continue to relax. At the same time, the U.S. has tightened its enforcement of regulations prohibiting any type of export to Chinese end-users involved in the proliferation of missiles or weapons of mass destruction.

Cultural Note: Just as the French Revolution renamed the days of the week, revolutionaries have made linguistic changes to signify a break with the past. After taking control of mainland China in 1949, the Communist Chinese made changes in their language, both written and verbal.

Outside the People's Republic of China, many Chinese have been slow to incorporate these changes. To this day, Taiwan primarily uses prerevolutionary forms of written and spoken Chinese. When you have your written materials translated for use in the PRC, make sure your translator uses the appropriate, "reformed" Chinese.

Comparative Data

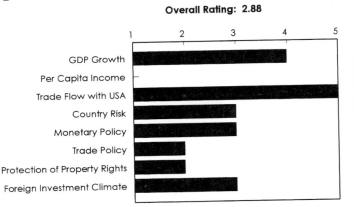

Overall Rating: 2.88

Country Risk Rating

Gross Domestic Product: $3 trillion*

GDP Growth: 11.8%

Per Capita Income: $2,500*

* Purchasing Power Parity

Trade Flows with the U.S.A.

Rank as Export Market for U.S.A. Goods & Services: 13th

U.S.A. Exports to China: $11.8 billion

Growth Rate of Exports: 27%

U.S.A. Imports from China: $45.5 billion

Growth Rate of Imports: 17%

Rank as a Supplier of Imports into the U.S.A.:   4th

Top U.S.A. Exports to China: Machinery; aircraft; fertilizers; electrical components; cotton/yarn/fabric; medical and optical equipment; motor vehicles; organic chemicals; plastics and resins; cereals.

Top U.S.A. Prospects for Export to China: Aircraft and parts; electric power systems; computers and peripherals; telecommunications equipment; agricultural chemicals; automotive parts; industrial chemicals; plastic materials and resins; pollution control equipment; machine tools.

Country Risk

Dun & Bradstreet rates China as having sufficient capacity to meet outstanding payment liabilities.

Letter of credit terms account for about 50% of trade transactions. More liberal terms such as open account are increasingly being used, but not recommended without prior knowledge of the China market. When open account terms are extended, 60 to 90 day terms are generally given.

Monetary Policy

Since the beginning of China's efforts to stabilize its economy in mid-1993, Chinese authorities have been reluctant to pursue tight macroeconomic policies that might lead to a sharp economic contraction. At the core of the government's monetary and fiscal problems remains the issue of state enterprise reforms. Despite the crippling financial costs of support for state-owned enterprises, there is little to suggest that the central government is prepared to risk the labor unrest which might follow any serious effort to tackle the problem. Strong inflationary pressures will continue to bedevil the economy unless the government introduces vital reforms required to address financial imbalances in the economy.

Inflation was at 21.7% in 1994 and projected at 14.5% in 1995. Dun & Bradstreet forecasts inflation to drop to 9.5% in 1996 and to 10.5% in 1997. *Monetary Unit*: yuan.

Trade Policy

TARIFFS: Import tariff rates are divided into two categories: the general tariff and the minimum (most-favored nation) tariff. Imports from the U.S. are assessed the minimum tariff rate since the U.S. has concluded an agreement with China containing reciprocal preferential tariff clauses.

China has gradually reduced tariffs on selected products, though the overall tariff levels are still very high. Tariffs range from 3% on promoted imports to more than 150% on discouraged imports such as automobiles.

Preferential duty reduction or exemption may be offered to firms located in Special Economic Zones, open cities, and foreign trade zones.

By adopting the harmonized system for customs classification and statistics on January 1, 1992, China indicated its interest in bringing its tariff system into conformity with international standards.

IMPORT LICENSING: China administers a complex system of nontariff trade barriers, including individual quotas on imports of machinery, electronic equipment and general goods like grain, fertilizer, textiles, and chemicals. While China is in the process of eliminating a great number of import licensing requirements, licenses will continue to be required for items including rubber products, wool, passenger vehicles, and hauling trucks. China's import licensing system still acts as an effective import barrier to many imported goods.

Numerous categories of commodities are affected by quotas, including watches, automobiles, motorcycles, machinery, electronic items and carbonated beverages. Under a bilateral Memorandum of Understanding (MOU) on Market Access signed in October 1992, China agreed to reduce trade barriers and gradually open its market to U.S. exports. Under the market access MOU, China is committed to curtailing most of these barriers by 1997.

IMPORT TAXES: In addition to assessment and collection of tariffs, a value-added tax generally equal to 17% is also collected on imported items. Certain imports are also subject to a consumption (excise) tax.

Protection of Intellectual Property Rights

The U.S. and China signed a Memorandum of Understanding on the Protection of Intellectual Property (IPR MOU) in 1992, pursuant to which China improved its laws governing intellectual property rights protection over the following two years and joined the Berne and Geneva Phonograms Conventions. The March 1995 extension of the IPR MOU sets out a plan for enforcing IPR and grants market access to certain products. In March 1995, the U.S. and China agreed to an extension to the 1992 MOU and the Chinese agreed to open the market to companies with intellectual property rights products and enforce rigorously Chinese IPR regulations.

China and the U.S. established bilateral copyright relations in March 1992, and China subsequently acceded to several international conventions. U.S. owners of computer software, books, films, sound recordings, and other subject matter now enjoy protection under China's copyright legislation, the Berne Convention, the Universal Copyright Convention, and the Geneva Phonogram Convention. Computer software programs will be protected for 50 years without mandatory registration requirements.

China's Patent Law, enacted in 1984, was extended in 1993 to protect chemical inventions. The period of patent protection was also lengthened to 20 years. China acceded to the Patent Cooperation Treaty in 1994 and will perform international patent searches and preliminary examinations of patent applications. Under the Patent Law, foreign parties must utilize the services of a registered Chinese agent to submit the patent application.

Trademark registration in China should be an integral part of any company's initial market entry. This is critical since China is a first-to-register system that requires no evidence of prior use or ownership. However, well-known trademarks are to receive protection even if there is no prior registration in China. Although problems remain with enforcement, China's trademark regime basically conforms to world standards. China joined in 1989 the Madrid Pact for the Protection of Trademarks, which grants reciprocal trademark registration to member countries. China amended its laws in

1993 to add special regulations allowing criminal prosecution for trademark infringement. Foreign companies must utilize the services of registered agents to submit the trademark application.

Foreign Investment Climate

Since 1978, China has actively sought foreign manufacturing investment and technology. The government is now seeking to attract foreign investment to poorer inland provinces and may increase incentives in inland areas.

In China's partially reformed command economy, numerous restrictions are placed on foreign ownership and the establishment of business enterprises. Large sectors of the Chinese economy, particularly in services and infrastructure, remain largely or completely closed to foreign investment. China has been gradually relaxing some restrictions on ownership and establishment. Since 1992, for example, new services sectors were opened on an experimental basis, including retailing, insurance, and tourism.

China is now also encouraging, on a limited basis, foreign investment in other previously closed sectors such as roads, railroads and harbors, Chinese airlines, and gold mines.

The 1994 Foreign Trade Law provides for extension of national treatment on a reciprocal basis to contracting parties of international treaties to which China is also a party. In practice, however, China's restrictive foreign trade and investment regulations deny foreign companies national treatment in all service and many industrial sectors. The U.S. is working bilaterally with other World Trade Organization (WTO) parties to encourage China to grant unconditional national treatment as part of its accession to the WTO.

In those sectors where foreign investment is allowed, foreign-invested enterprises (FIEs) can be established as holding companies, wholly foreign-owned enterprises, equity joint ventures, cooperative joint ventures, or, since January 1995, foreign-invested companies limited by share. Under China's 1994 Company Law, foreign firms can also now open branches in China. Potential investment projects usually go through a multitiered screening process. The first step is approval of the proposed project. The central government has delegated varying levels of approval authority to local governments. Formerly, only the Special Economic Zones of Shenzhen, Shantou, Zhuhai, Xiamen, and Hainan, and open cities could approve projects valued at up to $30 million. This approval authority has now been extended to many provincial capitals and coastal cities. The inland cities and regions are limited to approving projects valued below $10 million. Projects exceeding these limits are approved by the Ministry of Foreign Trade and Economic Cooperation (MOFTEC) and the State Planning Commission (SPC), for greenfield projects, or the State Economic and Trade Commission (SETC) for projects involving existing enterprises. If an investment involves $100 million or more, it must also obtain State Council approval, after MOFTEC's review and approval.

Current Leaders & Political Parties

(Update: International Academy at Santa Barbara *http://www.iasb.org/cwl*)

State, Government, and Political Party Leaders:

Pres.: Jiang Zemin

Vice Pres.: Rong Yiren

Central Committee of the Chinese Communist Party:

Gen. Sec.: Jiang Zemin

Members of the Political Bureau: Jiang Zemin, Li Ruihuan, LiPeng, Qiao Shi, Tian Jiyun, Li Tieying, Zhu Rongji, Liu Huaqing, Hu Jintao, Ding Guangen, Li Lanqing, Qian Qichen, Yang Baibing, Wu Bangguo, Zou Jiahua, Jiang Chunyun, Wei Jianxing, Xie Fei

State Council:

Prem.: Li Peng

Vice Premiers: Zhu Rongji, Zou Jiahua, Qian Qichen, Li Lanqing, Wu Banggao, Jiang Chun-yun

Sec. Gen.: Luo Gan

State Councillors: Li Tieying, Song Jian, Li Guixian, Chen Junsheng, Gen. Chi Haotian, Ismail Amat, Peng Peiyun, Luo Gan

State Council Ministers:

Foreign Affairs: Qian Qichen

Natl. Defense: Gen. Chi Hoatian

State Planning Comn.: Chen Jinhua

State Economic and Trade Comn.: Wang Zhongyu

State Comn. for Economic Restructuring: Li Tieying

State Education Comn.: Zhu Kaixuan

State Science and Technology Comn.: Song Jian

Comn. of Science, Technology, and Industry for Natl. Defense: Ding Henggao

State Nationalities Affairs Comn.: Ismail Amat

Public Security: Tao Siju

State Security: Jia Chunwang

Finance: Liu Zhongli

Labor: Li Boyong

Geology and Mineral Resources: Zhu Xun

Construction: Hou Jie

Power Industry: Shi Dazhen
Coal Industry: Wang Senhao
Machine-building Industry: He Guangyuan
Electronics Industry: Hu Qili
Metallurgical Industry: Liu Qi
Chemical Industry: Gu Xiulian
Railways: Han Zhubin
Communications: Huang Zhendong
Posts and Telecommunications: Wu Jichuan
Water Resources: Niu Maosheng
Agriculture: Liu Jiang
Forestry: Xu Youfang
Internal Trade: Chen Bangzhu
Foreign Trade and Economic Coop.: Wu Yi
Culture: Liu Zhongde
Radio, Film, and Television: Sun Jiazheng
Gov. of the People's Bank of China: Dai Xiang Long

Other Officials:

Pres. of the Supreme People's Court: Ren Jianxin
Chmn. of the Standing Comn. of the Natl. People's Congress: Qiao Shi
Chmn. of the Central Military Comn.: Jiang Zemin
Ambassador to U.S.: Li Daoyu
Perm. Rep. to U.N: Qin Huasun

Political Parties:

Chinese Communist Party, Revolutionary Com. of the Kuomintang, China
Democratic League, China Democratic Natl. Construction Assoc., China Assoc.
for Promoting Democracy, Chinese Peasants' and Workers' Democratic Party,
China Zhi Gong Dang, Jiu San Society, Taiwan Democratic Self-Government
League

 Political Influences on Business

China's top political leaders continue their strong commitment to foreign business
investment in China. In February 1995, the U.S. and China signed a major agreement
on protection of intellectual property which improved the atmosphere for bilateral
economic relations. But disagreements over human rights, proliferation, and trade
issues continue to affect bilateral relations.

Rapid price inflation, corruption, lay-offs from state-run enterprises, the growing gap between coastal regions and the interior, and economic disparities between rural and urban areas have contributed to dissatisfaction among the populace. Northwestern China has been troubled by occasional unrest among minority ethnic and religious groups. Dissatisfaction has not often been translated into widespread political activity since 1989, in part because the government is working to minimize tensions over its economic policies, but also because it has acted swiftly to repress any potential political protests.

In practice, major decisions are made by a few key leaders of the Chinese Communist Party. Ministries and/or the Standing Committee of the National People's Congress (China's legislature) formulate policy on day-to-day issues. Some provincial governments, especially those in fast-growing coastal regions, actively adopt local policy variations. Senior political figures generally agree on the need for further economic reforms and the need for political stability, but there are differences over the content, pace, and ending point of reforms. Most observers believe that the death of 90-year-old Party elder Deng Xiaoping will reshape leadership politics, but this readjustment is expected to be gradual. China is more likely be governed by a collective leadership for the foreseeable future rather than one predominant figure.

Faux Pas: Numbers can have significant impact on the Chinese psyche. When the number 4 is pronounced in Chinese, it suggests the word for "death." No Chinese would live or work at a building with an address of "444."

 # Contacts in the U.S.A. & in China

Contacts in the United States:

EMBASSY OF THE PEOPLE'S REPUBLIC OF CHINA
2300 Connecticut Ave., N.W.
Washington, D.C. 20008
Tel: (202) 328-2500 or 2520
Fax: (202) 232-7855

U.S. DEPARTMENT OF STATE
Bureau of Consular Affairs
Tel: (202) 647-5225
Country Desk Officer, China
Tel: (202) 647-6300

U.S. DEPARTMENT OF COMMERCE
China Desk
Int'l Trade Admin.
Tel: (202) 482-3583

CHINA CHAMBER OF INTERNATIONAL COMMERCE
Suite 139
4301 Connecticut Avenue, N.W.
Washington, D.C. 20008
Tel: (202) 244-3244

CHINA NATIONAL TOURIST OFFICE
333 W. Broadway #201
Glendale, C.A. 91204
Tel: (818) 545-7505
Fax: (818) 545-7506

Contacts in China:

U.S. EMBASSY
Xiu Shui Bei Jie 3
Bieijing, PRC or
100600, PSC 461, Box 50,
Beijing, PRC
(FPO AP 96521-0002)
Tel: [86] (1) 532-3831
Telex: AMEMB CN 22701
Fax: [86] (1) 532-3178

AMERICAN CHAMBER OF COMMERCE IN THE
PEOPLE'S REPUBLIC OF CHINA
Beijing
c/o Schenker & Co. GmbH 22
Jiaguomen Wai Dajie
Bejing, PRC 10004
Tel: [86] (671) 512-3712
Fax: [86] (671) 512-6871

DUN & BRADSTREET INTERNATIONAL
CONSULTANT (SHANGHAI) LTD.
3rd floor, Champion Building
363 Chang Ping Road
Shanghai 200041, PR China
Tel: 86 21 6218 9402
Fax: 86 21 6218 8184

PRESIDENT JIANG ZEMIN
Office of the President
Zhonganahai
Beijing, People's Republic of China

PREMIER LI PENG
Office of the Premier
Zhonganahai
Beijing, People's Republic of China

 Passport/Visa Requirements

Visa Information: Tel: (202) 663-1225

Entry Requirements: Passport and visa required.

Cultural Note: Food is extremely important in China. There are few better ways for a foreigner to ingratiate him or herself than to express interest in the fine points of Chinese cuisine.

In addition to several business lunches, all business transactions require at least one evening banquet. In fact, there should be at least two banquets: the first one given by the Chinese host, the second one by you. It is vital for you to give a banquet in return for one given by your hosts. (Reciprocity is the way networks are built in China.)

1. Banquets range in size and price. Your banquet should appear to cost the same, per person, as the banquet given by your Chinese host. (Actually, as a foreigner without connections, you will probably pay more for the same banquet.) Never surpass your host in the degree of lavishness at your banquet; such one-upmanship will cause your host to lose face.

2. Most banquets start between 6:30 and 7:00 P.M. and last for about two hours. You should arrive about 30 minutes before your guests; they will arrive on time. Be prepared to sample every dish. The Chinese may even test your fortitude on purpose with exotic delicacies like marinated, deep-fried scorpions (intact with stingers) on a bed of rice.

3. The Chinese use chopsticks rather than a fork. Since the use of chopsticks takes time to learn, it is useful to practice this skill in advance. In fact, dropping your chopsticks is considered bad luck. Chinese chopsticks are generally both heavier and thicker than the chopsticks used in Japan. Chopsticks are called *kuaitzu*, a word that also means *hurry*. Most Chinese can eat very hurriedly indeed with chopsticks.

4. The Chinese also use a curved porcelain spoon. This is generally reserved for soup. However, when eating rice out of a small bowl, it is permissible to use the spoon if one has added something to the rice (say, meat or vegetables). But pure rice is eaten just with chopsticks, a task most Westerners find quite difficult to manage without spilling a lot of rice. Hold the rice bowl close to your mouth; this will catch some of the rice you drop. Fortunately, rice is traditionally served at the end of a meal. Since you want to display that you have eaten your fill, you will leave part of your last course uneaten.

5. Most Chinese restaurants will provide a chopstick rest on which you may place your chopsticks. Traditionally, placing them parallel on top of your bowl was considered a sign of bad luck. And sticking your chopsticks straight up in your rice bowl was also frowned upon, since they then resembled the joss sticks used in religious ceremonies. But these traditions are no longer observed universally, especially in restaurants.

6. There is one other skill to learn with chopsticks: reversing them to use them as serving tongs. But again, most Chinese restaurants will provide a serving spoon with each dish, making this skill unnecessary.

7. Frequent toasts will be offered at a banquet. The host gives the first toast, and the ceremony continues all evening. It is acceptable to toast with a soft drink.

8. Never take the last bit of food from a serving dish. To do so would signify that you are still hungry.

9. The serving of fruit signals the end of the meal.

10. Where everyone sits has great significance in China. This is the traditional seating at a round Chinese table:

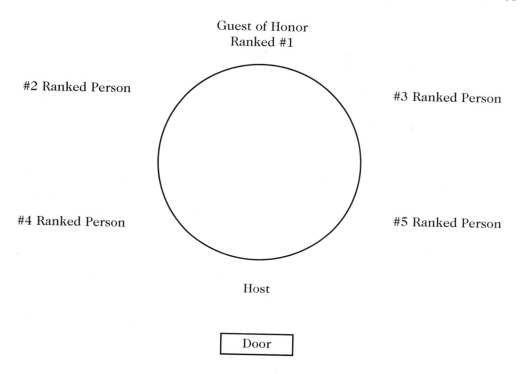

The host will sit closest to the door, so that he or she may direct the waiters as they come in and out. Interestingly, this seating pattern results in the least important people sitting next to the host.

Colombia

Official Name:	Republic of Colombia (República de Colombia)
Official Language:	Spanish
Government System:	Unitary multiparty republic
Population:	34.3 million (1995 est.)
Population Growth:	1.1% (1995 est.)
Area:	1.14 million sq. km. (440,000 sq. mi.); about the size of Texas, New Mexico, and Arkansas combined
Natural Resources:	crude oil, natural gas, coal, iron ore, nickel, gold, silver, copper, emeralds
Major Cities:	Bogotá (capital), Cali, Medellin, Barranquilla, Cartagena

Cultural Note: Colombia's rugged terrain has made it difficult for a strong central government to control the country. Colombia does have a tradition of democracy, but its governments have ranged from weak to ineffectual. It remains to be seen if that trend is being reversed. But the assassination of reformist candidates, usually by *narcoterrorists*, makes the reform process more difficult.

Age Breakdown

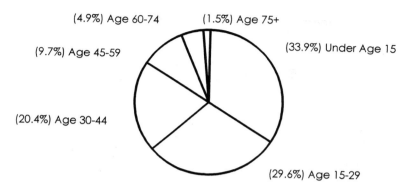

(4.9%) Age 60-74   (1.5%) Age 75+

(9.7%) Age 45-59   (33.9%) Under Age 15

(20.4%) Age 30-44

(29.6%) Age 15-29

Life Expectancy: 68 years male; 73 years female (1990)

 Time

Foreign executives are expected to be prompt to all business appointments.

Colombians do not interpret time as literally as do North Americans. To most Colombians, they have arrived promptly to a meeting if they are within 15 or 20 minutes of the scheduled time. Do not expect an apology if your Colombian counterpart is 20 minutes late; the Colombian considers him- or herself to be on time.

Everyone is expected to arrive late to a social engagement. Foreigners should arrive between 15 and 30 minutes late. Colombians may be a full hour late to a dinner or party.

Deadlines are similarly flexible in Colombia. Continued contact with a Colombian firm is necessary to insure completion on time, as well as reminders as to why it is important that the deadline is met. Before going to pick an item up, don't trust assurances that it is completed. Ask also if now is a good time to pick the item up. Something which a Colombian considers "essentially completed" may not actually be ready for pickup.

Colombia is five hours behind Greenwich Mean Time (G.M.T. − 5), which is the same as U.S. Eastern Standard Time.

 Holidays

(Updates: Getting Through Customs *http://www.getcustoms.com*)

This list is a working guide. Dates should be corroborated before final travel plans are made. In cases where holidays fall on Saturday or Sunday, commercial establishments may be closed the preceding Friday or following Monday.

New Year's Day	1 January
Saint Joseph's Day	19 March
Labor Day	1 May
Feast of the Sacred Heart	19 June
Saints Peter & Paul	29 June

Local holidays may be observed in addition to those listed above.

 ## Work Week

- Business hours are 9:00 A.M. to 5:00 P.M., Monday through Friday.
- Store hours vary, but are generally from 9:00 A.M. to 12:30 P.M., and then from 2:00 P.M. to 7:00 P.M., Monday through Saturday.
- Banking hours are from 9:00 A.M. to 3:00 P.M., Monday through Thursday, and until 3:30 on Friday.

Note: Unless you are traveling to the coastal lowlands, it is best to arrive a day early so you can adjust to the high altitude. This is especially true in the capital, Bogotá, which is 8,600 feet (2,600 meters) above sea level.

 ## Religious/Societal Influences on Business

There is no official religion in Colombia, but the majority of people belong to the Roman Catholic Church. Most Colombians would cite their families and the Church (in that order) as the most important influences on their lives.

Social pressure is intense. "*¿Que dirán?*" ("*What will people say?*") is a question asked frequently in Colombian families whenever propriety is threatened. Appearances must be kept up, which includes wearing fashionable clothes. Foreigners also need to be careful of their wardrobe, in order to be respected.

The greatest strains on Colombia's relationship with the U.S. came over the extradition issue. The fight against extradition was supported by the drug traffickers; the late drug kingpin Pablo Escobar donated millions to his antiextradition lobbying organization called Los Extraditables, which boasted the slogan "*Better a grave in Colombia than a jail in the United States.*" But there was also genuine sentiment among Colombians against being dictated to by the United States of America. Colombians have not forgotten past U.S. intervention in their internal affairs, most notably over Panama.

(In 1903, the U.S. recognized the breakaway Colombian province of Panama as an independent nation, so that the U.S. could build the Panama Canal.)

5 Cultural Tips

1. Regional differences are pronounced in Colombia. Expect a high level of formality in the interior, especially Bogotá. The coastal areas are far more relaxed. This is seen most clearly in the coastal preference for *tú* (the informal form of the pronoun *you* in Spanish) rather than the formal *usted*.

2. Greetings are very important in Colombia. Take the time to greet everyone formally. Give the person you are greeting your undivided attention. Men shake hands with each other and with women. Women choose whether or not to shake hands with other women; sometimes women will clasp each other's forearms instead. Friends are expected to hug and exchange kisses on the cheeks. When men hug each other, they often add a backslap or two.

3. Class consciousness is part of everyday life in Colombia. You must appear to be of the same class as your Colombian counterpart. There is no Colombian tradition for the "hands-on manager" or "getting your hands dirty," manual labor is seen as demeaning. Do not engage in an activity which would lower you in the eyes of Colombians.

4. As is common in class-conscious societies, most Colombians accept the basic inequality of their system as inevitable. A few people are rich, most people are poor; that is the way things are. Colombians find it puzzling when North Americans get upset over the plight of the poor.

5. Colombians are adaptable. They seem to have the ability to deal with any problem, no matter how disastrous. From earthquakes to terrorist bombings, they carry on as best they can. A foreigner who overreacts to a minor inconvenience will be treated with amusement or scorn. Colombians take care of themselves, and they do not depend on their government to do it for them.

Economic Overview

Colombia's long history of democratic governments, along with its steadily expanding economy, has made it one of Latin America's most attractive and stable markets for U.S. business. At the same time, the country has had to combat its international image as a narcotics producer, money launderer, human rights violator, and a place where street crime in the cities, guerrilla activity in the countryside, and violence often go unchecked.

Conscious of its need to improve its image, Colombia has worked to promote regional integration and security through active participation in regional and international organizations, and to reform its judicial and other institutions in an effort to stem the illicit drug trade. Business links between Colombia and the U.S. are well established. The United States is Colombia's main trading partner, supplying 39% of what Colombia buys from overseas and buying 37% of what it exports. Colombia represented the United States' fifth largest export market in Latin America in 1994.

The U.S. also holds the largest share of direct foreign investment in Colombia, $2.9 billion or 56% of total foreign direct investment. U.S. investment is diversified, covering the automotive, banking, chemical, communications, food, manufacturing, metal, paper, and pharmaceutical industries. The Colombian economy has changed dramatically in the years since the launching of the program of economic liberalization known as *apertura*, spearheaded by former President Cesar Gaviria. With the loosening of import and other controls and the privatization of many state-owned enterprises has come economic expansion, new domestic and foreign investment, and growing links with the U.S.

Colombia's rich energy and mineral resources and the improvement it is undertaking in infrastructure have attracted substantial new U.S. investment in recent years. The country should continue to draw U.S. capital and technology as the government adjusts its tax and regulatory regime, particularly in the oil and gas sector, and moves forward on privatization in the transport, utility, and telecommunications sectors.

Cultural Note: Colombian terrorist groups can cause serious problems, often by bombing oil pipelines and telephone networks. The far-left terrorist groups known as the Colombia Revolutionary Armed Forces (FARC) and the National Liberation Army (ELN) remain active, although the M-19 group has disbanded. Violent death in Colombia is roughly eight times as high as in the United States.

Kidnapping of business executives also continues, and foreign executives should consider themselves at risk. Never assume that you are safe because your company is small or your position is unimportant; criminals have frequently kidnapped the wrong people. Kidnap and ransom insurance is recommended; policies not only pay ransom but the cost of security consultants to handle negotiations and the kidnap victim's loss of income. As the country with the most kidnappings in the world, insurance premiums for Colombia are the most expensive.

Comparative Data

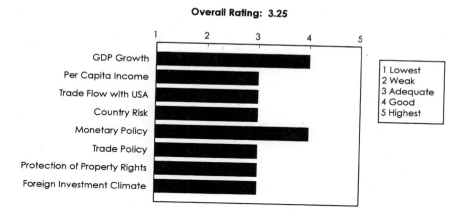

Overall Rating: 3.25

	1 Lowest
	2 Weak
	3 Adequate
	4 Good
	5 Highest

GDP Growth
Per Capita Income
Trade Flow with USA
Country Risk
Monetary Policy
Trade Policy
Protection of Property Rights
Foreign Investment Climate

Country Risk Rating

Gross Domestic Product: –$279 billion
GDP Growth: –6.5%
Per Capita Income: –$8,200

Trade Flows with the U.S.A.

Rank as Export Market for U.S.A. Goods & Services: 25th
U.S.A. Exports to Colombia: $4.6 billion
Growth Rate of Exports: 2%
U.S.A. Imports from Colombia: $3.7 billion
Growth Rate of Imports: 117%.
Rank as a Supplier of Imports into the U.S.A.: 30th

Top U.S.A. Exports to Colombia: Machinery; electrical components; motor vehicles; organic chemicals; aircraft and parts; plastics; medical and optical equipment; cereals; woven apparel; paper.

Top U.S.A. Prospects for Export to Colombia: Oil and gas field machinery and equipment; telecommunications equipment; computers/peripherals; electric power systems; automotive parts and accessories; plastic materials and resins; medical equipment; aircraft and parts; agricultural chemicals; construction equipment.

Country Risk

Dun & Bradstreet rates Colombia as having adequate capacity to meet outstanding payment liabilities.

A letter of credit is recommended. When open account terms are used, 60 to 180 days are the usual terms.

Monetary Policy

The government's goal of reducing inflation from 23% in 1994 to a target of 18% by the end of 1995 was thwarted by continued public spending on the national economic development plan, by wage settlements that have been above the government's guidelines, and by high interest rates. Fiscal laxity combined with accelerated peso weakness will make the government's 17% inflation target for year-end 1996 unlikely. *Monetary Unit:* Colombian peso.

Trade Policy

TARIFFS: Colombia's tariff reduction program was largely completed in 1992, lowering tariffs to a trade-weighted average of 12%, including duty-free entry for approximately 40% of tariff items.

IMPORT LICENSING: Imports must be registered with the Colombian Foreign Trade Institute.

A prior import license is required for the following: imports performed by government agencies and entities; imports of most used goods; nonreimbursable imports. The Ministry of Agriculture must approve import licenses for products that could compete with domestically produced commodities including malting barley, wheat, palm oil, and sorghum.

The prohibited import list has been eliminated except for used automotive vehicles, tires, used clothing, and firearms.

IMPORT TAXES: Most imports are subject to a 14% value-added tax (VAT). Some exceptions apply as in the case of imported vehicles for which there is a 35% sales tax.

A few products (primarily food items, health care products, and some medicines) are exempt from the payment of the VAT.

Protection of Intellectual Property Rights

Colombia continues to improve protection of intellectual property rights through the Andean Pact Decisions. It remained, however, on the U.S. government's Special 301 Watch List in 1995 due to continuing concerns over deficiencies in the patent regime and copyright enforcement efforts.

Colombia has signed the Paris Convention for the Protection of Industrial Property and has stated its intention to sign the Patent Cooperation Treaty (after approval of the Paris Convention). Colombia belongs to the Berne and Universal Copyright

Conventions. Andean Pact Decision 313 of 1991 provides patent protection for most products, including pharmaceuticals, biotechnology, and plant varieties. In 1993, the Andean Pact adopted Decision 344, which represented a significant improvement over previous standards used for the protection of industrial property. It provided for 20-year patent protection measured from filing date.

Colombia's copyright law is based on Law 23 of 1982, and Law 44 of 1993, which increases criminal penalties. Colombian law provides copyright protection for the life of the author plus 80 years. Although Colombia has a modern copyright law, lack of enforcement remains a serious problem.

Colombia's trademark protection requires registration and use of a trademark in Colombia. Trademark registrations have a 10-year duration and may be renewed for successive 10-year periods. Enforcement remains a weak area.

Foreign Investment Climate

Foreign investment policies are guided by two principles: equality, by which foreign and national investments receive the same legal and administrative treatment; and openness, by which few restrictions are applied regarding the amount of foreign investment or its destination.

Foreign investors are granted national treatment and are permitted 100% foreign ownership in virtually all sectors of the Colombian economy. Exceptions include national security, the disposal of hazardous waste products, and ownership of real estate and some real estate holding arrangements.

Liberalization of services has occurred in some sectors since 1991, especially in telecommunications, financial services, tourism, and television broadcasting.

All foreign investment in petroleum exploration and development in Colombia must be carried out by an association contract between the foreign investor and ECOPETROL, the state oil company. Generally, foreign investors are allowed to participate in privatization efforts without restrictions. Colombia does not impose any investment restrictions on foreign investments that it does not impose on national investors. However, some investors may find the provisions of the Colombian law burdensome. For example, many investments require a commercial presence in-country.

 Current Leaders & Political Parties

(Update: International Academy at Santa Barbara *http://www.iasb.org/cwl*)

Pres.: Ernesto Samper Pizano
Vice Pres.: Humberto De La Calle

Ministers:

Agriculture: Cecilia Lopez

Communications: Juan Manuel Turbay
Economic Dev.: Rodrigo Marin-Bernal
Education: María Emma Mejia
Finance and Public Credit: José Antonio Ocampo
Foreign Affairs: María Emma Majía
Foreign Trade: Morris Harf
Interior: Horacio Serpa-Uribe
Justice and Law: Carlos Medellin
Labor and Social Security: Orlando Obregon
Mines and Energy: Alberto Villamizar
Defense: Juan Carlos Esguerra
Health: Maria Teresa Forero-De-Saade

Other Officials:

Pres. of the Senate: Jose Guerra De La Espinella
Pres. of the House of Representatives: Rodrigo Rivera
Pres. of the Supreme Court: Hernando Herrera
Ambassador to U.S.: Carlos Lieras
Perm. Rep. to U.N.: Julio Londono

Political Parties:

Conservative Party, Liberal Party, Socialist Workers' Party, Patriotic Union Party (UP)

 # Political Influences on Business

The foreign policy of the government of Colombia has focused on enhancing Colombia's image as a responsible global and regional player. In pursuing this overall strategy, Colombia has concentrated its resources in three major areas: regional integration and security, economic growth, and counternarcotics. In developing pragmatic means to further these interests, the government of Colombia has pursued a foreign policy which in some areas parallels that of the U.S.A.

To promote regional integration and security, the government of Colombia has taken an active part of regional and international organizations such as the Rio Group, the APEC, CARICOM, the OAS, and the U.N. and its specialized agenices, and has developed close bilateral relation with its neighbors, the EU and the U.S.A. In international organizations, Colombia has taken an active role in seeking to limit the illegal transfer of arms and stop international narcotics trafficking. In October 1995,

Colombia assumed the presidency of the Nonaligned Movement (NAM). While Colombia's voting record in the U.N. generally does not coincide with U.S. positions, Colombia did join the consensus decision in May 1995 to extend indefinitely the Nuclear Nonproliferation Treaty. Regionally, Colombia joined Mexico and Venezuela (G-3) to encourage investment in Central America and the Caribbean and to seek and/or to solidify political solutions to civil strife in El Salvador, Nicaragua and Guatemala. Colombia has also been an active participant in reviewing and implementing the Plan of Action adopted at the Summit of the Americas in Miami in December 1994.

In the area of trade, Colombia's foreign policy has created lasting effects for Colombian citizens. President Samper, inaugurated on August 7, 1994, has generally followed his predecessor's *apertura* policy of liberalizing the economy.

Conscious of its international image as a narcotics-producing country and a human rights violator, Colombia has implemented some reforms in the judiciary, police, and military designed to improve the situation. The Colombian government ratified the U.N. Convention Against Illicit Traffic in Narcotic Drugs and Psychotropic Substances in 1993 (the Constitutional Court upheld the ratification in a 1994 decision) and the Second Protocol to the Geneva Conventions regarding human rights safeguards in internal civil conflicts in 1994 (the Constitutional Court upheld the ratification in a 1995 decision).

The all-encompassing issue of narcotics will continue to affect nearly all aspects of Colombia's political and economic environment. Narcotrafficking has had a negative effect on Colombian society, with several congresspersons and politicians under investigation in 1995 for illegal enrichment and/or other forms of corruption linked to the illicit drug trade. In addition to narcotraffickers, the high crime rate and guerrilla terrorism in Colombia adversely affects the business climate.

Notwithstanding Colombia's commitment to democratic institutions, its history has been plagued by violence. This situation has been exacerbated by the government's lack of a permanent presence in vast rural zones of the country. Guerrilla bands and narcotraffickers often have filled the resulting vacuum by establishing their own presence in these areas.

The 1991 constitution was intended to have far-reaching effects. It created the Office of the Prosecutor General (Fiscal) and the basis for a more aggressive prosecutorial system of criminal justice. The new constitution also granted the right of *tutela*, providing the citizens with a legal resource to protect their constitutional rights. The constitution also legalized participation of demobilized guerrilla factions as formal political parties with the prospect of securing, albeit temporarily, nonelected seats in Congress and opened the way for decentralization of state authority by elections of regional officials. However, implementing these multifaceted constitutional reforms has led to some differences in the government, as legislators, the executive, and the courts often promote their own interpretation of both the spirit and the letter of the constitution.

Contacts in the U.S.A. & Colombia

Contacts in the United States:

Contacts in Colombia:

THE EMBASSY OF THE REPUBLIC OF COLOMBIA
2118 Le Roy Place, N.W.
Washington, D.C. 20008
Tel: (202) 387-8338
Fax: (202) 232-8643

U.S. DEPARTMENT OF STATE
Bureau of Consular Affairs
Tel: (202) 647-5225
Colombia Desk
Tel: (202) 647-3023

U.S. DEPARTMENT OF COMMERCE:
Andean Division
Tel: (202) 482-1659
Fax: (202) 482-2218

COLOMBIA GOVERNMENT TOURIST OFFICE
140 E. 57th Street
New York, N.Y. 10022
Tel: (212) 688-0151

THE EMBASSY OF THE UNITED STATES
Calle 38, No.8-61, Bogota, Colombia or
P.O. Box A.A. 3831, Bogota, Colombia
APO AA 34038
Tel: [57] (1) 320-1300
Fax: [57] (1) 288-5687

COLOMBIAN-AMERICAN CHAMBER OF
COMMERCE
Apto. Aereo 8008, Calle 35, No.6-16
Bogota, Colombia
Tel: [57] (1) 285-7800
Fax: [57] (1) 288-6434
Telex: (396) 43326 CAMC CO

PRESIDENT ERNESTO SAMPER-PIZANO
Palacio de Nariño
Carrera 8, No. 7-26
Santafé de Bogotá, Republic of Colombia

Passport/Visa Requirements

Visa Information   (202) 663-1225

Entry Requirements: A passport and a return/onward ticket are required for stays up to three months. Minors (under 18) traveling alone, with one parent, or with a third party must present written authorization from the absent parent(s) or legal guardian, specifically granting permission to travel alone, with one parent, or with a third party. This authorization must be notarized, authenticated by a Colombian embassy or consulate, and translated into Spanish.

Faux Pas: Be careful when you measure height in Colombia! Colombians only measure *animals* by holding one hand horizontally, as if they were resting the hand on top of the animal's head. The height of a *person* is indicated by holding the hand *vertically* (palm out, thumb on top), as if it were resting on the *back* of the person's head.

Costa Rica

Official Name:	Republic of Costa Rica (República de Costa Rica)
Official Language:	Spanish
Government System:	Unitary multiparty republic
Population:	3.4 million (1995)
Population Growth:	2.3% (1992)
Area:	51,032 sq. km. (19,652 sq. mi.); slightly smaller than West Virginia
Natural Resources:	hydropower potential
Major Cities:	San José (capital), Alajuela, Cartago, Heredia, Limón, Golfito

Cultural Note: Because of its stability and tradition of democracy, Costa Rica (the name means Rich Coast) has long been known as the "Switzerland of Central America." The Costa Ricans (who call themselves *ticos*) are proud of their peaceful traditions. Costa Rica does not even have an army.

Age Breakdown

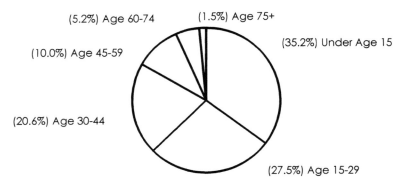

(5.2%) Age 60-74 (1.5%) Age 75+

(10.0%) Age 45-59   (35.2%) Under Age 15

(20.6%) Age 30-44

(27.5%) Age 15-29

Life Expectancy: 72 years male; 76 years female (1990)

 ## Time

Costa Ricans are generally the most punctual people in Central America. Foreigners are expected to be on time to all business appointments.

Costa Rica is six hours behind Greenwich Mean Time (G.M.T. − 6), which is one hour behind U.S. Eastern Standard Time (E.S.T. − 1).

 ## Holidays

(Update: Getting Through Customs *http://www.getcustoms.com*)

This list is a working guide. Dates should be corroborated before final travel plans are made. In cases where holidays fall on Saturday or Sunday, commercial establishments may be closed the preceding Friday or following Monday.

New Year's Day	1 January
Juan Santamaria	11 January
Sts. Peter and Paul	29 June
Our Lady of the Angels	2 August
Independence Day	15 September
Discovery or Columbus Day	12 October

Local holidays may be observed in addition to those listed above.

Work Week

- Business hours are 8:00 A.M. to 5:00 P.M., Monday through Friday, and 8:00 to 11:00 A.M. Saturday. Businesses close for lunch from 11:00 A.M. to 1:00 P.M. daily.
- Government offices are open 8:00 A.M. to 4:00 P.M., Monday through Friday.
- Banks are open 9:00 A.M. to 3:00 P.M. Monday through Friday.
- Good times to do business in Costa Rica are February to March, and September to November. The rainy season runs May through November (with rain heaviest on the Caribbean coast), and popular vacation times are December and January, and around Christmas and Easter holidays.

Religious/Societal Influences on Business

Roman Catholicism is the official religion of Costa Rica, but various Protestant groups have been making headway. A full 15% of the population follows an Evangelical Christian sect. Despite these inroads, the Catholic Church remains the most powerful organization (after the government) in Costa Rica.

Unlike other Latin American countries, race is not an issue in Costa Rica. Almost 97% of the population is European or *mestizo*, with virtually no difference between the two. Costa Rica's population is the lightest in color of any Central American nation. There is a miniscule number of African-Caribbeans, concentrated around the Atlantic port of Limón.

Although Costa Rica is not divided by race, class distinctions are important. Costa Rica had 44 presidents between the years of 1821 and 1970, and 33 of those presidents were descended from three of Costa Rica's original settlers! Despite the presence of this ruling oligarchy, Costa Rica has a larger middle class than many Latin American nations. Costa Rica cherishes its reputation as an egalitarian society of small independent farmers.

Costa Rica is pro-business and pro-United States. International trade is officially encouraged, promoted with the *"Exportar es Bueno"* (*"It's Good to Export"*) campaign.

5 Cultural Tips

1. All things American are popular in Costa Rica. U.S. products sell well. Costa Ricans often feel isolated from their less developed Central American neighbors, and prefer to associate themselves with the developed world.

2. Although 80% of Costa Ricans are Roman Catholics, Protestant sects are highly represented in the business classes. Many of the most successful and wealthiest Costa Ricans are Protestants.

3. Costa Rican manners tend to be "less Latin" than elsewhere in Central America. Men in Costa Rica greet each other with handshakes, not the back-thumping hug called an *abrazo*.

4. Although Costa Rica technically has no army, the functions of the military have been taken over by the police forces (many of whom have received military training by U.S. advisors). The Costa Rican police are divided into numerous divisions, each accountable to a different branch of the government. This prevents the police from unifying and exerting undue influence, as the military often does in other Latin American nations.

5. The slow pace of government environmental protection has led to the development of privately-owned nature preserves, which charge a fee for admission. Ecotourism is definitely on the increase in Costa Rica.

 ## Economic Overview

Costa Rica depends heavily on both agricultural and industrial imports. Although progress has been made in liberalizing its economy, promoting its domestic industry, and enhancing its role as a global trading partner via bilateral and multilateral agreements, the strong role of state monopolies, and the current fiscal crisis are also significant factors in the economy.

While Costa Rica's industrial base is growing, it is still an agriculturally-based economy where 47% of its economic base is food-related. However, in 1993 tourism surpassed banana exports as the nation's largest income producer. Costa Rica's economy grew at a healthy 4.5% pace in 1994.

Costa Rica's commercial environment is user-friendly with widespread national receptivity to U.S. products and services. The bilateral relationship between the U.S. and Costa Rica has traditionally been and continues to be excellent. With the exception of the country's monopolies on some critical services (which include telecommunications, electricity, insurance, petroleum refining, banking services, and so on), and deficiencies in the intellectual property regime, there are no trade barriers that affect the importation of most goods to Costa Rica.

Due to its perennial spring climate, stability, and hospitable atmosphere, the country has attracted some 30,000 U.S. expatriates as well as immigrants from such countries as Spain, Israel, Germany, China, and Japan, all of whom play a role in creating competition for U.S. products and services.

While foreign direct investment in Costa Rica is difficult to track, it is estimated that some $280 million flowed into Costa Rica in 1993, with the bulk of that investment from the U.S., Japan, Germany, Spain, and Korea. Textile and electronic component *maquilas*, located in most cases in attractive free trade zones, employ more than 70,000 Costa Ricans.

Cultural Note: Costa Rica is often promoted as a tropical paradise. Although the Costa Rican environment is still threatened, ecotourism is encouraging protection of the rain forest. But a growing number of landless peasants (who are demanding land to farm) oppose the expansion of national parks.

Comparative Data

Overall Rating: 2.38

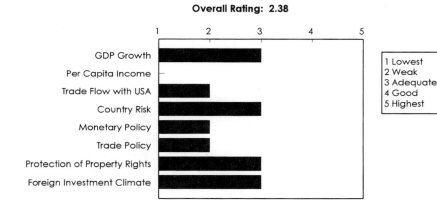

Country Risk Rating
Gross Domestic Product: $8.2 billion (1994)
GDP Growth: 4.5%
Per Capita Income: $2,687

Trade Flows with the U.S.A.
Rank as Export Market for U.S.A. Goods & Services: 40th
U.S.A. Exports to Costa Rica: $1.7 billion
Growth Rate of Exports: −10%
U.S.A. Imports from Costa Rica: $1.8 billion
Growth Rate of Imports: 12.5%
Rank as a Supplier of Imports into the U.S.A.:   41st

Top U.S.A. Exports to Costa Rica: Woven apparel; machinery; aircraft; electrical components; paper/paperboard; plastics and resins; motor vehicles; knit apparel; cereals; mineral fuel.

Top U.S.A. Prospects for Export to Costa Rica: Paper and paperboard; telecommunications equipment; hotel and restaurant equipment; construction equipment; medical equipment; water resources equipment and services; sporting goods and recreational equipment; shipbuilding equipment.

Country Risk

Dun & Bradstreet rates Cost Rica as having sufficient capacity to meet outstanding payment liabilities.

Sight drafts and open account terms predominate but letters of credit are recommended for new or small customers. When open account terms are used, 30 to 120 day terms are the norm.

Monetary Policy

The consumer price index (CPI) increased to 19.9% in 1994, more than double the 9.8% increase experienced in 1993. Inflation was forecast at 22% in 1995, 14% in 1996, and 10.2% in 1997. *Monetary Unit*: colón.

Trade Policy

TARIFFS: Customs duties range from 1 to 28% ad valorem. Tariff reductions resulting from the GATT Uruguay Round implementation have lowered tariff rates, but most food tariffs are still between 14 and 19%.

Costa Rica is a member of the Central American Common Market (CACM), which also includes Guatemala, El Salvador, Honduras, and Nicaragua. The CACM members are working toward the full implementation of a Common External Tariff which ranges between 5 and 20% for most products.

IMPORT LICENSING: Import licenses are not required for most products. However, pharmaceuticals, drugs, cosmetics, and chemical products require an import permit from the Costa Rican Ministry of Health. Import permits from the Ministry of Health are valid for five years.

Food products that are new to market require a registration, and phytosanitary and animal health certification are required by the Agriculture Ministry's *Sanidad Vegetal* division. These permits must be obtained by the Costa Rican importer.

IMPORT TAXES: A selective consumer tax ranging from 5% to 75% exists. This tax applies to about half of all products imported. A sales tax of 10% is levied on all products and services not destined for official use by the government of Costa Rica. Certain essential items are exempt.

A 1% surcharge is imposed on all imports. Items exempt from this surcharge are medicines, and raw materials for medicines for human use.

Protection of Intellectual Property Rights

Costa Rica is a signatory of all major international agreements and conventions on intellectual property, trademarks, copyrights, and patent protection. In May 1995, the Legislative Assembly ratified the country's adherence to the Paris Convention for the Protection of Industrial Property.

U.S. patents can be registered in Costa Rica in the patent office of the national registry. Costa Rican law stipulates 12 years patent protection for inventions, except in the case of medicines and agricultural inputs, for which the period of protection is limited to one year. Adherence to GATT and the possibility of obtaining desired foreign investment has motivated the government to contemplate extending patents on inventions, medicines, and agricultural chemicals to 20 years, although no such initiatives appear likely to be approved soon.

Any trademark registered abroad can be registered in Costa Rica, and in practice, the trademark is protected from copy even if not registered in Costa Rica upon showing proof of registration abroad. In May 1994, Costa Rica amended its copyright law to strengthen sanctions for piracy and provide explicit protection of computer programs.

Foreign Investment Climate

In general, Costa Rica has a relatively open international trade and investment regime. However, state monopolies in public utilities, insurance, bank demand deposits, the production and distribution of electricity, hydrocarbon and radioactive minerals extraction, refining and the wholesale distribution of petroleum, and operation of ports and airports limit investment opportunities in these sectors. In sectors not reserved to the state, there is widespread recognition in both public and private sectors that increased foreign investment is essential for increased exports and employment. Since mid-1982, the government has placed considerable emphasis on improving the investment climate, including the creation of the Ministry of Foreign Trade which is coordinating government efforts in the trade and investment areas.

Key to Costa Rica's attractiveness as a potential site for investment is the fact that Costa Rica is a beneficiary country of the U.S. Caribbean Basin Initiative (CBI) and Generalized System of Preferences (GSP). These programs grant Costa Rica duty-free access into the U.S.A. for some 4,000 products and have played a significant role in helping Costa Rica diversify its exports and increase two-way trade.

Laws governing private investment are identical for nationals and foreigners. Discrimination between these two groups is prohibited constitutionally. Foreign companies and persons may legally own equity in Costa Rican companies, including real estate, manufacturing plants and equipment, hotels, restaurants, and all kinds of commercial establishments. In general, laws controlling investment by foreigners are fairly transparent.

Current Leaders & Political Parties

(Update: International Academy at Santa Barbara *http://www.iasb.org/cwl*)

State, Government, and Political Party Leaders:
  Pres.: José Mariá Figueres
  First Vice President: Rodrigo Oreamuno
  Second Vice Pres.: Rebecca Grynspan

Cabinet Ministers:
  Foreign Affairs: Fernando Naranjo
  Foreign Commerce: José Rossi
  Presidency: Marco A. Vargas
  Health: Herman Weinstock
  Natural Resources, Energy, and Mines: René Castro
  Public Security: Bernardo Arce
  Economy and Industry: José León Desanti
  Public Education: Eduardo Doryan
  Culture, Youth, and Sports: Arnoldo Mora
  Planning: Leonardo Garnier
  Science and Technology: Eduardo Sibaja
  Agriculture and Livestock: Ricardo Garrón
  Housing: Rebecca Grynspan
  Labor and Social Security: Farid Ayales
  Justice: Juan Diego Castro
  Public Works and Transportation: Rodolfo Silva
  Regional Coor.: Sergio Quirós
  Finance: Francisco de Paula Gutiérrez
  Information: Alejandro Soto
  Interior: Mauren Clarke
  Tourism: Carlos Roesch
  State Reform: Mario Carvajal

Other Officials:

Pres. of the Supreme Court: Edgar Cervantes

Pres. of the Natl. Legislative Assembly: Antonio Alvarez

Pres. of the Central Bank of Costa Rica: Rodrigo Bolaños

Ambassador to U.S.: Sonia Picado

Perm. Rep. to U.N.: Fernando Berrocal

Political Parties:

Natl. Liberation Party (PLN), Social Christian Unity Party (PUSC), Democratic Force Party (PFD), Agricultural Union Party of Cartago (PUAC), Natl. Agrarian Party (PAN)

 Political Influences on Business

The bilateral relationship between the United States and Costa Rica has traditionally been and continues to be excellent. Although there have been and remain some bilateral irritants, these have been relatively minor in an otherwise excellent relationship.

Expropriation cases (most of which involve undeveloped land), long the main negative factor affecting U.S.-Costa Rican business relations, now appear on their way to resolution. However, a related problem has arisen with invasions of U.S. citizen-owned property by sometimes violent squatters that the Costa Rican police and judicial system have failed to deter.

The possible loss of Generalized System of Preferences (GSP) benefits because of alleged violations of international labor standards could have serious consequences for the Costa Rican export industry, particularly textiles. A 1993 petition filed by the AFL-CIO and accepted by the United States Trade Representative, although later withdrawn, caused considerable bilateral friction. A local labor confederation asked the AFL-CIO to file the petition again this year but no action was taken.

Costa Rica is a democratic republic governed according to the Constitution of 1949. This charter established a system of checks and balances among the executive, legislative and judicial branches. The 1949 Constitution abolished the Costa Rican Army and created a powerful independent body, the Supreme Electoral Tribunal (TSE), to oversee the impartiality and fairness of elections. A 1969 constitutional amendment limits the president to a single four-year term in office, although amendments allowing reelection or the extension of the presidential term to five years are currently under consideration by the Legislative Assembly.

The 57-member unicameral Legislative Assembly is elected concurrently with the president. Candidates for the legislature run on party slates in each province and not as individuals. The number of popular votes each party receives per province determines its quota of legislators in that jurisdiction. Deputies serve four-year terms and cannot be re-elected for successive periods. The current legislative assembly, for the term 1994–1998, took office on May 1, 1994.

In the February 6, 1994, election, José Mariá Figueres, the candidate of the National Liberation Party (Partido Liberacion Nacional or PLN), was elected to a four-year term in office, defeating his nearest rival Miguel Angel Rodriguez of the Social Christian Unity Party (Partido Unidad Social Cristiano or PUSC) by a margin of two percentage points. President Figueres' PLN party holds 28 seats in the Legislative Assembly. The PUSC won 25 seats. Three smaller parties won four seats. The next elections for President and the Legislative Assembly will be in February 1998.

The Supreme Court has 22 magistrates who sit in four chambers, including the Constitutional review chamber.

 Contacts in the U.S.A. & in Costa Rica:

Contacts in the United States:

EMBASSY OF THE REPUBLIC OF COSTA RICA
2114 S Street, N.W.
Washington, D.C. 20008
Tel: (202) 234-2945
Fax: (202) 265-4795

U.S. DEPARTMENT OF STATE
Bureau of Consular Affairs
Tel: (202) 647-5225
Country Desk Officer, Costa Rica
Tel: (202) 647-3381

U.S. DEPARTMENT OF COMMERCE, COSTA RICA DESK
Int'l Trade Admin.
Tel: (202) 482-5680

Contacts in Costa Rica:

U.S. EMBASSY
Pavas Road
San José
Mailing Address:
APO AA 34020
Tel: [506] 20-39-39
Fax: [506] 20-2305

THE COSTA RICAN-AMERICAN CHAMBER OF COMMERCE
Calle 3 Avenidas 1 y 3
Apartado 4946
San Jose

1000 Costa Rica
Tel: [506] 33-21-33
Telex: [323] 2186 POZUELO CR

PRESIDENT JOSÉ MARÍA FIGUERES
Casa Presidencial
Apdo 520, Zapote
San José, Republic of Costa Rica

Passport/Visa Requirements

Visa Information   Tel: (202) 663-1225

To obtain additional and updated information on entry and exit requirements, travelers can contact the Consular Section of the Embassy of Costa Rica or the nearest consulate.

Faux Pas: Be sure to learn some highlights about the political history of Central America before your visit. Never get in a position like the U.S. executive who did not know anything about the Costa Rican president who won the Nobel Peace Prize in 1987 for authoring the Central American Peace Plan (President Oscar Arias Sanchez).

Czech Republic

Official Name:	Czech Republic (Česká Republika)
Official Language:	Czech
Government System:	Multiparty parliamentary republic
Population:	10.4 million (1995)
Population Growth:	0.8% (1993)
Area:	78,864 sq. km. (30,441 sq. mi.); about the size of Virginia
Natural Resources:	coal, coke, timber, lignite, uranium, magnesite
Major Cities:	Prague (capital), Brno, Ostrava, Plzen, Olomouc

Cultural Note: After four decades of authoritarian Communist rule, the Czech Republic has moved faster towards democracy and capitalism than any other former Warsaw Pact nation. Still, the Czechs must deal with the legacies of the Communist regime. Besides massive environmental pollution, the Czechs need to overcome the dependency mentality of the Communist welfare state. They also have to deal with the former Communists within their midst. Former employees of the Secret Police and senior Communist Party officeholders have been banned from public office until the year 2000.

Age Breakdown

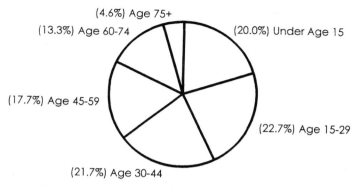

(4.6%) Age 75+

(13.3%) Age 60-74

(20.0%) Under Age 15

(17.7%) Age 45-59

(22.7%) Age 15-29

(21.7%) Age 30-44

Life Expectancy: 69 years male; 76 years female (1993)

Time

Punctuality is expected at both business appointments and social events.

The Czech Republic is one hour ahead of Greenwich Mean Time (G.M.T. + 1), which is six hours ahead of U.S. Eastern Standard Time (E.S.T. + 6).

Holidays

(Update: Getting Through Customs *http://www.getcustoms.com*)

This list is a working guide. Dates should be corroborated before final travel plans are made. In cases where holidays fall on Saturday or Sunday, commercial establishments may be closed the preceding Friday or following Monday.

New Year's Day	1 January
National Liberation Day	8 May
Saints Cyril & Methodius	5 July
Jan Hus Day	6 July
Saint Stephen's Day	26 December

While religion is not as important in the Czech Republic as in many other countries, Christian holidays are still observed.

Work Week

- As the business day begins early and ends in midafternoon, expect to schedule your appointments between 9:00 A.M. and 12 noon or between 1:00 and 3:00 P.M.
- Most Czechs receive four weeks of vacation per year. The traditional vacation time runs from mid-July to mid-August, so do not expect to be able to conduct business during this period.
- Business hours: 8:00 or 8:30 A.M. to 4:00 or 5:15 P.M., Monday through Friday.
- Banking hours: 8:00 A.M. to 2:00 P.M., Monday through Friday. Some banks close later on certain weekdays, and open from 8:00 A.M. until noon on Saturdays.
- Store hours: 8:00 or 9:00 A.M. to 5:00 or 6:00 P.M., Monday through Friday. Some establishments will be open on Saturdays until noon. Note that small shops may close for lunch from noon to 2:00 P.M.

Religious/Societal Influences on Business

More Czechs identify themselves as nondenominational (39.9%) than are members of the largest Church, the Roman Catholics (39.0%). The Czech Republic has no official religion, and organized religion plays a minor role in the daily lives of most citizens. Most other religions are represented in the Czech Republic. Some local Protestant variations include: Czechoslovak Brethren Reformed (2.0%), Czechoslovak Hussite (1.7%), and Silesian Evangelical (0.3%).

However, the Czech Republic has produced many profound thinkers and philosophers. Protestant reformer Jan Hus, who was burnt as a heretic in 1415, remains a national hero to many Czechs. Writer Franz Kafka (1883–1924) was a native of Prague; the themes of isolation in his work were inspired by being a German-speaking Jew in a Christian, Czech-speaking city. And Czech President Václav Havel, a playwright and essayist, is arguably the most profound chief of state in modern times.

Avoidance of violence is an important part of Czech philosophy. Czechs are proud of the way they endured two wrenching changes without violence: the 1989 Velvet Revolution in which the Communist regime gave way to democracy, and the peaceful separation of Czechoslovakia into the separate Czech and Slovak Republics in 1993.

5 Cultural Tips

1. Czech men shake hands both upon arrival and departure. Czech women may or may not shake hands, either with men or each other. Foreigners should wait to see if a Czech woman extends her hand for a handshake.

2. Age is respected. When a single representative is sent to the Czech Republic, he or she should be at least 40 years old, and preferably over 50. Sending a young person will give the impression that your company is not serious about doing business. (This is especially true since Prague has become a favorite destination for Generation X Slackers. Czechs see thousands of young American tourists, few of whom appear to have serious ambitions.)

3. Czechs insist that paperwork be properly filed and complete. Even during the Communist regime, the Czech Secret Police would dutifully issue a receipt for contraband materials they seized.

4. Business dealings in the Czech Republic must still cope with frequently changing regulations. Good legal advice from a Czech business lawyer is vital.

5. Czechs have a reputation as good hosts. Since business is conducted on a personal basis (Czechs must get to know you before they will do business with you), take advantage of social invitations. Business lunches are popular.

 Economic Overview

The Czech Republic is a small but growing market for U.S. products, and U.S. firms have had success selling computers and software, medical equipment, manufacturing technologies, energy and environmental technologies, and other industrial products. While the United States holds only a three to four percent share of the overall Czech import market, major investments by U.S. firms mean that U.S. products and services will continue to enjoy a high profile and demand.

The Czech Republic is considered by many to be the most economically advanced reemerging market of the former Eastern Bloc. It has a stable currency with few foreign exchange controls, low unemployment, low national debt, and strong foreign currency reserves. A sweeping privatization program has moved the majority of state-owned assets to private hands, and the process of restructuring these firms has been underway. By all accounts, the economic and commercial pictures are bright.

Czech firms are plagued, however, by a lack of capital, marketing, and financial expertise. Many firms are insolvent. Czech firms which do have local currency to buy U.S. goods and services are able to obtain U.S. currency to pay for them through the local bank with little difficulty. European competition for the Czech market is quite fierce. More than half of the country's trade is conducted with its four neighboring countries: Germany, Austria, Slovakia, and Poland. For American firms, the key to success is price, delivery, and service terms to compete with strong German and other European competition. Americans are among the most popular expatriates and visitors to the Czech Republic. American firms enjoy broad acceptance and are welcomed by nearly all Czech firms looking for contacts with foreign firms. Bilateral relations between the Czech Republic and the U.S. are as good as they have ever been.

Comparative Data

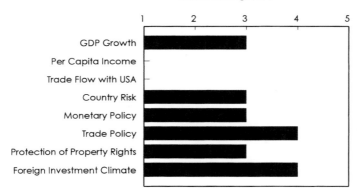

Country Risk Rating

Gross Domestic Product: $32.5 billion

GDP Growth: 2.5%

Per Capita Income: $3,155

Trade Flows with the U.S.A.

Rank as Export Market for U.S.A. Goods & Services: 65th

U.S.A. Exports to Czech Republic: $362 million

Growth Rate of Exports: 22%

U.S.A. Imports from Czech Republic: $364 million

Growth Rate of Imports: 15%

Rank as a Supplier of Imports into the U.S.A.:   66th

Top U.S.A. Exports to Czech Republic: Machinery; electrical components; medical and optical equipment; motor vehicles; aircraft and parts; animal feed; pharmaceutical products; cosmetics; wood pulp/paper waste; plastics and resins.

Top U.S.A. Prospects for Export to Czech Republic: Pollution control equipment; telecommunications equipment; medical equipment; security and safety equipment; building products; machine tools; electrical power systems; computer software; food processing and packaging equipment; insurance services.

Country Risk

Dun & Bradstreet rates the Czech Republic as having good capacity to meet outstanding payment liabilities.

Open account terms are the most common credit terms, with up to 75% of transactions taking place on open account. However, letters of credit or cash in advance are recommended for new customers.

Monetary Policy

The government is convinced it can keep its yearly inflation figures below 10%. Inflation reached 10% in 1994 and dropped to about 9.1% in 1995. Annual inflation is forecast at 8.2% for 1996 and 7.3% in 1997. *Monetary Unit*: crown.

Trade Policy

TARIFFS: The Czech Republic has adopted a GATT tariff code, which has an average tariff of 5% to 6%.

IMPORT LICENSING: Import licenses are required for certain classes of goods into the Czech Republic. These are listed in a special appendix to the trade law. Appendix A goods, for which a license is automatically granted after payment of an administrative fee, include uranium ore, scrap metals, and textile products, as well as certain agricultural products and food.

Appendix B, C, D, and E products, which include agricultural and food products, some minerals, chemicals, pharmaceuticals, raw hides and other hide products, poisonous and toxic substance,s and military and dual-use items, are subject to license granted to a certain extent in relation to a limited value or quantity.

All licenses are issued by the Ministry of Trade and Industry.

IMPORT TAXES: A two-tiered value-added tax is in effect. Basic articles such as fuel, energy, staple foodstuffs, and pharmaceuticals are subject to a 5% VAT. A 22% VAT is imposed on the remaining categories of goods and services.

Excise taxes are levied on gasoline, tobacco, alcohol, wines, and spirits.

Protection of Intellectual Property Rights

The Czech Republic is bound to the Berne, Paris, and Universal Copyright Conventions. The government is working to ensure that laws for the protection of intellectual property in the Republic match or exceed those of western Europe. Thus, existing legislation guarantees protection of all forms of property rights, including patents, copyrights, trademarks, and semiconductor chip layout design. Patents are valid for 20 years after application. Patent applications are examined for usefulness.

Trademarks are licensed for periods of 10 years from the date of application and are renewable for like periods. The protection of intellectual property does remain a problem, especially regarding the manufacture and sale of software and the sale of counterfeit videotapes and designer clothing produced outside the country.

Foreign Investment Climate

An open investment climate has been a key element of the economic transformation of the Czech Republic. The transformation process, including the establishment of an open and stable investment climate, has continued without disruption in the Czech Republic following the break-up of Czechoslovakia at the end of 1992. The Czechoslovak government focused on improving the investment climate at the initial stages of economic reform in 1990. It was considered to be critical for attracting foreign capital and investment much needed by undercapitalized state enterprises undergoing privatization. Additionally, the Czechoslovaks and Czechs set a high priority on economic integration with the world's advanced economies. The Czech government has set full membership in the European Union (EU) as its highest priority, and hopes the Czech Republic will become a member of the Organization of Economic Cooperation and Development (OECD) in the near future.

Foreign investors can, as individuals, establish sole proprietorships, joint ventures, and branch offices in the Czech Republic. Foreign and domestic investors are treated identically and both are subject to the same tax codes and other laws. The government does not screen foreign investment projects other than for those few industries which are considered sensitive. Industries considered sensitive include defense-related industries, national or cultural monuments, salt production, and companies involved in the distillation of pure alcohol. The government does, however, evaluate all investment offers for state enterprises undergoing privatization.

Foreign firms operating in the Czech republic conduct business under the law as Czech firms. Foreign firms are able to repatriate profits and liquidate investments, and are protected from expropriation under both international and domestic law and under treaty.

Current Leaders & Political Parties

(Update: International Academy at Santa Barbara *http://www.iasb.org/cwl*)

State, Government, and Political Party Leaders:
   Pres.: Václav Havel

Ministers:
   Prime Min.: Václav Klaus
   Dep. Prime Ministers: Ivan Kocarnik

Dep. Prime Min. and Min. of Agriculture: Josef Lux
Dep. Prime. Min. and Prime Min. of Justice: Jan Kalvoda
Finance: Ivan Kocarnik
Foreign Affairs: Josef Zieleniec
Industry and Trade: Vladimir Dlouhy
Economic Policy and Dev.: Karel Dyba
Health: Jan Strasky
Interior: Jan Ruml
Culture: Jaromir Talir
Education, Youth, and Physical Education: Ivan Pilip
Labor and Social Affairs: Jindrich Vodicka
State Control: Igor Nemec
Natl. Property and Privatization: Jiri Skalicky
Environment: Jiri Skalicky
Economic Competition: Stanislav Belehradek
Transportation: Martin Riman
Defense: Hiloslav Vyborny

Other Officials:

Chmn. of the Supreme Court: Otakar Motejl
Ambassador to U.S.: Michael Zantovsky
Perm. Rep. to U.N.: Karel Kovanda

Political Parties:

Civic Democratic Party-Christian Democratic Party, Civic Democratic Alliance, Liberal Social Union, Mov. for Self-Governing Democracy of Moravia and Silesia, Christian Democratic Union, Christian Social Union, Czech Social Democratic Party, Agrarian Party, Green Party, Assembly for the Republic, Czech Communist Party, Party of the Democratic Left

 Political Influences on Business

Bilateral relations with the United States are as good as they have ever been. Since the establishment of the Czech Republic at the beginning of 1993, a series of high-level visits (including presidential visits to both countries, top-level military and cabinet contacts, and countless working-level meetings) have reaffirmed the breadth of cooperation and mutual interest. The United States is in the process of phasing out assistance programs to the Czech Republic. This phase-out, expected to be completed by 1996, is a clear indicator of the Czech Republic's role as emerging partner with the U.S. That partnership ranges from close bilateral military ties, cooperation in combatting transnational challenges such as organized crime and narcotics, working together in the United Nations Security Council, and working closely through a series of cultural, educational, and legal programs to deepen Czech progress in democratization and to ensure better U.S. understanding of the Czech achievement.

The political issues affecting the business climate are few. The Czech Government is committed to early entry into Western institutions, first the Organization for Economic Cooperation and Development (OECD), and then the European Union (EU). Theirs is an export-driven economy, and European markets are the first priority. The U.S. has expressed concerns about some elements of the Czech business culture which are less than transparent, and sometimes too bureaucratic. There are only tangentially political issues, inasmuch as they represent the ongoing transformation in the already established democratic institutions of the country. Most problems of business representatives are also widely acknowledged by government officials, who are frequently cited by business as being open and available to listen to business problems. The U.S. makes its concerns known to Czech officials and partners on a case-by-case basis, and while conflicts in some areas continue to exist, the seriousness with which the Czechs take foreign commercial concerns is encouraging.

The Czech Republic is a parliamentary democracy. The coalition government is led by the Civic Democratic Party (ODS), a conservative, secular, free-market-oriented party whose leader, Prime Minister Václav Klaus, is the architect of the country's economic reform. President Václav Havel, the head of state, is an internationally recognized advocate of human rights and social justice. The parliamentary Chamber of Deputies is elected every four years; the next election is scheduled for 1996.

Contacts in the U.S.A. & the Czech Republic

Contacts in the United States:

EMBASSY OF CZECH REPUBLIC
3900 Spring of Freedom St., N.W.
Washington, D.C. 20008
Tel: (202) 363-6315
Fax: (202) 966-8540

EMBASSY OF THE SLOVAK REPUBLIC
2201 Wisconsin Ave., N.W.
Suite 380
Washington, D.C. 20007
Tel: (202) 965-5160
Fax: (202) 965-5166

U.S. DEPARTMENT OF STATE
Country Desk Officer
Czech Republic
Tel: (202) 647-3187

U.S. DEPARTMENT OF COMMERCE
Eastern European Desk
Int'l Trade Admin.
Tel: (202) 482-2645

*Contacts in the Czech
and Slovak Republics:*

U.S. EMBASSY CZECH REPUBLIC
Trziste 15
118 01 Prague 1
Prague
Mailing Address:
Unit 1330
APO AE 09213-5630
Tel: [42] (2) 2451-0847
Telex: 21196 AMEMBC
Fax: [42] (2) 2451-1001

U.S. EMBASSY SLOVAK REPUBLIC
Hviezdoslavovo Namestie 4
81102 Bratislava
Mailing Address:
Use Embassy street address
Tel: [42] (2) 330-861, 333-338
Fax: [42] (2) 330-096

AMERICAN CHAMBER OF COMMERCE IN THE
CZECH REPUBLIC
Karlovo nam
24, Praha 1
Tel: [42] (2) 299-887, 296-778
Fax: [42] (2) 291-481

DUN & BRADSTREET SPOL S R.O.
Postal Address: Spalena 17, 110 00
Praha 1, Czech Republic
Street Address: Spalena 17, 110 00
Praha 1, Czech Republic
Tel: [42] (20 24909-111 Operator)
Fax: [42] (2) 298-076
   [42] (2) 249-11834

PRESIDENT VÁCLAV HAVEL
Office of the President
119 08 Praha 1-Hrad
Czech Republic

PRIME MINISTER VÁCLAV KLAUS
Office of the Prime Minister
Nabr. E. Benese 4
125 09 Praha 1
Czech Republic

Passport/VISA Requirements

Visa Information: (202) 663-1225

Entry Requirements: For U.S. citizens, a passport is needed but a visa is not required for stays of up to 30 days. For stays of over 30 days, U.S. citizens must present visa request to the Czech Embassy in Washington, D.C.

For further information concerning entry requirements for the Czech Republic, contact the Embassy of the Czech Republic

Cultural Note: The Czech Republic, Poland, and Hungary are often grouped together as the three most economically successful nations of the Eastern Bloc. Of all the former Warsaw Pact countries, they have the most democratic societies and stable economic systems. Social scientists who index national levels of anxiety have placed Czechs at a middle level, between the anxious Hungarians and the placid Poles.

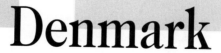

Denmark

Official Name:	Kingdom of Denmark (Kongeriget Danmark)
Official Language:	Danish
Government System:	Constitutional monarchy
Population:	5.2 million (1995)
Population Growth:	0.3% (1994)
Area:	43,076 sq. km. (16,632 sq. mi.); slightly smaller than Vermont and New Hampshire combined
Natural Resources:	crude oil, natural gas, fish, salt, limestone
Major Cities:	Copenhagen (capital), Aarhus, Odense, Aalborg

Cultural Note: One thing the Danes know how to do is take meetings. Like the Danes themselves, these meetings are well organized. They always have specific, stated agendas; they both start and finish on schedule. Participants prepare carefully, and everyone gets to express his or her opinion (as long as he or she is well informed on the matter). These meetings are an integral part of the Danish management style.

Age Breakdown

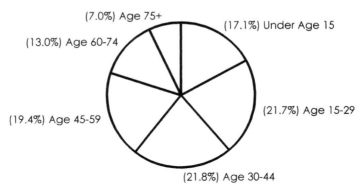

Life Expectancy: 72 years male; 78 years female (1993)

 Time

Strict punctuality is expected in Denmark, both in business and social situations. Tardiness gives an impression of incompetence and poor time management.

Denmark is one hour ahead of Greenwich Mean Time (G.M.T. + 1), which is six hours ahead of U.S. Eastern Standard Time (E.S.T. + 6).

 Holidays

(Update: Getting Through Customs *http://www.getcustoms.com*)

This list is a working guide. Dates should be corroborated before final travel plans are made. In cases where holidays fall on Saturday or Sunday, commercial establishments may be closed the preceding Friday or following Monday.

New Year's Day	1 January
General Prayer Day	3 May
Constitution Day	5 June
Boxing Day	26 December
New Year's Eve	31 December

Be sure to confirm your appointments with local representatives before taking your trip. Regional holidays may present a conflict.

- As in the rest of Scandinavia, summer is a time of leisure. It is both difficult and inconsiderate to try to conduct serious business during July and August. Many firms close for extended periods during these two months to allow their employees to take summer vacations. Danes have 5 weeks of paid vacation per year.

Work Week

- Business hours vary throughout Denmark. Opening times range from 8:00 to 9:00 A.M. and closing times from 4:30 to 5:30 P.M. Offices operate on a five-day schedule. Banks are open from 9:30 A.M. to 4:00 P.M. on weekdays with the exception of Thursday, when they stay open until 6:00 P.M.

Religious/Societal Influences on Business

Denmark's official religion is the Evangelical Lutheran Church, to which 87.7% of the population belongs. Generally, religion does not play a large part in the everyday lives of the Danes.

Fierce independence is a national characteristic of the Danes. (This should not be surprising; without it, tiny Denmark could never have maintained its independence in proximity to Germany.)

It is not easy to be in a position of authority in Denmark. The egalitarian nature of Danish culture means each person has an opinion, an opinion which will be listened to. Danes do not simply take orders; they must be allowed their say and then be convinced to go along with the program. But once a decision is made, everyone is expected to be supportive. Bosses are seen more like coaches than leaders, and they have to earn the respect of their employees.

Social scientists have observed that the Danes have a highly nurturing culture. Both men and women are very concerned with social welfare and the quality of life. As one would expect in a country with a high proportion of women in business, Denmark offers generous child care and paternity leave.

The Danes consider truthfulness and modesty to be important virtues. Wealth is downplayed, and ostentation is frowned upon. Denmark is a meritocracy. Nepotism is not unheard of, but if relatives are hired, they are expected to be highly competent.

5 Cultural Tips

1. While most Danes speak English, the greeting they traditionally give (which sounds like hi) is Danish, not English. This Danish word is *heij*, and it is used both upon greeting and farewell. A handshake accompanies the traditional greeting. Danes shake hands with both men and women.

2. Leadership among the independent-minded Danes requires consensus-building. There is a great deal of give-and-take among all levels of a Danish company. Strong negative input from even a minor member of a company could sink your proposal.

3. Since Danes are both slow to decide and independent-minded, the hard sell is the worst technique one can take. Present your pitch, supply all the follow-up data requested (no matter how extraneous this data may seem to you), and wait. The Danes cannot be rushed.

4. Work and homelife are kept separate in Denmark. Take an invitation to a Danish home as a great honor. Be sure to arrive on time. As a dinner guest, you may be led straight from the door to the dining table. In Denmark, drinks are served during and after a meal, but not before.

5. The fierce independence and individualism of the Danes has worked against the development of large corporations. The majority of Danish companies are small. More than half the population works in companies with fewer than 200 employees.

 ## Economic Overview

The United States is Denmark's largest trading partner outside the European Union. There are approximately 250 American subsidiaries in Denmark representing about 12% of foreign direct investment. Direct investment from the U.S. totals about $2 billion. Political and commercial relations with the United States are excellent. Denmark's standard of living, per capita GDP, and rate of personal taxation are among the highest in the world. It is a good market and investment site for American companies, its location is excellent, and improving infrastructure and the skills of its labor force make it an attractive location for regional offices serving Scandinavia and the Baltics.

U.S. exports to Denmark should take advantage of an improved competitive position resulting from the present low value of the dollar.

Cultural Note: Denmark has the highest percentage of women in business in the European Union. Be prepared to find women at all levels of Danish business and government.

Comparative Data

Overall Rating: 4.25

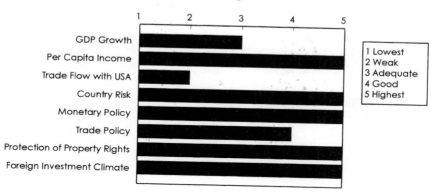

Country Risk Rating

Gross Domestic Product: $146 billion
GDP Growth: 4.4%
Per Capita Income: $28,072

Trade Flows with the U.S.A.

Rank as Export Market for U.S.A. Goods & Services: 45th
U.S.A. Exports to Denmark: $1.5 billion
Growth Rate of Exports: 25%
U.S.A. Imports from Denmark: $1.9 billion
Growth Rate of Imports: −10%
Rank as a Supplier of Imports into the U.S.A.:   40th

Top U.S.A. Exports to Denmark: Machinery; electrical components; aircraft and parts; medical and optical equipment; books and newspaper; tobacco; motor vehicles; fruits and nuts; mineral fuel; wood.

Top U.S.A. Prospects for Export to Denmark: Software; computers; engineering services; tourism; pollution control equipment; electrical power systems; oil field machinery; medical equipment; telecommunications equipment; auto parts.

Country Risk

Dun & Bradstreet rates Denmark as having excellent capacity to meet outstanding payment liabilities. It carries the lowest degree of risk.

Credit terms depend on sector and size of transaction but are usually open account with 30 to 60 days normal.

Monetary Policy

The Danish economy was expected to slow down in 1996. Inflation will remain low, between 2% and 3%. Inflation has averaged below 3% for the last four years. *Monetary Unit:* kroner.

Trade Policy

TARIFFS: Because of its European Union membership, Denmark imposes common external tariffs on goods entering from non-EU countries, including the U.S. These duties run from 5 to 14% on manufactured goods.

Agricultural products, including cereal grains, rice, milk and milk products, beef and veal, olive oil, and sugar, are governed by the common agricultural policy in which duties are supplemented by a system of variable levies. The purpose is to equalize prices of imported commodities with those produced within the EU. Because of these levies, some U.S. processed food products are not competitive in the Danish market.

IMPORT LICENSING: With very few exceptions, which include alcoholic beverages, weapons and arms, certain drugs and chemicals, and certain food products, Denmark requires no import licenses.

There are no special import restrictions or license requirements which constitute problems for U.S. industrial product exporters.

IMPORT TAXES: Although not an import tax, all goods imported into Denmark are also subject to a 2% value-added tax (VAT). The VAT is applied on a nondiscriminatory basis to all goods and most services, whether imported or produced locally.

Protection of Intellectual Property Rights

Denmark is party to (and an enforcer of) a large number of international conventions and treaties concerning protection of intellectual property rights. Denmark offers adequate protection for intellectual property rights. Denmark is a member of the World Intellectual Property Organization. It adheres to the Paris Convention for the Protection of Industrial Property, the Patent Cooperation Treaty, the Strasbourg convention, and the Budapest convention. Denmark has ratified the European Patent Convention and the EU Patent Convention.

Denmark is also a party to the 1886 Berne Convention and its subsequent revisions, and the 1952 Universal Copyright Convention and its 1971 revision. There is little piracy in Denmark of records or video cassettes, but software piracy is estimated to cost the industry more than $100 million annually.

A new Danish trademark act entered into force January 1, 1992, which also implements the EU trademark directive harmonizing EU member countries' trademark legislation.

Foreign Investment Climate

Because Denmark is heavily dependent on foreign trade and international cooperation, it follows liberal trade and investment policies and encourages increased foreign investment. Denmark welcomes foreign investors on a nondiscriminatory, national treatment basis, including allowing them to benefit from national investment incentive programs. As a general rule, foreign direct investment in Denmark may take place without restrictions and screening and there are no major foreign investment barriers.

Ownership restrictions apply to only a few sectors, including those subject to national security considerations.

There is a well-established system of commercial law and expropriation is almost entirely limited to public construction purposes, in which case full compensation is paid. There are no restrictions on capital transfers and no foreign exchange restrictions. Worker productivity is high, inflation low, and corporate taxation one of the lowest in the EU. Ownership restrictions apply in a few sectors including: hydrocarbon exploration, arms production, aircraft, and shipping.

There are about 250 U.S. subsidiaries in Denmark representing approximately 12% of the present total value of total foreign direct investment in Denmark. Between 1983 and 1994, U.S. investors acquired about 75 Danish companies.

Current Leaders & Political Parties

(Update: International Academy at Santa Barbara *http://www.iasb.org/cwl*)

State, Government, and Political Party Leaders:
    Head of State: Queen Margrethe II

Ministers:
    Prime Min.: Poul Nyrup Rasmussen
    Economic Affairs and Nordic Coop.: Marianne Jelved
    Industry and Trade: Mimi Jakobsen
    Finance: Mogens Lykketoft
    Foreign Affairs: Niels Helveg Petersen
    Environment and Energy: Svend Auken
    Dev. Coop.: Poul Nielson
    Interior and Ecclesiastical Affairs: Birte Weiss

Defense: Hans Haekkerup
Cultural Affairs: Jytte Hilden
Transportation: Jan Trojborg
Social Affairs: Karen Jespersen
Housing and Building: Ole Lovig Simonsen
Research: Frank Jensen
Agriculture and Fisheries: Henrik Dam Kristensen
Taxation: Carsten Koch

Other Officials:

Ambassador to U.S.: K. Erik Tygesen
Perm. Rep. to U.N.: B. Haauonsen

Political Parties:

Social Democratic Party, Conservative People's Party, Socialist People's Party, Center Democratic Party, Christian People's Party, Liberal Democratic Party, Left Socialist Party, Progressive Party, Single Tax Party, Communist Party

 # Political Influences on Business

Although U.S.-Danish relations were strained in the early 1980s over security issues, the relations between the two countries are now excellent. NATO is popular in Denmark, perhaps more so than in any other country in Europe. More than 70% of the Danes favor Danish membership of NATO, and the Danes are also adamant that progress toward European integration should not come at the expense of transatlantic ties. Concern for retaining NATO was one of the arguments consistently invoked by opponents of Danish membership in the European Union.

While political issues rarely affect the Danish business climate, the business sector fears that the government's new series of environmental taxes imposed on business, pending introduction of similar taxes in Denmark's major competing countries, may jeopardize Danish competitiveness.

Denmark is a constitutional monarchy. The Parliament, known as the Folketing, is elected for a four-year term, but usually elections are held before the four years are up, either because the government is toppled in a vote of confidence, or because the Prime Minister calls an election (which he can do at any time) in an attempt to increase the government coalition's parliamentary position. Denmark has a history of minority governments. The last election was held September 21, 1994.

With a few amendments (the latest and most comprehensive in 1953), the Constitution dates from 1849, when the King renounced absolutism (the "royal dictatorship"). Today Denmark is among the most politically stable democracies. The Queen nominally rules through the Prime Minister and his Cabinet. As the Prime Minister is accountable to the Folketing (Denmark's unicameral parliament), the Queen "chooses" him based on recommendations from the leaders of the political parties.

The Prime Minister works through Cabinet Ministers and their ministries. Cabinet Ministers need not be members of Parliament, although most usually are. Ministers have no political Deputy Ministers or Secretaries of State as in other parliamentary democracies. Rather, they have one or more Permanent Under Secretaries, who are the highest-ranking civil servants within the ministry. There are no political appointees among the civil servants, who remain unaffected by changes of government.

The parliament has 175 members, plus two each from Greenland and the Faroes, which are autonomous parts of the Danish realm.

Judicial power rests solely with the courts, although the monarch on rare occasions grants pardons.

In 1995, eight political parties were represented in the Folketing and there was one unaffiliated member. Four of the parties have a parliamentary history of 79 years or longer. Political parties play a much greater role in Danish politics than in the United States, for two major reasons. The first is the system of awarding seats on the basis of proportional representation. The second reason is the fact that Folketing members have no personal staff (nor, for that matter, do parliamentary committees). As a result, Danish parliamentarians rely on their parties for support and technical expertise, and party discipline is very tight.

The government that was reelected in 1994 is a minority coalition composed of three parties: the Social Democrats, the Radicals, and the Center Democrats. Together, these parties control 76 of the 179 seats in the Folketing.

Denmark has made an impressive economic recovery under the leadership of Prime Minister Poul Nyrup Rasmussen. Ficscal policies were tightened in 1995 to insure that the economy would not become overheated.

Contacts in the U.S.A. & in Denmark

Contacts in the United States:

EMBASSY OF THE KINGDOM OF DENMARK
3200 Whitehaven St., N.W.
Washington, D.C. 20008
Tel: (202) 234-4300
Fax: (202) 328-1470
E-mail: ambadane@erols.com

U.S. DEPARTMENT OF STATE
Bureau of Consular Affairs
Tel: (202) 647-5225
Country Desk Officer, Denmark
Tel: (202) 647-5669

U.S. DEPARTMENT OF COMMERCE
Denmark Desk
Int'l Trade Admin.
Tel: (202) 482-2841

DANISH TOURIST BOARD
655 Third Avenue
New York, N.Y. 10017
Tel: (212) 949-2326
Fax: (212) 983-5260

Contacts in Denmark:

U.S. EMBASSY
Dag Hammarskjolds Alle 24
2100 Copenhagen O
Mailing Address:
APO AE 09716
Tel: [45] (31) 42-31-44
Fax: [45] (35) 43-0223
Telex: 22216 AMEMB DK

DUN & BRADSTREET INTERNATIONAL A/S
(D&B/HYLDAHL)
Postal Address: Egegaardsvej 39, DK
2610 Rodovre, Denmark
Street Address: Egegaardsvej 39, DK
2610 Rodovre, Denmark
Tel: [45] (36) 709-000
Fax: [45] (36) 709-129

QUEEN MARGRETHE II
Office of the Queen
Amalienborg Palace
Copenhagen K., Kingdom of Denmark

PRIME MINISTER POUL NYRUP RASMUSSEN
Christiansborg Palace
Prins Jorgens Gaard II
1218 Copenhagen K., Kingdom of
Denmark

 Passport/Visa Requirements

Visa Information   (202) 663-1225

Entry Requirements: A passport is required. U.S. citizens do not need a visa for a three-month tourist stay, as long as they have not accumulated a total of three months' stay in any Nordic country within the past six months. For current information concerning entry and customs requirements for Denmark, travelers can contact the Denmark Embassy.

Faux Pas: A visitor from the U.S.A. was embarrassed when he attempted to chat with other patrons while waiting to be seated in a Danish restaurant. The Danes did not respond; they thought it very odd that someone would try to strike up a conversation with total strangers.

Egypt

Official Name:	Arab Republic of Egypt (Jumhuriyah Misr al-'Arabiyah)
Official Language:	Arabic
Government System:	Republic
Population:	59 million
Population Growth:	2.3%
Area:	1,001,450 sq. km. (386,650 sq. mi.); slightly smaller than Texas, Oklahoma, and Arkansas combined
Natural Resources:	crude oil, natural gas, iron ore, phosphates, manganese, limestone, gypsum, talc, asbestos, lead, zinc
Major Cities:	Cairo (capital), Alexandria, Aswan, Asyut, Port Said, Suez, Ismailia, Tanta

Cultural Note: Egyptians tend to have large extended families. They are rarely alone, and solitude is not often a chosen condition. As a result, Egyptians gravitate toward others in public. If you are sitting in an empty movie theater, an Egyptian will probably choose a seat next to you. If you are seated at one end of a bench, an Egyptian is likely to sit next to you, rather than at the other end of the bench. This is just force of habit; it does not mean that the Egyptian wishes to speak to you.

Age Breakdown

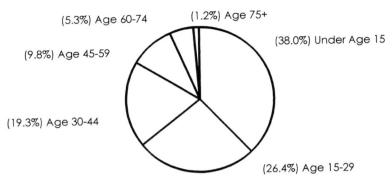

(5.3%) Age 60-74

(1.2%) Age 75+

(9.8%) Age 45-59

(38.0%) Under Age 15

(19.3%) Age 30-44

(26.4%) Age 15-29

Life Expectancy: 58 years male; 62 years female (1992)

 ## Time

Arabs often find it amusing how dependent Westerners are on the clock. Punctuality does not have a high priority in Egypt. Your Egyptian counterpart may be late for an appointment or might not show up at all. You, as a Westerner, should try to be prompt. Everything will take longer in Egypt, including the decision-making process.

Egypt is two hours ahead of Greenwich Mean Time (G.M.T. = 2), which is seven hours ahead of U.S. Eastern Standard Time (E.S.T. + 7).

 ## Holidays

(Update: Getting Through Customs *http://www.getcustoms.com*)

This list is a working guide. Dates should be corroborated before final travel plans are made. In cases where holidays fall on Saturday or Sunday, commercial establishments may be closed the preceding Friday or following Monday.

Remember that the Islamic calendar uses lunar months of 28 days, so an Islamic year of 12 months is only 354 days long. Holidays will thus be on different dates (by the Western calendar) every year. Muslim holiday dates are also approximations since they depend upon actual lunar observations. Paperwork should carry two dates, the Gregorian (Western) date and the Hijrah (Arabic) date. Be aware that Christian Egyptians (Coptics) have yet another calendar, different from both of the above.

New Year's Day	1 January
Ramadan Bairam	varies
Liberation of the Sinai Day	25 April
Labor Day	1 May
Islamic New Year	varies
National Day	23 July
Armed Forces Day	6 October
(Anniversary of the 1973 War)	

There are additional Islamic and Eastern Orthodox Christian holidays which vary in observance date from year to year. Confirm your appointments with local representatives to avoid conflicts with regional festivals.

Work Week

- Friday is the Muslim holy day; no business is conducted on Fridays. Most people do not work on Thursdays either. The work week runs from Saturday through Wednesday.
- Working hours for businesses, banks, and government offices are truncated during the month of Ramadan.
- Government hours are 8:00 A.M. to 2:00 P.M. They are closed on either Thursday and Friday or Friday and Saturday (the variation is designed to reduce traffic on congested Cairo streets).
- Banking hours tend to be 8:30 A.M. to 1:30 P.M., Monday through Wednesday. Some banks keep Sunday morning hours from 10 A.M. to 12 noon. Most international hotels offer 24-hour banking services.
- Business hours vary widely. In the winter, many close for much of the afternoon and reopen for a few hours in late afternoon.
- A typical business schedule would be: 8 A.M. to 2 P.M. in the summer; 9 A.M. to 1 P.M. and 5 P.M. to 7 P.M. in the winter.

Religious/Societal Influences on Business

Islam is the official religion of Egypt, and 90% of Egyptians are Sunni Moslems. The remaining 10% are primarily Coptic Christians. The Coptic religion predates the arrival of Islam in Egypt, but the Coptics feel that the majority of Muslims discriminate against them. Coptics are not well represented either in business or the Egyptian government.

Egyptians are intensely nationalistic and are quick to take offense at foreign interference in their affairs. Sensitive areas include Egypt's former colonial overlords (France and Britain), economic and cultural influences from the U.S., Islamic fundamentalism, and Israel. After fighting (and losing) three wars with Israel, Egypt became the first Arab country to make peace with Israel. However, the Egyptian people might not have stood for a peace treaty had not the Egyptian Army "redeemed" itself in the Yom Kippur War. After being routed in the previous two wars, the Egyptian armed forces put up a stubborn fight in the Yom Kippur War. Even though they were defeated, this resistance allowed the military to "save face," something that is always important in Egypt.

As in all Islamic countries, piety and decorum are valued. Alcohol and pork are prohibited to observant Muslims, but Islam in Egypt is not as strict as in Saudi Arabia (where foreigners are jailed for possessing alcohol). Most international hotels in Egypt serve alcohol.

With the largest Arab population in the world, Egypt considers itself the leading Arab nation. Yet Egypt is essentially a poor country, with a growing population that can only be supported by vast amounts of foreign aid. As usual, poor Arabs tend toward fundamentalism, and fundamentalist terrorism remains a problem in Egypt.

 5 Cultural Tips

1. Egypt is one of the most Westernized nations of the Middle East. You will encounter some international executives who are very familiar with Western business customs. Other Egyptian executives may have traditional Arab manners. Be prepared for any extreme.

2. The traditional Arab business appointment follows a general pattern. First, you would be made to wait. (The lower your status, the longer you wait.) Then you would be shown into a room with several people. One will take the position of host, and will make extensive inquiries into your health and journeys before starting to talk about business. The other people may or may not be introduced. Your host may interrupt your sales pitch at any time to converse with others in the room. The others in the room might pay attention to your pitch, or they may carry on conversations of their own. Your host may ask you to repeat all or part of your presentation to a new arrival. You may have no idea who the decision maker is (although it's probably an older man who watches everything yet says nothing). Finally, you will be served coffee, encouraging things will be said (but no contracts signed), and your appointment is over.

3. Adjustments foreigners must make include the work week (Friday is the Islamic Sabbath, so the work week runs Saturday through Wednesday) and Ramadan (the month of fasting, when no one eats during the day and many people seem cranky).

4. Exaggeration and Arabic go hand-in-hand. Acceptance is blown up to enthusiasm; disapproval becomes a dire threat. Learn to take this in stride. When you hear an Egyptian say yes in answer to a question, always consider the cultural context. A mild yes is probably a polite no; at best, it means possibly.

5. Saving face is always a consideration in Egypt. Never cause someone to lose face in public. Be prepared to go to great lengths to protect someone's dignity.

Economic Overview

Since launching an economic reform program in 1991, Egypt has opened its doors wider to foreign trade and foreign investment. Egypt is one of a handful of markets where the U.S. has a multibillion dollar trade surplus.

By far the largest Arab country by population, Egypt is in the heart of the Middle East and has a reasonably well educated, English-speaking labor force. Between 5 and 10 million of Egypt's population enjoy Western consumption patterns. The rest are poor, but habits and consumption are changing fast.

U.S. exporters enjoy a solid position with one-third of the $11 billion import market. Egyptians like American goods and technology and the American image overall is quite positive. While progress has been made in liberalizing Egypt's trade regime, domestic industry remains protected by nontariff import barriers and relatively high tariff rates.

Challenges to doing business in Egypt include the relative poverty of the majority of the population which limits the consumer market, the slow pace of business deregulation under the economic reform program, and bureaucratic red tape.

Cultural Note: Foreigners who inadvertently violate Egyptian taboos sometimes underestimate the seriousness of their transgressions. But a single incident, when it gets out of hand, can ruin your reputation in Egypt. For example: A visiting British poetry professor, while lecturing at Ain Shams University in Cairo, unthinkingly displayed the sole of his foot to his audience. In Egypt, as in other Muslim countries, this is a serious insult. The professor's failure to respect Egyptian decorum resulted in a student protest, followed by newspaper headlines denouncing British arrogance.

Comparative Data

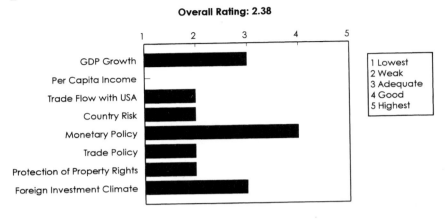

Overall Rating: 2.38

Legend:
1 Lowest
2 Weak
3 Adequate
4 Good
5 Highest

Country Risk Rating

Gross Domestic Product: $146 billion
GDP Growth: 4.5%
Per Capita Income: $2,500

Trade Flows with the U.S.A.

Rank as Export Market for U.S.A. Goods & Services: 33rd
U.S.A. Exports to Egypt: $2.9 billion
Growth Rate of Exports: 3%
U.S.A. Imports from Egypt: $606 million
Growth Rate of Imports: 10%
Rank as a Supplier of Imports into the U.S.A.:   60th

Top U.S.A. Exports to Egypt: Cereals; motor vehicles; aircraft; machinery; arms and ammunition; electrical products; medical and optical equipment; mineral fuel (fuel from coal); paper and paperboard; plastics.

Top U.S.A. Prospects for Export to Egypt: Telecommunications equipment; electrical power systems; aircraft and parts; plastic materials and resins; oil and gas field machinery; paper and paperboard; airport and ground support equipment; architectural/construction/engineering services; computers and peripherals; food processing and packaging equipment.

Credit Terms

Dun & Bradstreet rates Egypt as an adequate credit risk with a reasonable capacity to meet outstanding payment liabilities.

A confirmed irrevocable letter of credit is recommended when doing business with Egyptian concerns.

Monetary Policy

Inflation in 1996 and 1997 is forecast between 5.5% and 7%. *Monetary Unit*: Egyptian pound.

Trade Policy

TARIFFS: Tariffs range between 5 and 70%. Egyptian tariff rates are considered relatively high compared to other developing countries.

IMPORT LICENSING: Import licenses are no longer required in Egypt. Import bans apply to textiles, apparel, and poultry, although poultry was expected to be removed from the banned list in 1995.

Approximately 130 items are inspected for quality control prior to admittance into Egypt. These include foodstuffs, spare parts, construction products, electronic devices, appliances, and many consumer goods.

IMPORT TAXES: Egypt assesses a 3 to 6% service fee on imports, depending on the tariff applied. Egypt has committed to the World Bank to reduce this service fee to a flat 2%.

A sales tax ranging between 5 and 25% is added to the final customs value of the imported item.

Protection of Intellectual Property Rights

Egypt's legal system provides protection for most forms of intellectual property. Enforcement of laws, while improving, is still considered ineffective. Egypt is a party to the Berne Copyright and Paris Patent Conventions.

Egypt's patent law excludes certain categories of products, including pharmaceuticals and food products. The patent term is only 15 years from the application of the filing date, compared with the international standard of 20 years. A five-year renewal may be obtained only if the invention is of special importance and has not been worked adequately to compensate patent holders for their efforts and expenses.

A new copyright law was passed in 1992 which increased penalties substantially against piracy. Computer software was afforded specific protection. Copyright piracy is still widespread and affects all categories of works.

Egypt's trademark law is not enforced strenuously and the courts have only limited experience in adjudicating infringement cases.

Foreign Investment Climate

The government of Egypt is open to foreign direct investment. The U.S. and Egypt implemented a Bilateral Investment Treaty in 1992.

Investments are automatically approved unless the sector is on a "negative list" of projects. Only two items are on the negative list, military products and related industries, and tobacco and tobacco products.

Most foreign investment is under Investment Law 230, which allows 100% foreign ownership of ventures and guarantees the right to remit income earned in Egypt and to repatriate capital. Under Law 230, enterprises may own land necessary for their objectives without obtaining the specific approval of the Prime Minister, regardless of the foreign ownership percentage.

Privatization guidelines clearly state that there shall be no discrimination against foreign investors, but the sale of sector assets to foreigners remains controversial.

 # Current Leaders & Political Parties

(Update: International Academy at Santa Barbara *http://www.iasb.org/cwl*)

State, Government, and Political Party Leaders:

Pres.: Mohamed Hosni Mubarek

Cabinet Ministers:

Dep. Prime Min. and Min. of Planning: Dr. Kamal Ahmed El-Ganzouri

Dep. Prime Min. and Min. of Agriculture and Land Reclamation:
   Dr. Youssef Amin Wali

Insurance and Social Affairs: Dr. Amal Abdel Rahman Othman

Transportation and Telecommunications: Suliman Metwalli

Electricity and Energy: Mohamed Maher Abaza

Defense and Military Production: Fd. Mar. Mohammed Hussein Tantawy

Information: Mohamed Safwat El-Sherif

Foreign Affairs: Amr Mahmoud Moussa

Business, Environment, and Admin. Dev.: Dr. Atef Mohamed Ebeid

Supplies and Trade: Dr. Ahmed El Guweili

Finance: Mohieddin Abu Kakr Al-Gharib

Awqafs (Islamic Trusts): Dr. Mahmoud Hamdy Zagzoug

Justice: Farouk Mahmoud Seif El-Nasr

Culture: Farouk Abdel Aziz Hosni

Cabinet Affairs and Monitoring: Tala't Sayed Ahmed Hammad

Local Admin.: Dr. Mahmoud Ahmed Sherif

Education: Dr. Hussein Kamel Bahaa El-Din

Petroleum: Dr. Hamdy Ali El-Banbi

Interior: Gen. Hassan El-Alfi

State for Cabinet Affairs: Dr. Youssef Boutros Ghali

Housing and Public Utilities: Mohamed Ibrahim Suleiman

State for People's Assembly and Shoura Cncl. Affairs: Dr. Mohamed Zaki Abu-Amer

Tourism: Dr. Mamdouh Ahmed El Beltagui

Economy and International Cooperation: Dr. Nawal Abdelmoneim/El Tatawi

Irrigation and Water Resources: Mohamed Abdel-Hady Radi

Health and Population: Dr. Ismail Awadallah Sallam

Industry and Mineral Resources: Suleiman Reda Ali Soliman

Housing, Public Utilities: Mohamed Ibrahim Suliman

State for Scientific Research: Dr. Venice Kamel Goudah

State for Military Production: Dr. Mohamed EL-Ghamrawy Daoud

Labor and Employment: Ahmed Ahmed El-Amawi

Other Officials:

Speaker of the People's Assembly: Dr. Ahmed Fathi Surour

Speaker of the Shura Cncl.: Dr. Mustafa Kamal Helmy

Ambassador to U.S.: Ahmed Maher El-Sayed

Perm. Rep. to U.N.: Nabil El Araby

Political Parties:

Natl. Democratic Party, Labor Socialist Party, Liberal Socialist Party, Natl. Progressive Unionist Party, New Wafd Party, Al-Umma Party, Egyptian Green Party, New MISR Al-Fatah Party, Unionist Democratic Party, Nasserist Party, Social Justice Party, Egyptian Arab Party

Political Influences on Business

President Hosni Mubarak has supported a strong U.S.-Egyptian relationship based on shared interests in promoting regional peace and stability, revitalizing the Egyptian economy, and strengthening trade ties. Over the years, Egypt and the U.S. have worked closely to help further the Middle East peace process. In 1993–94, Egypt hosted many of the negotiating rounds for the Gaza-Jericho autonomy agreement which was signed in Cairo in May 1994 by former Israeli Prime Minister Yitzhak Rabin and PLO leader Yasir Arafat.

The threat of terrorism remains an impediment to foreign business investment. Since 1992, extremist groups seeking to overthrow the Egyptian government have staged attacks on Egyptian government officials, security forces, foreign tourists, and Egyptian Coptic Christians. Although the terrorist attacks have hurt Egypt's tourist industry, they are not at this time considered a substantial threat to the government or its ability to make overall progress.

The Egyptian political system has undergone significant liberalization since the Nasser era of a few generations ago. Today, citizens enjoy a substantial degree of freedom of expression and the judiciary regularly demonstrates its independence from the executive branch. Further progress on political reform has taken a back seat to meeting the challenge posed by terrorist groups. The government's antiterrorism campaign has raised serious allegations of such human rights abuses as torture, arbitrary arrest, prolonged detention without trial, and the use of military courts to try persons accused of terrorism. Moreover, the governing National Democratic Party (NDP) dominates the political scene to such an extent that, as a practical matter, people do not have a meaningful ability to change their government. In 1994, the People's Assembly approved a three-year extension of the Emergency Law and Egypt has been under an official state of emergency continuously since 1981.

The Egyptian Constitution provides for a strong president, who is empowered to appoint one or more vice presidents, the prime minister, the cabinet, and the governors of Egypt's 26 provinces. In 1993, President Hosni Mubarak was endorsed in a national referendum, in which he ran unopposed, to serve a third six-year term as president by the People's Assembly.

The People's Assembly has 454 members, 444 of which are popularly elected with 10 appointed by the president. The constitution reserves 50% of the Assembly seats for workers and farmers. Assembly members sit for five-year terms. There is also a 210-member *Shura* (Consultative) Council which has an advisory role on public policy but little legislative power.

 ## Contacts in the U.S.A. & in Egypt

Contacts in the United States:

EMBASSY OF THE ARAB REPUBLIC OF EGYPT
3521 International Court, N.W.
Washington, D.C. 20008
Tel: (202) 895-5400
Fax: (202) 244-4319

U.S. DEPARTMENT OF STATE
Bureau of Consular Affairs
Tel: (202) 647-5225
Egypt desk
Tel: (202) 647-1228

U.S. DEPARTMENT OF COMMERCE
Int'l Trade Administration
Office of the Near East
Egypt desk
Tel: (202) 482-1860 or 5506

TOURISM OFFICE
Egyptian Tourist Authority
323 Geary Street
San Francisco, CA 94102
Tel: (415) 781-7676

In the Arab Republic of Egypt:

U.S. EMBASSY
8 Kamal El-Din Salah St.
Garden City, Cairo, Egypt
U.S. Mailing Address:
APO AE 09839
Tel: [20] (2) 355-7371
Telex: 93773 AMEMB
Fax: [20] (2) 355-8368

AMERICAN CHAMBER OF COMMERCE IN EGYPT
Cairo Marriott Hotel
Suite 1541
P.O. Box 33 Zamalek
Cairo, Egypt
Tel: [20] (2) 340-8888
Fax: [20] (2) 340-6667
Telex: 20870 AMCHE UN

PRESIDENT MOHAMED HOSNI MUBARAK
Office of the President
Cairo, Arab Republic of Egypt

PRIME MINISTER DR. KAMAL AHMED EL GANZOURI
Office of the Prime Minister
Cairo, Arab Republic of Egypt

Passport/Visa Requirements

Visa information   (202) 663-1225

Entry Requirements: A passport and visa are required.

For additional entry information, U.S. citizens can contact the Embassy of the Arab Republic of Egypt.

Faux Pas: Don't make assumptions about Egyptians not understanding English. A U.S. executive from an aircraft manufacturer, assuming his limo driver did not speak English, scoffed to a colleague about the inability of the Egyptians to fly the airplanes he was selling. Not only did the driver understand, but he reported the remark to his superiors. The information reached the Egyptian Minister of Defense, who asked the U.S. Ambassador to have this executive sent home. This incautious executive was gone within 48 hours.

France

Official Name:	French Republic (République Française)
Official Language:	French
Government System:	Multiparty republic
Population:	58 million
Population Growth:	0.50%
Area:	551,670 sq. km. (220,668 sq. mi.); largest West European country, about four-fifths the size of Texas
Natural Resources:	coal, iron ore, bauxite, fish, timber, zinc, potash
Major Cities:	Paris (capital), Marseille, Lyon, Toulouse, Strasbourg, Nice, Bordeaux

Cultural Note: The French attitudes on money and sex are the reverse of those in the United States. Unlike Americans, the French are almost impossible to embarrass about sex or nudity. On the other hand, money (and how you get it) is embarrassing to the French. Having money, or having the ability to make money, garners little respect in France. In fact, the simple question "What do you do?" is considered too personal to ask a stranger in France. To most French men and women, their jobs and incomes are none of your business.

Age Breakdown

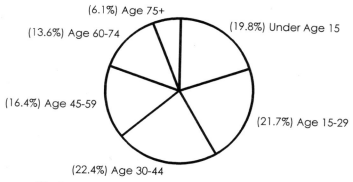

(6.1%) Age 75+
(13.6%) Age 60-74
(19.8%) Under Age 15
(16.4%) Age 45-59
(21.7%) Age 15-29
(22.4%) Age 30-44

Life Expectancy: 73 years male; 81 years female (1991)

Time

Punctuality is treated very casually in France. People are often late, and no offense is taken. But the person in the subservient position is usually prompt. If you are trying to sell something to a French executive, you must be on time, while the executive is free to be late.

The rules for social events vary. People try to be punctual for lunch, since everyone will be returning to work afterward (although lunch itself can easily span two hours!). At dinner, they can easily be half an hour late.

In general, the French hate commitment. They will wait until the last minute before scheduling anything. Meetings and appointments will be rescheduled frequently.

France is one hour ahead of Greenwich Mean Time (G.M.T. + 1), which is six hours ahead of U.S. Eastern Standard Time (E.S.T. + 6).

Holidays

(Update: Getting Through Customs *http://www.getcustoms.com*)

This list is a working guide. Dates should be corroborated before final travel plans are made. In cases where holidays fall on Saturday or Sunday, commercial establishments may be closed the preceding Friday or following Monday.

New Year's Day	1 January
Good Friday	varies
Easter Monday	varies
Labor Day	1 May
Veteran's Day (WWII)	8 May
Bastille Day/French National Day	15 July
Christmas Day	25 December

When a holiday falls on a Sunday, it is observed on Monday.

 ## Work Week

- Most French get four or five weeks summer vacation, and take it in July and August. Indeed, except for the tourist industry, France virtually shuts down in August. Try to conduct business during other months.
- The fiscal year in the public sector runs on a calendar-year basis.

 ## Religious/Societal Influences on Business

France has no official religion. Most religions are represented in France, but the majority of people (over 75%) are Roman Catholic. Recent immigrants from Algeria and other Mediterranean areas have increased the number of Muslims to 3%. An additional 3% of the French describe themselves as atheists.

Religion does not play a large part in the everyday lives of most French citizens. Anticlerical doctrines were made law during the French Revolution, and some of these survive to this day. Education, however, is the seminal event in the lives of most French citizens. French schools are rigorous, assigning so much homework that children have little time for either mischief or other activities. Linguistic capability and wit are valued highly. Children are encouraged to develop their verbal skills from an early age. In order to discourage mundane topics of conversation, many parents respond to straightforward comments from children by saying "That's boring!"

France is a highly stratified society, with sharply defined and competing classes. This "us against them" attitude is seen not only in politics, but in everyday interaction. Foreigners often find customer service in France to be below their standards, and complain to the manager. Yet the manager nearly always sides with the employee. Manager and employee are part of a "family," and they unite against outsiders, even when it costs the company money! (But remember, earning money is not as high a personal priority in France as it is in the U.S.A.)

France remains a patriarchal country. Women's rights have come late to France; it wasn't until 1923 that women acquired the right to open their own mail! Sexual harassment has been illegal only since 1992.

 ## 5 Cultural Tips

1. The French handshake is brief, almost a hand clasp, accompanied by a short span of eye contact. There is good reason for this: French employees shake hands with each fellow employee every day . . . *twice*! When an employee arrives, he or she goes around the building shaking hands with everyone. When they leave, the process is repeated. Even in a small office, this can involve several hundred hand-shakes every single day. While some French (of both sexes) kiss their friends on both cheeks, this is rarely done in a business setting.

2. The French have a great appreciation for the art of conversation. However, be aware that the French frequently interrupt each other. *French conversation is not linear.* Instead, conversation is considered a dynamic process of give-and-take, where every possibility is articulated. Argument is a form of entertainment. Well-expressed opinions are appreciated, even if they are diametrically opposed to everyone else's. The French often complain that North Americans lecture, rather than converse. Note that you do not have to answer every single objection to your proposal. The French want every opinion to be expressed, not necessarily refuted.

3. Food is important in France, and business always involves sharing meals. At a business lunch or dinner, show enthusiasm about the food before beginning a business discussion. Whoever initiates the meal is expected to pay. Reservations are necessary in most restaurants, except in brasseries and in hotels. In choosing a restaurant, stick to French, rather than ethnic ones.

4. Respect privacy. The French close doors behind them; you should do the same. Knock and wait before entering.

5. Pay attention to voices. It is a sign of closeness in France to be able to recognize someone over the telephone by their voice alone. A friend is liable to be hurt if you have to ask "Who is this?" on the phone. Also be sensitive to the volume of your voice. It is no secret that U.S. executives are known to offend everyone in a restaurant, meeting, or on the street with their loud voices and braying laughter.

 ## Economic Overview

France has the world's sixth largest economy and is the United States' tenth largest trading partner. The market for U.S. goods and services in France has been, and will continue to be, of major importance in industry, agriculture, and in the *invisibles* accounts, particularly in travel and franchising. As the economic recovery continues in France, there is expected to be improved demand for building materials, equipment related to air and surface transportation, and machine tools.

The French market is mature, sophisticated, and well served by suppliers from around the world. Competition, both local and third-country, confronts American business at every corner in the coveted French market. With the increasingly free flow of goods and persons among European Union member nations, there is a natural tendency to buy within the community. U.S. businesses should keep this in mind so as to be competitive in shipping expenses and in timely delivery. The French commercial environment is generally receptive to U.S. goods and services. It is dynamic and reflects consumer trends as well as the effect of comparative advantage in an interdependent world marketplace. The complex French society includes a strong market for high quality, high-tech consumer goods, particularly for its affluent cities where the distribution system still uses independent specialty stores as well as the more modern discount stores.

France and the U.S. are close allies. Despite occasional differences of view, the U.S. and France work together on a broad range of trade, security, and geopolitical issues.

Most U.S. companies face no major obstacles in doing business in France with a few significant exceptions; namely, these are restrictions on the TV broadcast of non-European firms and programs and the limitations on the performance of legal services by non-French lawyers. U.S. companies sometimes complain of France's complex technical standards and of unduly long testing procedures.

Comparative Data

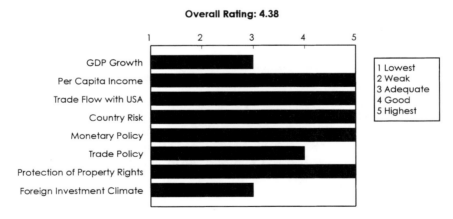

Overall Rating: 4.38

	1 Lowest
	2 Weak
	3 Adequate
	4 Good
	5 Highest

Country Risk Rating

Gross Domestic Product: $1.3 trillion
GDP Growth: 2.2%
Per Capita Income: $22,138

Trade Flows with the U.S.A.

Rank as Export Market for U.S.A. Goods & Services: 10th

U.S.A. Exports to France: $14.2 billion

Growth Rate of Exports: 4%

U.S.A. Imports from France: $17.1 billion

Growth Rate of Imports: 2%

Rank as a Supplier of Imports into the U.S.A.:   11th

Top U.S.A. Exports to France: Machinery; electrical components; medical and optical equipment; aircraft and parts; precious stones and metal; organic chemicals; motor vehicles; plastics and resins; mineral fuel/oil; pharmaceutical products.

Top U.S.A. Prospects for Export to France: Travel and tourism; computer software; industrial chemicals; aircraft and parts; computers and peripherals; security and safety equipment; insurance services; electrical power systems; electronic components; medical equipment.

Country Risk

Dun & Bradstreet rates France as having excellent capacity to meet outstanding payment liabilities. France carries the lowest degree of risk.

Credit terms vary according to sector and size of transaction, but are usually between 60 and 90 days. Most transactions are on open account.

Monetary Policy

Inflationary pressures will remain well contained. The annual inflation rate for consumer prices has fallen from 3.6% in 1989 to 1.7% in 1995, the lowest rate in France in 37 years. Inflation will remain modest in the 2% to 2.5% range. *Monetary Unit:* French franc.

Trade Policy

TARIFFS: Tariffs levied on imports from non-EU countries, including the U.S., are moderate. Most raw materials enter duty-free or at low rates, while most manufactured goods are subject to rates of between 5 and 17%. Most agricultural product imports are covered by the Common Agricultural Policy (CAP), under which many items are subject to variable levies designed to equalize the prices of imported commodities with those produced in the EU.

IMPORT LICENSING: Most products can be imported without an import license.

Products which are subject to restrictive regulations include: poultry meat, enriched flour, genetic material, crayfish, and certain fruits and vegetables which are subject to seasonal price restrictions.

IMPORT TAXES: In addition to the duties levied under the Common External Tariff, goods imported into France are also subject to a Value-Added Tax (VAT). Currently, the VAT in France is generally charged at one of two rates: the standard rate of 18.6%; the reduced rate of 5.5% applicable to most agricultural products and foodstuffs and certain medicines.

Most processed products entering the European Union and France are subject to additional import charges based on the percentage of sugar, milk fat, milk protein, and starch in the product. This situation should improve in the future because these charges will be converted to fixed tariff equivalents and reduced under the Uruguay Round Agreement.

Protection of Intellectual Property Rights

Under the French intellectual property rights regime, industrial property is protected by patents, trademarks, and designs and models, while literary/artistic property is protected by copyrights.

U.S. nationals are entitled to receive the same protection of industrial property rights in France as French nationals. In addition, U.S. nationals have a right of priority period after filing a U.S. patent, trademark, design, or model, in which to file a corresponding application in France. This period is 12 months for patents and six months for trademarks, designs, and models.

In order to qualify for patent protection, the invention must have an industrial or agricultural application; imply a nonobvious procedure and have an absolute novelty. Patents for inventions have a 20-year life span, after which they become part of the public domain. Patents of addition are only valid for the unexpired term of their parent patents. Trademark protection can apply to both goods and services. In a general sense, trademarks recognize and protect indicators which serve to distinguish one product or service from similar products or services. A trademark has a 10-year life span and is renewable every 10 years.

Copyrights cover artistic works, literary works, and software. In the French intellectual property rights regime, in order to qualify for a copyright, the language used to express the idea must be original, not the idea itself. Copyrights are valid for 50 years after the death of the author, with two major exceptions: music copyrights are valid for 70 years after the death of the composer, and software copyrights are valid for 25 years after creation.

Foreign Investment Climate

With its central location in a dynamic and unified European market, excellent infrastructure, productive and disciplined workforce, and high quality of life, France has become one of the most attractive potential locations for U.S. direct investment.

The French government actively courts foreign investment and has progressively liberalized its investment approval regime. Direct foreign investment is regarded as one of the best potential sources of new jobs. However, U.S. investors still do not receive full national or EU treatment. The French state has a centuries-old tradition of extensive control of business and the economy. Today, even after a decade of rapid and comprehensive economic deregulation, and despite massive foreign investment by French companies, foreign investors in France occasionally face interference from government officials.

France offers a variety of financial incentives to foreign investors and its investment promotion agency, DATAR, provides extensive assistance to potential investors both in France and through its agencies around the world.

 Current Leaders & Political Parties

(Update: International Academy at Santa Barbara *http://www.iasb.org/cwl*)

State, Government, and Political Party Leaders:

Pres.: Jacques Chirac

Cabinet Ministers:

Prime Min.: Alain Juppé

Natl. Education, Higher Learning, and Research: François Bayrou

Defense: Charles Millon

Public Works, Housing, Transportation, and Tourism: Bernard Pons

Foreign Affairs: Hervé De Charette

Interior: Jean-Louis Debré

Economy and Finance: Jean Arthuis

Relations with Parliament: Roger Romani

Environment: Corinne Lepage

Industry, Posts, and Telecommunications: Franck Borotra

Agriculture, Fisheries, and Food: Philippe Vasseur

Regional Dev., Urban Affairs, and Integration: Jean-Claude Gaudin

Small and Medium Business, Commerce, and Crafts: Jean-Pierre Raffarin

Other Officials:

Pres. of the Natl. Assembly: Philippe Seguin

Pres. of the Senate: René Monory

Ambassador to U.S.: François Bujon de L'Estang

Perm. Rep. to U.N.: Jean-Bernard Merimee

Political Parties:

>   Socialist Party (PS), Leftist Radical Mov. (MRG), Communist Party (PCF), Rally
>   for the Republic (RPR), Union for French Democracy (UDF), Green Party,
>   Republican Party (PR), Center for Social Democrats (CDS), Natl. Front (FN)

 Political Influences on Business

France and the U.S. are close allies. France is a democratic republic whose political system is based on a written constitution approved by referendum in 1958. According to the French Constitution, the President of the Republic is elected by direct suffrage every seven years. The President names the Prime Minister, presides over the cabinet, commands the armed forces and concludes treaties. He is also empowered to dissolve the National Assembly and, in certain emergency situations, may assume full power. France's political system is a hybrid of presidential and parliamentary systems, resulting occasionally in the President and Prime Minister being of opposing parties. From March 1993 to April 1995, for example, the Socialist President had a Prime Minister from a different party.

The Constitution provides for a bicameral parliament consisting of a National Assembly and a Senate. National Assembly deputies are elected directly by universal suffrage for five-year terms. Senators are elected indirectly for nine-year terms; one-third of the Senate is renewed every three years.

The late French President Francois Mitterrand, a Socialist, left office in May 1995, ending 14 years (two seven-year terms) in power.

In the 1995 elections, the former Mayor of Paris, Jacques Chirac, edged out another Gaullist, Edouard Balladur (the former French Prime Minister) and Socialist Lionel Jospin for the Presidency. This had been Chirac's third attempt at the Presidency.

Chirac appointed Alain Juppé as Prime Minister. Mr. Juppé soon faced a scandal over revelations that he and several relatives were paying some 40% under market price to rent government-owned apartments in expensive Paris neighborhoods.

Concentrating on such issues as welfare and health care reform, Mr. Chirac has had limited effect on the French business climate. His greatest effect on French business resulted from a national security decision to conduct a series of thermonuclear tests on the South Pacific Island of Mururoa. The French underestimated the virulence of the opposition to these tests from Pacific Rim nations, notably Japan, Australia, and New Zealand. In retaliation, various nations temporarily banned the import of French products.

Contacts in the U.S.A. & in France

Contacts in the United States:

EMBASSY OF FRANCE
4101 Reservoir Road, N.W.
Washington, D.C. 20007
Tel: (202) 944-6000

U.S. DEPARTMENT OF STATE
Bureau of Consular Affairs
Tel: (202) 647-5225
Country Desk Officer, France
Tel: (202) 647-2663

U.S. DEPARTMENT OF COMMERCE
France Desk
Int'l Trade Admin.
Tel: (202) 482-6008

FRENCH GOVERNMENT TOURIST OFFICE
610 Fifth Street
New York, N.Y. 10020-2452
Tel: (212) 757-1125
Fax: (212) 247-6468

Contacts in France:

U.S. EMBASSY
2 Avenue Gabriel
75382 Paris Cedex 08
Paris, France
Mailing Address:
APO AE 09777
Tel: [33] (1) 42 96 12 02
Telex: 285319 AMEMB
Fax: [33] (1) 42 66 97 83

THE AMERICAN CHAMBER OF COMMERCE IN
FRANCE
21 Avenue George V
F-75008 Paris, France
Tel: [33] (1) 47 23 70 28
Fax: [33] (1) 47 20 18 62

DUN & BRADSTREET FRANCE S.A.
Postal and street Address: 345 avenue
George Clemenceau, Immeuble Defense
Bergeres, TSA 5003, 92882 Nanterre
CTC Cedex 9, France
Tel: [33] (1) 41 35 17 00
Fax: [33] (1) 41 35 17 77

PRESIDENT JACQUES CHIRAC
Palais de l'Elysee
55-57 rue de Faubourg Sant Honore
75008 Paris, France

PRIME MINISTER ALAIN JUPPÉ
Office of the Prime Minister
57 rue de Varenne
75700 Paris, France

Passport/Visa Requirements

Entry Requirements: A passport is required. For a stay not exceeding three months, the nationals of the countries listed do not need a visa to enter France, its overseas departments (French Guyana, Guadeloupe, Martinique, Mayotte, Reunion, St. Pierre, and Miquelon), and its overseas territories (French Polynesia, New Caledonia, Wallis and Futuna); Andorra, Argentina, Austria, Belgium, Brunei, Canada, Chile, Croatia, Cyprus, the Czech Republic, Denmark, Finland, Germany, Great Britain, Greece, Hungary, Iceland, Israel, Ireland, Italy, Japan, Korea (ROK), Liechtenstein, Luxembourg, Malaysia, Malta, Monaco, Netherlands, New Zealand, Norway, Poland, Portugal, San Marino, Singapore, the Slovak Republic, Slovenia, Spain, Sweden, Switzerland, the United States, Uruguay, and the Vatican.

A visa is still required for a U.S. citizen for a short stay of less than 3 months if the individual is 1) intending to study in France, 2) a journalist on assignment, 3) a member of a plane or ship crew on a mission, or 4) holder of diplomatic or official passports if on a mission.

Cultural Note: If you don't speak French, it is very important that you apologize for your lack of knowledge. The French are proud of their language, and believe everyone should be able to speak it. (After all, for several hundred years, just about every Western diplomat did speak French.)

Germany

Official Name:	Federal Republic of Germany
Official Language:	German
Government System:	Democratic federal multiparty republic
Population:	81 million
Population Growth:	0.9%
Area:	356,854 sq. km. (137,821 sq. mi.); about the size of Montana
Major Cities:	Berlin (capital), Bonn (government seat), Hamburg, Munich, Frankfurt, Cologne, Leipzig, Dresden
Natural Resources:	iron ore, coal, potash, timber, copper, natural gas, salt

Cultural Note: Keep your thinking linear in Germany. Thorough, methodical planning is how Germans have achieved their reputation for quality. Every aspect of every project will be examined in detail. This process can be very time-intensive.

Germans do not like the unexpected. Sudden changes, even if they may improve the outcome, are unwelcome.

Present your ideas in an organized manner. Be aware that the tendency of U.S. citizens to precede blunt criticism by first saying something positive is not done in Germany. A juxtaposition of good news/bad news may cause them to ignore your entire statement. In fact, Germans do not need or expect compliments. They just assume everything is satisfactory unless they hear otherwise.

Age Breakdown

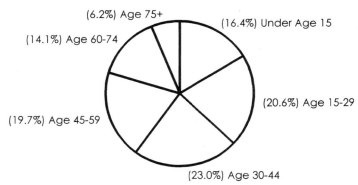

(6.2%) Age 75+

(16.4%) Under Age 15

(14.1%) Age 60-74

(20.6%) Age 15-29

(19.7%) Age 45-59

(23.0%) Age 30-44

Life Expectancy: 72 years male; 79 years female (1993)

 Time

Punctuality is all-important in Germany. Arrive on time for every appointment, whether for business or social engagements. Being tardy, even by just two or three minutes, is very insulting to a German executive.

Since planning is so important, appointments are made several weeks in advance. Do not expect to be able to wrangle an appointment on short notice.

Curiously, punctuality in Germany does not include delivery dates. Goods or services may be delivered late by Germans without either explanation or apology.

Germany is one hour ahead of Greenwich Mean Time (G.M.T. + 1), or add six hours to U.S. Eastern Standard Time (E.S.T. + 6).

 Holidays

(Update: Getting Through Customs *http://www.getcustoms.com*)

This list is a working guide. Dates should be corroborated before final travel plans are made. In cases where holidays fall on Saturday or Sunday, commercial establishments may be closed the preceding Friday or following Monday.

New Year's Day	1 January
Epiphany	6 January
[in Baden-Wuerttemberg & Bavaria only]	

Good Friday	varies
Easter Monday	varies
Labor Day (May Day)	1 May
Ascension Day	varies
Whitmonday	varies
Corpus Christi [Baden-Wuerttemberg, Bavaria, North Rhine-Westphalia, Rhineland- Palinate, & Saarland]	6 June
German Unity Day	varies
Reformation Day [Brandenburg, Mecklenburg- Vorpommern, Saxony, Saxony-Anhalt, & Thuringia only]	31 October
All Saints Day [Baden-Wuerttemberg, Bavaria, North Rhine-Westphalia, Rhineland-Palinate, & Saarland]	1 November
Christmas Holiday	25 & 26 Christmas

There are also many regional holidays which are observed in addition to this list.

Work Week

- Business hours are generally 8:00 or 9:00 A.M. to 4:00 or 5:00 P.M. Monday through Friday.

- The preferred times for business appointments are between 11:00 A.M. and 1:00 P.M. or between 3:00 P.M. and 5:00 P.M. Late afternoon appointments are not unusual.

- Do not schedule appointments on Friday afternoons; some offices close by 2:00 or 3:00 P.M. on Fridays. Many people take long vacations during July, August, and December, so check first to see if your counterpart will be available. Also be aware that little work gets done during regional festivals, such as the Oktoberfest or the three-day Carnival before Lent.

- Banking hours: 8:30 A.M. to 1:00 P.M. and 2:00 to 4:00 P.M., Monday through Friday Closing time on Thursday is extended to 5:30 P.M.

- Store hours: 8:00 or 9:00 A.M. to 5:00 or 6:00 P.M., Monday through Friday. On Saturday, most shops close by 2:00 P.M., except for one Saturday per month, when they remain open into the evening.

Note: The government-mandated lack of evening shopping hours poses considerable difficulties for working women, who do the bulk of family shopping in Germany.

Religious/Societal Influences on Business

Germany is split evenly between Roman Catholics (who are concentrated in the South) and Protestants (who are found in the North). With the exception of a few issues, such as abortion, there is little conflict between the churches.

Environmental consciousness approaches the level of religious belief in many Germans. Germany has some of the strictest packaging and recycling laws on Earth. Veneration of nature, especially forests, has deep historical roots.

Social factors are as important as religion towards regulating German behavior. There is a great desire for order and control. Every citizen has a responsibility to maintain order. This covers a huge range of behavior, from public deportment (which is quiet and serious) to automobile maintenance (cars are kept amazingly clean). Life is considered serious, and humor confined to very specific times and places.

5 Cultural Tips

1. In business situations, most Germans shake hands at both the beginning and the end of a meeting. Note that the handshake may be accompanied by a very slight bow, little more than a nod of the head. Although this bow is subtle, it is important. Failure to respond with this nod/bow (especially to a superior) may get you off to a bad start.

2. Germans are sticklers for titles. Try to address people by their full, correct title, no matter how extraordinarily long that title may seem to foreigners. This is especially important when addressing a letter.

    Most Germans expect to be addressed as Mr. or Mrs./Ms. followed by her/his surname

    Mr. = Herr   Mrs./Ms. = Frau

    Note that *Fraulein (Miss)* is no longer used except for women under age 18. A businesswoman should be addressed as *Frau*, no matter what her marital status.

    If someone has one or more titles, retain the Mr. or Mrs./Ms. but substitute the title(s) for the surname. Many professionals use their title, including engineers, pastors, politicians, and lawyers. Anyone with a doctorate is entitled to the title of *Doktor*. A college professor with a Ph.D. is addressed as *Herr Profesor Doktor*.

3. Germans reserve their smiles to indicate affection. In the course of business, they rarely smile, and laughter is certainly not considered appropriate for business. Along with their formal deportment, Germans avoid slouching, gesticulating wildly, and putting their hands in their pockets.

4. Germans love to talk on the telephone. While important business decisions are not made over the phone, expect many follow-up calls or faxes. Cellular phones insure that many Germans are never out of reach. However, Germans jealously guard their private life, so do not phone a German executive at home without permission. Since reunification, great effort has been placed in bringing the poor phone system of the former East Germany up to West German standards.

5. In business encounters, age takes precedence over youth. In a delegation, the eldest person enters first. When two people are introduced, the younger person is introduced to an older person. This assumes that the eldest person has the highest rank. In business settings, a young CEO would take precedence over an older, lower-ranking executive. In social settings, a young person of nobility (Germany has many royal families) takes precedence over commoners.

 Economic Overview

Germany remains the largest economy in Europe and one which U.S. companies must address. Unification of Germany made it all the more important for U.S. products; Germany is the sixth largest export market for U.S. products worldwide. The western German market is a wealthy one, whose population enjoys a very high standard of living. Long-term prospects are bright for the eastern states, but the road to prosperity will be rocky and tardy in reaching some corners of the region. The top priorities of the German government are to maintain economic growth and to continue fostering the development of eastern Germany.

The German economy is the world's third largest, behind only the U.S. and Japan. It accounts for approximately 25% of the European Union's GDP by itself. Germany's broadly diversified economy affords its citizens one of the highest standards of living in the world. To a far greater degree than its European neighbors, Germany's population and industry are decentralized and distributed evenly. Major cities and businesses dot the countryside in a landscape which features no single business center. U.S. suppliers must ensure that their distributors, or own dealerships, have countrywide capability.

Success in the German market requires long-term commitment to market development and sales support.

Comparative Data

Overall Rating: 4.5

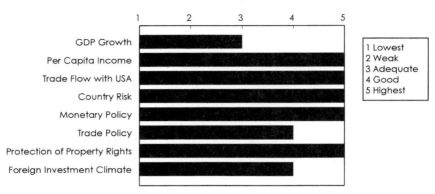

Country Risk Rating

Gross Domestic Product: $2.3 trillion
GDP Growth: 2.0%
Per Capita Income: $29,000

Trade Flows with the U.S.A.

Rank as Export Market for U.S.A. Goods & Services: 6th
U.S.A. Exports to Germany: $22.3 billion
Growth Rate of Exports: 16%
U.S.A. Imports from Germany: $36.8 billion
Growth Rate of Imports: 16%
Rank as a Supplier of Imports into the U.S.A.:   5th

Top U.S.A. Exports to Germany: Machinery, electronic components, medical and optical equipment, motor vehicles, aircraft, plastics, chemical products, pharmaceuticals, precious stones and metals, organic chemicals.

Top U.S.A. Prospects for Export to Germany: Computer software, computer equipment and peripherals, information services, franchising, electronic components, telecommunications equipment, aircraft/parts, laboratory scientific equipment, industrial chemicals, automotive parts.

Credit Terms

Dun & Bradstreet rates Germany as having the highest creditworthiness with an excellent capacity to meet payment liabilities when compared with other countries. Germany carries the lowest degree of risk.

Most business is done on an open-account basis with 30 to 90 day terms the norm. Closer scrutiny of creditworthiness is advised on eastern German companies, and moderately secure terms are recommended. Discounts are often expected for prompt payment.

Monetary Policy

Inflationary pressure remains firmly under control and will continue to be slow in the short term. The inflation rate in 1994 was 2.7% and 2.0% in 1995, forecast at 2.0% for 1996. *Monetary Unit*: Deutsche mark.

Trade Policy

TARIFFS: Most manufactured goods are subject to tariff rates of between 5 and 8%. Most raw materials enter either duty-free or at low rates. Most agricultural imports are covered by the Common Agricultural Policy (CAP) where many items are subject to variable levies designed to equalize the prices of imported commodities with those produced in EU member countries.

IMPORT LICENSING: Germany has one of the world's strongest market economies and one that poses few formal barriers to U.S. firms. Safety standards can at times complicate access to the market for some U.S. products. Firms interested in exporting to Germany should be well prepared to ensure they know precisely which standards apply to their products, and that timely testing and certification is obtained.

IMPORT TAXES: Germany levies a 15% value-added tax on industrial goods.

Protection of Intellectual Property Rights

Intellectual property is generally well protected in Germany. Germany is a member of the World Intellectual Property Organization and a party to the Berne Convention for the Protection of Literary and Artistic Works, the Paris Convention for the Protection of Industrial Property, the Universal Copyright Convention, and the Patent Cooperation Treaty.

German patent law provides for issuance of a basic patent for a period of 20 years following the effective filing date of application. Trademark registrations are valid for 10 years from the application filing date and are renewable for similar periods. Under the German Copyright Law, works of literature, music, and art are protected for the life of the author and 70 years after his/her death; photographs are protected for 25 years after publication, or if never published, 25 years after creation of the work.

Foreign Investment Climate

One hundred percent foreign ownership is permitted in almost all sectors open to private investment. Firms in certain sectors, such as the media, can only be owned up to 49% by any one individual or company, however.

Under German law, foreign-owned companies registered in Germany as a GmbH (limited liability company) or an AG (joint stock company) have domestic status.

The U.S. remains the single largest source of foreign investment in Germany, providing approximately 26% of all foreign direct investment in 1993.

Current Leaders & Political Parties

(Update: International Academy at Santa Barbara *http://www.iasb.org/cwl*)

Sate, Government, and Political Party Leaders:
President.: Roman Herzog
Federal Chancellor: Dr. Helmut Kohl

Cabinet Ministers:
Fed. Chancellor: Dr. Helmut Kohl
Special Tasks and Min. of the Fed. Chancellery: Friedrich Bohl
Foreign Affairs: Dr. Klaus Kinkel
Interior: Manfred Kanther
Justice: Dr. Edzard Schmidt-Jortzig
Finance: Dr. Theo Waigel
Labor and Social Affairs: Norbert Blüm
Defense: Volker Rühe
Family, Elderly, Women, and Youth: Claudia Nolte
Health: Horst Seehofer
Transportation: Matthias Wissmann
Environment, Nature Protection, and Nuclear Safety: Angela Merkel
Posts and Telecommunications: Dr. Wolfgang Bötsch
Regional Planning and Urban Dev.: Klaus Töpfer
Education, Science, Research, and Technology: Jürgen Rüttgers
Economic Coop. and Dev.: Carl-Dieter Spranger

State Ministers:

    Chancellery: Bernd Schmidbauer

    Foreign Affairs: Helmut Schäfer

    Pres. of the Bundestag (parliament): Rita Süssmuth

Other Officials:

    Ambassador to U.S.: Jürgen Chrobog

    Perm. Rep. to U.N.: Detlev Graf von Rantzau

Political Parties:

    Christian Democratic Party (CDU), Christian Social Union (CSU), Social Democratic Party (SPD), Free Democratic Party (FDP), Green Party/Alliance 90, Republicans, Party of Democratic Socialism (PDS)

 Political Influences on Business

The top priorities of the German government are to maintain economic growth and to continue fostering the development of eastern Germany. The new states are now an integral part of Germany, contain millions of voters, and are being brought up to the economic standards of western Germany as quickly as possible. Accordingly, a high priority continues to be placed on financing eastern development, implying the likelihood of a flow of major project opportunities for years to come.

In addition, Germany's political leadership also wants to promote Germany's competitiveness and various proposals are being considered to modernize the country's economic situation. Since unification on October 3, 1990, Germany has placed a high priority on improving its relations with its neighboring countries as well as strengthening trans-Atlantic relations. Recognizing that political stability is nurtured by economic prosperity, Germany has been one of the major sources of assistance to Central European and CIS countries.

The country continues to emphasize close ties with the United States, membership in NATO, progress toward further European integration, and improved relations with Central Europe. German-American political, economic, and security relationships regardless of which administration has been in power in either country have been based on close consultation and coordination at the most senior levels. High-level visits take place frequently, and the United States and the FRG cooperate actively in international forums. U.S. government officials enjoy good access to policy makers and decision makers, and are able to raise issues directly affecting U.S. business active in Germany.

Under the German Constitution, known as the Basic Law, the Federal Republic of Germany (FRG) is a parliamentary democracy with a bicameral legislature, an independent judiciary, and executive power exercised by a Prime Minister, whose title is Chancellor.

The lower house of Parliament, the *Bundestag*, currently consists of 672 deputies elected for a 4-year term. Members are elected through a mixture of direct constituency candidates and party lists. The Basic Law and the *Laender* (state) constitutions stipulate that parties must receive at least 5 percent of the national vote (or at least three directly elected seats in federal elections) in order to be represented in the federal and state parliaments. The last national elections took place on October 16, 1994. One must be 18 years old to vote in Germany.

The president may be elected to two 5-year terms and his duties as chief of state are largely ceremonial. Executive power is exercised by the Chancellor who is elected by and responsible to the Bundestag. The Chancellor cannot be removed from office during a 4-year term unless the Bundestag has agreed on a successor.

The upper house, the *Bundesrat*, is composed of delegations from the 16 state governments and has a proportional distribution of its 68 votes, depending on the population of the state. The role of the Bundesrat is limited but it can exercise substantial veto powers over legislation passed in the Bundestag when the proposed legislation would affect the numerous prerogatives of the Laender. Among these are matters relating to tax reform, law enforcement and the courts, culture and education, the environment, and social assistance.

 Contacts in the U.S.A. & in Germany

Contacts in the United States:

EMBASSY OF THE FEDERAL REPUBLIC OF GERMANY
4645 Reservoir Road, N.W.
Washington, D.C. 20007
Tel: (202) 298-4000
Fax: (202) 298-4249

U.S. DEPARTMENT OF STATE
Country Desk Officer, Germany
Tel: (202) 647-2155

U.S. DEPARTMENT OF COMMERCE
Germany Desk
Int'l Trade Admin.
Tel: (202) 482-2435 or 482-2434

Contacts in Germany:

U.S. EMBASSY
Deichmanns Ave
53179 Bonn 2
Bonn, Germany
Tel: [49] (228) 3392063
Fax: [49] (228) 334649

THE AMERICAN CHAMBER OF COMMERCE IN GERMANY
Rossmarkt 12, Postfach 100 162
D-6000 Frankfurt/Main 1
Frankfurt, Germany
Tel: (69) 28 34 01
Telex: 4189679 ACC D

Dun & Bradstreet Schimmelpfeng GmbH
Postal Address: Postfach 71 08 51, 60498
Frankfurt/M, Germany
Street Address: Hahnstr. 31-35, 60528
Franfurt/M, Germany
Tel: [49] (69) 66303-0
Fax: [49] (69) 66303-175,
    [49] (69) 66303-624 (RMS)

President Dr. Roman Herzog
Office of the Federal President
Schloss Bellevue
Spreeweg 1, 10557 Berlin
Federal Republic of Germany

Chancellor Dr. Helmut Kohl
Office of the Federal Chancellor
Bundeskanzleramt
Adenauerallee 141
53113 Bonn, Federal Republic of
Germany

Cultural Note: Germans keep a slightly larger personal space around them than most North Americans. Stand about 6 inches further back than you would in the U.S.A. The position of office furniture follows this rule. Do not move your chair closer; a German executive could find that very insulting.

This expanded personal space extends to their automobiles. Expect a violent outburst from a German driver if you so much as touch his or her car. Never put a package down on any car except your own.

Passport/Visa Requirements

Visa information   (202) 663-1225

Entry Requirements: Citizens of the United States of America who plan to visit the Federal Republic of Germany as tourists or for business purposes for a period of up to three months do not need a visa. A valid U.S. passport is sufficient. Citizens of other countries (except citizens of member states of the European Union) may require a visa.

All persons who wish to stay in the Federal Republic of Germany for a period of more than three months are required to obtain a residence permit in the form of a visa.

Faux Pas: A Baltimore manufacturer of cabinet hardware was seeking a European distributor, and decided to approach a Frankfurt firm. To make a sales pitch the firm sent a bright young executive who was fluent in German. He was an accomplished speaker, and a past president of the local Toastmasters Club. The executive even had a local connection, as his grandparents had immigrated from the Frankfurt region.

Despite these advantages, his presentation was not well received, and the Frankfurt firm did not become a distributor. The executive later discovered that the Germans had been put off by the start of his speech. Following American speaking customs, he opened with some humorous anecdotes. Germans find nothing funny about business, so his amusing opening caused them to immediately reject him as a serious prospect. Furthermore, he was too young to be sent alone to a country like Germany, where age conveys respect. The Germans assumed that if this was an important offer, an older executive would have been sent.

Hong Kong

Official Name:	Hong Kong (English) Hsiang Kang (Chinese)
Official Languages:	English & Chinese
Government System:	Colonial administration by the United Kingdom; the territory reverts to Chinese sovereignty on July 1, 1997
Population:	6.15 million (1995)
Population Growth:	2.4%
Area:	1,077 sq. km. (416 sq. mi.); slightly less than six times the size of Washington, D.C.
Natural Resources:	deepwater harbor, feldspar

Cultural Note: Hong Kong's population is 97% Chinese, and most of those Chinese speak Cantonese, not the Mandarin Chinese that is the official language of the People's Republic of China. While written Chinese is understood by speakers of all versions of Chinese, spoken Cantonese is very different from Mandarin; the two are not mutually intelligible. With the upcoming incorporation of Hong Kong into the PRC, Mandarin Chinese (known as *Putonghua*) is becoming more important.

Age Breakdown

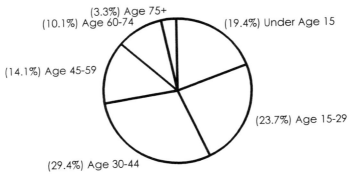

(3.3%) Age 75+
(10.1%) Age 60-74
(19.4%) Under Age 15
(14.1%) Age 45-59
(23.7%) Age 15-29
(29.4%) Age 30-44

Life Expectancy: 75 years male; 81 years female (1994)

 ## Time: Be Punctual!

Everyone in Hong Kong seems to be rushing. This is evident as soon as you land in Hong Kong, as passengers rush to disembark from the airplane. Expect a mob instead of a neat line; people seem to be jostling for position. Given the aggressive nature of business in Hong Kong, it's not surprising that every bottleneck is seen as another test of "the survival of the fittest."

Time is money in Hong Kong, and punctuality is expected from foreigners. While your Hong Kong counterpart will not always be prompt, you will lose face if you make him or her wait for you. Be sure to apologize if you are late, even if it was not your fault.

Hong Kong is eight hours ahead of Greenwich Mean Time (G.M.T. + 8), which is thirteen hours ahead of U.S. Eastern Standard Time (E.S.T. + 13).

 ## Holidays

(Updates: Getting Through Customs *http://www.getcustoms.com*)

The first weekday in January	1 January
Lunar New Year's Day	January - February
The second day of Lunar New Year	January - February
The third day of Lunar New Year	January - February
Ching Ming Festival	early spring
Good Friday	March - April
The day following Good Friday	March - April

Easter Monday	March - April
The Birthday of Her Majesty the Queen	15 June
The Monday following Queen's Birthday	17 June
Tuen Ng Festival	spring
Bank Holiday	The Saturday preceding the last Monday in August
Liberation Day	last Monday in August
Day after the Chinese Mid-Autumn Festival	September - October
Day after Chung Yeung Festival	autumn
Christmas Day	25 December
Boxing Day	26 December (or first weekday after Christmas)

Work Week

Business hours are 9 to 5, Monday through Friday. Saturday has traditionally been a half day but, due to the competition to keep staff, many companies now advertise a 5-day workweek.

Religious/Societal Influences on Business

To identify the influences on Hong Kong's culture, one first has to define it. And in polyglot, multicultural, expatriate-filled Hong Kong, there is little agreement on what that culture is.

Narrowing it down to the two predominant cultures, British and Chinese, we have a Hong Kong that is overwhelmingly Chinese demographically, but has an overlay of British tradition. British ideals of law, freedom, and democracy (although Hong Kong had little public participation in government until recently) have permeated the consciousness of the citizenry. Nevertheless, traditional Chinese Confucian values predominate. To the foreigner, two of the most evident values are the importance of saving face and the desirability of harmony.

Hong Kong's religious denominations include Buddhist, Taoist, Christian, plus small numbers of Moslems, Hindus, Jews, and Sikhs.

Traditional religions do not play a large part in Hong Kong's society. (Some have said that Hong Kong's only religion is money!) However, Chinese folk beliefs are very important. *Feng shui* (a type of geomancy) has a wide following. Many words, items, and numbers are thought to impart good luck or bad luck. Foreigners ignore these at their peril, since it can be virtually impossible to get Chinese to associate themselves with something deemed "unlucky."

For example, the numbers 3, 5, and 8 are considered lucky. In some Chinese dialects, the pronunciation of the number 3 sounds like the word for "life." The number 5 is significant in Chinese tradition; there are five traditional elements, five colors, five sacred mountains, and so on. The number 8 is the luckiest of all, since its pronunciation sounds like the word for "prosperous." Series of numbers with 8 are in great demand, such as street addresses, phone numbers, and license plates. As a matter of fact, Chinese executives will pay thousands of dollars extra for a car with lots of 8s in the serial number or license plate.

On the other hand, the pronunciation of the number 4 suggests the word for "death." No Chinese would live or work at a building with an address of "444."

 5 Cultural Tips

1. As a foreigner with no blood relatives in Hong Kong, you will be introduced by your name, employer, and job description. This will occur not only at business meetings but at social ones as well. In Hong Kong, you are what you do. Make sure that you have a sufficient number of business cards; you will exchange them frequently. Your card is an important method of identifying your status. If you run out of cards, you will lose status every time you fail to offer your card during an exchange.

2. Despite the traditional frugality of the Chinese, Hong Kong has the highest per-capita amount of cellular phones in the world! Hong Kong businesspeople are always on the go, yet they are always reachable; you will see them talking on their cell phones everywhere. Make sure you are accessible while you are in Hong Kong via cell phone, pager, e-mail, and so on.

3. Hong Kong workers are known for being highly productive. However, only a small proportion could be called "self-starters." Most Hong Kong Chinese prefer to be given specific, well-defined duties, which they will perform to the best of their abilities. But they may not do well when asked to do something outside those duties. This reluctance to keep to one's specific job extends from high-ranking executives on down, including the office tea-cart lady, who may get upset if you ask her to make coffee instead of tea.

4. Rank and status are always important in Hong Kong. If you ask someone to do a job they consider demeaning or beneath their station, the job won't get done. (Of course, since harmony demands that no one give an outright refusal, they won't tell you they won't do it.) Always try to find the correct person for the job.

5. The flip side of "sticking to one's own job" is that relatively few Hong Kong Chinese will work on their business skill outside the office. When they need to gain new skills, they expect to be trained on the job. It is not part of Chinese tradition for adults to take work home and study (if for no other reason than the crowded, noisy living quarters of most Chinese are not conducive to quiet studying). But assigned to a training course during office hours at company expense, the average worker will once again tackle it to the best of his or her ability.

Economic Overview

No international executive can afford to ignore Hong Kong. It is probably the world's best example of free enterprise with its free-market philosophy, entrepreneurial drive, absence of trade barriers, low and predictable taxes, transparent regulations, and complete freedom of capital movement. Hong Kong is simply one of the most desirable places to do business in the world.

Hong Kong's economy is services-dominated, accounting for some 80% of GDP and employing more than 70% of the work force. Major sectors include travel/tourism, transportation, trading, and financial services. Manufacturing continues to decline, now accounting for just 11% of GDP and 20% of the work force. The textile and clothing/apparel industries remain the backbone of Hong Kong's manufacturing sector.

With a per capita GDP of $21,750, Hong Kong's sophisticated, bilingual consumers offer outstanding opportunities for sales of a full range of U.S. products and services.

Housing, food, telecommunications, transportation and health care are all available at levels comparable to major cities in the U.S.A. While Hong Kong is one of the most expensive cities in the world, especially for housing, it is also very efficient, making it possible to accomplish a great deal in a short time.

Effective July 1, 1997, Hong Kong will revert to Chinese sovereignty after more than 150 years under British rule. The Chinese government has pledged that the social and economic systems, lifestyle, rights, and freedoms that Hong Kong people now enjoy will remain unchanged for 50 years. Geographic proximity and cultural and linguistic ties, particularly to the adjacent Guangdong province, have greatly accelerated Hong Kong's economic integration with China. Trade and investment with the People's Republic of China have surged as China's economy continues its fast-track growth. China is Hong Kong's largest trading partner and an estimated 66% of cumulative foreign investment in China is from Hong Kong.

U.S. companies with offices in Hong Kong's territories:	approximately 1,000
U.S. citizens residing in the territories:	approximately 34,000

Cultural Note: As one might expect from one of the most crowded places on Earth, Hong Kong is noisy. On the streets, the rumble of incessant traffic is underscored by car horns and radios. Inside, a lack of soundproofing makes the atmosphere even noisier. Chinese restaurants usually consist of one large, open space, rather than the sound-deadening, partitioned maze of upscale restaurants in the U.S.A. And the Cantonese language (with its multiple tonalities and harsh glottal stops) is often hard on Western ears, particularly at the escalated volume commonly spoken!

Comparative Data

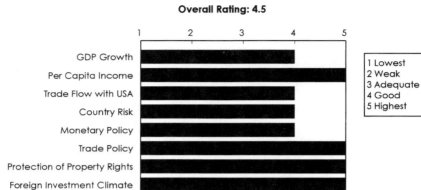

Overall Rating: 4.5

Country Risk Rating

Domestic Product: $131.9 billion

GDP Growth: 5.5%

Per Capita Income: $21,750

Trade Flows with the U.S.A.

Rank as Export Market for U.S.A. Goods & Services: 11th

U.S.A. Exports to Hong Kong: $14.2 billion

Growth Rate of Exports: 23%

U.S.A. Imports from Hong Kong: $10.3 billion

Growth Rate of Imports: 6%

Rank as a Supplier of Imports into the U.S.A.: 14th

Top U.S.A. Exports to Hong Kong: Electronic components, machinery, precious stones and metal, plastics, motor vehicles, medical and optical equipment, aircraft, meat, paper and paperboard.

Top U.S.A. Prospects for Export to Hong Kong: Construction equipment, telecommunications equipment, electric power systems, electronic parts/components, insurance, drugs and pharmaceuticals, travel and tourism services, scientific and analytical equipment, waste-water treatment technologies, plastic materials and resins.

Credit Terms

Dun & Bradstreet rates Hong Kong as having good capacity to meet outstanding payment liabilities. The majority of transactions are performed on open account or sight draft terms. Credit terms of 30 to 90 days are common, although up to 180 days may be requested in some sectors. Credit checks on individual firms are advised.

Monetary Policy

Hong Kong's annual inflation rate has been stable for the last several years, averaging about 8.5% since 1992. Inflation is expected to continue to average from 7% to 9%.
Monetary Unit: Hong Kong Dollar

Trade Policy

TARIFFS: The Hong Kong government levies no import tariffs.

IMPORT LICENSING: Textiles are subject to import licensing. Importers of "reserved commodities" which include rice and frozen meat, must obtain an importer's license before they can import these commodities.

The import of munitions, firearms, and fireworks is strictly forbidden.

IMPORT TAXES: Domestic consumption taxes are imposed on certain goods including tobacco (including cigarettes), alcoholic beverages, methyl alcohol, and some fuels. These taxes are levied on both local manufactures and imports.

Protection of Intellectual Property Rights

Hong Kong has developed comprehensive laws covering trademarks, trade descriptions, copyrights, industrial designs, and patents. Patent and copyright laws are currently dependent on the United Kingdom. The Customs and Excise Department is responsible for the enforcement of protection for intellectual property rights. The department has a special unit with more than 100 investigators. Enactment of substantially stiffer penalties in 1995 should help deter retailers from carrying pirated products.

Hong Kong has acceded to the Paris Convention for the Protection of Industrial Property, the Berne Convention for the Protection of Literary and Artistic Works, and the Geneva and Paris Universal Copyright Conventions.

Patent protection extends as long as the original patent in the U.K. Copyrights are protected under the U.K. Copyright Act and the Hong Kong Copyright Ordinance. Foreign works are protected provided ownership is vested in a country which is a signatory to one of the international conventions. There is no need to register a copyright; protection under the Copyright Ordinance is automatic.

All trademark registrations originally filed in Hong Kong are valid for seven years and renewable for 14-year periods.

Foreign Investment Climate

Hong Kong pursues a free market philosophy with minimum interference with corporate initiative. The territory welcomes foreign investment. There is no distinction in law or practice between investments by foreign-controlled companies and those controlled by local interests. There is no capital gains tax nor are there withholding taxes on dividends and royalties. There are no disincentives to foreign investment such as limitations on the use or transfer of foreign currency, or any system of quotas, performance requirements, bonds, deposits, or other similar regulations.

With few exceptions, the Hong Kong government does not attempt to limit the activities of foreign investors either in specified projects or sectors. U.S. direct investment in Hong Kong totaled $12 billion at year-end 1994, making the U.S. one of Hong Kong's largest investors. More than 80 of the world's top 100 banks have operations in Hong Kong and more than 40 U.S. banks have offices in the territory.

Current Leaders & Political Parties

(Update: International Academy at Santa Barbara *http://www.iasb.org/cwl*)

State, Government, and Political Party Leaders:

Head of State: Queen Elizabeth II

Gov.: Christopher Francis Patten

Other Officials:

Chief Secretary: Ms. Anson Chan Fang On Sang

Chief Justice: Sir Ti Liang Yang

Political Parties:

Liberal Party, Liberal Democratic Federation, Democratic Party, Democratic Alliance for Betterment of Hong Kong, Hong Kong Democratic Foundation, Assoc. for Democracy and People's Livelihood, Hong Kong Progressive Alliance

Political Influences on Business

As a British dependency, Hong Kong is a free society with legally protected rights. Its constitutional arrangements are defined by the letters patent and royal instructions. Executive powers are vested in a governor (appointed by the British crown); the governor holds extensive authority. The judiciary is an independent body adhering to English common law with certain variations. Fundamental rights ultimately rest on oversight by the British Parliament. In practice, however, Hong Kong largely controls its own internal affairs. The governor appoints an advisory executive council, and a partially representative Legislative Council has limited powers. The main functions of the 60-member Legislative Council (Legco) are to enact laws, control public expenditure, and monitor performance of the government by putting forward questions on matters of public interest.

Three major political parties are represented in Legco: the Democratic Alliance for the Betterment of Hong Kong, the Democratic Party, and the Liberal Party. The first has a pro-Beijing orientation, the second strongly advocates broader democracy in the territory, and the third is probusiness.

When Hong Kong becomes a Special Administrative Region (abbreviated as HKSAR) under China in July 1997, the Basic Law will guarantee the rights and freedoms that Hong Kong residents now enjoy. These include the continued rule of law and the maintenance of Hong Kong's capitalist system for 50 years. The HKSAR will maintain its capitalist economic and trade systems, shall retain the status of a free port and continue a free trade policy with free movement of goods and capital. It will retain its status as an international financial center. It will, on its own, formulate monetary and financial policies and safeguard the free operation of business and financial markets.

The Basic Law states that the HKSAR will maintain its own currency and use revenues exclusively for its own purposes. The Hong Kong Dollar will continue to be freely convertible and foreign exchange, gold, and securities markets will continue to operate. Systems currently in place, including Hong Kong's regulatory and supervisory framework, will remain unchanged. Hong Kong's legal system, including the independence of the judiciary and obligation of the executive authorities to abide by the law, are slated to continue. Beijing will be responsible for foreign affairs and defense of the HKSAR.

 Contacts in the U.S.A. & in Hong Kong

Contacts in the United States:

DEPARTMENT OF COMMERCE
International Trade Administration
Country Desk Officer
Office of China, Hong Kong and Mongolia
Herbert C. Hoover Bldg.
14th and Constitution Ave, N.W.
Washington, D.C. 20230
Tel: 1 (202) 482-3932
Fax: 1 (202) 482-1576

U.S. DEPARTMENT OF EAST ASIA AND PACIFIC
Office of International Operations
Herbert C. Hoover Bldg.
14th and Constitution Ave, N.W.
Washington, D.C. 20230 U.S.A.
Tel: 1 (202) 482-2422
Fax: 1 (202) 482-5179

DEPARTMENT OF STATE
Country Desk Officer
Office of Chinese and Mongolian Affairs
Room 4318
Washington, D.C. 20520 U.S.A.
Tel: 1 (202) 647-6802
Fax: 1 (202) 647-6820

GOVERNMENT OF HONG KONG ECONOMIC
OFFICE
1150 18th St., N.W.,
Suite 475
Washington, D.C. 20036
Tel: 202-331-8947

Contacts in Hong Kong:

GOVERNMENT OF HONG KONG
Central Government Offices
Lower Albert Rd.
Hong Kong, Asia

U.S. CONSULATE GENERAL TRADE
Foreign Commercial Service
Hong Kong
26 Garden Road
Hong Kong
Tel: (852) 2521-1467
Fax: (852) 2845-9800

U.S. CONSULATE GENERAL
ECONOMIC/POLITICAL SECTION
Tel: (852) 2841-2101
Fax: (852) 2526-7382

AMERICAN CHAMBER OF COMMERCE
HONG KONG
1030 Swire House
Central Hong Kong
Tel: (852) 2526-0165
Fax: (852) 2810-1289

DUN & BRADSTREET (HK) LTD.
Postal and street Address: 12/F, K. Wah
Centre,
191 Java Road, North Point, Hong Kong
Tel: (852) 2516-1111
Fax: (852) 2562-6149

Contacts in the United Kingdom:

QUEEN ELIZABETH II
Buckingham Palace
London, SW1A 1AA
United Kingdom of Great Britain and Northern Ireland

Passport/Visa Requirements

Visa Information   (202) 663-1225

Entry Requirements: Passports are required by all persons visiting Hong Kong. Visas are not necessary for United States citizens for visits of not more than one month, provided they hold return or onward tickets and have with them sufficient funds for their stay. For visits of longer than one month, but less than three months, a visa is required and can be given on application to a British visa office.

For more current information the traveler can consult the British Embassy.

Faux Pas: One of the most difficult tasks a new Westerner in Hong Kong must face is adapting his or her name into Chinese. Usually, this begins with a phonetic translation: each English phoneme (sound) is given the closest equivalent Chinese phoneme. In this way, when a Chinese says your name, it will sound something like your name in English. Then a written form which corresponds to those phonemes is chosen. Here things can get very complex, because many Chinese ideographs have multiple meanings. Furthermore, each ideograph may be pronounced differently in each Chinese variant. In other words, an ideograph spoken in Mandarin may sound very different when spoken in Cantonese.

The previous Governor of Hong Kong, Lord Wilson, had a Chinese name long before he was appointed in 1987. But while his name was acceptable in Mandarin, it had unfortunate connotations in Cantonese. When the characters in his Chinese surname were broken down, they included the character in Cantonese for the word *ghost*. Wisely, the Governor chose alternate ideograph characters for his name.

India

Official Name:	Republic of India (English)
	Bharat (Hindi)
Official Languages:	English and Hindi
Government System:	Multiparty federal republic
Population:	936 million
Population Growth:	1.8%
Area:	3,287,263 sq. km. (1,268,884 sq. mi.); about twice the size of Alaska
Natural Resources:	coal, iron ore, manganese, mica, bauxite, titanium ore, chromite, natural gas, diamonds, crude oil, limestone
Major Cities:	New Delhi (capital), Calcutta, Bombay, Madras, Bangalore, Hyderabad, Ahmedabad

Cultural Note: In the U.S.A., people think in terms of dominating or controlling the environment. For example, the West was "won," rivers are "tamed," and land is "developed." India has the opposite viewpoint of nature. Perhaps because Indians are faced with the overwhelming power of yearly monsoons, they traditionally consider themselves to be at the mercy of their environment. In India, it is the *people* who are tamed by the land.

Age Breakdown

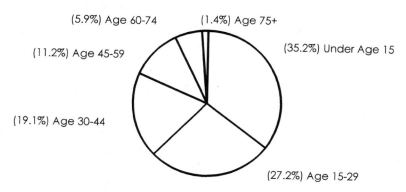

(5.9%) Age 60-74   (1.4%) Age 75+

(11.2%) Age 45-59   (35.2%) Under Age 15

(19.1%) Age 30-44

(27.2%) Age 15-29

Life Expectancy: 57 years male; 59 years female (1990)

Time

As a foreign businessperson, you are expected to be relatively prompt. However, punctuality has never been considered a virtue in India. Your Indian counterpart may be late, or even not show up at all.

India is five and one-half hours ahead of Greenwich Mean Time (G.M.T. + 5-1/2), which is ten and one-half hours ahead of Eastern Standard Time (E.S.T. + 10-1/2).

Holidays

(Update: Getting Through Customs *http://www.getcustoms.com*)

- The best time of year to visit India is between October and March (bypassing the seasons of extreme heat and monsoons).
- Business is not conducted during religious holidays, which are numerous throughout the many regions and states of India. As dates for these holidays change from year to year, check with the Indian Tourist Office, Consulate, or Embassy before scheduling your visit.

This list is a working guide. In cases where holidays fall on Saturday or Sunday, commercial establishments may be closed the preceding Friday or following Monday.

The dates of Islamic holidays are approximations, since they depend upon actual lunar observations. Islamic holidays translated into English also vary in spelling. Many Islamic-owned businesses are closed on Fridays.

Republic Day	26 January
Mahashivratri	usually February - March
Idu'l Fitr	varies
Good Friday	usually March - April
Ramnavami	usually March - April
Buddha Purnima	usually May - June
Muharram	varies
Bakrid (Idu'l Zuha)	varies
Independence Day	15 August
Janmashtami	usually August - September
Dussehra	usually October - November
Diwali	usually Ocober - November
Guru Nanak's Birthday	25 November
Christmas	25 December

Again, many religous holidays are observed in different states in India, and cannot be pinpointed exactly because of some of their reliance on the Lunar Calendar.

Work Week

- Indian executives prefer late morning or early afternoon appointments, between 11:00 A.M. and 4:00 P.M.
- Business hours: 9:30 A.M. to 5:00 P.M., Monday through Friday (lunch is usually from 1:00 to 2:00 P.M.)
- Bank hours: 10:00 A.M. to 2:00 P.M., Monday through Friday, and 10:00 A.M.to 12:00 noon on Saturdays
- Government office hours: 10:00 A.M. to 5:00 P.M., Monday through Saturday (closed for lunch from 1:00 to 2:00 P.M.). Note that government offices are closed the second Saturday of each month.

Religious/Societal Influences on Business

India has such a plethora of cultures, religions, and castes that it would take several volumes to explain them all.

The majority of Indians are Hindu. Unlike many religions which are traced to a particular founder, Hinduism grew out of Indian mythology. Hinduism has many variants and lacks a single, authoritative text (like the Bible or the Koran). It is a religion with multiple gods, and it teaches a belief in karma and reincarnation. To escape the cycles of reincarnation and achieve nirvana, one must stop committing both bad deeds and good deeds, a difficult process which requires virtual nonintervention with humanity. India's caste system is supported by most variants of Hinduism. Cows are venerated by many Hindus, who neither eat beef nor wear leather. Many Hindus are vegetarian.

A minority of Indians are Muslim. Islam is a monotheistic religion with ties to both Judaism and Christianity. Shiite Muslims outnumber Sunni Muslims by about three-to-one in India. Surrender to the will of Allah is a central belief. Pork and alcohol are prohibited to observant Muslims.

Since India's two major religions abjure beef and pork, it is not surprising that Indian cuisine uses mostly chicken, lamb, or vegetables. These religions also share an acceptance of fate, and have a fatalistic view of man's ability to change that fate.

About 2% of Indians are Sikhs. Sikhism combines tenets of both Hinduism and Islam. Sikhs believe in reincarnation but do not recognize caste distinctions. Unlike Hindus, Sikhs reject nonintervention with the world as cowardly.

India also has Christians, Buddhists, Jains, and Zoroastrians.

 5 Cultural Tips

1. Business relationships in India are based on personal relationships. You must establish a relationship of mutual respect with Indian decision makers. To do this, you may need to make your initial contacts with middle managers. While they do not make the final decision, they can bring your proposal to the attention of their bosses. They will be much more accessible than the executives at the top.

2. With fourteen major languages and some three hundred minor ones, English has become a unifying force in India. Generally, you will be able to conduct business in English, and it is not necessary to have your written materials translated.

3. Traditionally, Indians used a greeting called a *namaste* rather than shaking hands. The namaste is done by holding the palms together at chin level, as if praying. This is accompanied by a nod or short bow and the word namaste (*nah-mahs-tay*). Like the *aloha* in Hawaiian, namaste means either hello or goodbye.

4. Body language in India is very different from North America. Head gestures for yes and no are virtually reversed. Indians show agreement by tossing their head from side to side, which Westerners can misinterpret as no. To show disagreement, Indians nod up-and-down, or rather toss their heads up and back. This is similar to the gesture Americans use to indicate yes.

5. Gift-giving is an important part of doing business in India. Remember that gifts are not opened in the presence of the giver. Wrap the gifts carefully, but avoid using

black or white paper, which many people consider unlucky. If you have occasion to give money to an Indian, give an odd number, such as $11 rather than $10.

 ## Economic Overview

The United States is India's leading foreign investor and largest trading partner. Bilateral trade between the two countries exceeded $9.0 billion in 1995. The U.S. has identified India as one of the 10 "Big Emerging Markets" where future growth rates are poised to exceed those in the developed markets. India's economy is a mixture of traditional village farming, modern agriculture, handicrafts, a wide range of industries, and a multitude of support services. Faster economic growth in the 1980s permitted a significant increase in real per capita private consumption.

Financial strains in 1990 and 1991 prompted government austerity measures that slowed industrial growth but permitted India to meet its international payment obligations without rescheduling its debt. Production, trade, and investment reforms since 1991 have provided new opportunities for Indian businesses and an estimated 100 million to 200 million middle class consumers.

India has a dynamic private sector, a need for capital and technology that cannot be met domestically, a growing middle class hungry for opportunity, and a consensus favoring opening India to foreign trade and investment. Positive factors for the remainder of the 1990s are India's strong entrepreneurial class and the central government's recognition of the continuing need for market-oriented approaches to economic development. The progress of India's economic reforms offer investment and trade opportunities to U.S. firms willing and able to accept some measure of uncertainty as the process matures. Negative factors include the desperate poverty of hundreds of millions of Indians and the impact of the huge and expanding population on an already overloaded environment.

Cultural Note: In a culture with a history of scarcity, complex traditions often develop. In India you will be offered refreshment (usually tea) at virtually every business meeting. Tradition requires you to turn down at least the first offer, and, if you wish, the second. However, you must accept the third offer, or risk insulting your host. The object of these refusals is not to be coy, but to avoid appearing greedy.

Comparative Data

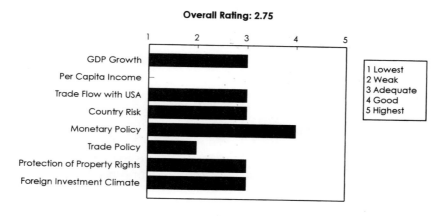

Overall Rating: 2.75

| | 1 | 2 | 3 | 4 | 5 |

GDP Growth
Per Capita Income
Trade Flow with USA
Country Risk
Monetary Policy
Trade Policy
Protection of Property Rights
Foreign Investment Climate

1 Lowest
2 Weak
3 Adequate
4 Good
5 Highest

Country Risk Rating

Gross Domestic Product: $300 billion
GDP Growth: 5%
Per Capita Income: $320

Trade Flows with the U.S.A.

Rank as Export Market for U.S.A. Goods & Services: 30th
U.S.A Exports to India: $3.3 billion
Growth Rate of Exports: 43%
U.S.A. Imports from India: $5.7 billion
Growth Rate of Imports: 7.5%
Rank as a Supplier of Imports into the U.S.A.:   24th

Top U.S.A. Exports to India: Machinery, aircraft, electrical products, organic chemicals, medical and optical equipment, fertilizers, iron and steel, precious stones and metals, plastic, copper.

Top U.S.A. Prospects for Export to India: Aircraft and parts, oil and gas field machinery, electronic and scientific equipment, telecommunications equipment and services, medical equipment, chemical production machinery, machine tools and metal working equipment, computer software and services, mining equipment, computers.

Country Risk

Dun & Bradstreet rates India as having sufficient capacity to meet outstanding payment liabilities.

Fully secured terms such as confirmed letter of credit are advised for initial transactions. Use of letters of credit is declining, representing less than 50% off all transactions.

Monetary Policy

Inflation was in double digits for most of the 1994/95 fiscal year. Tightening of the monetary policy in April 1995 helped in bringing inflation down under 9% in mid-1995. The government's goal was to bring inflation down to about 8% by year-end 1995 and to 5% or less in following years. *Monetary Unit*: Indian rupee.

Trade Policy

TARIFFS: The Indian government continues to reduce tariff rates. A 50% tariff ceiling was set in the 1995/96 budget, down from 300% in 1991. The import-weighted tariff is 33%.

Despite reforms, Indian tariffs are still some of the highest in the world, especially for goods that can be produced domestically.

IMPORT LICENSING: The import licensing regime has been liberalized but still limits many U.S. goods.

Importation of consumer goods is virtually banned except for some imports under the special import license (SIL) arrangement. Consumer goods are defined as goods which can directly satisfy human need without further processing. Thus, products of agricultural or animal origin must be licensed and are, in most cases, banned effectively. India has liberalized many restrictions on the importation of capital goods.

IMPORT TAXES: India maintains a variety of additional duties and countervailing duties which raise the effective tariff rates well above the tariff ceiling for some products.

Protection of Intellectual Property Rights

Inadequate protection of intellectual property rights, particularly for pharmaceuticals, trademarks, and copyrighted material, has been a source of controversy between India and the United Sates for a number of years. As of June 1995, India remains a priority foreign country under the "Special 301" section of U.S. trade law as a result of its failure to provide adequate patent protection to U.S. commerce. Present Indian law prohibits product patents for any invention intended for use or usable as a food, medicine, or drug.

The Indian Patents Act of 1970 also forbids product patents for substances prepared through or produced by chemical processes. India does grant patents to products which are not chemicals or drugs. The life of a product patent on such inventions is 14 years from the date of filing. India's commitment to the Uruguay Round Agreement will require full patent protection no later than 2005.

The Indian parliament passed new copyright legislation in May 1994 and implemented it in May 1995. This legislation improves protection for copyrighted works, especially software. India is a member of the Universal Copyright Convention and the Berne Convention. Trademark protection in India is considered good. U.S. firms may register a trademark in accordance with the Trade and Merchandise Marks Act of 1958. Amendments to the existing law have been introduced and were expected to be enacted by the end of 1995.

Foreign Investment Climate

Four years after launching a concerted drive to modernize its economy, India is beginning to attract the attention of the international investment community. With its 200-million-strong middle class, vast pool of skilled labor and relatively well-developed financial system, India offers both a rich market and tremendous potential productive capacity.

The rush of foreign direct investment to India has been doubling annually in the last four years. The U.S. is the leading foreign investor, accounting for 24% of the total investment approved in 1994 and about 16% in 1995. During 1994, U.S. firms obtained $1.1 billion of new investment approvals. Total foreign investment inflows in 1994/95 reached an estimated $4.8 billion, up from $4.2 billion the previous year. Since July 1991, Indian government approvals for equity investments of up to 51% in most manufacturing industries have been automatic. Foreign equity investments in excess of 51%, or those which fall outside the specified "high priority" areas, must be approved by the Foreign Investment Promotion Board and approved by a Cabinet Committee. The only sectors of the Indian economy excluded specifically from foreign investment are the defense sector, railways, and atomic energy.

For investors, the crux of the 1991 economic reforms consisted of the deregulation of most domestic industries, removing licensing requirements, and permitting foreign and domestic firms far more independence in investment and marketing decisions. Regulatory reform has been accompanied by a far more positive attitude toward private enterprise and foreign investment on the part of regulators.

 ## Current Leaders & Political Parties

(Update: International Academy at Santa Barbara *http://www.iasb.org/cwl*)

Pres.: Dr. Shankar Dayal Sharma
Vice Pres.: K. R. Narayanan

Cabinet Ministers:

    Prime Min. and Min. of Home and Agriculture: H. D. Deve Gowda

    Defense: Mulayam Singh Yadav

    Finance, Law, and Justice: P. Chidambaram

    Food and Commerce: Devendra Prasad Yadav

    Human Resource Dev.: S. R. Bommai

    Urban Dev.: M. Arunachalam

    Railways: Ram Vilas Paswan

    External Affairs and Water Resources: I. K. Gujral

    Civil Aviation, Tourism Information, and Broadcasting: C. M. Ibrahim

    Industry: R. Murasoli Maran

Other Officials:

    Speaker of the Lok Sabha (Lower House of Parliament): Shiv Raj Patil

    Chief Justice of the Supreme Court: Manepalli Narayanarao Venkatachaliah

    Ambassador to U.S.: Naresh Chandfra

    Perm. Rep. to U.N.: C. R. Gharekhan

Political Parties:

    Congress (I) Party, Congress (S) Party, Lok Dal, Janata Dal, Bhartiya Janata Party, Communist Party, Communist Party (Marxist)

Political Influences on Business

Former Prime Minister Rao's tenure was marked by his sweeping economic reform program, launched in 1991, which helped move India from a planned to a market economy. Individual states are increasingly seeking foreign investments on their own. Somewhat mitigating this otherwise "business friendly" environment are India's stultifying (and still largely unreformed) bureaucracies; New Delhi's ongoing dispute with Pakistan (which has resulted in three wars); and caste and communal tensions that have worsened (sometimes exploding into violence) in recent years. Nevertheless, on balance, India is becoming an increasingly attractive business environment and most industrialized nations are rapidly expanding their commercial presence in the country.

India is a multiethnic, multireligious, federal republic composed of 25 states and 7 union territories. The country has a bicameral parliament, including the Upper House, the *Rajya Sabha* (government assembly), and the Lower House, the *Lok Sabha* (people's assembly). The judiciary is relatively independent and the legal system is based on English common law. National and state elections are ordinarily held every five years, although they maybe postponed in an emergency and may be held more frequently if the government loses a confidence vote.

Despite tremendous obstacles and the ever-present potential for disorder, the 1996 elections displayed a degree of orderliness and honesty which would do any nation proud. Election sites were set up even in remote mountain regions and accommodations were made for India's large numbers of illiterate voters. Once again, the world's most populous democracy showed the world that it can manage its own affairs quite adeptly.

Contacts in the U.S.A. & in India

Contacts in the United States:

EMBASSY OF THE REPUBLIC OF INDIA
2107 Massachusetts Ave., N.W.
Washington, D.C. 20008
Tel: (202) 939-7000
Fax: (202) 483-3972

U.S. DEPARTMENT OF STATE
Overseas Travel Advisories
Tel: (202) 647-5225
Country Desk Officer, India
Tel: (202) 647-2141

U.S. DEPARTMENT OF COMMERCE
India Desk
Int'l Trade Admin.
Tel: (202) 482-2954

Contacts in India:

U.S. EMBASSY
Shanti Path
Chanakyapuri 110021
New Delhi
Tel: [91] (11) 600651
Telex: 031-82065 USEM IN
Fax: [91] (11) 687-2028

DUN & BRADSTREET INFORMATION SERVICES
Postal and Street Address: 106 Free
Press House, Nariman Point, Bombay
400 021, India
Tel: [91] (22) 284-1898, 282-1866
Fax: [91] (22) 284-6380

PRESIDENT DR. SHANKAR DAYAL SHARMA
Office of the President
Rashtrapati Bhavan
New Delhi 110004, Republic of India

PRIME MINISTER H. D. DEVE GOWDA
Office of the Prime Minister
South Block
New Delhi 110011, Republic of India

Passport/Visa Requirements

Visa Information   Tel: (202) 663-1225

Entry Requirements: A passport and visa (obtained in advance) are required. Tourist, Entry, Business, Student, Research, Transit, and Missionary visas are issued.

Passports should be valid for a period of at least six months from the date of application.

Persons entering India from, or through, a yellow fever infected area are required to be in possession of a valid certificate of vaccination against yellow fever. No other health certificates are obligatory (at present) but immunization against smallpox and cholera is recommended.

Faux Pas: At an appointment with a high-ranking Indian bureaucrat, a U.S. salesman of data-processing equipment was invited to give his pitch in the presence of a third person. The bureaucrat did not introduce this third man, nor did the third man speak. The presence of this man totally unnerved the salesman. He imagined worst-case scenarios, such as the third man being employed by his competitors. He became so distracted that he gave a poor presentation, and failed to make a sale.

In India (as in the Middle East), there is no guarantee that a business appointment will be private. Your Indian client may be joined by an advisor, a relative, or just an interested party. The silent person may be the real decision maker, observing you while you pitch to an underling. Do not become distracted by their presence.

Names and Titles in India

Each ethnic group in India has different nomenclature patterns. All Indians, however, value professional titles. For someone who does not have a title, use *Mr., Mrs.,* or *Miss.*

Historically, Hindus did not have family surnames. A Hindu man used the initial of his father's name first, followed by his own personal name. For example, for a man named *Thiruselvan* whose father was named *Vijay*, the everyday usage would be *V. Thiruselvan*. People would address him as *Mr. Thiruselvan*. On important documents, both names would be written out in full, separated by *s/o* (for *son of*). This same man would sign his name as *Thiruselvan s/o Vijay*. Note that long Indian names are often shortened. A man named *Thiruselvan* could shorten it to either *Mr. Thiru* or *Mr. Selvan*.

Hindu women's names follow the same pattern, except that instead of *s/o* she would use *d/o* (for *daughter of*). When an Indian woman marries, she usually drops her father's initial; instead she follows her personal name with her husband's name. For instance: if *S. Kamala* (female) marries *V. Thiru* (male), she will go by *Mrs. Kamala Thiru*.

Some Indians use Western-style surnames. Christian Indians often have Biblical surnames (*Abraham, Jacob,* and so on). Indians from the former Portuguese colony of Goa may have surnames of Portuguese origin, like *Rozario* or *DeSilva*. Such a person could be addressed as *Dr. Jacob* or *Mr. DeSilva*.

Sikh men use a given name followed by *Singh*. Sikh women follow their given name with *Kaur*. Address a Sikh by title and first name, not *Singh* or *Kaur*. To call to a Sikh male *Mr. Singh* is as meaningless as saying *Mr. Man* in English.

Indonesia

Official Name:	Republic of Indonesia
Official Language:	Bahasa Indonesia (modified form of Malay)
Government System:	Unitary multiparty republic
Population:	193 Million
Population Growth:	1.6%
Area:	2,027,665 sq. km. (782,000 sq. mi.); slightly smaller than Alaska and California combined
Natural Resources:	crude oil, tin, natural gas, nickel, timber, bauxite, copper, fertile soils, coal, gold, silver
Major Cities:	Jakarta (capital), Bandung, Semarang, Surabaya, Medan, Palembang, Ujung Pandang

Cultural Note: Status is very important in Indonesia, and every individual has a ranking on the "totem pole" of importance. In the native language (called Bahasa Indonesia) it is difficult to even converse with a person until you know if she or he is your superior, inferior, or equal. Even when the conversation is in English, Indonesians will not feel comfortable until they know your ranking. This is one reason why Indonesians will ask you very personal questions about your job, your education, and your salary.

Age Breakdown

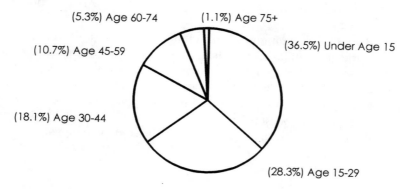

(5.3%) Age 60-74

(1.1%) Age 75+

(10.7%) Age 45-59

(36.5%) Under Age 15

(18.1%) Age 30-44

(28.3%) Age 15-29

Life Expectancy: 60 years male; 64 years female (1992)

 Time

Indonesia spans three time zones. Java and Bali are in West Indonesia Standard Time, which is seven hours ahead of Greenwich Mean Time (G.M.T. + 7). Central Indonesia Standard Time is eight hours ahead of Greenwich Mean Time (G.M.T. + 8); Lombok and Nusatenggara are on Central Time. The East Indonesia Standard Time zone, which includes Maluku and Irian Jaya, is nine hours ahead of Greenwich Mean Time (G.M.T. + 9).

 Holidays

(Update: Getting Through Customs *http://www.getcustoms.com*)

- The holidays in Indonesia represent an attempt to accommodate the celebrations of Islam, Hinduism, and Christianity.

New Year	1–2 January
Idul Fitri	varies
Good Friday	usually March - April
Ascension of Christ	usually April - May
Idul Adha [Haj New Year]	varies
First of Muharram [Moslem New Year]	varies
Independence Day	17 August
Maulid An-Nabi [Mohammed's birthday]	varies
Christmas Day	25 December

- Observant Muslims fast from dawn to sundown during the month of Ramadan. Expect this to have a negative effect on business dealings. Also, do not eat or drink in front of fasting persons.
- Three calendars are in common use in Indonesia. The Western (or Gregorian) calendar is the official calendar in use. Islamic holidays are dated via the Arabic calendar, which loses about 11 days each year against the Western calendar. Finally, there is a Hindu-influenced Javanese calendar.
- Certain days are considered lucky when different calendars coincide. For example, when the 5th day of the Western week falls on the 5th day of the Javanese week (which is only 5 days long), the occasion is considered auspicious.

 ## Work Week

- Although the majority of Indonesians are Muslim, Indonesia does not follow the traditional Islamic work-week pattern (Friday is the Islamic Holy Day, so the traditional Muslim "weekend" is Thursday and Friday). Instead, the work week runs for four full days, Monday through Thursday, then two half days on Friday and Saturday.
- Business hours are generally from 8:00 A.M. to 4:00 P.M., Monday through Thursday, with additional hours on Friday and Saturday mornings. Some businesses have a full workday on Friday, although Muslim employees will take at least one hour off on Friday to pray. Saturday hours generally end by 1:00 P.M.
- The traditional lunchtime is from 12 noon (or 12:30 P.M.) to 1:30 P.M.; it is often the largest meal of the day.
- Most government offices keep an 8:00 A.M. to 4:00 P.M. schedule, with a half day on Friday and Saturday.
- Many Indonesian banks open from 8:00 A.M. to 4:00 P.M. from Monday to Thursday, with half days on Friday and Saturday. Other hours are possible; banks on Bali are often open only from 8:00 A.M. to 12 noon daily.
- Shop hours vary. Most shops will be open five or six days a week, beginning at 9 or 10 A.M., and closing at 6 or 7 P.M.

Cultural Note: The Indonesian term *jam karet* ("rubber time") refers to the indigenous casual attitude towards time. Only a great emergency such as a death or disaster will impel many Indonesians to haste or punctuality.

Religious Influences on Business

In common with other multiethnic societies spread out over an archipelago, Indonesia must contend with divisiveness. Although the majority (87.2%) of Indonesians are Muslim, Islam has not been established as Indonesia's official religion. Instead, Indonesia has declared itself to be officially "monotheistic." The government has established an official doctrine called Pancasila, which affirms the existence of a single Supreme Being. This is in harmony with both Islam and Christianity, Indonesia's second largest religious grouping (9.6% of the population). It is, however, in opposition to Indonesia's minority Hindus (1.8%).

The five principles of Pancasila are:

- Belief in One Supreme God
- Belief in a just and civilized humanity
- Belief in the unity of Indonesia
- Belief in democracy
- Belief that adherence to Pancasila will bring social justice to all the peoples of Indonesia

All Indonesian government employees and all students are indoctrinated in Pancasila.

Despite its Muslim plurality, Indonesia does not follow the traditional Islamic work week. (The Muslim Sabbath is Friday, so the standard "weekend" in the Islamic world is Thursday and Friday). In Indonesia, the work week extends over six days: full workdays from Monday through Thursday, followed by two half days on Friday and Saturday.

Both Islamic and Hindu tradition call for modesty in dress. This applies to foreigners as well. Due to Indonesia's equatorial heat and humidity, business dress is often casual. The standard office wear for men is dark trousers and a light-colored long-sleeved shirt and tie, without a jacket. Many businessmen wear a short-sleeved shirt with no tie. However, businesswomen must wear long-sleeved blouses with a skirt; their upper arms must be covered and their skirts should be knee-length or longer. (Indonesians manage to remain well-groomed despite the climate, often bathing several times a day.)

5 Cultural Tips

1. Appointments can be scheduled at relatively short notice. Be punctual; as a foreign businessperson, you are expected to be on time for all business appointments. However, it would be unrealistic to expect punctuality from all Indonesians, since promptness was not traditionally considered a virtue. Furthermore, making people wait can be an expression of Indonesia's social structure. It is the prerogative of a person of higher standing to make a person of lower-standing wait, and it is very poor manners for a person of lower rank to show anger or unhappiness toward a person of higher rank.

2. Even foreigners are expected to be late to social events. As a general rule, arrive about half an hour late. But be aware that there is a complex social interplay even at social events. When invited to a social event, Indonesians try to discover the guest list. They will then attempt to arrive later than lesser personages but earlier than more important ones. (For this reason, invitations to some events may state a time, but will add "please arrive fifteen minutes early." This is to insure that no one arrives after the most important guest.)

3. Indonesians show great deference to a superior. Consequently, superiors are often told what they want to hear. The truth is conveyed in private, "up the grapevine," often by a friend of the superior. Indonesians honor their superior by shielding him from bad news in public. This Indonesian trait, called *asal bapak senang* (which translates "keeping father happy") is instilled in Indonesians since childhood. A foreign executive must establish a network whereby s/he can be told the truth in private.

4. Since it is impolite to disagree with someone openly, Indonesians rarely say "No." The listener is expected to be perceptive enough to discern a polite *"Yes (but I really mean No)"* from an actual "Yes." This is rarely a problem when speaking in Bahasa Indonesia, since the language has at least 12 ways to say "No" and many ways to say *"I'm saying 'Yes' but I mean 'No.'"* This subtlety is lost in English.

5. Indonesians are comfortable with silence, in both business and social settings. A silent pause does not necessarily signal either acceptance or rejection. Westerners often find such pauses uncomfortable, but Indonesians do not "jump" on the end of someone else's sentences. Politeness demands that they leave a respectful pause (as long as 10 to 15 seconds) before responding. Westerners often assume they have agreement and resume talking before an Indonesian has the chance to respond.

Economic Overview

Indonesia's structural changes are developing a marketplace that U.S. companies should not ignore. Indonesia has a free-market economy which is dominated by the private sector. The government does play a role in the economy, however, through state-owned firms and the imposition of price controls in selected industries.

Designated as one of the 10 "Big Emerging Markets" by the U.S. Department of Commerce, the Republic of Indonesia is abundantly endowed with natural resources and a population approaching 200 million. U.S. exports have doubled since 1988, totaling $3.3 billion in 1995. The country has an unbroken record of stable economic growth over the last 25 years with prospects of continued growth in GDP averaging 6% annually.

The middle class is widening and deepening. The latest World Bank report classified Indonesia as an Asian growth tiger, and graduated the country to lower middle income status.

In 1994, Indonesia's per capita GDP passed $875, more than double that of India. Life expectancy has risen dramatically, from 41 in 1965 to 63 in 1994.

Indonesia has made considerable progress in trade and investment deregulation. In mid-1994, Indonesia lowered investment barriers to among the lowest in the Asian region. In May 1995, the government unveiled a comprehensive tariff reduction package which covered roughly two-thirds of all traded goods.

Foreign investment approvals in 1994 and 1995 exceeded $20 billion, double that of the highest previous year. A steady stream of government deregulation packages continue to liberalize the investment and trade regimes. Evolving privatization measures should yield billions of dollars of sales opportunities well into the next century, particularly in infrastructure development such as power, transportation, telecommunications, and environmental projects.

Comparative Data

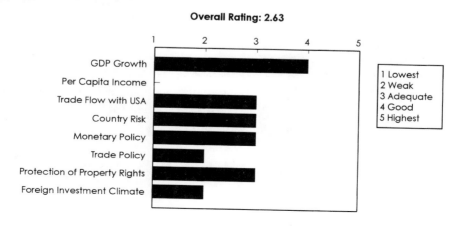

Overall Rating: 2.63

1	Lowest
2	Weak
3	Adequate
4	Good
5	Highest

GDP Growth
Per Capita Income
Trade Flow with USA
Country Risk
Monetary Policy
Trade Policy
Protection of Property Rights
Foreign Investment Climate

Country Risk Rating
Gross Domestic Product: $166 billion
GDP Growth: 7.3%
Per Capita Income: $875

Trade Flows with the U.S.A.
Rank as U.S.A. Export Market: 29th
U.S.A. Exports to Indonesia: $3.3 billion
Growth Rate: 18%
U.S.A. Imports from Indonesia: $7.4 billion
Growth Rate: 14%
Rank as Supplier of U.S.A. Imports: 18th

Top U.S.A. Exports to Indonesia: Machinery; aircraft; electrical equipment; cotton, yarn, and fabric; organic chemicals; woodpulp and paper waste; plastics; miscellaneous grain, seeds, and fruit; motor vehicles; miscellaneous chemicals.

Top U.S.A. Prospects to Indonesia: Household consumer goods; building products; architectural, construction and engineering services; electrical power systems; franchising; telecommunications equipment; pollution control equipment; construction equipment; computer systems and peripherals; food processing; and packaging equipment.

Credit Terms
Dun & Bradstreet rates Indonesia as having sufficient capacity to meet outstanding payment liabilities. Approximately 60% of all trade transactions occur on letter of credit terms, but more liberal transaction methods including open account and sight draft are being used increasingly. Credit terms of 60–90 days are common. Unsecured terms are not advised for new customers.

Monetary Policy
A downside to the economy's otherwise stellar performance is the high inflationary environment. Inflation topped 9% in 1994 and 1995. Foreign capital inflows are a primary reason for the high inflation. *Monetary unit:* rupiah.

Trade Policy

TARIFFS: A May 1995 tariff reform package reduced import duties and taxes on most tariff categories by 5 to 10%. According to the Indonesian schedule for future tariff reform, tariffs below 20% will be reduced by 5% by the year 2000, and tariffs greater than 20% will be reduced to 20% by 1998 and to 10% by 2003.

The trade-weighted average tariff in 1995 was 9.5%, but the effective tariff rate is much lower due to imported goods which are exempted from duty. Capital goods for approved investments, imports used to produce exported goods, and imports exempted by the Ministry of Finance are not subject to the duties.

IMPORT LICENSING: Nontariff barriers continue to protect a large share of both agricultural and manufacturing production. Products in 189 tariff categories are subject to import licensing restrictions, covering $2 billion, or 6.3% of total imports in 1994. Major affected products are motor vehicles, rice, wheat, sugar, salt, soybean meal, alcoholic beverages, cloves, explosives, and petroleum products.

Importers of most goods must obtain a license from the Department of Trade. Importers of food and drug-related products must be registered with the Department of Health. Importers of oil and gas products must also register with the appropriate department.

All ocean-borne imports valued at more than $5,000 must undergo a preshipment inspection.

IMPORT TAXES: Indonesia imposes import surcharges, or supplemental import duties, on approximately 200 tariff lines. These surcharges range from 5 to 30% with imports in the automotive sector subjected to surcharges of 75%.

Additionally, the government levies a 10% value-added tax on the sale of all domestic and imported goods, and a luxury tax of 10 to 35% on a number of products. For imports, these sales taxes are collected at the point of import and are calculated based on the value of the product, including import duties.

Protection of Intellectual Property Rights

Protection of intellectual property rights in Indonesia is hampered by inadequate enforcement of the laws and regulations passed in 1987. Foreign companies must therefore be vigilant in protecting their products from IPR infringement.

Indonesia is a member of the World Intellectual Property Organization. The government is revising its patent, copyright, and trademark laws.

Products and production processes are in principle patentable subject to certain requirements for a period of 14 years commencing from the filing of the patent application. The patent can be extended for another two years.

A new trademark law offers protection for service marks and collective marks and sets forth a procedure for opposition prior to examination by the trademark office. It also provides well-known mark protection. Cancellation actions must be lodged within five years of the trademark registration date.

An amended copyright law affords protection to foreign works, expands the scope of coverage and raises the terms of protection for most categories of works to international standards.

Foreign Investment Climate

The Indonesian government actively encourages foreign investment. Foreign investment in industry, particularly in export-oriented and labor-intensive activities, is strongly encouraged. Although some sectors remain closed or restricted, the government periodically updates its negative investment list and list of sectors reserved for small business. Recently, several previously restricted sectors were opened to foreign investment, including harbors, electricity generation, telecommunications, shipping, airlines, railways, and water supply. Foreign investment in many services remain restricted, however.

Foreign investors may purchase domestic firms except in sectors prohibited by the negative list. In June 1994, requirements for minimum equity in most foreign investments were eliminated. Foreign investors who open with 100% equity must divest some percentage of their holdings after 15 years. Foreign investors may not hold majority ownership in retail operations, although franchise, licensing, and technical service agreements are common. Foreign companies are also forbidden from providing domestic distribution services.

Most foreign investments must be approved by the Capital Investment Coordinating Board (BKPM). Investments in the oil and gas, mining, banking, and insurance industries are handled by the relevant technical government departments.

Current Leaders & Political Parties

(Update: International Academy at Santa Barbara *http://www.iasb.org/cwl*)

Pres.: Soeharto
Vice Pres.: Gen. Try Sutrisno

Cabinet Ministers:
Home Affairs: Yogie Suardi Memed
Foreign Affairs: Ali Alatas
Defense and Security: Gen. Edi Sudradjat
Justice: Oetojo Oesman

Information: H. Harmoko
Finance: Mar'ie Muhammad
Industry and Trade: T. Ariwibowo
Agriculture: Dr. Syarifudin Baharsjah
Mining and Energy: I. B. Sudjana
Public Works: Radinal Moochtar
Forestry: Djamaloedin Soeryohadikoesoemo
Communications: Dr. Haryanto Dhanutirto
Tourism, Posts, and Telecommunications: Joop Ave
Cooperatives and Small Business: Subiakto Tjakrawerdaja
Manpower: Abdul Latief
Transmigration: Siswono Yudohusodo
Education and Culture: Dr. Wardiman Djojonegoro
Health: Prof. Sujudi
Religious Affairs: Dr. Tarmizi Taher
Social Affairs: Endang Kusuma Inten Soeweno

Other Officials:

Gov. of the Bank of Indonesia: Dr. J. Soedrajad Djiwandono
Attorney Gen.: Singgih
Cdr.-in-Chief of the Armed Forces: Gen. Feisal Tanjung
Chmn. of the People's Consultative Assembly: H. Wahono
Chmn. of the Supreme Court: Purwoto Gandasubrata
Ambassador to U.S.: Dr. Arifin Mohamad Siregar
Perm. Rep. to U.N.: Nugroho Wisnumurti

Political Parties:

Indonesian Democratic Party (fusion of all natl. and Christian parties), Golongan Karya (functional group), United Dev. Party (fusion of all Muslim parties)

Political Influences on Business

The current leadership of Indonesia favors foreign investment. Business has been growing, as has the standard of living for many Indonesians. However, human rights concerns continue to hamper Indonesia's future. The Indonesian occupation of East Timor is considered illegal by many nations. Note that politics and business are closely related; when a nation lodges protests against Indonesian actions, expatriate business executives from that country are liable to experience Indonesian disapproval.

For the past three decades, President Soeharto, whose current term ends in 1998, has ruled unchallenged with the support of the military. Under a "dual function" concept that justifies military involvement in the social and political life of the nation, the military holds many key civilian government positions and parliamentary posts. However, the number of military in such posts has been on the decline during the last decade.

Mr. Soeharto is only the second president of Indonesia in nearly five decades, and the mechanisms that are supposed to guide the presidential succession process are essentially untested. No obvious replacement to Soeharto, who is 75, is currently visible. These factors make the succession issue a key one in assessing the future stability for business ventures, both because of Soeharto's relatively probusiness policies and because of the political uncertainties involved.

Other stability factors with business implications are ones that are related to perceived inequalities in income and rising complaints over labor issues, especially the continued failure of a number of employers to pay the legally mandated minimum wage, despite stepped up government enforcement efforts. These issues could lead to localized problems; more widespread upheavals appear unlikely, however, for the foreseeable future. Concern over human rights issues led the United States to cut back its military training program in Indonesia in 1992.

Indonesia is one of the world's most important nonaligned nations (a distinction which has less importance since the Cold War ended). Under the 1945 Constitution, supreme governmental authority in Indonesia is vested in the 1,000-member People's Consultative Assembly (MPR), which meets every five years to select the president and vice president and establish the broad outlines of government policy for the next five years. Half of the MPR's members come from the partially elected Parliament (DPR), and the other half are appointed by the government.

Of the 500 members of the DPR, 400 are selected through nationwide elections held every five years, and 100 are active duty members of the armed forces (ABRI) appointed by the military. The number of appointed members in both the DPR and the MPR will drop by 25 in the 1997 election cycle. Parliaments also exist at the provincial and district level. The last national and local parliamentary elections were held in 1992; the next will be held in 1997.

The signing on December 14, 1995, of a security agreement between Australia and Indonesia was a positive sign. Since the defeat of the Japanese in World War II, the expansionist Indonesians have been seen as Australia's primary (non-Communist) security threat. Australian troops fought Indonesian forces on the island of Borneo in the 1960s. But Indonesia's economic interdependence has reduced the chances of war. And, to the chagrin of other nations, Australia has recognized Indonesian sovereignty over East Timor.

Contacts in the U.S.A. & in Indonesia

Contacts in the United States:

EMBASSY OF INDONESIA
2020 Massachusetts Ave., N.W.
Washington, D.C. 20036
Tel: (202) 775-5200
Fax: (202) 775-5365

U.S. DEPARTMENT OF STATE
Overseas Travel Advisories
Tel: (202) 647-5225
Indonesia Desk
Tel: (202) 647-3276

U.S. DEPARTMENT OF COMMERCE
Indonesia Desk
Tel: (202) 482-3877

TOURISM OFFICE
Indonesian Tourist Promotion Office
3456 Wilshire Blvd.
Suite 104
Los Angeles, CA 90010
Tel: (213) 387-2078

Contacts in Indonesia:

THE EMBASSY OF THE UNITED STATES
Medan Merdeka Selatan 5, Box 1
Jakarta, Indonesia (APO AP 96520)
Tel: [62] (21) 360-360
Telex: 44218 AMEMB JKT
Fax: [62] (21) 386-2259

AMERICAN CHAMBER OF COMMERCE IN
INDONESIA
The Landmark Center, 22nd Floor
Suite 2204
Jl. Jendral Sudirman I
Jakarta, Indonesia
Tel: [62] (21) 571-0800 ext. 2222
Telex: 62822 LMARK IA
Fax: [62] (21) 571-0656

PRESIDENT SOEHARTO
Office of the President
Bina Graha
Jl. Veteran No. 17
Jakarta, Republic of Indonesia

Passport/Visa Requirements

Visa Information   Tel: (202) 663-1225

Entry Requirements: Passports valid for a minimum of six months at time of admission and onward return tickets are required. Visas are not required for tourist/business stays of up to two months (nonextendable). Special permits are required for some areas of Indonesia.

For longer stays and more current information, the traveler may contact the Embassy of the Republic of Indonesia.

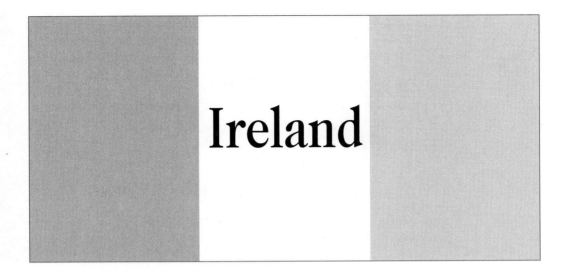

Ireland

Official Name:	Eire (Irish), Ireland (English)
Official Languages:	Irish and English
Government System:	Parliamentary multiparty republic
Population:	3.6 million
Population Growth:	–0.7%
Area:	70,282 sq. km. (27,136 sq. mi.); slightly smaller than West Virginia
Natural Resources:	zinc, lead, natural gas, crude oil, barite, copper, gypsum, limestone, dolomite, peat, silver
Major Cities:	Dublin (capital), Cork, Limerick, Galway, Waterford

---

Cultural Note: The Republic of Ireland joined the European Community in 1973, yielding favorable gains for Ireland. Trade with the EU took Ireland out from Britain's shadow. Multinational corporations have placed their headquarters in Ireland. As one of the poorest members of the EU, Ireland became eligible for EU loans and assistance.

EU influence is also helping women to achieve equality in Ireland. Historically a male-dominated society, Ireland now has many women in politics, including its Chief of State, President Mary Robinson.

Age Breakdown

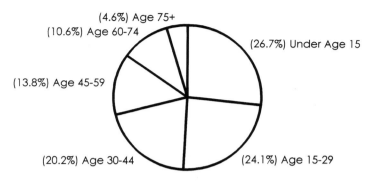

Life Expectancy: 70 years male; 76 years female (1990)

 Time

Promptness is expected for business appointments. The rules for social engagements, especially between friends, are more flexible.

Punctuality has not historically been valued in Ireland. In order to encourage people to pay their bills promptly, the Irish telephone and electric utilities automatically enter paid-on-time bills into a raffle! Even Irish schools have a fairly relaxed attitude about tardiness.

Irish attitudes toward time also extend to deadlines and delivery dates. Don't expect something to be executed at the time or date promised, unless you have been careful to explain why that deadline must be met.

In rural areas, everything shuts down at lunchtime from 1 P.M. to 2 or 2:30 P.M. for lunch. (For many people this includes a trip to the pub.) Shops and offices close down, and only food-service establishments remain open. In fact, one day a week, many rural businesses close for the day at 1 P.M., giving their employees an afternoon off.

In the cities, people take lunches in shifts, allowing businesses to remain open.

Ireland, like England, is on Greenwich Mean Time. This is five hours ahead of U.S. Eastern Standard Time (E.S.T. + 5).

 Holidays

(Update: Getting Through Customs *http://www.getcustoms.com*)

New Year's Day	1 January
Saint Patrick's Day	17 March

Easter Monday	varies
May Holiday	First Monday
June Holiday	First Monday
August Holiday	First Monday
October Holiday	Last Monday
Christmas Day	25 December
Saint Stephen's Day	26 December

If New Year's Day, Saint Patrick's Day, Christmas Day, or Saint Stephen's Day fall on a weekend, the following Monday is a public holiday.

Work Week

- A 39-hour, 5-day workweek is the norm for offices and factories. For offices, the customary working hours are 9:00 A.M. to 5:30 P.M. with lunch from 1:00 P.M. to 2:00 P.M.; banking hours are from 10:00 to 4:00 P.M. with banks having various evening hours posted. Most retail stores are open from 9:00 A.M. to 6:00 P.M., Monday through Saturday, although some have later hours to permit evening shopping.
- Because of vacations in July and August, many Irish executives may not be available except by appointment. Most businesses also close from December 24 through January 2 during the Christmas festive period.

Religious/Societal Influences on Business

It is not possible to define the Irish identity without reference to two seminal influences: the British Empire and the Catholic Church.

Ireland was invaded by the British many times. Subjugation began in earnest after Henry VIII changed England's official religion from Catholicism to Protestantism, which had the side effect of making wealthy Catholic monasteries into legitimate military targets. The Irish were dispossessed and Protestant gentry set up farms known as plantations. In the North of Ireland, even the plantations' tenant farmers were Protestant Englishmen. Southern Ireland was brutally subjugated by Cromwell the Protector in the 1650s. Catholic Irish lands were confiscated. By the 18th Century, Catholics owned less than 15% of Irish lands.

The height of British misrule of Ireland occurred during the Potato Famine of the 1840s. The potato crop failed in 1842, then failed again in 1846. While a million Irish starved and another million fled Ireland, British-owned plantations in Ireland continued to export grain. By the time the famine eased, the population of Ireland had dropped from over eight million to some six million. Emigration had become a way of life, and has continued to the present time.

The Irish pressed for reform. Aided by some English and Irish-Protestants, they sought first Home Rule, then outright independence for Ireland. The Republic of Ireland became a reality in 1921, but the Northern six counties remained part of Great Britain. (It is over the fate of Northern Ireland that the violence, which the Irish call "the troubles," continues today.) Not a single tourist has been killed or seriously injured by political violence since the troubles began in 1968.

As in other occupied countries, the Church became a guardian of the national identity. While Ireland has no official religion, about 92% of the citizens of Eire are Catholic. The Church's influence can be seen in Ireland's legal obstacles to divorce, contraception, and abortion. Condoms were illegal until 1980; after that, they could only be sold to married couples by prescription! Divorce and abortion are still essentially proscribed in Ireland.

Despite centuries of subjugation, the Irish are nevertheless proud of their history and heritage. Many consider the glory days of Ireland to be between the fall of the Roman Empire and the rise of Charlemagne. During this time span, Western scholarship and literacy was virtually isolated to Ireland. Once Charlemagne had restored stability to Europe, Irish scholars spread throughout the continent, reviving educational traditions which were lost in the Dark Ages.

 ## 5 Cultural Tips

1. The Irish character can seem complex and contradictory at times. (Sigmund Freud is alleged to have said that the Irish are the only people who cannot be helped by psychoanalysis.) Ireland is a conservative Catholic country, yet the Irish people are inevitably described as rebellious by nature and sarcastic about authority. Ireland has the lowest rate of marriage per capita in the European Union yet the highest fertility rate (2.1 children per woman), plus an 18% illegitimacy rate. A poor country with high unemployment, Ireland often gives more per capita to charities than far wealthier nations.

2. Irish hospitality and friendliness are well known. Most Irish look forward to chatting with friends and strangers alike over a cup of tea or a pint of Guinness. It would be considered impolite not to talk to anyone (even a stranger) in whose company you found yourself, whether in a waiting room or a pub. This has its drawbacks, especially in supermarkets, where everyone in line talks to each other and the checkout clerk, making a simple transaction far longer than necessary.

3. The Irish frequently use the points of a compass to describe location. Not only will a site (such as a shop or office) be described as *"east of here,"* but small objects within reach will be so located (*"the directory is south of you on the table"*). It is useful to know the cardinal points at all times while in Ireland. Curiously, *below*

is used to mean *north;* *"Dunmanway is the next village below"* means *"Dunmanway is the next village to the north."*

4. The Irish have an ambivalent attitude toward wealth. The founding father of the Irish Republic, Eamon De Valera, envisioned Ireland as a pastoral land of simple virtues. Moneymaking was not included a virtue. People who have achieved financial success are not respected automatically. Ostentation is frowned upon, except in giving to charity.

5. Leisure time is valued in Ireland. Only in sport is leisure highly structured. Most Irish enjoy simply chatting with their friends. (Naturally, in a country with such a changeable climate, the weather is a constant topic.) When encountering strangers, the favorite Irish pastime is to find out as much as possible about them while revealing as little as possible about oneself. In social situations, people quickly move to a first name basis, but business acquaintances often retain the use of the surname.

Economic Overview

The commercial environment in Ireland is highly conducive for U.S. companies interested in trade and investment. The U.S. and Ireland enjoy long-standing political, economic, and commercial relations, and a close cultural affinity.

The Irish economy is now growing strongly. The past three years have witnessed real economic growth of 3 to 5% per year. The outlook for 1996 and beyond is positive with growth rates of 5 to 6% forecast. While the Irish market is small, many U.S. firms see Ireland as a gateway to the larger European market.

Comparative Data

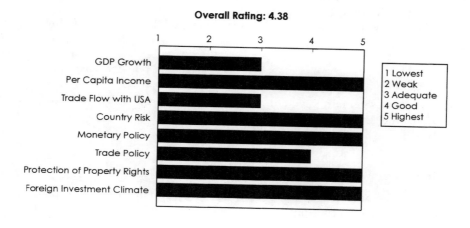

Overall Rating: 4.38

GDP Growth	
Per Capita Income	
Trade Flow with USA	
Country Risk	
Monetary Policy	
Trade Policy	
Protection of Property Rights	
Foreign Investment Climate	

1 Lowest
2 Weak
3 Adequate
4 Good
5 Highest

Country Risk Rating
Gross Domestic Product: $53 billion
GDP Growth: 5.7%
Per Capita Income: $15,000

Trade Flows with the U.S.A.
Rank as Export Market for U.S.A. Goods & Services: 27th
U.S.A. Exports to Ireland: $4.0 billion
Growth Rate of Exports: 17%
U.S.A. Imports from Ireland: $4.0 billion
Growth Rate of Imports: 38%
Rank as a Supplier of Imports into the U.S.A.:   27th

Top U.S.A. Exports to Ireland: Machinery; electronic components; medical and optical equipment; organic chemicals; pharmaceuticals; animal feed; aircraft; plastics; precious stones and metals; mineral fuels.

Top U.S.A. Prospects to Ireland: Computers and peripherals; electronic components; industrial chemicals; computer software; electrical power systems; medical equipment; drugs and pharmaceuticals; building products; air conditioning and refrigeration equipment.

Country Risk
Dun & Bradstreet rates Ireland as having the highest creditworthiness with an excellent capacity to meet outstanding payment liabilities. Ireland carries the lowest degree of risk when compared to other countries.

Usual credit terms are open account, 30 to 90 days, but sight drafts are recommended.

Monetary Policy
Inflationary pressures remain subdued. Inflation in 1993 was 1.5%, 2.5% in 1994 and 2.5% in 1995. Dun & Bradstreet forecasts inflation in 1996 to be 2.5%. *Monetary Unit:* Irish punt (pound).

Trade Policy
TARIFFS: As a member of the European Union (EU), Ireland applies EU tariffs. Duty rates on manufactured goods from the U.S. generally range from 5 to 8%. Most raw

materials enter duty-free or at low rates. In accordance with EU regulations, agricultural and food items are often subject to import levies which vary depending on world market prices.

IMPORT LICENSING: Only a small number of goods of U.S. origin require import licenses, mostly agricultural and food items. Other items subject to licensing include coal and lignite fuel, a few products from the chemical and related industries, specified iron and steel products, various textiles and textile products, natural and synthetic precious and semi-precious stones, zinc, and controlled items such as arms and munitions. Import licenses are generally granted quickly for goods of U.S. origin.

IMPORT TAXES: A 21% value-added tax (VAT) is charged on the import of goods and services into Ireland. The importer is liable for payment of the VAT at the time of customs clearance.

Excise taxes are levied on a limited number of products such as gasoline and diesel fuel, spirits, beer, wine, bottled water, cider, tobacco, motor vehicles, and liquid petroleum gas. Excise rates vary depending on the products.

Protection of Intellectual Property Rights

Ireland has legislation for the protection of patents, trademarks, and industrial designs. It is a member of the Paris Union which adheres to the International Convention for the Protection of Industrial Property. Ireland is also a signatory to the European Patent Convention which provides for a centralized European-wide patent protection system.

The European Patent Convention has simplified the process for obtaining patent protection in the EU member states. Under this convention, a patent applicant is granted a preexamined 20-year, nonrenewable European patent that has the effect of a national patent in all 16 countries that are signatories of the convention. Trademark laws are embodied by the Trademark Law of 1963.

Ireland and the U.S. are signatories of the Universal Copyright Convention which provides for mutual copyright protection. Copyright protection in Ireland is generally considered to be good.

Foreign Investment Climate

Successive Irish governments for the last 30 years have actively sought to attract foreign private investment to Ireland. In recent years, Ireland's membership in the European Union, its reservoir of well-trained workers, its close access to the European marketplace and significant investment incentives have been the primary attractions to foreign investors.

Central Bank of Ireland approval is required for investments by foreign companies in new projects and existing entities in Ireland. One hundred percent foreign ownership is permitted in sectors open to private investment, except where restricted for national security purposes. Foreign ownership of land, however, is prohibited, except for stud farms and agricultural land associated with horses and horse racing.

The U.S.A. is the largest foreign investor in Ireland.

Current Leaders & Political Parties

(Update: International Academy at Santa Barbara *http://www.iasb.org/cwl*)

President.: Mary Robinson

Ministers:
Taoiseach (Prime Min.): John Bruton
Tanaiste (Dep. Prime Min.) and Min. of Foreign Affairs: Dick Spring
Finance: Ruairi Quinn
Employment and Enterprise: Richard Bruton
Defense and Marine Affairs: Sean Barrett
Health: Michael Noonan
Environment: Brendan Howlin
Equality and Law Reform: Mervyn Taylor
Tourism and Trade: Enda Kenny
Arts, Culture, and Gaeltacht: Michael D. Higgins
Agriculture, Food, and Forestry: Ivan Yates
Transport, Energy, and Communications: Michael Lowry
Chief Whip: Jim Higgins

Other Officials:
Chief Justice of the Supreme Court: Liam Hamilton
Ambassador to U.S.: Dermot Gallagher
Perm. Rep. to U.N.: John Campbell

Political Parties:
Fianna Fá áil (FF), Fine Gael (FG), Labour Party (LAB), Progressive Democrats, Democratic Left, Green Party

Political Influences on Business

Ireland and the United States enjoy uniformly good bilateral relations. The same language, similar values, frequent visits back and forth, and the presence of some 44 million Americans of at least partial Irish descent guarantee that they will continue to do so indefinitely.

There are no outstanding bilateral disputes. A few minor disagreements on specific trade issues (e.g., corn-gluten feed and malt-sprout pellets) occurred in the recent past but have been resolved. That is not to say that others could not arise, given Ireland's membership in the European Union (EU) and its support of the EU consensus on most issues. However, if any disagreement should arise, approval of the Uruguay Round of the GATT negotiations and the reservoir of goodwill built up on both sides should temper them.

Ireland, which has traditionally followed a policy of neutrality, has pledged to support the Common Foreign and Security Policy (CFSP) provided under the Maastricht Treaty on European Union. This commitment implies an eventual change in Irish neutrality. In any case, the end of the Cold War and the collapse of communism render the concept of neutrality largely perfunctory.

Ireland has on occasion been critical of some aspects of U.S. Foreign Policy (such as U.S. involvement in Central America in the 1980s and support for Israel), but recent world developments have practically eliminated any negative rhetoric. The only U.S. foreign policy stance that continues to draw Irish criticism is the maintenance of the U.S. embargo against Cuba. If anything, the Irish want the U.S. to play an even greater role in the resolution of critical international problems.

Although not an ally in technical terms, Ireland remains one of the United States' oldest and closest friends. Recent developments, such as the White House Conference for Trade and Investment in Ireland (convened in Washington in May 1995), together with President Clinton's 1995 visit to Ireland (under the aegis of the Presidential Economic Initiative for Ireland), have helped reinforce these strong historical ties. Further enhancement of this relationship has been effected by the active role the U.S. has taken in promoting the peace process and the economic confidence and stability.

Few major political issues significantly affect the business climate. The Irish economy is "on a roll," performing better than any other in Europe. The outlook is for continued strong growth of at least 5% per year, low inflation and interest rates, declining unemployment and (thanks in part to European Union assistance) significant renovation and extension of the country's transportation and communications infrastructures. If the government continues the appropriate policies, the country will keep making steady progress in paying off the national debt, which now stands at 90% of GNP. The Fianna Fail/Labor coalition government, which assumed office following the November 1992 general election, collapsed in November 1993 after Prime Minister Reynolds forced through a court appointment over the strong opposition of his junior coalition partner. In December 1994, a new three-party "rainbow" coalition was formed, consisting of Fine Gael, Labor, and the Democratic Left. Fine Gael leader John Bruton became Prime Minister, while Labor leader Dick Spring remained Deputy Prime Minister and Foreign Minister.

One of the major issues in the political arena which is sure to influence the business climate is the current coalition government's program, "A Government for Renewal." This program outlines the path which the "rainbow" coalition has chosen for the three years remaining in the parliamentary term. The program attempts to fuse the differing economic philosophies and priorities held by the coalition partners into a single agenda. It attempts to combine the Fine Gael priority of tax reduction with the Labor/Democratic Left priority of increased government spending into one general fiscal policy. Although these objectives may in most cases seem contradictory, the government believes that the robust growth of the Irish economy can provide for the simultaneous, albeit moderate pursuit of these goals. Such a program would work to remove disincentives for hiring while still providing for the strong social welfare system. In implementing the program, the coalition pledges to maintain the fiscal discipline of the preceding government, and given Ireland's desire to be an early participant in the forthcoming European Monetary Union, ensure that all commitments will adhere to Maastricht guidelines.

Despite continued high levels of taxation, consumer confidence and spending have shown strong growth in recent years. The strong performance of the Irish economy and the generally favorable economic climate in Europe have reinforced this growth. Although taxation is high, international companies enjoy significant tax breaks under government incentive programs.

Given Ireland's extensive social welfare system, employers often find the marginal cost of employing another worker excessively high. Strikes in the private sector are relatively rare, but unions strenuously oppose proposals to lay off or dismiss workers.

Ireland is a parliamentary democracy. Its president or head of state is a largely ceremonial figure elected to a 7-year term. According to the Irish Constitution, the president needs advance cabinet approval of speeches and travel. The incumbent is Mary Robinson, elected in November 1990.

The Bicameral Legislature is comprised of the *Seanad* or Senate with 60 members and the *Dail* or House of Representatives with 166 members. The 166 Dail representatives are elected by universal suffrage for a maximum 5-year term. Members of the Senate also hold office for a similar 5-year term; however, 11 Senate members are nominated by the Prime Minister and the remaining 49 are elected by local universities and from panels of candidates in the following five areas: Cultural and Educational, Agricultural, Labor, Industrial and Commercial, and Administrative. The Dail is the more powerful body. The electoral system features proportional representation in multicandidate constituencies. The last election was in November 1992; the current government assumed office on December 15, 1994. The next election must be held by November 1997.

Contacts in the U.S.A. & in Ireland

Contacts in the United States:

EMBASSY OF IRELAND
2234 Massachusetts Ave., N.W.
Washington, D.C. 20008
Tel: 202-462-3939
Fax: 202-232-5593

U.S. DEPARTMENT OF STATE
Bureau of Consular Affairs
Tel: 202-647-5225
Country Desk Officer
Ireland
Tel: 202-647-8027

U.S. DEPARTMENT OF COMMERCE
Ireland Desk
Tel: 202-482-3748

IRISH TOURIST BOARD
757 Third Avenue
New York, N.Y. 10017
Tel: 212 418-0800 or 1-800 223-6470

Contacts in Ireland:

U.S. EMBASSY
42 Elgin Road, Ballsbridge
Dublin, Ireland
Tel: [353] (1) 68-87-77
Telex: 93684

UNITED STATES CHAMBER OF COMMERCE
20 College Green
Dublin 2, Ireland
Tel: [353] (1) 79-37-33
Telex: 31187 UCIL EI

DUN & BRADSTREET LTD.
Postal Address: P.O. Box 455A, Dublin 2,
Ireland
Street Address: Holbrook House, Holles
Street, Dublin 2, Ireland
Tel: [353] (1) 676-4239
Fax: [353] (1) 678-9301

PRESIDENT MARY ROBINSON
Office of the President
'Aras an Uachtaráin
Phoenix Park
Dublin 8, Ireland

PRIME MINISTER JOHN BRUTON
Office of the Taoiseach
Government Buildings
Upper Merrion Street
Dublin 2, Ireland

Passport/Visa Requirements

Visa Information   Tel: (202) 663-1225

Entry Requirements: A passport is required. Tourists are not required to obtain visas for stays under 90 days, but may be asked to show onward or return tickets. To reside in the country, U.S. citizens must satisfy the Immigration authorities that they can support themselves for the period of the proposed stay.

For further information concerning entry requirements for Ireland, travelers can contact the Embassy of Ireland.

Cultural Note: The Irish propensity for talk is somewhat exaggerated; not all of the Irish chatter, nor do they all speak with great cleverness. But enough do to give foreigners this impression. Many Irish will take it upon themselves to talk to any foreigner they meet. A stranger's name, marital status, occupation, and reason for visiting is quickly ascertained, and this information is passed around from person to person. The contrast with cultures that ignore strangers is striking.

Israel

Official Name:	State of Israel
	Medinat Yisra'el (Hebrew) Isra'il (Arabic)
Official Languages:	Hebrew and Arabic
Government System:	Parliamentary multiparty democracy
Population:	5.6 million
Population Growth:	2.7%
Area:	20,325 sq. km. (7,850 sq. mi.); not including the Israeli-occupied Arab territories of the West Bank and Gaza Strip, about the size of New Jersey
Natural Resources:	copper, phosphates, bromide, potash, clay, sand, sulfur, asphalt, manganese, small amounts of natural gas and crude oil
Major Cities:	Jerusalem (capital), Tel Aviv, Haifa, Beersheba

Cultural Note: Israel has a diverse population. Jews make up only about 82% of the population, and almost half of the Israeli Jews were born outside Israel. The remainder includes Palestinians (who can be Muslim or Christian) and Druze (all of whom worship an offshoot of Islam).

Age Breakdown

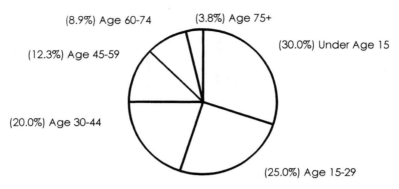

(8.9%) Age 60-74

(3.8%) Age 75+

(12.3%) Age 45-59

(30.0%) Under Age 15

(20.0%) Age 30-44

(25.0%) Age 15-29

Life Expectancy: 75 years male; 78 years female (1994)

 Time

As a foreigner, you will be expected to be on time to business appointments. Many Israelis familiar with North American business customs will likewise be punctual. However, punctuality is not a custom in most Middle Eastern cultures.

Israel is two hours ahead of Greenwich Mean Time (G.M.T. + 2), which is seven hours ahead of U.S. Eastern Standard Time (E.S.T. + 7).

 Holidays

(Update: Getting Through Customs *http://www.getcustoms.com*)

- Both Judaism and Islam use lunar calendars which are different from the Gregorian (Western) calendar. However, for official business purposes (and when dealing with foreigners), most Israelis will use the Gregorian calendar.
- The Jewish and Islamic lunar calendars use lunar months of 28 days, so a lunar year of 12 months is only 354 days long. Holidays will thus be on different dates (by the Western calendar) every year.
- Note that when a schedule is agreed upon in terms of months (i.e., delivery in two months), an Israeli may be thinking in terms of 28-day months while a Westerner may be assuming 30-day months.

This list is a working guide. Dates should be corroborated before final travel plans are made. In cases where holidays fall on Saturday or Sunday, commercial establishments may be closed the preceding Friday or following Monday.

Passover (First and Last Days)	spring
Yom Ha'Atzma'ut (Independence Day)	15 April
Shavuot (Pentecost)	late spring
Rosh Hashanah (Jewish New Year)	usually September
Yom Kippur (The Day of Atonement)	usually September
Sukkot (Feast of Tabernacles)	September - October
Simhat Torah (Celebration of the Law)	usually October
Hanukkah (Festival of Lights; First and Last Days)	late November - mid December

- The dates of Islamic holidays are based upon actual lunar observations. Thus, the dates given below are only approximations; the holidays could be celebrated the day before or the day after the given date.

In Islamic neighborhoods, the most important holidays are:

The three-day feast celebrating the end of the fasting of the month of Ramadan (Id al Fitr)

The Feast of the Sacrifice (Id al Adha)

Work Week

- The Jewish holy day, the Sabbath, begins at sunset on Friday and ends at sunset on Saturday. In deference to the religious Jewish community, no business is conducted on the Sabbath. The work week runs from Sunday through Thursday.
- Government hours are generally: 8:00 A.M. to 3:00 P.M., Sunday through Thursday. Many offices close at 2:00 P.M. during the summer.
- Banking hours vary. Main banks in commercial districts are open from 8:30 A.M. to 2:00 P.M., Sunday through Thursday; some extend their hours until 7:00 P.M. Branch banks which cater primarily to the public operate on a split schedule. They are usually open from 8:30 A.M. to 12:30 P.M., Sunday through Thursday, plus 4:00 to 5:30 P.M. on Sundays, Tuesdays, and Thursdays. Many banks close at noon on Fridays.
- Business hours vary widely. Even the days businesses are open depends upon the religion of the owner. Most Jewish businesses close on Fridays (especially in the afternoon) and Saturdays. Islamic-owned establishments will be closed all day on Fridays; Christian-owned ones will be closed Sundays. (Remember that Palestinians may be either Muslim or Christian.)
- A typical schedule for a Jewish-owned business would be: 8:00 A.M. to 4:00 P.M., Sunday through Thursday, and 8:00 A.M. to 1:00 P.M. on Fridays.

Religious/Societal Influences on Business

Although Israel is the Jewish homeland, the State of Israel has no official religion. The Jewish population is divided into different groups. The Ashkenazi Jews came from Germany, Poland, and Russia. Most Jews in the U.S. came from this group. The native language of the Ashkenazim is Yiddish (although many also spoke the language of their country of residence).

The Sephardic Jews were exiled from Spain and Portugal in 1492. They spread throughout the Mediterranean, especially the Middle East. Before the Zionist movement encouraged Jews to move back to the Holy Land in the 20th century, most Jews in Israel were Sephardim. The native language of the Sepahrdic Jews is *Landino*. After Israel's neighbors declared war on Israel, most Sephardim outside of Israel emigrated. The large Jewish communities in cities like Cairo and Baghdad left for Israel.

For years, Israel had approximately equal numbers of Ashkenazim and Sephardim. But the recent influx of Ashkenazim from the former U.S.S.R. has irrevocably tipped the balance in favor of the Ashkenazim. Some Sephardim resent the dominant position of the Ashkenazi community.

The Yemeni and Ethiopian Jews are two smaller groups. They have been much less successful in Israel, and tension exists over their place in Israeli society. In January of 1996, the Ethiopian community was outraged to discover that their blood donations were routinely destroyed. The black Ethiopians charged the government with racism, but the health service defended the practice, since the Ethiopian Jews come from an area of Africa where AIDS is endemic.

Aside from their ethnic origins, Israeli Jewry runs the gamut from fundamentalist belief to atheism. Many Jews consider themselves "secular," and rarely participate in their religion. In fact, some of the recent immigrants from Russia had never practiced Judaism, and needed to study even the basics of Jewish belief. On the other hand, some very religious Jews want to make their beliefs part of daily life in Israel. Because of the Parliamentary system in Israel, small religious-oriented parties can have a disproportionate amount of power.

5 Cultural Tips

1. Jerusalem, the new capital of Israel, contains some of the most important shrines of Christianity and Islam, as well as Judaism. If this is your first trip, do not underestimate the tremendous impact these shrines may have on you. (The city of Jerusalem has one of the busiest asylums in the world, full of tourists who lost touch with reality after visiting the Holy Places.) Even the most hard-headed business executives may be distracted.

2. The official work week in Israel runs from Sunday through Thursday, as the Jewish Sabbath begins at sunset on Friday and ends at sunset on Saturday. No business is conducted on the Sabbath, but many Jewish-owned business are open until 1 P.M. on Fridays. The Muslim holy day begins at dawn on Friday, and Muslims do not work on Friday afternoons. Some Christian business owners do not open on Sunday. So the only days that everyone in Israel works are Monday, Tuesday, Wednesday, and Thursday.

3. For many Orthodox and fundamentalist Jews, the Sabbath is devoted to God, and "not working" on the Sabbath is interpreted very broadly. Even turning on a light switch can be interpreted as work. Some will hire a non-Jew to do necessary chores on the Sabbath.

4. A large number of Israeli businesspeople speak English. If you have your materials translated into Hebrew, remember that Hebrew is read right-to-left (the opposite of English's left-to-right). Graphic design is also reversed; the back page of a booklet in the U.S. is the front page in Israel.

5. Most Israelis love to talk. Business meetings usually begin with long discussions, during which the parties get to know each other. Business will not be discussed until this process has concluded.

Economic Overview

The historic ties between the U.S. and Israel give distinct advantages to U.S. firms wishing to do business in Israel. A free trade agreement between the U.S. and Israel, concluded in 1985, was fully implemented on January 1, 1995, and is a key factor in keeping the U.S. as Israel's largest trading partner. U.S. loan guarantees, a cheaper dollar, and programs which encourage joint research and development have helped maintain an advantage for U.S. firms.

Two major factors influencing Israel's economy in the 1990s are the influx of nearly 600,000 immigrants from the former Soviet Union and the peace process in the Middle East. Both have had positive effects on the Israeli economy and Israel led the developed world with 7% real GDP growth in 1994. Remarkably, since Israel's massive immigration wave began in 1990, more jobs have been created than exist for the new labor market entrants.

Two main issues affect the business climate in Israel: regional instability and terrorism. These two issues have led some foreign business to move cautiously on investments in Israel. The assassination of Prime Minster Yitzhak Rabin in November 1995 underlines that there remains opposition from some Israelis to the Arab-Israeli peace process. Israel has an increasingly open, modern, and sophisticated commercial environment with a well-educated population. The market for U.S. goods and services exists now and will continue to expand.

Cultural Note: All countries change, but few countries have had to deal with the changes Israel has seen in the past few years. The influx of Russian Jews, the peace agreement with the Palestinians, and the constant threat of terrorism have all changed Israel. Each of these have had unexpected effects:

Many of the Russian immigrants were highly educated, and Israel does not have enough high-level jobs to fully employ them. Israel is now the most "over educated" nation in the world, with Russian engineers and musicians working as manual laborers.

As part of the peace agreement, Israel began disengaging from the Occupied Territories. Opposition to the "peace-for-land" policy has rent Israeli society, as reflected in the assassination of Prime Minister Rabin by an Israeli fundamentalist. This policy is currently stalled under Prime Minister Netanyahu.

After every terrorist attack attributed to a Palestinian group (such as Hamas), the Israeli government closes the Israeli-Palestinian border. This punishes the many Palestinians whose economy depends on Israel. But the frequent loss of Palestinian day-laborers also hurts their Israeli employers. To offset this, the Israelis have invited some Asians into Israel as replacement labor. (This is common in other Middle Eastern nations, where Filipinos and other Asians are brought in to supplement the work force.)

Comparative Data

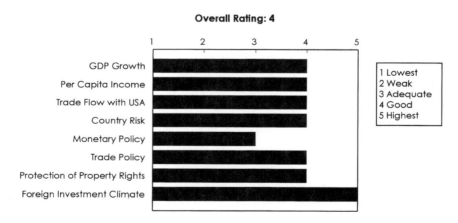

Country Risk Rating

Gross Domestic Product: $73.6 billion
GDP Growth: 6.7%
Per Capita Income: $13,700

Trade Flows with the U.S.A.

Rank as Export Market for U.S.A. Goods & Services: 21st
U.S.A. Exports to Israel: $5.6 billion
Growth Rate of Exports: 12%
U.S.A. Imports from Israel: $5.7 billion
Growth Rate of Imports: 10%
Rank as a Supplier of Imports into the U.S.A.:   25th

Top U.S.A. Exports to Country: Aircraft; electronic components; machinery; precious stones and metals; motor vehicles; medical and optical equipment; cereals; ships and boats; miscellaneous grain, seed and fruit; tobacco.

Top U.S.A. Prospects for Export to Country: Electrical power systems; pollution control equipment; medical equipment and supplies; computer software; electronic components; sporting goods; industrial process controls; hotel furnishings, fixtures and equipment; machine tools; trucks, trailers and buses; construction equipment.

Credit Terms

Dun & Bradstreet rates Israel as having good capacity to meet outstanding payment liabilities.

Open account terms are the dominant vehicle of payment, with 60 to 90 day terms the norm. A letter of credit is recommended for new accounts.

Monetary Policy

Inflation reached 14.5% in 1994, but returned to single digit rates in 1995. To reach its goal of 8% to 11% inflation in 1995, the Bank of Israel employed a restrictive monetary policy which slowed levels of economic growth and led to real interest rate levels of close to 5%. Inflation in 1996 is expected to reach 12% to 14%. *Monetary Unit:* new Israeli shekel.

Trade Policy

TARIFFS: Under the U.S.-Israeli Free Trade Agreement, all remaining duties imposed on U.S.-made products were eliminated on January 1, 1995.

IMPORT LICENSING: All import licensing requirements for U.S.-made consumer and industrial goods have been eliminated under the Free Trade Agreement. However, licensing requirements and quantitative restrictions still exist for a wide range of food and agricultural products. All medical devices and equipment are subject to supervision by the Ministry of Health.

Israel maintains extensive restrictions on agricultural imports ranging from quotas, licensing restrictions, and variable levies to outright prohibitions.

IMPORT TAXES: A value added tax of 17% is levied on almost all imported and domestically produced goods and services, other than capital goods, exports, fresh fruits and vegetables, most foreign tourists' services, and travel tickets. The VAT applies to all imports, based on the landed cost of an item plus the customs duty and taxes.

A purchase tax (ranging from 25 to 180%) is applied on items traditionally considered luxury goods such as automobiles, home electronics, cosmetics, and agriculture and food items. By law, purchase taxes apply to both local and foreign products. However, when there is no local production, the purchase tax becomes a duty equivalent charge.

Other indirect taxes include fuel taxes on gasoline and kerosene, an entertainment tax, and excise taxes on alcoholic beverages, tobacco, and other goods produced locally for domestic consumption.

Protection of Intellectual Property Rights

Patent protection is available comprehensively. A patent is granted for 20 years from the date of application. Methods of medical treatments, plant or animal varieties, and computer programs are not, at present, patentable.

As Israel is a member of the Berne Convention, no formal application is required to obtain copyright protection. Computer software is protected under the general copyright laws as "literary works." Copyright protection continues for the length of the author's life plus 50 years. Trademarks are protected under the Trade Marks Ordinance, and appellations of origin are protected under the Appellations of Origin (Protection) Law. Any proprietor of a trademark used, or proposed to be used in Israel, may apply for registration of the mark. The term of protection for a trademark is seven years, which may be renewed indefinitely for periods of 14 years.

Foreign Investment Climate

The Israeli government places a high priority on encouraging foreign investment in the Israeli economy. There are generally no restrictions for foreign investors doing business in Israel and, except in certain departments of the defense industry which are closed to outside investors, there are no restrictions on foreign investment in the private sector. Investments in regulated industries (e.g., banking and insurance) require prior government approval.

All benefits available to Israelis are available to foreign investors, and there is specific legislation to encourage foreign investment which gives the foreign investors certain advantages, such as reduced tax rates for longer periods of time than for residents.

Foreign investors are granted national treatment and are encouraged to participate in the ongoing Israeli privatization program.

Current Leaders & Political Parties

(Update: International Academy at Santa Barbara *http://www.iasb.org/cwl*)

State, Government, and Political Party Leaders:

Pres.: Ezer Weizman

Ministers:

Prime Min. and Min. of Defense: Benjamin Netanyahu

Foreign Affairs: David Levy

Finance: Dan Meridor

Education and Culture: Zevulun Hammer

Construction and Housing: Benjamin Ben-Eliezer

Internal Security: Avigdor Kahalani

Science and Technology: Binyamin Begin

Communications: Limor Livnat

Health: Dr. Ephraim Sneh

Economics and Planning: Yossi Beilin

Industry and Trade: Natan Sharansky

Religious Affairs: Prof. Shimon Shitreet

Interior: Haim Ramon

Labor and Social Affairs: Ora Namir

Energy and Infrastructure: Dr. Gonen Segev

Transportation: Yisrael Kessar

Other Officials:

Speaker of the Knesset (Parliament): Shevah Weiss

Ambassador to U.S.: Itamar Rabinovich

Perm. Rep. to U.N.: Gad Ya'acobi

Political Parties:

Likud, Labor, Natl. Religious Party, Democratic Front (Communist), Shas, Moledet, Arab Democratic Party, Meretz, Tsomet, United Torah Judiasm, Yi'ud

Political Influences on Business

It is expected that the recent agreements between Israel and her Arab neighbors will promote a climate conducive to business investment in the region.

Many aspects of Israeli life are governed by religious law. In observance of Shabbat (sundown Friday to sundown Saturday), most public transportation and Israel's national airline do not operate. Most businesses and government offices are closed from Friday afternoon to Sunday morning. Laws of *Kashrut* (kosher requirements for food) also restrict the importation and selling of certain foods and beverages in Israel.

Israel is a parliamentary democracy. The president is elected by the *Knesset*, a unicameral parliament, for a five-year term. Traditionally, the president has selected the leader of the party most able to form a government to become prime minister. The prime minister exercises executive power. A new law which will affect the 1996 elections calls for direct election of the prime minister rather than presidential selection. This experiment is part of an effort to democratize Israel's political process even further.

The Knesset's 120 members are elected to four-year terms, although the prime minister may decide to call for new elections before the end of the term or the prime minister's government can fall on a vote of no-confidence in the Knesset. The president then has the option of asking the current prime minister to form a new government. If he cannot, new elections take place for the Knesset. A total of eleven political parties are currently represented in the 13th and current Knesset. They include: Labor, Likud, Meretz, Tzomet, Shas, National Religious Party, United Torah Judaism, Hadash, Moledet, Yi'ud, and the Arab Democratic Party.

Following the assassination of Yitzhak Rabin in November 1995, Shimon Peres became Prime Minister. In 1996, Peres' Labor Party lost a close election to the Likud Party. Likud's Benjamin Netanyahu became the new Prime Minister.

Contacts in the U.S.A. & in Israel

Contacts in the United States:

EMBASSY OF THE STATE OF ISRAEL
3514 International Drive, N.W.
Washington, D.C. 20008
Tel: (202) 364-5500 or 364-5590
Fax: (202) 364-5423

U.S. DEPARTMENT OF STATE:
Bureau of Consular Affairs
Tel: (202) 647-5225
Israel Desk
Tel: (202) 647-3930

U.S. DEPARTMENT OF COMMERCE
Israel Desk
Tel: (202) 482-1870
Fax: (202) 482-1857

ISRAEL GOVERNMENT TOURIST OFFICE
350 Fifth Avenue
19th Floor
New York, N.Y. 10118
Tel: (212) 560-0650
Fax: (212) 629-4368

GOVERNMENT OF ISRAEL TRADE CENTER
350 Fifth Avenue
New York, N.Y. 10118
Tel: (212) 560-0660
Fax: (212) 564-8964

AMERICA-ISRAEL CHAMBER OF COMMERCE
AND INDUSTRY, INC.
The Empire State Bldg.
350 Fifth Avenue
Suite 1919
New York, N.Y. 10118
Tel: (212) 971-0310

Contacts in Israel:

THE INTERNATIONAL COUNTRY CODE FOR
ISRAEL IS [972].

THE EMBASSY OF THE UNITED STATES
71 Hayarkon Street
PSC 98, Box 100
Tel Aviv 63903
APO AE 09830
Tel: [972] (3) 517-4338
Telex: 33376 USFCS IL
Fax: [972] (3) 663449

ISRAEL-AMERICAN CHAMBER OF COMMERCE
AND INDUSTRY
35 Shaul Hamelech Boulevard
P.O. Box 33174
Tel Aviv, Israel
Tel: [972] (3) 252-341
Telex: 32129 BETAM IL

THE COMMITTEE FOR ECONOMIC GROWTH OF
ISRAEL (CEGI)
5301 North Ironwood Road
Milwaukee, Wisconsin 53217
Tel: (414) 961-1000

DUN & BRADSTREET (ISRAEL) LTD.
Postal Address: P.O. Box 50200, 61500
Tel Aviv, Israel
Street Address: City Palace, 27 Hamered
Street, Floor C-2, 68125 Tel Aviv, Israel
Tel: [972] (3) 510-3355
Fax: [972] (3) 510-3397

PRESIDENT EZER WEIZMAN
Beit Hanasi
3 Hanasi Street
92188 Jerusalem, State of Israel

PRIME MINISTER BENJAMIN NETANYAHU
3 Kaplan Street
Kiryat Ben-Gurion
91919 Jerusalem, State of Israel

 Passport/Visa Requirements

Visa Information   Tel: (202) 663-1225

U.S. citizens do not require a tourist or business visa to visit Israel provided that they possess a passport valid for at least nine further months of travel and that they have either a return (or onward) ticket or funds to purchase such a ticket.

On arrival, U.S. passports are endorsed gratis for a three month's stay; this endorsement can be renewed.

Faux Pas: A visiting U.S. executive assumed that an Israeli businessman wanted to be bribed when the Israeli stabbed the forefinger of one hand at the open palm of his other hand (like an impatient bellhop demanding a tip). The American soon found that he had completely misread the situation. The Israeli's action was an idiomatic negative gesture meaning "grass will grow on my palm before this comes to pass."

Italy

Official Name:	Italian Republic (Republica Italiana)
Official Language:	Italian
Population:	58.2 million (1995)
Population Growth:	0.2% (1992)
Area:	301,230 sq. km. (120,492 sq. mi.); about the size of Georgia and Florida combined
Natural Resources:	mercury, potash, marble, sulfur, dwindling natural gas and crude oil reserves, fish, coal
Major Cities:	Rome (capital), Milan, Turin, Naples

Cultural Note: The Italians, and their ancestors, the Romans, invented many of the business practices we use today. Their innovations included banking, insurance, and even double-entry bookkeeping. Do not let Italian friendliness and chatter lull you into forgetting that they are very astute businesspeople.

Age Breakdown

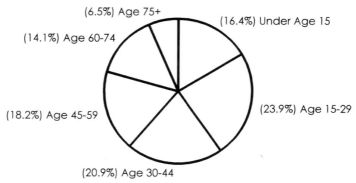

(6.5%) Age 75+

(14.1%) Age 60-74

(16.4%) Under Age 15

(23.9%) Age 15-29

(18.2%) Age 45-59

(20.9%) Age 30-44

Life Expectancy: 73 years male; 80 years female (1990)

 ## Time

"Time is money" is not an Italian aphorism. Although foreign business executives are expected to be relatively punctual for business appointments, Italians may not be. However, you should phone if you expect to be more than five minutes late.

Foreigners are generally expected to be on time for social engagements.

Italy is one hour ahead of Greenwich Mean Time (G.M.T. + 1), which is six hours ahead of U.S. Eastern Standard Time (E.S.T. + 6).

 ## Holidays

(Update: Getting Through Customs *http://www.getcustoms.com*)

New Year's Day	1 January
Easter Monday	varies
Anniversary of the Liberation	25 April
Labor Day	1 May
St. John (Florence and Genoa)	24 June
Sts. Peter and Paul (Rome)	29 June
St. Rosalia (Palermo)	15 July
Ferragosto and Assumption	varies
All Saints Day	1 November

St. Ambrogio (Milan)	7 December
St. Stephen's Day	26 December
New Year's Eve	31 December

In addition, the observance of many regional holidays may close businesses. July and August are poor months for conducting business since many firms close for vacation. The same is true during Christmas and New Year. Be sure to check with local contacts to confirm these and additional holidays.

Work Week

Normal business hours are from 8 or 9 A.M. to noon or 1 P.M. and from 3 to 6 or 7 P.M. Working hours for the various ministries of the government are normally from 8 A.M. to 2 P.M. without intermission. Bank hours are from 8:30 A.M. to 1:30 P.M. and 3:00–4:00 P.M.; they are closed on Saturdays.

Religious/Societal Influences on Business

The vast majority of Italians are raised Roman Catholic, although the Republic of Italy has no official religion. The Catholic Church remains influential in Italy, although it was unable to prevent the legalization of divorce and abortion in the 1970s.

If the Church has diminished importance in Italy, so does the other icon of Italian culture, the family. Long before Italy was united into one country, the family was the institution which provided stability and order. Several generations lived under one roof, and most of the adults worked in the family business.

Today, both a falling birth rate and economics have changed the family. Households now need two incomes, so more women work. Many Italians have moved away from their traditional homes in search of employment. Today the extended family with several generations under one roof is the exception, not the rule.

5 Cultural Tips

1. The Italian bureaucracy and legal system is notoriously slow. One reason for this is that Italy is burdened by over 2,000 years of law. New laws are added but old ones are rarely taken off the books, even laws dating back to the Roman Empire! The recent influx of EU regulations has only made things more difficult.

2. Sooner or later, everyone falls afoul of the extensive and sometimes contradictory Italian legal system. The tax codes are similarly hazardous. One Italian president

claimed that if Italians paid all of their taxes, they'd owe 150% of their income! Get good local legal representation; you will need it.

3. Italian firms tend to have a fairly rigid hierarchy, with little visible fraternization between the ranks. This doesn't necessarily indicate a lack of communication. Even though you may be dealing with the top ranks of executives, the lower ranks of employees may also be evaluating your proposal.

4. Everyone tends to speak at once in Italian gatherings. This goes for business meetings as well as social events. It is possible for Italians to conduct a meeting in a more orderly fashion, but only if those rules are established in the beginning.

5. Italian executives often have more than one business card. One card will contain all important business information, including the person's educational degrees and/or professional titles, plus all contact information, phone and fax numbers, Internet address, and so on. They may have a second card without the extensive professional titles. (Italians who lack this second card may instead cross out these titles on their card. This does not mean that those titles have been revoked! Instead, it means that the two of you have established a less formal relationship, and you do not have to address the Italian by his or her title.) Finally, there is a third card for social occasions. This is a visiting card, and contains only the person's name, with no titles, addresses, or phone numbers.

 Economic Overview

Italy, representing the world's fifth largest economy, continues to transform itself. The government continues on a path of privatization and is reducing its role in the economy. As this rationalization of the economy moves forward, the economy is expected to offer even more opportunities to the U.S. as both a buyer of U.S. goods and for investment.

The Italian economy has recovered strongly from the 1993 recession. Growth in 1994 was 2.2% and 3.2% in 1995. A strong export performance, driven by the weak lira, has been key to this recovery.

Cultural Note: It has been suggested that Italians add numerous gestures to their speech because the Italian language is fractured into many different dialects, and the gestures assist comprehension. Speakers of some dialects do have difficulty communicating with other Italians. The dialect of Tuscany has been selected as the national dialect and is taught in schools.

Comparative Data

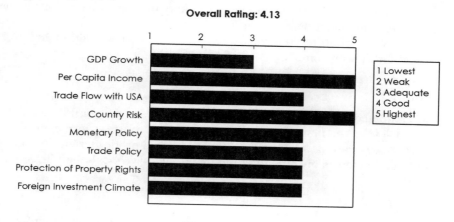

Overall Rating: 4.13

	1	2	3	4	5
GDP Growth					
Per Capita Income					
Trade Flow with USA					
Country Risk					
Monetary Policy					
Trade Policy					
Protection of Property Rights					
Foreign Investment Climate					

1 Lowest
2 Weak
3 Adequate
4 Good
5 Highest

Country Risk Rating

Gross Domestic Product: $1.01 trillion
GDP Growth: 2.2%
Per Capita Income: $18,276

Trade Flows with the U.S.A.

Rank as Export Market for U.S.A. Goods & Services: 16th
U.S.A. Exports to Italy: $8.8 billion
Growth Rate of Exports: 22%
U.S.A. Imports from Italy: $16.5 billion
Growth Rate of Imports: 12%
Rank as a Supplier of Imports into the U.S.A.: 12th

Top U.S.A. Exports to Italy: Machinery; aircraft and parts; electrical components; medical and optical equipment; mineral fuel; organic chemicals; woodpulp/paper, wood; motor vehicles; pharmaceuticals.

Top U.S.A. Prospects for Export to Italy: Aircraft and parts; computer software; industrial chemicals; computer services; telecommunications equipment; computers and peripherals; electronic components; process controls; laboratory scientific equipment.

Credit Terms

Dun & Bradstreet rates Italy as having excellent capacity to meet outstanding payment liabilities. It carries the lowest degree of risk.

Open account terms of 30 to 90 days are most commonly used, although letter of credit is advised for new customers.

Monetary Policy

Inflation was estimated at 5.2% in 1995 and is predicted at 4.5% for 1996. Inflation, which was below 4% for the first time in 25 years in 1994, returned as a central problem in 1995. Lira devaluation, tax increases, and increased profit margins by industry are cited as the main factors pushing inflation up. *Monetary Unit*: Italian lira.

Trade Policy

TARIFFS: Italy applies the European Union tariffs. Duty rates on manufactured goods from the United States generally range from 5 to 8%. Agricultural products face higher rates and special levies. Most raw materials enter duty free or at low rates.

IMPORT LICENSING: With the exception of a small group of primarily agricultural goods, practically all goods originating from the United States can be imported without import licenses. Import licenses, when required, are generally granted quickly for goods of U.S. origin.

Various apparel and textile products, and controlled items such as arms and munitions are the most frequently regulated items.

IMPORT TAXES: A 19% value-added tax is applied to most goods and services. A 9% VAT applies to processed foods and a 4% rate applies to basic foods and medicines.

Excise taxes are levied on a small number of products such as soft drinks, wine, beer, spirits, tobacco, sugar, and petroleum products.

Protection of Intellectual Property Rights

Italy is a member of the World Intellectual Property Organization, a party to the Berne and Universal Copyright conventions, the Paris Industrial Property convention, the Patent Cooperation Treaty, and the Madrid Agreement on International Registration of Trademarks.

Patents are granted for 15 years from the effective filing date of application. Trademarks are registered for 20 years from the effective filing date and are renewable for similar periods. Copyright protection for an author's work exists for the life of the author, plus 50 years after his death.

Foreign Investment Climate

Official Italian policy is to encourage foreign investment. For the most part, foreign investors will not find major impediments to investing in Italy. One hundred percent foreign ownership of corporations is allowed. The government does, however, have the authority to block mergers involving foreign firms for reasons essential to the national economy or if the home government of the foreign firm applies discriminatory measures against Italian firms.

There are several industry sectors which are either closely regulated or prohibited outright to foreign investors. These include domestic air transport and aircraft manufacturing. The government operates several monopolies, including petroleum, railroads, electrical generation and transmission, and production of cigars and cigarettes. A privatization program is reducing the state role in these sectors. Italy maintains restrictions and/or limits on foreign investment in banking, insurance, and shipping. Outside these sectors, there are no screening or blocking procedures directed solely at foreign investment.

Companies can bring in foreign workers only after certifying that no unemployed Italian is available to perform the expected duties.

Switzerland has the largest stock of foreign direct investment in Italy, followed by the U.S.A. *Monetary Unit*: Italian lira.

 ## Current Leaders & Political Parties

(Update: International Academy at Santa Barbara *http://www.iasb.org/cwl*)

State, Government, and Political Party Leaders:
President: Oscar Luigi Scalfaro

Council of Ministers:
Prime Min. and Min. of Treasury: Romano Prodi
Foreign Affairs: Lamberto Dini
Interior: Giorgio Napolitano
Finance: Vincenzo Visco
Defense: Beniamino Andreatta
Education: Luigi Berlinguer
Public Works and Environment: Antonio DiPietro
Transport and Merchant Marine: Claudio Burlando
Dep. Prime Min. and Min. of Posts and Telecommunications: Antonio Maccanico
Industry, Commerce, Crafts, and Foreign Trade: Pierluigi Bersani
Health: Rosi Bindi
University, Scientific, and Technological Research: Giorgio Salvini

Other Officials:

> Pres. of the Cncl. of State: Giorgio Crisci
>
> Pres. of the Senate: Nicola Mancino
>
> Pres. of the Chamber: Luciano Violante
>
> Pres. of the Constitutional Court: Francesco Paolo Casavola
>
> Ambassador to U.S.: Ferdinando Salleo
>
> Perm. Rep. to U.N.: Francesco Paolo Fulci

Political Parties:

> Go Italy, Italian Popular Party, Christian Democratic Center, Democratic Party of the Left, Natl. Alliance, Socialist Party, Democratic Alliance, Italian Socialist Mov., Northern League, Italian Republican Party (PRI), Union for Federalism, Centrist Union, People's Party, Radical Party, Union of Democratic Socialists, Green Party

 Political Influences on Business

Italy is a republic whose government is divided into three spheres of power: the Parliament, the government (which performs an executive function), and the judicial. The President of the Republic (who has limited responsibilities in all three spheres) and the constitutional court help to maintain an equilibrium between these branches. The President of the Republic's most important functions are to nominate the prime minister and his cabinet, and to dissolve parliament.

Parliament consists of the Chamber of Deputies and the Senate. Over time, the Chamber of Deputies has become the leading body, but each is equivalent in power. A large part of the work of Parliament takes place in committees.

The executive functions are exercised by the government, which consists of the Prime Minister and his Council of Ministers. The Prime Minister is the President of the Council and the leading figure in the government. His power is derived from the day-to-day running of the government, chairing the council and setting its agenda, as well as signing legislation. There are twenty-two ministers, including four without portfolio. The ministries form the basic structure of the state's public administration by implementing the policies and laws of the state.

The justice system consists of four branches (constitutional, common, administrative, and special), which are essentially independent of each other.

Although the power of the State is primarily centralized, the twenty regions have authority for the administration of some public functions and for enacting certain specific legislation (e.g. healthcare).

An important factor in the government and the state is the power of the political parties. Because no party commanded a parliamentary majority for almost 45 years, coalition government was the norm. Any return to a political government following elections is expected to be based on a coalition, whether of the center-right or center-left.

Contacts in the U.S.A. & in Italy

Contacts in the United States:

THE EMBASSY OF THE REPUBLIC OF ITALY
1601 Fuller Street, N.W.
Washington, D.C. 20009
Tel: (202) 328-5500
Fax: (202) 462-3605

THE HOLY SEE APOSTOLIC NUNCIATURE
3339 Massachusetts Avenue, N.W.
Washington, D.C. 20008
Telephone: (202) 333-7121

U.S. DEPARTMENT OF STATE
Bureau of Consular Affairs
Tel: (202) 647-5225
Country Desk Officer, Italy
Tel: (202) 647-4426

U.S. DEPARTMENT OF COMMERCE
Country Desk Officer, Italy
Tel: (202) 482-2177

ITALIAN GOVERNMENT TOURIST BOARD
(ENIT)
630 Fifth Avenue
Suite 1565
New York, N.Y. 10111
Tel: (212) 245-4822
Fax: (212) 586-9249

Contacts in Italy:

U.S. EMBASSY
Via Veneto 119/A
Rome, Italy or
Box 100 APO AE 09624
Tel: [39] (6) 46741
Telex: 622322 AMBRMA
Fax: [39] (6) 488-2672

U.S. INFORMATION SERVICE
Via Boncompagni 2,
00187, Rome, Italy
Tel: 011-39-6-4674-2655

DUN & BRADSTREET KOSMOS S.P.A.
Postal Address: Casella Postal 10052,
20100 Milan, Italy
Street Address: Via dei Valtorta 48,
20127 Milan, Italy
Tel: [39] (2) 284-551
Fax: [39] (2) 884-55500

PRESIDENT OSCAR LUIGI SCALFARO
Office of the President
Palazzo del Quirinale
00187 Rome, Republic of Italy

PRIME MINISTER ROMANO PRODI
Office of the Prime Minister
Palazzo Chigi
Piazza Colonna 370
00100 Rome, Republic of Italy

THE HOLY SEE (EMBASSY)
Vatican City
Villino Pacelli, Via Aurelia 294
00165 Rome; APO AE 09624
Tel: 011-396-46741
Telex: 622322 AMBRMC

THE AMERICAN CHAMBER OF COMMERCE IN ITALY
Via Cantu 1
20123 Milano
Tel: [39] (2) 869-0661
Telex: 352128 AMCHAM I
Fax: [39] (2) 805-7737

There are further U.S. Consular contacts available locally in: Genoa, Milan, Naples, Palermo, and Florence. Contact the Department of Commerce Desk, or State Desk listed above for further information.

 ## Passport/Visa Requirements

Visa Information   Tel: (202) 663-1225

U.S. citizens traveling to Italy as tourists, in possession of a valid U.S. passport, do not need a visa to enter Italy for a stay not exceeding 90 days. For any other reason or for a tourist stay longer than three months, a visa is necessary.

All persons or entities engaging in business in Italy in any capacity must be registered with the local Chamber of Commerce, Industry, and Agriculture, a quasi-government office operating essentially as a field office of the Ministry of Industry and Commerce. Depending on the kind of company, additional registrations may be necessary.

Faux Pas: After being briefed by her male colleagues, an American businesswoman visited Italy expecting to encounter a touch-oriented culture. To her surprise, she encountered very little touching at all. In point of fact, it is Italian men whose gestures include frequent touching, and that is only with other men. Italian women rarely touch other women. And tactile contact between genders in Italy is primarily reserved for sexual situations.

A 1977 study comparing the touching behaviors of North Americans, Germans, and Italians found that Italian men touch each other more than either North American or German men. However, North American men engaged in tactile behavior more often than Italian women!

Japan

Official Name:	Japan (Nihon)
Official Language:	Japanese
Government System:	Parliamentary democracy under constitutional monarch
Population:	125.3 million (1995)
Population Growth:	0.32% (1994)
Area:	377,765 sq. km. (145,711 sq. mi.) slightly smaller than California
Natural resources:	negligible mineral resources, fish
Major Cities:	Tokyo (capital), Yokohama, Osaka, Kyoto, Nagoya, Sapporo, Kobe

Cultural Note: Most Japanese know what will be discussed in a meeting, how everyone feels about it, and how it will impact their business before they ever get there. The purpose of a Japanese meeting is for the participants to reach some sort of consensus. A flexible agenda is necessary so that the discussions may flow more freely. When a foreigner tries to adhere religiously to an agenda, it inhibits the creation of consensus. Even worse, this implies that the foreigner's time in Japan is limited, which weakens the foreigner's bargaining position.

Age Breakdown

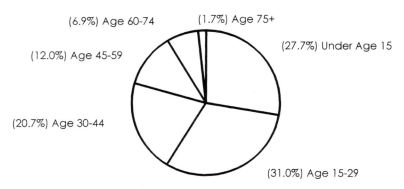

(6.9%) Age 60-74
(1.7%) Age 75+
(27.7%) Under Age 15
(12.0%) Age 45-59
(20.7%) Age 30-44
(31.0%) Age 15-29

Life Expectancy: 76 years male; 82 years female (1993)

 Time

Japan is nine hours ahead of Greenwich Mean Time (G.M.T. + 9), or you can add 14 hours to U.S. Eastern Standard Time (E.S.T. +14). It is important to be punctual to all business engagements in Japan.

 Holidays

(Update: Getting Through Customs *http://www.getcustoms.com*)

When a national holiday falls on a Sunday in Japan, the following Monday is a compensatory day off. In addition, many Japanese companies and government offices traditionally close during the New Year's holiday season (December 28–January 3), "Golden Week" (April 29–May 5), and the traditional O-Bon Festival (usually August 12–15).

New Year's Day	January 1
Adult's Day	January 15
National Foundation Day	February 11
Vernal Equinox Day	late March
Greenery Day	April 29
Constitution Memorial Day	May 3
(Declared Official Holiday)	May 4
Children's Day	May 5

Respect-for-the-Aged	September 15
Autumnal Equinox Day	late September
Health-Sports Day	October 10
Culture Day	November 3
Labor Thanksgiving Day	November 23
Emperor's Birthday	December 23

Work Week

Monday through Friday, 9:00 A.M. to 5:00 P.M.; many companies also work Saturday mornings, 9:00 A.M. to 12:00 noon; 42.9 average weekly hours worked (April 1995).

Religious/Societal Influences on Business

Many Japanese say that they are not religious. However, since the philosophy known as Shinto is so pervasive, it does influence Japanese behavior.

As Confucianism is to China, so is Shinto to Japan.

Both Confucianism and Shinto are usually described as philosophies rather than religions. It is quite possible to adhere to Confucian or Shinto precepts while being a practicing Buddhist or Christian.

Shinto, or "the way of the gods," is deeply interwoven with Japanese tradition. It is so interconnected to the traditions of the Japanese State that the two cannot be entirely separated.

Shinto does not establish specific deities to be worshiped, as do most religions. (In fact, it asserts that minor deities are everywhere in nature; each mountain or river has a god.) However, it does detail numerous rituals and customs, which foreigners often perceive as religious ceremonies.

It is Shinto that maintained that the Japanese Emperor was a God, a concept which the U.S. Occupation Forces insisted be denied. The 1946 radio announcement by the late Emperor Hirohito that he was not divine was a traumatic event for the Japanese. Shinto was also dethroned as Japan's state belief system; Japan now has no official religion.

The Japan-centric beliefs of Shinto reinforce the Japan-first attitude which is so vexing to foreign negotiators.

Buddhism is the largest conventional religion in Japan. While officially followed by 38.3% of the population, many more Japanese will participate in occasional Buddhist observances. In fact, there is a saying that "Japanese are born Shinto but die Buddhist." This reflects the preference for Shinto celebrations at birth and for Buddhist ritual at funerals.

Only about 1.2% of Japanese describe themselves as Christian.

5 Cultural Tips

1. Do not expect to make Japan the headquarters for all your Pac Rim/Asian operations. There are vast differences among cultures in Japan, China, Korea, Malaysia, and so on. Neither is it generally wise to place an executive from any other Asian country in a management position in Japan.

2. It is important to view your company's objectives in a global, high-level manner, with an understanding of how all the pieces relate. Be prepared to communicate this big picture to the Japanese, and be ready to answer questions about any and all aspects of the presentation in depth, and in a nonlinear manner. While U.S. executives generally consider it logical to resolve each item one-by-one, and will "hammer" at a point of disagreement, the Japanese look at the overall picture. The Japanese believe that many issues may be explored (and resolved) simultaneously.

3. Emphasize and build on points of agreement with your Japanese counterparts. A persuasive, positive presentation is compatible with Japanese culture, a high-pressure, confrontational approach is not.

4. Always give your Japanese contacts time, whether it entails: a) e-mailing your questions two weeks ahead of your meeting so you know they will be able to answer them comfortably in person; b) waiting through what may seem an interminable amount of silence for a Japanese executive to respond to a question; or c) allowing the Japanese negotiating team weeks to reach their consensus. Never impose a U.S. concept of time on Japanese culture.

5. Do not be offended by the many personal questions the Japanese may ask you. Expect to be asked about your job, your title, your responsibilities, the number of employees that report to you, and so on. Japanese is a very complex language with many forms of address. The Japanese will need a lot of information in order to decide which form to use when speaking to you. (Most of this subtlety will be lost when translated into English, but it is important to the Japanese.)

Cultural Note: Do not be surprised if your Japanese interpreter translates Japanese into English almost simultaneously, but waits for you (the English speaker) to finish before translating your statements into Japanese. Unlike English, Japanese is a very predictable language. By the time a Japanese executive is halfway through a sentence, the translator probably knows how the sentence will end. Indeed, it would be very impolite of a Japanese to end a sentence with an unexpected choice of words.

Economic Overview

As the world's second largest economy and second largest export market for U.S. goods and services, Japan offers large-scale opportunities and strategic benefits for U.S. firms. As an expensive, highly competitive and highly complex market, Japan remains a challenging place to do business. U.S. firms hoping to succeed in Japan must take a long-term approach to entering the market and building a market presence.

Although Japan's overall economic outlook remains cloudy, the outlook for U.S. exports to Japan remains positive. Japan's imports of U.S. goods increased by 20% in 1995 to $64.3 billion. The U.S. government has worked with the Japanese to eliminate trade barriers in Japan through trade negotiations and high visibility trade promotions.

Japan remains a highly homogenous society and business practices are characterized by long-standing, close-knit relations among individuals and firms. Regulatory processes and local business practices in Japan reflect systems designed for indigenous needs with little or no consideration given for potential participation by foreign companies. Even for Japanese businesspeople, it takes time to develop relationships and become an "insider." For the non-Japanese businessperson, the task is formidable, but not impossible.

The Japanese consumer has traditionally been conservative and brand-conscious. However, during the recessionary environment of the past few years, opportunities are emerging for purveyors of "value." More fragmented buying habits are emerging among a new generation of more individualistic consumers. As a result of this, Japan's complex distribution system is now changing dramatically.

Comparative Data

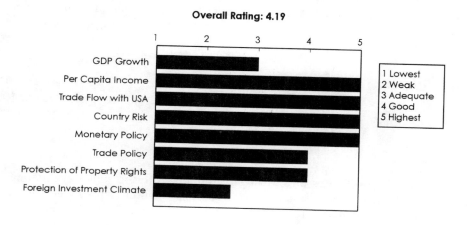

Overall Rating: 4.19

Country Risk Rating
Gross Domestic Product: $5.6 trillion
GDP Growth: 0.8%
Per Capita Income: $44,455

Trade Flows with the U.S.A.:
Rank as Export Market for U.S.A. Goods & Services: 2
U.S.A. Exports to Japan: $64.3 billion (1995)
Growth Rate of Exports: 20%
U.S.A. Imports from Japan: $123.5 billion (1995)
Growth Rate of Imports: 4%
Rank as a Supplier of Imports into the U.S.A.:   2

Top U.S.A. Exports to Japan: Machinery, electronic components, aircraft, medical and optical equipment, wood, motor vehicles, cereals, meat, fish and seafood, tobacco.

Top U.S.A. Prospects for Export to Japan: Computers and peripherals, electronic components, autos/light trucks/vans, medical equipment, computer software, architectural/engineering/construction services, apparel, paper and paperboard, telecommunications equipment, pet foods and supplies.

Country Risk Rating
Dun & Bradstreet rates Japan as having an excellent capacity to meet outstanding payment liabilities. It carries the lowest degree of risk when compared with other countries. Open account terms of 30 to 60 days are commonly used, with few cases of default reported.

Monetary Policy
Inflation is almost nonexistent; 1995 inflation was under 2% as were the rates in 1994 and 1993. *Monetary Unit* :Yen.

Trade Policy
TARIFFS: At 2%, tariff rates on industrial products entering Japan are among the lowest in the world. Almost all machinery imports are entered duty-free. However, import duties remain relatively high on some agricultural items and certain manufactured goods.
Goods with a value less than 10,000 yen are excluded from duty.

IMPORT LICENSING: Most goods qualify as freely importable and do not require an import license. The only exception are those commodities that fall under import quotas in which case the Japanese importer must apply for license approval. Rice, wheat, beef, and leather products are among the few remaining products subject to import quotas.

Use of chemicals and other additives in foods and cosmetics is regulated heavily.

IMPORT TAXES: In addition to customs duty, a 3% consumption tax is levied on all goods sold in Japan. Payment is required at the time of import declaration. Goods with a value of less than 10,000 yen are excluded from the consumption tax.

Protection of Intellectual Property Rights

It is necessary to file applications to register patents and trademarks in Japan to obtain protection, but prior filing in the United States can provide certain advantages if applications are filed promptly in Japan. It will be necessary to hire a Japanese attorney or patent practitioner to prosecute the patent or trademark application. Except for voluntary registration of computer programs, there is no system of copyright registration and U.S. copyrights and sound recordings are recognized in Japan by international treaty.

Patents are granted to the first to file an application for a particular invention, rather than to the first to invent. Patents are granted and valid for 20 years from the date the application is filed. It can take as long as five to six years on average to obtain a patent in Japan. An applicant can request accelerated examination.

Japan's trademark registration process is also slow. It takes on average four years to process a trademark registration in Japan.

Foreign Investment Climate

Japan has progressively liberalized its foreign direct investment regime and is open to foreign direct investment with certain exceptions. The level of foreign direct investment in Japan remains quite low when compared to its trading partners. In fact, Japan has 15 times as much direct investment abroad as foreign investment at home. U.S. external investment is 1.2 times the foreign investment within the country, and Britain is 1.3.

Although most Japanese legal restrictions on foreign direct investment have been eliminated, considerable bureaucratic discretion remains. While Japan's foreign exchange laws have shifted to expost notification of planned investments in most cases, in numerous sectors (e.g. agriculture, mining, forestry, fishing) prior notification is still required.

In the sectors which still require prior notification, the Japanese government retains the right to restrict foreign direct investment if it determines that the investment would seriously and adversely affect the smooth performance of the national economy.

Recent changes have made it easier for foreign retailers to invest in Japan.

Current Leaders & Political Parties

(Update: International Academy at Santa Barbara *http://www.iasb.org/cwl*)

Symbol of the State: Emperor Akihito
Prime Min.: Ryutaro Hashimoto
Foreign Affairs: Yukihiko Ikeda
Finance: Wataru Kubu
Internat. Trade: Shupei Tsukahara
Transport: Shizuka Kamei

Other Officials:

Ambassador to U.S.: Takakazu Kuriyama
Perm. Rep. to UN: Yoshio Hatano

Political Parties:

Liberal Democratic Party (LDP), Social Democratic Party (SDPJ), Komei Party (KMP), Democratic Socialist Party (DSP), New Frontier Party, Communist Party (JCP), Progressive United Social Democratic Party Alliance (P/USDP), Rengo, Japan New Party

Political Influences on Business

Japan is a strong democracy in which basic human rights are well respected. Under the constitution and in practice, the Emperor's role is essentially symbolic. Japan has a parliamentary form of government. The head of government, the prime minister, is elected by Japan's parliament, the National Diet. Elections to the Lower House, the more powerful of the Diet's two chambers, are held at least once very four years.

Upper House elections are held every three years, at which time half of the membership is up for election. Most of Japan's political parties espouse moderate or conservative domestic and foreign policies.

Japan's entrenched bureaucracy is often blamed for Japan's slowness to liberalize its policies toward foreign trade. However, Japan is a highly insular culture. Protection of the Japanese homeland is ingrained, and protectionist policies have widespread support. Even a massive overhaul of Japan's bureaucracy would not guarantee a change in trade policy.

Contacts in the U.S.A. & in Japan

Contacts in the United States:

EMBASSY OF JAPAN
2520 Massachusetts Ave., N.W.
Washington, D.C. 20008
Tel: (202) 939-6700
Fax: (202) 328-2187

U.S. DEPARTMENT OF STATE
Bureau of Consular Affairs
Tel: (202) 647-5225
Country Desk Officer, Japan
Tel: (202) 647-2912

U.S. DEPARTMENT OF COMMERCE
Office of Japan Trade Policy (OJTP)
Japan Export Information Center (JEIC)
International Trade Administration
Room 2320, Washington D.C. 20230
OJTP Tel: (202) 482-1820
Fax: (202) 482-0469
JEIC Tel: (202) 482-2425
Fax: (202) 482-0469
Japan Desk
Int'l Trade Admin.
Tel: (202) 482-2425
Japan National Tourist Organization
(JNTO)
Tel: (212) 757-5640

Contacts in Japan:

U.S. EMBASSY
Akasaka 1-chome
Minato-ku (107)
Tokyo
Mailing Address:
Unit 45004, Box 258
APO AP 96337-0001
Tel: [81] (3) 3224-5000
Fax: [81] (3) 3505-1862

THE AMERICAN CHAMBER OF COMMERCE OF
JAPAN
Fukide Bldg.
No. 2, 4-1-21 Toranomon
Minato-Ku
Tokyo
Tel: (03) 433-5381
Telex: 2425104 KYLE J

AMERICAN BUSINESS INFORMATION CENTER
(ABIC)
Tel: [81] (3)3225-5075
Fax: [81] (3)3589-4235
(U.S. Address: Unit 45004, Box 204, APO
AP 96337-5004)

THE AMERICAN CHAMBER OF COMMERCE IN
JAPAN (ACCJ)
5F, Bridgestone Toranomon Bldg.
3-25-2 Toranomon, Minato-ku, Tokyo
105
Tel: [81] (3) 3433-5381
Fax: [81] (3) 3436-1446

JAPANESE GOVERNMENT AGENCIES
JETRO
Import Promotion Dept.
2-2-5 Toranomon, Minato-ku, Tokyo 105
Tel: [81] (3) 3582-5562
Fax: [81] (3) 3582-5027

DUN & BRADSTREET INFORMATION SERVICES
JAPAN K.K.
Postal and Street Address: 5F Aobadai
Hills, 4–7–7 Aobadai, Meguro-ku,
Tokyo 153, Japan
Tel: [81] (3) 3481-3561

PRIME MINISTER RYUTARO HASHIMOTO
Prime Minister's Office
1-6-1, Nagata-cho
Chiyoda-ku
Tokyo 100, Japan

 ## Passport/Visa Requirements

Visa Information   Tel: (202) 663-1225

Entry Requirements: Passports are required. Onward/return tickets are required for visitors arriving on the visa waiver and may be requested for visitors arriving on other types of visas. Visas are not required for U.S. citizens for tourist/business stays of up to 90 days. However, anyone arriving under the terms of the 90-day visa waiver will not be allowed to extend his/her stay or adjust status. There are no exceptions to this rule.

Faux Pas: Japan is a "high-context" culture, where much information is communicated by subtle cues. This subtlety is far removed from the clear, dramatic nonverbal behavior of North Americans. The broad expressions and gestures of Westerners are sometimes disconcerting to the Japanese. A female executive found this out during a presentation when she noticed a man in the front row making faces at her. During her entire presentation, he was grimacing and pursing his lips. She felt he was being rude, and after her speech, she mentioned the man's behavior to a Japanese associate. An abject apology came back immediately from the Japanese man in question. He said that he was so mesmerized by her dramatic facial expressions and hadn't realized he was unconsciously mimicking her!

Malaysia

Official Name:	Malaysia
Official Language:	Bahasa Malaysia
Government System:	Federal parliamentary democracy with constitutional monarch
Population:	20 million (1995)
Population Growth:	2.4%
Area:	329,749 sq. km. (127,316 sq. mi.); slightly larger than New Mexico
Natural Resources:	Tin, crude oil, timber, copper, iron ore, natural gas, bauxite
Major Cities:	Kuala Lumpur (capital), Penang, Petaling Jaya, Ipoh, Malacca

Cultural Note: For the Pacific Rim, Malaysia has a relatively low population density (152.9 persons per square mile, compared with 258.2 per square mile in neighboring Indonesia). This low density has allowed Malaysia to keep large areas of its territory undeveloped. The Malaysian Timber Council estimates that as much as 75% of Malaysia's forests are protected (although many environmentialists would dispute this claim). Some forests are now being modified for recreation and eco-tourism. Environmental preservation has a high profile in Malaysia.

Age Breakdown

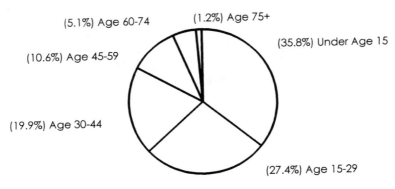

(5.1%) Age 60-74
(1.2%) Age 75+
(10.6%) Age 45-59
(35.8%) Under Age 15
(19.9%) Age 30-44
(27.4%) Age 15-29

Life Expectancy: 69 years male; 74 years female (1994)

 Time

Long-term planning is very big in Malaysia. The government continually announces goals to be met by specific dates. For example, Kuala Lumpur's new airport is to be completed by 1998. Malaysia is building a new capital city, Putrajaya, to be completed by 2008. And Prime Minister Mahathir Mohamad's ambitious "Vision 2020" program details the development of his country by the year 2020.

On a daily basis, however, time is more fluid. Foreigners are expected to arrive on time to business appointments, but Malaysians are not always prompt.

Arrival times at social events can involve complex rules of precedence. But as a general guideline, foreigners should arrive about fifteen minutes late.

Malaysia is eight hours ahead of Greenwich Mean Time (G.M.T. + 8), which is thirteen hours ahead of U.S. Eastern Standard Time (E.S.T. + 13).

 Holidays

(Update: Getting Through Customs *http://www.getcustoms.com*)

This list is a working guide. Dates should be corroborated before final travel plans are made. In cases where holidays fall on Saturday or Sunday, commercial establishments may be closed the preceding Friday or following Monday.

The scheduled Islamic holidays dates are approximations since they depend upon lunar observations; the actual celebrations could be a day or two off. Islamic holidays can be spelled different ways in English.

The holidays in Malaysia vary from state to state. The heavily Muslim states do not celebrate any non-Islamic holidays (including Easter, Christmas, and Western New Year's Day).

New Year's Day	1 January
Kuala Lumpur City Day	1 February
First Day of Chinese New Year	varies
Hari Raya Puasa	varies
Hari Raya Haji	varies
Labor Day	1 May
Wesak Day [Buddhist holiday]	varies
Awal Muharam	varies
Agong's Birthday	1 June
Prophet Mohammed's Birthday	varies
Malaysian National Day	31 August
Deepavali	varies
Christmas	25 December

Work Week

Although most Malays are Muslim, not all of Malaysia follows the traditional Islamic work week pattern (Friday is the Islamic Holy Day, so the traditional Muslim "weekend" is Thursday and Friday). In those areas where Friday is a work day, Muslim workers will take a two-hour break on Friday afternoons to attend a mosque.

Malaysia is divided into thirteen states. Only the following five states follow the Islamic work week (Saturday through Wednesday): Perlis, Kedah, Kelantan, Terengganu, and Johor. All of these are in West (Peninsular) Malaysia. The Malaysian capital city, Kuala Lumpur, is in the state of Selangor, where the work week is Monday through Friday.

Business hours are generally from 8:00 A.M. to 5:00 P.M., Monday through Friday. Some offices will be open for a half-day on Saturdays, generally in the morning. In the 5 states which follow the Islamic work week (Saturday through Wednesday), some people work a half-day on Thursday.

The traditional lunchtime was from 12 noon (or 12:15 P.M.) to 2 P.M., but this generally has been reduced to a single hour, beginning at noon or 1 P.M. Nevertheless, many people will take longer than an hour for lunch.

Most government offices keep an 8:30 A.M. to 4:45 P.M. schedule, with a half day from 8:30 A.M. to noon on Saturday (on Thursday in the five aforementioned Muslim states).

Many Malaysian banks keep the traditional banking hours of 9:00 A.M. to 3:00 P.M., with a few hours on Saturday mornings (Thursday mornings in the five aforementioned Muslim states).

Shop hours vary. Most shops will open at 9 or 10 A.M., and will close at 6 or 7 P.M., 5 or 6 days a week.

Executives will often work far longer days than their subordinates. The Chinese especially, have reputations as workaholics.

Religious/Societal Influences on Business

Malaysia is a multicultural nation. Ethnic Malays, known as the *Bumiputera*, make up over 60% of the population; they hold the political power in Malaysia. Ethnic Chinese constitute the next largest group, followed by ethnic Indians. The latter are well-represented in the professional arena (especially in law). The Chinese dominate the business spheres.

Most religions are represented in Malaysia. Ethnic Malays and many Indians are Muslims. When forced to choose, most Chinese will list themselves as "Buddhist," but they are quite capable of following several religious traditions simultaneously.

The strident defense of Asian traditions by Malaysian Prime Minister Mahathir Mohamad has been summarized in his 1996 book, *The Voice of Asia*, coauthored by Shintaro Ishihara (Japanese politician and coauthor of *The Japan That Can Say No*). In this book, Mahathir proclaims:

> Westerners generally cannot rid themselves of (their) sense of superiority. They still consider their values and political and economic systems better than any others. It would not be so bad if it stopped at that; it seems, however, that they will not be satisfied until they have forced other countries to adopt their ways as well. Everyone must be democratic, but only according to the Western concept of democracy; no one can violate human rights, again according to their self-righteous interpretation of human rights. Westerners cannot seem to understand diversity.

The Malaysians are intent on maintaining their own cultural tradition, whether or not the West approves.

5 Cultural Tips

1. In multicultural Malaysia, your first job is to find out who you are talking to. Each of the three main ethnic groups, Malay, Indian, and Chinese, has their own traditions. The majority of Malaysian businesspeople are Chinese, and they share the

habits of overseas Chinese in Singapore, Hong Kong, or Taiwan. Their native language will be a Southern Chinese dialect, but they will probably speak to you in English. Ethnic Malays, called *Bumiputera*, dominate Malaysia's government. Although many educated Malays speak English, the law mandates that official correspondence with the Malaysian government be written in the native language, *Bahasa Malaysia*. Finally, while the native tongue of members of the Indian community could be one of several Indian languages, educated Indians speak English. Foreigners are most likely to encounter Indian Malaysians as lawyers or journalists.

2. Although the Chinese and Indians are immigrants to Malaysia, don't assume that they are newcomers. The Chinese began arriving in the 15th century! And, while many Indians came to Malaysia after World War I, it was Indian traders who brought Islam to Malaysia over 400 years ago. There is a good chance that a Chinese or Indian's ancestors were in Malaysia long before the U.S.A. was born!

3. Historically, there has been animosity between the majority of Malays and the Chinese who controlled Malaysia's wealth. As a result, the redistribution of wealth from Chinese to ethnic Malays has become official policy in Malaysia. This is done in several ways, including a law that requires that 30% of all new stock offerings must go to Bumiputera. Although they must pay for the stock, the value of many stocks rises quickly from the initial offering price. (The official Anticorruption Agency watches the government stock-allocation committees, preventing committee members from allocating promising stocks to themselves.)

4. Remember to follow the taboos typical of Islamic societies: eat only with your right hand (since the left hand is unclean), never expose the soles of your feet, dress modestly, and never touch anyone, even a child, on the head.

5. Malaysia is a country undergoing a rapid transition to a modern, industrialized society. Consequently, many old traditions are being lost. For example, the Chinese traditionally wore black only to a funeral, but black is now a preferred color for young Chinese on the dance floor. And both Malays and Indians speak softly, except at parties, when they can be just as raucous as any group on Earth. And Malaysians find dairy products disgusting, except for ice cream, which is quite welcome in the tropical climate.

Economic Overview

The Malaysian economy has grown more than 8% a year for the last eight years. Economic growth has averaged almost 7% per annum for the past three decades. Most sectors of the economy are very open to international trade, and U.S. products have been successful in almost all of them. U.S.-Malaysian bilateral relations are close and productive across the board.

Malaysia has been transformed from a low-income producer of commodities like tin, rubber, and palm oil into a middle income exporter of manufactured products. For example, Malaysia is the world's third largest producer (and largest exporter) of semiconductors. It is also the world's largest exporter of room air conditioners, color TV tubes, and VCRs. Although the population of Malaysia is only 20 million, it is a more important market for U.S. exports than many countries of much larger size. This market continues to grow rapidly in line with the ongoing expansion and transformation of the economy. The United States is Malaysia's second largest trading partner, accounting for 19% of its total trade. The U.S. was the largest foreign investor in Malaysia from 1991 through 1993, and third largest in 1994. The cumulative value of U.S. investments in Malaysia is more than $8 billion. The majority of foreign investment is in the oil and gas sector, with the rest in manufacturing, especially semiconductors and other electronic products.

Cultural Note: In the brave new world of Malaysia, there is no room for drug addiction. Draconian sentences are given for offenses. Any Malaysian citizen can be ordered to take a drug test, and failure to pass means a mandatory one-to-three year sentence in a rehabilitation camp.

Comparative Data

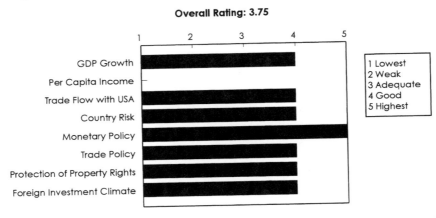

Overall Rating: 3.75

GDP Growth				
Per Capita Income				
Trade Flow with USA				
Country Risk				
Monetary Policy				
Trade Policy				
Protection of Property Rights				
Foreign Investment Climate				

1 Lowest
2 Weak
3 Adequate
4 Good
5 Highest

Country Risk Rating

Gross Domestic Product: $42 billion
GDP Growth: 8.5%
Per Capita Income: $3,627

Trade Flows with the U.S.A.

Rank as Export Market for U.S.A. Goods & Services: 17th

U.S.A Exports to Malaysia: $8.8 billion

Growth Rate of Exports: 25%

U.S.A. Imports from Malaysia: $17.4 billion

Growth Rate of Imports: 24%

Rank as a Supplier of Imports into the U.S.A.:   10th

Top U.S.A. Exports to Malaysia: Electronic components; machinery; aircraft and parts; medical and optical equipment; paper/paperboard; organic chemicals; plastics; ceramics; inorganic chemicals; iron and steel.

Top U.S.A. Prospects for Export to Malaysia: Electronic components; aircraft and parts; computer software; computers and peripherals; telecommunications equipment; franchising; industrial chemicals; pollution control equipment; oil and gas field machinery and services; medical equipment; sporting goods.

Credit Terms

Dun & Bradstreet rates Malaysia as having good capacity to meet outstanding payment liabilities.

Liberal credit terms such as open account are now widely acceptable, with letters of credit now accounting for just one-third of transactions. More secure terms (letters of credit) are still recommended on deals with smaller concerns and/or new accounts.

Monetary Policy

The government is aware of the inflationary potential of the economy's rapid development and expansion and closely monitors fiscal and monetary policies to ensure low inflation.

As a result, Malaysia's annual inflation rate has been below 5% for the last four years and is forecast at 4.1% in 1996. *Monetary Unit*: ringitt.

Trade Policy

TARIFFS: Import duties range from 0 to 200%, with the average duty rate being less than 10%. Higher rates apply to luxury goods.

Raw materials used directly for the manufacture of goods for export are exempted from import tariffs if such material is not produced locally or if local materials are not of acceptable quality and price.

IMPORT LICENSING: Import permits are required for arms and explosives, motor vehicles, dangerous drugs and chemicals, plants, soil, tin ore, and certain essential foodstuffs.

IMPORT TAXES: A sales tax of 10% is levied on most imported goods. The sales tax is not applied to raw materials and machinery used in export production.

Protection of Intellectual Property Rights

Malaysia has an effective legal system and adequate legislation to protect private property. It also has a strong regime for protecting intellectual property rights (IPR). In 1986 the government passed a strong patent law, and in 1987 it enacted a copyright law that explicitly protects computer software. Trademark infringement has not been a major problem for U.S. companies, and patent protection is good. Malaysia has acceded to the Berne Convention, and the Paris Convention, and is a member of the World Intellectual Property Organization.

Patents registered in Malaysia generally have a 15-year duration. Copyright protection extends to computer software and lasts for life of the author plus 50 years. Under provisions of the Copyright Act of 1987, as amended in 1990, Malaysian authorities are allowed to enter and search premises suspected of infringement and to seize infringing copies and reproduction equipment.

Foreign Investment Climate

The Malaysian government welcomes manufacturing investment, especially in high-tech areas. One-hundred-percent foreign ownership in manufacturing is permitted only in certain instances.

Investment approval depends on the size of the investment, whether or not it includes local equity participation, the type of financing required, the ability of existing and planned infrastructure to support the effort, and the existence of a local or foreign market for the output. The criteria are applied in a local nondiscriminatory manner, except in the rare case when a local and a foreign firm propose identical projects.

Domestic services industries are protected tightly, with foreign firms generally limited to 30% equity shares in new ventures. The government severely restricts establishment in the financial service industry with the notable exception of fund management firms. No banking or insurance licenses are being awarded.

On a manufacturing project approval basis, the U.S. has been one of the top foreign investors in Malaysia for the last several years. In 1994, the approved proposed investment from the U.S. was $501 million, behind only Japan and Taiwan. These three countries made up approximately 75% of the total foreign investment in Malaysia in 1994.

Current Leaders & Political Parties

(Update: International Academy at Santa Barbara *http://www.iasb.org/cwl*)

Head of State: His Majesty Tuanku Jaafar Ibni Almarhum Tuanku Abdul Rahman

Cabinet Ministers:

Prime Min. and Min. of Home Affairs: Datuk Seri Dr. Mahathir Mohamad

Dep. Prime Min. and Min. of Finance: Datuk Seri Anwar Ibrahim

Human Resources: Datuk Lim Ah Lek

Youth and Sports: Tan Sri Muhyiddin Yassin

Land and Coop. Dev.: Datuk Osu Sukam

Works: Datuk Seri S. Samy Vellu

Foreign Affairs: Datuk Abdullah Haji Ahmed Badawi

Defense: Datuk Syed Hamid Albar

Rural Dev.: Datuk Annuar Musa

Information: Datuk Mohamad bin Rahmat

Transport: Dr. Ling Liong Sik

Internat. Trade and Industry: Datuk Seri Rafidah Aziz

Entrepreneur Dev.: Datuk Mustapa Mohamed

Primary Industries: Dr. Lim Keng Yaik

Science, Technology, and Environment: Law Hieng Ding

Energy, Telecommunications, and Posts: Datuk Leo Moggie

Culture, Arts, and Tourism: Datuk Haji Sabbaruddin Chik

Domestic Trade and Consumer Affairs: Dato Abu Omar Hassan

Natl. Unity and Community Dev.: Datin Paduka Hajah Zaleha Ismail

Other Officials:

Dir. Gen. of the Environment Dept.: Dr. Abu Bakar Jaafar

Pres. of the Senate: Dato' Seri Chan Choong Tak

Speaker of the House of Representatives: Datuk Mohamed Zahir Haji Ismail

Ambassador to U.S.: Dato' Dali Mahmud Hashim

Perm. Rep. to U.N.: Tan Sri Razali Ismail

Political Parties:

Natl. Front (BN), Democratic Action Party (DAP), Pan Malaysian Islamic Party (PAS)

Political Influences on Business

The Malaysian political environment is strongly favorable to international and domestic business development. U.S.-Malaysian bilateral relations are close and productive across the board.

Malaysia is a constitutional monarchy with a parliamentary system of government. In practice, power is strongly concentrated in the Prime Minister. He has traditionally been head of UMNO (the United Malays National Organization), the principal party in the governing coalition which has ruled Malaysia continuously since independence from the U.K. in 1957. The ruling coalition scored an impressive victory in the general elections held in April 1995. The position of monarch, the Yang di Pertuan Agong, is rotated among the rulers of nine of the thirteen states of Malaysia. The role has over time become almost entirely ceremonial and symbolic.

The government has taken a strong proactive role in the development and industrialization of the Malaysian economy. This has included significant state sector investment, a close alliance between government and the private business community, and a variety of policies and programs to bolster the economic status of the Malay and indigenous communities, commonly referred to as bumiputras. Tensions between the Malay, Chinese, and Indian communities were serious in the past. However, with rapid economic growth over the past several decades (in which all groups in the country have shared) these tensions have been reduced greatly.

Malaysia enjoys friendly relations with the United States and has worked with the U.S. on many issues, including for example the U.N. peacekeeping operations in Somalia. Malaysia has also contributed forces to U.N. operations in Cambodia and Bosnia. Malaysia is a member of ASEAN (Association of South East Asian States), founded in 1967 with Indonesia, the Philippines, Singapore, Thailand, and Brunei. The U.S. has strongly supported ASEAN, and participates in an annual dialogue with ASEAN members at the level of Foreign Ministers. ASEAN is working to create AFTA (an ASEAN Free Trade Area), which if successful would create a single market of over 330 million people. If, as expected, Laos, Cambodia, and Burma also join ASEAN in the future, the group would include over 400 million people. Malaysia is also a member APEC (Asia-Pacific Economic Cooperation), which includes the U.S., China, Japan, and most of the other countries of the Pacific Rim.

Faux Pas: Following the lead of Prime Minister Mahathir, the Malaysian government strongly rejects foreign interference in internal affairs. While Malaysia promotes ecotourism, it is not willing to put up with foreign environmentalists. There has been massive logging of the Borneo rain forests. (The portions of Malaysia on the island of Borneo are semiautonomous; they are not subject to the logging restrictions in force on peninsular Malaysia.) But when eight foreigners protested the logging by chaining themselves to some trees in Borneo, they did not reckon on the backlash from the Malaysian government. The official government news agency roared that these eight protesters were part of an "international infrastructure that can attack and topple the sovereign governments of third-world nations, using the excuse of saving the environment" and that their actions constituted "a war against Malaysia." The cause of Malaysian environmentalism was not advanced by their actions.

Contacts in the U.S.A. & in Malaysia

Contacts in the United States:

EMBASSY OF MALAYSIA
2401 Massachusetts Avenue, N.W.
Washington, D.C. 20008
Tel: (202) 328-2700
Fax: (202) 483-7661

U.S. DEPARTMENT OF STATE
Bureau of Consular Affairs
Tel: (202) 647-5225
Country Desk Officer, Malaysia
Tel: (202) 647-3276

U.S. DEPARTMENT OF COMMERCE
Malaysia Desk
Int'l Trade Admin.
Tel: (202) 482-3647

TOURISM OFFICE
Malaysia Tourist Promotion Board
818 W. 7th Street
Los Angeles, C.A. 90017
Tel: (213) 689-9702
Fax: (213) 689-1530

Contacts in Malaysia:

U.S. EMBASSY
376 Jalan Tun Razak
50400 Kuala Lampur or
P.O. Box 10035, Malaysia
Tel: [60] (3) 248-9011
Fax: [60] (3) 242-2207
APO AP 96535-8152

AMERICAN BUSINESS COUNCIL OF MALAYSIA
15.01, 15th Floor, AMODA
22 Jalan Imbi
55100 Kuala Lumpur, Malaysia
Tel: [60] (3) 248-2407
Fax: [60] (3) 242-8540

D&B INFORMATION SERVICES (M) SDN BHD
Postal Address: Suite 50D, 50th Floor,
Empire Tower
Jalan Tun Razak
50400 Kuala Lumpur, Malaysia
Tel: [60] (3) 262-7995
Fax: [60] (3) 264-4877

HIS MAJESTY TUANKU JAAFAR IBNI ALMARHUM TUANKU ABDUL RAHMAN
Office of the Supreme Head of State
Istana Negara
50500 Kuala Lumpur, Malaysia

PRIME MINISTER DATUK SERI MAHATHIR MOHAMED
Office of the Prime Minister
Jalan Dato Onn
50502 Kuala Lumpur, Malaysia

Passport/Visa Requirements

Visa Information   Tel: (202) 663-1225

Entry Requirements: A passport is required. Visas are not required for stays of up to three months. Yellow fever and cholera immunizations are necessary, if arriving from infected areas. On arrival in Malaysia, the Immigration Authorities will usually grant a two to three weeks' stay which may be extended up to a maximum period of three months. For purposes of employment, research, educational purposes, and other professional visits, visas are required.

A waiting period of between 6 to 8 weeks is required before the result of the visa application can be notified to the applicant.

Those wishing to enter the Borneo States of Sabah and Sarawak will need additional visa approval from the immigration authorities for visits involving a stay exceeding three (3) months. Applicants are required to give the names of the sponsors or references in Malaysia in their application forms.

Visitors allowed to stay in Malaysia for more than a year are required to obtain National Registration Identity Cards from the nearest registration office where they are staying.

For further information, travelers can call the Embassy of Malaysia.

Faux Pas: An expatriate American businessman who had rented a house in Kuala Lumpur was outraged to receive a municipal bill for *air* in the mail. He complained bitterly that no civilized country charged for air, let alone the polluted air of Kuala Lumpur. Eventually, a fellow expatriate explained that his *"air bill"* was actually a *water* bill. *Air* is the Bahasa Malaysian word for *water* (it is pronounced *"ayer"*). The Malays he complained to were too embarrassed to point out his error.

Mexico

Official Name:	United Mexican States (Estados Unidos Mexicanos)
Official Language:	Spanish
Government System:	Federal republic
Population:	92 million
Population Growth:	1.8%
Area:	1.972 million sq. km. (762,000 sq. mi.); about three times the size of Texas
Natural Resources:	crude oil, silver, copper, gold, lead, zinc, natural gas, timber
Major Cities:	Mexico City (capital), Guadalajara, Monterrey, Tijuana, Juárez, León

Cultural Note: At every first meeting, expect to be asked some variation of "What have you done (or seen) in Mexico?" This is a polite way of inquiring about your respect for Mexican culture and traditions. To establish your credentials as someone who cares about Mexico and its people, you are expected to see the usual sights and gain an appreciation of Mexican culture. If you haven't seen any, at least know the names of some tourist sights and say that you are looking forward to seeing them.

Age Breakdown

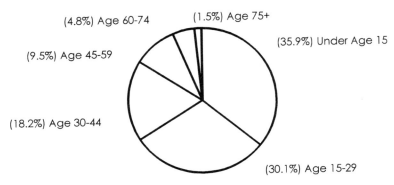

(4.8%) Age 60-74   (1.5%) Age 75+

(9.5%) Age 45-59   (35.9%) Under Age 15

(18.2%) Age 30-44

(30.1%) Age 15-29

Life Expectancy: 69 years male; 75 years female (1994 est.)

 Time

Time is flexible in Mexico. Although foreign businesspeople are expected to be on time to business appointments, Mexican executives may be late, sometimes considerably late.

Not even *norteamericanos* (U.S. citizens; Canadians are *canadienses*) are expected to be prompt to social occasions. In general, arrive about 30 minutes late to social events. But in Mexico City, guests often arrive as much as two hours late. When in doubt as to what time you are really expected, ask.

Be aware when you are told that something will be done mañana, this probably does not mean tomorrow (its literal translation). In this context, mañana refers to some indeterminate date in the near future. Deadlines are always flexible. Many foreigners recommend placing your contracted delivery date two weeks to a month ahead of the date you really need the product. With this much leeway, you stand a good chance of getting it on time.

Mexicans are well aware of the U.S. attitude toward time. Manipulating the use of time is one way they can control this relationship.

Most of Mexico is six hours behind Greenwich Mean Time (G.M.T. − 6), which is one hour behind U.S. Eastern Standard Time (E.S.T. − 1), or the same as U.S. Central Standard Time.

A portion of west-central Mexico is seven hours behind Greenwich Mean Time (G.M.T. − 7), which is in the Mountain Time Zone (E.S.T. − 2). The Mexican states of Sonora, Sinaloa, and Nayarit are in this time zone.

Finally, North and South Baja California are eight hours behind Greenwich Mean Time (G.M.T. − 8), which places them in the Pacific Time Zone (E.S.T. − 3).

Holidays

(Update: Getting Through Customs *http://www.getcustoms.com*)

This is a working guide. Dates should be corroborated before final travel plans are made. In cases where holidays fall on Saturday or Sunday, commercial establishments may be closed the preceding Friday or following Monday.

New Year's Day	1 January
Constitution Day	5 February
Birthday of Benito Juarez	21 March
Spring Equinox	late March
(Chichen Itza's Temple of Kukulkan special alignment with the sun)	
Labor day	1 May
Victory at Puebla	5 May
(defeat of the French army) Cinco de Mayo	
Independence Day	16 September
Columbus Day–Dia de la Raza	12 October
Anniversary of the 1910 Revolution	20 November
The Day of the Virgin of Guadalupe	12 December
New Year's Eve	31 December

- Avoid scheduling business trips around Christmas and Easter.

Work Week

- Business hours are generally 9:00 A.M. to 6:00 P.M. with lunch between 1:00 and 3:00 P.M., Monday through Friday. Banks are open 9:00 A.M. to 1:30 P.M., Monday through Friday. Government offices operate 8:00 A.M. to 2:30 P.M., Monday through Friday.

Religious/Societal Influences on Business

The majority (89.7%) of Mexicans are Roman Catholic. Protestant sects (especially Evangelical) have enjoyed rapid growth in recent years, but they are still a small part of the population. Mexico has no official religion.

Mexico has been harsh on many of its inhabitants. Except for the elite, most Mexican families have experienced hardship and tragedy. By U.S. standards, most Mexican laborers work long hours for very low wages. Yet Mexicans are known for maintaining a positive outlook despite hardship. They maintain a zest for life, and enjoy their numerous celebrations to the fullest.

The family is the most important institution in Mexico. Nepotism is an accepted practice. Mexican executives generally put a higher importance on the best interest of their families than on the company they work for. Firing a high-ranking executive can be difficult, since he (Mexican business executives are overwhelmingly male) may have several relatives and friends working for the company, who feel great loyalty toward him.

While competence and achievement are appreciated in Mexico, they are by no means the most important consideration of an individual's worth. Mexicans find all people worthy of respect, regardless of their talents. Furthermore, each person is considered not only as an individual, but as a part of a family. Deference is shown to the elderly and status of one's family in the social hierarchy.

Mexico is a male-dominated society. But foreign female executives find few problems, since Mexican machismo requires male executives to be gentlemanly and polite. They may even grant a meeting to a female executive more quickly than a male one. Mexican women who find success in business have a reputation for toughness and efficiency while maintaining their femininity.

 ## 5 Cultural Tips

1. Subordinates in Mexico do not make extended eye contact with their bosses. Instead, they display respect by looking at the ground. This should not be interpreted as disinterest. As a foreign businessperson, you may engage in intermittent eye contact. Eye contact is yielded to the person talking, while the listener mainly looks away. Avoid intense, constant eye contact; this is interpreted as aggression.

2. The handshake is the traditional greeting between men. Women have the option of shaking hands with men; men usually wait to see if a woman extends her hand. A man may include a slight bow while shaking hands with a woman. Good friends embrace. Women often kiss each other on the cheek while embracing.

3. Mexico has many resources but most Mexicans are poor, and this has engendered a sense of national thrift. While some wealthy Mexicans live very well indeed, ostentation is frowned upon. Foreigners should dress stylishly but avoid expensive jewelry. (Note that Mexican frugality does not include hospitality; Mexicans often spend lavishly to celebrate or entertain guests.)

4. Lunch is traditionally the largest meal of the day in Mexico, so business lunches tend to be expansive. Lunch usually lasts for two hours, from 2 P.M. to 4 P.M. (However, near the U.S. border, some businesses have adopted 12 noon to 2 P.M.

lunchtime.) Wine is often consumed with lunch; some executives will have some tequila as well. Foreigners in Mexico City (altitude 7,349 feet) should remember that high altitudes increase the negative effects of alcohol.

5. Socializing is an integral part of doing business in Mexico. Accept invitations to social events, even though business will not be discussed. An invitation into a Mexican home is a great honor. Be assured that the phrase *"Mi casa es su casa"* *("My house is your house")* is not uttered lightly. It means that you are being accepted as a friend of the family, a position of both honor and obligation.

Economic Overview

Mexico, under the guidance of President Ernesto Zedillo, entered 1995 in the midst of a severe financial crisis. Mexico's membership in the North American Free Trade Agreement (NAFTA) with the United States and Canada, its solid record of economic reforms, and its strong growth in the second and third quarters of 1994, at an annual rate of 3.8% and 4.5% respectively, seemed to augur bright prospects for 1995. However, an overvalued exchange rate and widening current account deficits created an unbalance that ultimately proved unsustainable. To finance the trade gap, the government had become increasingly reliant on volatile portfolio investment.

A series of political shocks in 1994, an uprising in the southern state of Chiapas, the assassination of a presidential candidate, several high-profile kidnappings, the killing of a second high-profile political figure, and renewed threats from the Chiapas rebels, combined with rising international interest rates and concerns of a devaluation to undermine investor confidence and prompt massive outflows of capital. The dwindling of foreign exchange reserves, which the central bank had been using to defend the currency, forced the new administration to change the exchange rate the last few days of 1994. The adjustment roiled Mexican financial markets, leading to a 30% to 40% weakening of the peso relative to the dollar. In response to the devaluation and the resulting financial crisis, Mexico negotiated a package of international support in early 1995 to bolster the balance of payment position including a $20 billion package provided by the U.S. in short- and medium-term funds and guarantees.

Mexico is evolving toward a multiparty democracy after 60 years of uninterrupted rule by the Institutional Revolutionary Party (PRI). The Zedillo Administration is committed to advancing this process through a political reform program. The financial crisis which began shortly after President Zedillo took office has complicated the reform process. Nonetheless, the government has made good on its commitment by holding free and fair elections in which opposition parties have won important vacancies. The reform process, which favors underlying social stability, is expected to continue.

On the positive side, the upturn in Mexican export activity shows no sign of abating, at least through 1996. Exports will continue to provide the main dynamic to growth in 1996, with consumption remaining relatively flat. Mexico's trade surplus in

1995 exceeded $7 billion, a stark contrast to the trade deficit of more than $17 billion in 1994. While the devaluation has helped Mexican exporters (since their products are now cheaper), it also raises the specter of an inflationary spiral if domestic producers increase their prices and workers demand wage hikes.

There are considerable opportunities for U.S. products related to the new strength of Mexican exports. U.S. firms would do well to target those Mexican companies which are gearing up to export and which will require increasing amounts of capital and intermediate goods. Some government measures to improve the country's infrastructure will also provide opportunities for U.S. firms as Mexico continues its plans to privatize its airports, railroads, utilities, and other state-run enterprises.

As Mexico entered 1996, questions still remained about the government's ability to regain the confidence of investors. Paramount to this is the government's ability to subdue inflationary pressures. In 1995, inflation ran at a 52% rate. Forecasts call for an improved inflation rate of between 20% and 25% in 1996, but consumer prices were expected to undergo further upward hikes (partly due to the elimination of food subsidies).

In the wake of the peso devaluation, American exports to Mexico declined in 1995, by about 10% compared to 1994. The impact on each exporter, however, has varied depending on the nature of the product. Nonessential products such as consumer goods experienced the greatest decline in 1995. Other product sectors, such as intermediate goods, have fared better while experiencing slower growth rates.

Despite the problems, there are still plenty of opportunities in this important market. Mexico, even after the peso devaluation, remains the third largest export market for U.S. products, trailing only Canada and Japan. Mexico's economic fundamentals are still sound. Public finances are in balance. The private sector, not the government, is the driving force in an increasingly deregulated economy. NAFTA has locked in many of the reforms in progress; there has been no turning back from the agreement on the part of the Mexican government. U.S. exporters should keep in mind that more than 60% of U.S. goods now enter Mexico duty-free. During the first year of the NAFTA, U.S.-Mexico trade increased by 23% to more than $100 billion. NAFTA is also bearing fruit in financial services. As of June 1995, eight U.S. banks, three insurance companies, and one brokerage house had opened Mexican subsidiaries.

Cultural Note: Directness is not considered a virtue in Mexico. U.S. citizens used to being bluntly honest will not do well here. Courtesy and tact are valued more than truth; it is considered polite to tell someone what they (apparently) want to hear, even if that is untrue. Flattery is commonly used. While bargaining is enjoyed, arguing is not. Every effort is made to avoid a loss of face.

Comparative Data

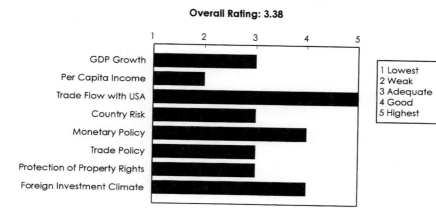

Overall Rating: 3.38

Scale:
1 Lowest
2 Weak
3 Adequate
4 Good
5 Highest

Country Risk Rating

Gross Domestic Product: $377 billion
GDP Growth: 4.5%
Per Capita Income: $4,200

Trade Flows with the U.S.A.

Rank as Export Market for U.S.A. Goods & Services: 3rd
U.S.A. Exports to Mexico: $46.3 billion
Growth Rate of Exports: −10%
U.S.A. Imports from Mexico: $61.7 billion
Growth Rate of Imports: 25%
Rank as a Supplier of Imports into the U.S.A.: 3rd

Top U.S.A. Exports to Mexico: Electrical components; machinery; motor vehicles; plastics and resins; medical and optical equipment; paper/paperboard; iron and steel products; organic chemicals; mineral fuel/oil; cereals.

Top U.S.A. Prospects for Export to Mexico: Automotive parts and service; franchising; pollution control equipment; chemical production machinery; telecommunications equipment; building products; management consulting services; apparel; aircraft and parts; electronic components.

Country Risk

Dun & Bradstreet rates Mexico as having reasonable capacity to meet outstanding payment liabilities.

Many U.S. companies sell to Mexico via open account. When open account terms are extended, 90 to 180 day terms are the norm. With prudent credit review practices, open account sales in Mexico need not be inherently risky.

Monetary Policy

Inflation jumped to 52% in 1995. Forecasts are for inflation to drop to between 20% and 25% in 1996. Consumer prices will undergo a further upward hike in 1996 as food subsidies are eliminated. *Monetary Unit:* Mexican peso.

Trade Policy

TARIFFS: With the entry in force of the NAFTA on January 1, 1994, Mexico further lowered its tariffs on U.S. and Canadian origin goods. Mexican tariffs on U.S. goods are between 10% and 20%. The highest Mexican tariffs tend to be on agricultural products and finished motor vehicles. Under NAFTA, tariffs on U.S. goods will be phased out over a maximum period of 10 years, varying by type of good. Many U.S. goods now enter Mexico duty-free.

IMPORT LICENSING: Under NAFTA, Mexico abolished its import licensing requirements for U.S. origin goods. Various agricultural products and finished motor vehicles, however, remain subject to tariff rate quotas.

The NAFTA provides that for the first 10 years of the agreement, Mexico may adopt or maintain prohibitions or restrictions on the importation of certain used goods. These are (primarily), construction machinery and heavy equipment, industrial machinery, electronic data processing equipment, motorcycles, motor homes and campers, and most trailers and tankers.

IMPORT TAXES: Mexico imposes a 15% value-added tax (VAT) on most sales transactions, including foreign sales. Basic products such as food and drugs are exempt from VAT. Mexican customs collects the VAT on imports upon entry of the merchandise into Mexico.

A 0.8% customs processing fee is also charged on the value of imports.

Protection of Intellectual Property Rights

Mexico is a member of most international organizations regulating the protection of intellectual property rights (IPR).

The Mexican government strengthened its domestic legal framework for protecting intellectual property in 1991 with the promulgation of a new industrial property law (patents and trademarks), and an extensive revision of its copyright law.

Product patent protection was extended to virtually all processes and products, including chemicals, alloys, pharmaceutical, biotechnology, and plant varieties. The term of patent protection was extended from 14 to 20 years from the date of filing. Trademarks are now granted for 10-year renewable periods. The enhanced copyright law provides protection for computer programs against unauthorized reproduction for a period of 50 years. Sanctions and penalties against infringements were increased and damages now can be claimed regardless of the application of sanctions.

Mexico actively enforces its intellectual property laws and has seized and destroyed millions of dollars worth of pirated merchandise. In an effort to improve enforcement and put teeth into its IPR laws, the Mexican government formed an intersecretarial commission in October 1993 to cut through the bureaucratic obstacles hindering effective action.

Foreign Investment Climate

In December 1993, the government passed a foreign investment law that replaced a restrictive 1973 statute. The law is consistent with the foreign investment chapter of NAFTA and opened more areas of the economy to foreign ownership.

It also provided national treatment for most foreign investment, eliminated all performance requirements for foreign investment projects, and liberalized criteria for automatic approval of foreign investment proposals. Most foreign investors operate in Mexico through corporations. Foreign-owned corporations are subject to the same laws as local companies as well as any special regulations governing foreign investment. A Mexican corporation must have at least five shareholders and, except in certain sensitive sectors, can usually be established in one or two months. Non-Mexican citizens cannot own property within 50 kilometers of the sea coasts or within 100 kilometers of the Mexican border. Property within those areas can be leased through 30 year trusts held by Mexican banks. Foreign investors can acquire such property for commercial purposes by establishing a Mexican subsidiary.

Under the NAFTA, Mexico may not expropriate property, except for a public purpose on a nondiscriminatory basis. Expropriations are governed by international law and require rapid, fair market value compensation, including accrued interest. Investors have the right to international arbitration for violations of this or any other rights included in the investment chapter of the NAFTA.

Current Leaders & Political Parties

(Update: International Academy at Santa Barbara *http://www.iasb.org/cwl*)

State, Government, and Political Party Leaders:

Pres.: Dr. Ernesto Zedillo Ponce De León

Cabinet Secretaries:

Internal Affairs: Esteban Moctezuma Barragán
Foreign Relations: José Angel Gurría Treviño
Natl. Defense: Gen. Enrique Cervantes Aguirre
Finance and Public Credit: vacant
Navy: José Ramón Lorenzo Franco
Social Dev.: Carlos Rojas Gutiérrez
Commerce and Industrial Dev.: Herminio Blanco Morales
Communications and Transportation: Guillermo Ortiz Martínez
Labor and Social Welfare: Santiago Oñate Laborde
Energy, Mines, and Parastatal Industry: Jesus Reyer Heroles
Agriculture and Water Resources: Francisco Labastida Ochoa
Agrarian Reform: Arturo Warman
Fisheries: Julia Carabias
Tourism: Silvia Hernández

Other Officials:

Leader of the House of Representatives: Humberto Roque Villanueva
Leader of the Senate: Fernando Ortíz Arana
Ambassador to U.S.: Jorge Montaño
Perm. Rep. to U.N.: Victor Flores Olea

Political Parties:

Institutional Revolutionary Party (PRI), Party of the Cardenista Front of Natl. Reconstruction (PFCRN), Natl. Action Party (PAN), Authentic Party of the Mexican Revolution (PARM), Party of the Democratic Revolution (PRD), Socialist Workers' Party (PST), Popular Socialist Party (PPS), Mexican Green Ecology Party

Political Influences on Business

Rarely have the vagaries of politics and economics been so well illustrated as in Mexico in the mid-1990s. Until the end of 1994, Mexico was riding high. Prosperity was increasing, and the signing of the North American Free Trade Agreement was augured to bring a golden age to Mexican trade. Newly installed President Ernesto Zedillo and his predecessor, Carols Salinas, were heroes.

On 20 December 1994, that all changed. On that date, a botched devaluation of the Mexican peso precipitated the collapse of the Mexican economy. Not all of this was Mexico's fault. The global investment market and instantaneous communications are relatively new phenomena. Some economists have called the Mexican collapse "the first crisis of the 21st century." Now, Ernesto Zedillo and Carlos Salinas are discredited, along with their Institutional Revolutionary Party (PRI), which may face the end of six decades in power.

All economic crises have winners and losers. Those who can buy Mexican goods or labor with foreign currency are the winners. Although the bargains fade as economic stability returns, Mexican goods and services are still attractive. Businesses who need to sell to the Mexican consumer have had a difficult time. Mexico needs to export its way out of this financial crisis.

Mexico's current difficulties include the demand for debt relief by thousands of ordinary citizens. While international loans shored up big industrial debtors, thousands of small businesspeople find they are saddled with high-interest debts which they can never repay. New measures designed to make it easier and quicker for creditors to attach the funds or properties of debtors have outraged Mexican citizens. Yet the low savings and high debt levels of the Mexican people contributed to the crisis. If the Mexican government had discouraged debt and encouraged savings, as do many Asian governments, the Mexican economy would be much healthier.

It was international politics, not Mexican policy makers, which rescued the bond market. This came in the form of billions of dollars in guarantees from the United States and the International Monetary Fund. Mutual funds and bonds had superseded bank loans as Mexico's largest source of private financing. But this is liable to be the last time that such bond markets are rescued so easily.

Most international economists still view NAFTA as Mexico's best hope for revival. Thanks to the devalued peso and free trade, Mexican exports are booming. Continued privatization offers good long-term investment opportunities for investors.

It is hoped that true multiparty government will also make Mexico more attractive to investors. Political reforms are underway. Of the five elections for state governors in 1995, the PRI won only two.

Contacts in the U.S.A. & in Mexico

Contacts in the United States:

EMBASSY OF MEXICO
1911 Pennsylvania Avenue, N.W.
Washington, D.C. 20006
Tel: (202) 728-1600
Fax: (202) 728-1718

U.S. DEPARTMENT OF STATE
Bureau of Consular Affairs
Tel: (202) 647-5225
Country Desk Officer, Mexico
Tel: (202) 647-9894

U.S. DEPARTMENT OF COMMERCE
Mexico Desk
Int'l Trade Commission
Tel: (202) 482-0300

U.S./MEXICO CHAMBER OF COMMERCE
1730 Rhode Island Ave., N.W., #1112
Washington, D.C. 20036
Tel: (202) 296-5198
Fax: (202) 728-0768
Tourism Office

MEXICO GOVERNMENT TOURIST OFFICE
405 Park Ave.
Suite 1401
New York, N.Y. 10022
Tel: (212) 755-7261
Fax: (212) 753-2874

Contacts in Mexico:

U.S. EMBASSY
Paseo de la Reforma 305
Colonia Cuauhtemoc
06500 Mexico D.F.
Mailing address:
P.O. Box 3087
Laredo, TX 78044-3087
Tel: [52] (5) 211-0042
Fax: [52] (5) 511-9980

AMERICAN CHAMBER OF COMMERCE OF
MEXICO, A.C.
Lucerna 78–4,
Col Juarez 06600
Mexico 6, D.F.
Tel: [52] (5) 724-3800
Fax: [52] (5) 703-3908

DUN & BRADSTREET, S.A. DE C.V.
Postal Address: Apartado Postal 40 BIS
06700 Mexico, D.F.
Street Address: Durango 263
4th & 5th Floors
Col. Roma
Delagacion Cuauhtemoc
06700 Mexico, D.F.
Tel: [52] (5) 208-5066,
      [52] (5)229-6900
Fax: [52] (5) 514-7502

PRESIDENT ERNESTO ZEDILLO PONCE DE
LEÓN
Office of the President
Palacio Nacional
Patio de hono, 20 Piso
Mexico City, D.F. 06067
Mexico

Passport/Visa Requirements

Visa Information   Tel: (202) 663-1225

Entry Requirements: Proof of citizenship is required for entry by U.S. citizens. A passport and visa are not required for a tourist/transit stay of up to 180 days. A tourist card issued by Mexican consulates and most airlines serving Mexico is required. Minors traveling without a valid passport require notarized consent from parents or at the international border if traveling alone, with one parent, or in someone else's custody.

Evidence of U.S. citizenship must be presented and carried during the trip: U.S. passport, birth certificate, naturalization certificate or voter's registration certificate, if it shows place of birth.

In compliance with NAFTA, the Mexican government, through the National Immigration Institute (NII) of the Secretariat of the Interior, drafted and implemented the FM-N immigration form. This form may be used by businesspersons of U.S. or Canadian nationality who wish to enter Mexico under the protection of NAFTA.

Cultural Note: Many Mexicans consider themselves "Guadalupeños," a nickname for those who believe in the miracle of the Virgin of Guadalupe. The miracle asserts that the Virgin Mary appeared three times to a poor Aztec, Juan Diego, in 1513. She told him to build a church in Tepeyac, where the Aztec goddess Tonantin was worshipped. Today that church has become a basilica, and is visited by more than one million pilgrims annually. Images of the Virgin of Guadalupe are everywhere, a symbol of unity between the Aztec and Spanish cultures, and of Mexican nationality.

The Netherlands

Official Name:	Kingdom of the Netherlands (Koninkrijk der Nederlanden)
Official Language:	Dutch
Government System:	Multiparty parliamentary democracy under constitutional monarch
Population:	15 million
Population Growth:	0.52%
Area:	41,526 sq. km. (16,033 sq. mi.); about half the size of Maine
Natural Resources:	natural gas, crude oil, fertile soil
Major Cities:	Amsterdam (capital), The Hague (seat of government), Rotterdam, Utrecht

Cultural Note: The Dutch have always been good businesspeople. Success in business is not new to them; they were the world's leading economic power during the seventeenth century. The modern conception of the limited-liability corporation was largely invented in the Netherlands.

Age Breakdown

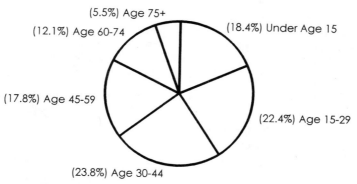

(5.5%) Age 75+

(12.1%) Age 60-74

(18.4%) Under Age 15

(17.8%) Age 45-59

(22.4%) Age 15-29

(23.8%) Age 30-44

Life Expectancy: 74 years male; 80 years female (1992)

 ## Time

Punctuality is vital. Be on time to both business and social engagements.

The efficient use of time is considered an important virtue in the Netherlands. Tardiness is seen as indicative of other negative traits as well. People who cannot use their time wisely are not trusted!

The Netherlands is one hour ahead of Greenwich Mean Time (G.M.T. + 1), which is six hours ahead of U.S. Eastern Standard Time (E.S.T. + 6).

 ## Holidays

(Update: Getting Through Customs *http://www.getcustoms.com*)

This list is a working guide. Dates should be corroborated before final travel plans are made. In cases where holidays fall on Saturday or Sunday, commercial establishments may be closed the preceding Friday or following Monday.

New Year's Day	1 January
The Queen's Birthday	30 April
Liberation Day	5 May
Christmas Holidays	25–26 December

Work Week

- Many Dutch executives take long vacations during June, July, August, and late December, so confirm that your counterparts will be available.
- Business hours: 8:30 A.M. to 5:30 P.M., Monday through Friday.
- Banking hours: 9:00 A.M. TO 4:00 P.M., Monday through Friday. Some banks have Thursday night hours as well.
- Store hours: 8:30 or 9:00 A.M. to 5:30 or 6:00 P.M., Monday through Friday. Some shops will have extended evening hours on Thursday or Friday. Note that most shops will be closed for a half day each week.

 ## Religious/Societal Influences on Business

Although the Netherlands has no official religion, the Calvinist ethics of the Dutch Reformed Church have great influence over everyday life. Honesty is one such virtue. Not only do the Dutch dislike evasiveness and duplicity, they do not deal well with secrecy. They may even be uncomfortable when forced to conceal proprietary information.

Another Dutch virtue is frugality. Wealth is downplayed. Even the rich in the Netherlands display a lack of ostentation, often living in modest homes.

Planning is seen as important to success. This makes the decision-making process quite slow, since every aspect of a deal will be examined in detail. (This is a trait the Dutch share with their German neighbors.)

While there are many areas of commonality between the Netherlands and Germany, there are also substantial differences. Social scientists use a scale called the *Uncertainty Avoidance Index*, which determines how far people will go to avoid uncertainty. Germany scores high on this scale. To try and eliminate as much uncertainty as possible, Germans generally legislate for every possibility (in their view, rules and regulations help give structure and stability to life). The Dutch feel no need to do this. (For example, in Germany everyone is required to carry their I.D. card. This is not the case in the Netherlands.)

The Netherlands has an extensive welfare system, which they are having increasing difficulty affording. But each Dutch citizen is considered valuable and worthy of respect. It is in this area of social welfare requirements that U.S. corporations investing in the Netherlands report some of their greatest difficulties. A report issued by the Dutch Ministry of Economic Affairs found that U.S. management styles in general seemed ill-suited to the Netherlands, while Scandinavian managers report few problems at all.

As is common in small European countries, the Dutch do not expect foreigners to know their language. Most Dutch are multilingual, and many speak English. In a business setting, and English-speaking person is usually close at hand.

5 Cultural Tips

1. Since so many people in the Netherlands speak English, it is not necessary to translate business materials into Dutch. Be sure that your business cards note any advanced educational degrees, and keep your business correspondence neat and formal. The Dutch feel that if they are going to the trouble of reading your correspondence in English, the least you can do is write a letter that is grammatically correct.

2. In keeping with Dutch egalitarianism, greet everyone in a small, enclosed space with a *"good day"* upon entering. They will respond in kind, then return to their work. This covers not only offices, but shops, waiting rooms, elevators, and railroad compartments as well. At a social event, if you have not been introduced to everyone, you should then go around the room and introduce yourself.

3. Data collection is very important to the Dutch. (Do not be surprised if, when you arrive for your first meeting, your Dutch counterpart has a complete dossier on you!) Be prepared to supply reams of information on every aspect of your deal. This is especially true for U.S. businesspeople, whose reputation for hyperbole engenders distrust among the pragmatic Dutch.

4. Never give the impression that you consider yourself superior in the Netherlands. The Dutch accord everyone a degree of respect, and respond badly to anyone who "puts on airs." This unwillingness to place oneself in a subservient position can result in poor customer service. Foreigners often complain that Dutch store clerks and waiters "act like they're doing you a favor to wait on you."

5. The Dutch value diversity and tolerance, which makes them well-suited to the international business arena. Curiously, they also exhibit a large degree of conformity of behavior. From its clockwork punctuality to its clean-swept streets, the Netherlands would not run so smoothly unless most of its citizens agreed on proper behavior.

Economic Overview

The Netherlands is one of the top dozen trading countries in the world. It is ranked thirteenth in GNP, ninth in imports of goods and services from the United States, and third in foreign investment in the U.S., behind only the United Kingdom and Japan.

The U.S. is the largest foreign investor in the Netherlands and has its largest bilateral trade surplus in the world with this country.

Economic growth picked up in the Netherlands in 1994. Real Gross Domestic Product (GDP) grew 3.4%, but slowed to 2.1% in 1995. The range of export potential for products and services in the Netherlands is amazingly broad-based. From high-tech to low-tech, all manner of goods coming into Europe can take advantage of Dutch distribution, warehousing, and value-added manufacturing.

American industrial goods, as well as consumer goods, are popular and have a reputation for quality. An estimated 7,000 U.S. companies have appointed Dutch agents and distributors in the Netherlands. Of the top 500 U.S. companies, 105 have formed European Distribution Centers in the Netherlands. Approximately 1,100 American and American-affiliated companies have operations in the Netherlands. The country's strategic location combined with the relative ease of doing business makes the Netherlands an ideal European operations location for American companies. The country's advanced transport and logistical infrastructure is second to none in Europe. Historically, the U.S. and Netherlands have had a close bilateral relationship, encompassing a full agenda of political, economic, military, and social issues.

Comparative Data

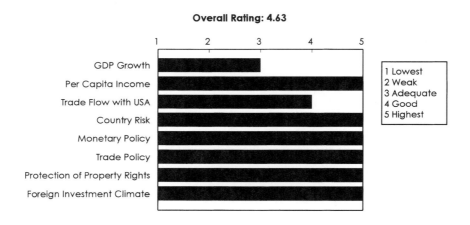

Overall Rating: 4.63

GDP Growth	
Per Capita Income	
Trade Flow with USA	
Country Risk	
Monetary Policy	
Trade Policy	
Protection of Property Rights	
Foreign Investment Climate	

1 Lowest
2 Weak
3 Adequate
4 Good
5 Highest

Country Risk Rating

Gross Domestic Product: $330 billion

GDP Growth: 2.5%

Per Capita Income: $21,500

Trade Flows with the U.S.A.

Rank as Export Market for U.S.A. Goods & Services: 8th
U.S.A. Exports to the Netherlands: $16.5 billion
Growth Rate of Exports: 25%
U.S.A. Imports from the Netherlands: $6.4 billion
Growth Rate of Imports: 7%
Rank as a Supplier of Imports into the U.S.A.:   21st

Top U.S.A. Exports to the Netherlands: Machinery; aircraft and parts; electrical components; medical and optical equipment; organic chemicals; plastics and resins;grain/feed/seed/fruit; motor vehicles; animal feed; mineral fuel/oil.

Top U.S.A. Prospects for Export to the Netherlands: Computer software; telecommunications services; electronic components; computer services; computers and peripherals; telecommunications equipment; pollution control equipment; aircraft and parts; building products; automotive parts and service equipment.

Country Risk

Dun & Bradstreet rates the Netherlands as having excellent capacity to meet outstanding payment liabilities. It carries the lowest degree of risk.

Open account terms of 30 to 60 days are normally extended with few problems reported with payments.

Monetary Policy

Inflation has remained low for several years and is forecast to remain in the 2% to 2.5% range through 1997. *Monetary Unit:* Dutch guilder.

Trade Policy

TARIFFS: Duty rates on manufactured goods from the United States generally range from 5 to 8%. Most raw materials enter duty-free or at low rates while agricultural products face higher rates and special levies.

IMPORT LICENSING: Only a small number of goods of U.S. origin require import licenses, mostly agricultural and food items. Other items subject to import licensing requirements include coal and lignite fuel, a few specified base metal products, various apparel and textile products, and controlled items such as arms and munitions. Licenses are generally granted quickly for goods of U.S. origin.

IMPORT TAXES: A value-added tax is charged on the sale of goods and services within the country. A 6% rate applies to necessities of life such as food, medicines, and transportation. A 17.5% rate is the general or standard rate and applies to most goods. Excise taxes are levied on a small number of products such as soft drinks, wine, beer, spirits, tobacco, sugar, and petroleum products. The EU plans to harmonize excise taxes.

Protection of Intellectual Property Rights

The Dutch legal system provides adequate protection, and facilitates acquisition and disposition of all property rights including intellectual property.

The Netherlands belongs to the World Intellectual Property Organization, it is a signatory of the Paris Convention for the Protection of Industrial Property, and conforms to accepted international practices for protection of technology and trademarks.

Patents for foreign inventions are granted retroactively to the date of original filing in the home country, provided the application is made through a Dutch patent lawyer within one year of the original filing date. Patents are valid for 20 years.

Trademarks are protected for 10 years from the date of filing of the application for registration. Registrations can be renewed for periods of 10 years. The Netherlands is a member of the Universal Copyright Convention and the Berne Convention. The EU copyright agreement establishes protection for the life of the author plus 70 years.

Foreign Investment Climate

The Dutch government maintains liberal policies toward foreign direct investment. With the exception of public and private monopolies (military production, aviation, shipping, distribution of electricity, gas and water, railways and radio and television broadcasting), foreign firms are able to invest in any sector and entitled under the law to equal treatment with domestic firms.

Provision of government incentives, rules of incorporation, access to the capital market, etc., are all non-discriminatory. The Dutch actively recruit foreign investment through the Netherlands Foreign Investment Agency.

There are no apparent foreign investment screening mechanisms, and 100% foreign ownership is permitted in those sectors open to foreign private investment. All firms must conform to certain rules of conduct on mergers and takeovers. These are administered by the Socio-Economic Council, an official advisory board composed of representatives of business, labor, and government. Since 1993, anti-takeover measures have liberalized significantly. Draft legislation to further curtail corporate protective measures is under preparation. During the last decade, the number of foreign companies with establishments in the Netherlands has grown to more than 6,300, employing close to 352,000 workers. Included are 1,680 U.S. companies accounting for 123,000 jobs. Foreign companies in the Netherlands account for a quarter of industrial production and about 20% of employment in industry. Close to one-third (29%) of foreign establishments in the Netherlands are of U.S. origin, with 5% Japanese, 51% from the EU and 13% from other European companies.

Current Leaders & Political Parties

(Update: International Academy at Santa Barbara *http://www.iasb.org/cwl*)

State, Government, and Political Party Leaders:

Head of State: Queen Beatrix

Cabinet Ministers:

Prime Min. and Min. of Gen. Affairs: W. Kok

First Dep. Prime Min. and Min. for Home Affairs: H. F. Dijkstal

Second Dep. Prime Min. and Min. for Foreign Affairs: H. A. F. M. O. Van Mierlo

Dev. Coop.: J. P. Pronk

Finance: G. Zalm

Economic Affairs: G. Wijers

Defense: J. J. C. Voorhoeve

Justice: W. Sorgdrager

Education, Cultural Affairs, and Science: J. M. M. Ritzen

Social Affairs and Employment: A. P. W. Melkert

Transportation, Public Works, and Water Management: A. Jorritsma-Lebbink

Health, Welfare, and Sports: E. Borst-Eilers

Housing, Planning, and Environment: M. De Boer

Agriculture, Nature Management, and Fisheries: J. J. Van Aartsen

Other Officials:

Ambassador to U.S.: Adrian P. R. Jacobovits De Szeged

Perm. Rep. to U.N.: N. H. Biegman

Political Parties:

Christian Democratic Alliance (CDA), Labor Party (PvdA), People's Party for Freedom and Democracy (VVD), Democrats '66 (D'66), Reformational Political Federation (RPF), Centre Party (CP), Green Left (GL)

Political Influences on Business

The Netherlands has an historically close bilateral relationship with the United States, encompassing a full agenda of political, economic, military, and social issues. The Netherlands and the United States work closely together in NATO, the United Nations, the GATT, the Organization on Security and Cooperation in Europe, the OECD, and other international organizations.

A three-party coalition consisting of the left-leaning Labor Party (PvdA), the right-leaning Liberal Party (VVD) and center-left Democrats (D66), has been in power since August 1994. The government is implementing its coalition agreement to trim budget deficits and to streamline the generous social welfare system. Among priorities for addressing business needs are reducing company tax contributions for social programs, and easing employment rigidities. In foreign affairs and defense policy, there is a strong consensus in the Netherlands in favor of continued close ties with the United States, support for NATO, and further European integration through the EU.

The Netherlands is a constitutional monarchy with a parliamentary form of government. The monarch (Queen Beatrix) is the titular head of state; however, the Council of Ministers (the Cabinet plus representatives of the Netherlands Antilles) is responsible for government policy. The ministers, collectively and individually, are responsible to the Parliament, but do not serve in Parliament.

The Dutch Parliament (also known as the "States General") consists of two houses: the First and Second Chambers. The Second Chamber is the more influential of the two chambers. It consists of 150 members elected on party slates for four-year terms under a system of proportional representation. As a result, members represent the whole country rather than individual districts as in the United States. The difficulty of winning an absolute majority under this system has given rise to a tradition of coalition government.

The First Chamber, composed of 75 members, is elected by provincial legislatures for four-year terms. While it can neither initiate nor amend legislation, it must approve all legislation passed by the Second Chamber before it becomes law.

The next national elections are due to be held in 1998.

Contacts in the U.S.A. & in the Netherlands

Contacts in the United States:

EMBASSY OF THE KINGDOM OF THE NETHERLANDS
4200 Linnean Avenue, N.W.
Washington, D.C. 20008
Tel: (202) 244-5300
Fax: (202) 362-3430

U.S. DEPARTMENT OF STATE
Bureau of Consular Affairs
Tel: (202) 647-5225
Country Desk Officer,
The Netherlands
Tel: (202) 647-6664

U.S. DEPARTMENT OF COMMERCE
Netherlands Desk
Int'l Trade Admin.
Tel: (202) 482-5401

THE NETHERLANDS CHAMBER OF COMMERCE
IN THE U.S., INC.
One Rockefeller Plaza
11th Floor
New York, N.Y. 10020
Tel: (212) 265-6460
Fax: (212) 265-6402

Contacts in The Netherlands:

U.S. EMBASSY
The Hague
Lange Voorhout 102
2514 EJ The Hague, Netherlands
PSC 71, Box 1000
APO AE 09715
Tel: (31) (70) 310-9209
Fax: (31) (70) 361-4688

AMERICAN CHAMBER OF COMMERCE IN THE
NETHERLANDS
Carnegieplein 5
2517 KJ The Hague, The Netherlands
Tel: (31) (70) 3-65-98-08/9
Fax: (31) (70) 3-64-69-92

CONSULATE GENERAL OF THE NETHERLANDS
One Rockefeller Plaza
11th Floor
New York, N.Y. 10020
Tel: (212) 246-1429
Fax: (212) 333-3603

TOURISM OFFICE
Netherlands Board of Tourism
355 Lexington Ave.
21st floor
New York, N.Y. 10017
Tel: (212) 370-7367
Fax: (212) 370-9507

DUN & BRADSTREET B.V.
Postal Address: P.O. Box 278
3000 AG Rotterdam
The Netherlands
Street Address: Westblaak 138
3012 KM Rotterdam
The Netherlands
Tel: [31] (10) 400-9400
Fax: [31] (10) 414-7380

PRIME MINISTER W. KOK
Office of the Prime Minister
Binnenhof 20
P.O. Box 20001
2500 EA The Hague
Kingdom of the Netherlands

QUEEN BEATRIX WILHELMINA ARMGARD
Noordeinde 68
Postbus 30412
2500 GK The Hague
Kingdom of the Netherlands

Passport/Visa Requirements

Entry Requirements: A passport is required. A visa is not required for tourist or business stays up to 90 days. Possession of a return ticket or ticket to destination outside the Netherlands is required.

For further information concerning entry requirements for the Netherlands, travelers can contact the Embassy of the Netherlands, or the nearest Dutch Consulate General.

Cultural Note: The Netherlands is a constitutional monarchy. And unlike the disdain with which some British hold their royal family, most Dutch like their royals.

Peru

Official Name:	Republic of Peru (República del Perú)
Official Language:	Spanish, Quechua, Aymara
Government System:	Unitary multiparty republic
Population:	23.4 million
Population Growth:	2.1%
Area:	1.285 million sq. km. (496,222 sq. mi.); three times larger than California
Natural Resources:	copper, silver, lead, zinc, crude oil, gold, crude oil, timber, fish, iron ore, coal, phosphates, potash
Major Cities:	Lima (capital), Arequipa, Chiclayo, Piura, Cuzco, Huancayo, Trujillo

Cultural Note: Industry, ingenuity, and perseverance are considered part of the Peruvian heritage. These characteristics are necessary for survival in this harsh Andean nation. Much of Peru is mountainous and inhospitable, yet Indians scrape out a living there, often through subsistence agriculture. But in the past decade, millions of poor people have left the countryside, fleeing the violent conflict between the Peruvian armed forces and various revolutionary groups, primarily the Sendero Luminiso (Shining Path). Some 25,000 Peruvian civilians have died in the conflict.

Age Breakdown

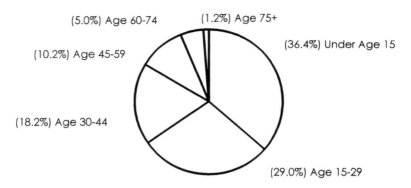

(5.0%) Age 60-74

(1.2%) Age 75+

(10.2%) Age 45-59

(36.4%) Under Age 15

(18.2%) Age 30-44

(29.0%) Age 15-29

Life Expectancy: 62 years male; 66 years female (1990)

 Time

The omnipresent historical sites, both pre-Columbian and Spanish Colonial, give Peru a sense of timelessness. Punctuality was never a part of this culture. However, foreign businesspeople are expected to be prompt.

Peru is five hours behind Greenwich Mean Time (G.M.T. − 5), which is the same as U.S. Eastern Standard Time.

 Holidays

(Update: Getting Through Customs *http://www.getcustoms.com*)

This list is a working guide. Dates should be corroborated before final travel plans are made. In cases where holidays fall on Saturday or Sunday, commercial establishments may be closed the preceding Friday or following Monday.

New Year's Day	1 January
Labor Day	1 May
Saints Peter and Paul	29 June
Independence Day	28/29 July
Saint Rosa of the Americas or Saint Rose of Lima	30 August
New Year's Eve	31 December

Confirm these dates as well as local holidays which may be celebrated regionally prior to scheduling appointments.

Work Week

- The work week is longer in Peru since businesses are often open six days a week. Business hours generally run from around 8:00 A.M. to 5 or 6:00 P.M. People may return home for lunch, so offices sometimes close between 1:00–3:00 P.M.
- Government offices and banks work different hours between summer (January to March) and winter (April to December).
- Many Peruvians go on vacation between January and March, and two weeks before and after Christmas and Easter. Therefore, try not to schedule major appointments then or during national holidays.

Religious/Societal Influences on Business

The overwhelming majority of Peruvians are Roman Catholic. Nevertheless, many of the Indians and mestizos retain their ancient Incan folk beliefs, as well as their native Quechua language. The sun festival of Inti Raymi each June is one remnant of Incan tradition. Another is stated in this Inca precept: *ama sua, ama qella, ama llulla* (meaning *do not steal, do not be idle, do not lie*).

Peruvians are divided by geography, ethnicity, and class. Animosity exists between the majority poor (who are all or partially Indian) and the white oligarchy (who own the bulk of Peru's wealth and businesses). There is friction between the residents of Lima (known as Limeños) and everyone else.

Peru's abundant natural resources make the plight of Peru's poor all the more bitter. Blessed with minerals, petroleum, fishing, and timber, Peru also has archaeological wonders for tourism. In the illegal economy, Peru produces billions in cocaine every year. It is no surprise that the phrase *Vale un Perú* (*It's worth a Peru*) became an expression of incalculable wealth throughout the Spanish-speaking world.

5 Cultural Tips

1. Peru was the seat of the Spanish Colonial Empire in South America. Because of its mineral wealth, the Spanish held on to Peru as long as possible. Peruvians still maintain a higher level of formality than many other Latin Americans.

2. Blunt, frank speech is not valued in Peru. Politeness demands a less direct approach. When spoken to aggressively, many Peruvians will tell you what they think you want to hear. It is best to avoid questions that can be answered with *yes* or *no.*

3. Peru is the southernmost nation where bullfighting is still popular. In fact, Lima has the oldest bullfighting ring in the Americas. Bullfighting is considered an art, not a sport. Whatever your feelings about bullfighting, do not speak disparagingly about it in Peru.

4. Historically, the role of women in Peruvian society was quite restricted. But the social and economic dislocations of the past few decades have forced women into public life. The need to feed their children led to the creation of all-women's organizations such as *Vaso de Leche* (*Glass of Milk*). Women have been elected to political office, especially at the local level.

5. Abbreviations and acronyms (collectively known as *siglas*) are common in Peru. Some utilize the first letter of each word, such as APRA for the Alianza Popular Revolucionaria Americana (the American Popular Revolutionary Alliance, one of Peru's major political parties). Other words can be derived from siglas; an *aprista* is a member of APRA. Others combine several initial letters, such as *Dincote* for Peru's Dirección Nacional Contra de Terrorismo (the National Counter-Terrorism Department).

 Economic Overview

After nearly 25 years of negative per capita GDP growth, Peru was the fastest growing economy in the world in 1994 (based on national GDP growth rate), and was expected to be the fastest growing in Latin America in 1995. A landslide victory by President Fujimori in 1995 and diminished terrorist activity allow Peru to continue with its disciplined economic course. Since coming into power in July 1990, the Fujimori administration has liberalized trade, investment, and foreign exchange regulations. U.S. products and services are well-regarded in the market and Peruvian companies are interested in expanding their business ties with the U.S.

Cultural Note: It is hard to exaggerate the changes President Fujimori has brought to Peru. Just twelve days after his accession to the presidency in July 1990, he instituted an economic austerity program. (Ironically, this was virtually the same program proposed by the man Fujimori defeated for the presidency, internationally acclaimed author Mario Vargas Llosa.) The cost of living soared with the removal of price controls. The Peruvian poor and middle classes were hit hard. As one columnist put it, Peruvians faced "Japanese prices on African incomes." Yet the majority of Peruvians continued to support Fujimori, for the same reason they elected him: Fujimori is not one of the white oligarchs who have ruled Peru since its inception. In racially divided

Peru, where the majority of citizens are poor and of mixed or Indian descent, the son of a Japanese grocer was seen as "one of us."

The economic austerity program, sometimes called *Fujishock*, successfully reduced inflation, which had reached a high of 7000% a year! Money from abroad once again flows into Peru, and the budget has been balanced.

Two further events secured Fujimori's position. In April of 1992 he closed down the Peruvian Congress, a notoriously corrupt and useless body. This move was tremendously popular with the people. Just a few months later, the legendary leader of the Shining Path terrorist group was captured in Lima, crippling his organization. The constitution has been amended to allow Fujimori to succeed himself as President.

Comparative Data

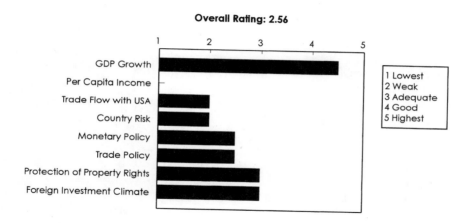

Overall Rating: 2.56

1	Lowest
2	Weak
3	Adequate
4	Good
5	Highest

Country Risk Rating

Gross Domestic Product: $32.5 billion
GDP Growth: 13%
Per Capita Income: $1,400

Trade Flows with the U.S.A.

Rank as Export Market for U.S.A. Goods & Services: 39th
U.S.A. Exports to Peru: $1.8 billion
Growth Rate of Exports: 28%
U.S.A. Imports from Peru: $1.0 million
Growth Rate of Imports: 19%
Rank as a Supplier of Imports into the U.S.A.:   54th

Top U.S.A. Exports to Peru: Machinery; mineral fuel; electronic components; cereals; motor vehicles; plastics; organic chemicals; aircraft; medical and optical equipment; paper and paperboard.

Top U.S.A. Prospects for Export to Peru: Telecommunications equipment; construction equipment; computers and peripherals; auto parts; mining and industry equipment; oil and gas equipment; medical equipment; food processing and packaging equipment; agricultural machinery; franchising.

Country Risk

Dun & Bradstreet rates Peru as having reasonable capacity to meet outstanding payment liabilities. Secured terms are advised on initial deals. Only reputable banks should be used.

Monetary Policy

Inflation has dropped from 7,650% in 1990 to 15.4% in 1994 as a result of tight monetary and fiscal policies. Inflation is expected to hover around 10% in 1996. *Monetary Unit*: nuevo sol.

Trade Policy

TARIFFS: Peru maintains 15% tariffs on 95% of the items on the tariff schedule and 25% tariffs on the remaining 5%. The trade-weighted average tariff is 16%, down from 80% in 1990. The government plans to move to a flat 15% tariff rate, which will eventually be reduced to 12%. This could change, however, if Peru joins the Andean Customs Union and adopts its common external tariff schedule of varying rates between 5 to 20%.

IMPORT LICENSING: The government has abolished import licenses for the vast majority of products. The only remaining products needing licenses are firearms, munitions, and explosives imported by private persons, chemical precursors (used in cocaine production), and ammonium nitrate fertilizer, which has been used for terrorist car bombs.

IMPORT TAXES: Most imports are subject to an 18% value added tax. Additionally, selective consumption taxes ranging from 10 to 50% are applied to certain luxury items. Peru in 1991 introduced temporary import surcharges on six basic agricultural commodities: wheat, wheat flour, rice, corn, sugar, and milk products. The government began reducing the surcharges in increments in April 1994 and has agreed to phase out the surcharges over a three-year period ending in 1997. Port fees have been reduced but are still relatively high for Latin America.

Protection of Intellectual Property Rights

The United States continues to raise intellectual property rights issues with Peru. While Peru has made improvements in its intellectual property rights protection, it does not yet appear to provide adequate and effective protection. In late 1993, the Andean Pact passed two new decisions on the protection of patents and trademarks. These Decisions took effect in Peru on January 1, 1994. The decisions offer a significant improvement over previous standards of protection for intellectual property in the Andean Pact countries; there is now a 20-year term of protection for patents.

In late 1993, the Andean Pact passed a decision on copyright protection which establishes a generally effective system. This decision took effect in Peru on January 1, 1994. However, copyrights are widely disregarded. The Peruvian government has conducted raids on vendors of pirated books, cassettes, and videos.

Foreign Investment Climate

The Fujimori government seeks to attract foreign investment in all sectors of the economy. Peru's liberal investment laws offer national treatment to all investors. An ambitious program of privatization has resulted in more than 90 privatizations since 1991. The goal is to sell off all remaining state-owned enterprises by the end of 1996.

Foreign investors have the same rights as national investors and thus would benefit from any investment incentives such as tax exonerations. Foreign investors also have international arbitration rights to settle investment contract disputes. Industries established in free trade zones are allowed to import manufacturing components free of all duties and fees. Zone users are also exempt from all taxes for a period of 15 years.

Current Leaders & Political Parties

(Update: International Academy at Santa Barbara *http://www.iasb.org/cwl*)

State, Government, and Political Party Leaders:
   Pres.: Alberto Fujimori
   Vice Pres.: vacant

Cabinet Ministers:
   Pres. of the Cncl. of Ministers and Min. of Education: Dante Cordova Blanco
   Foreign Affairs: Dr. Francisco Tudela
   Agriculture: Absalon Vasquez Villanueva
   Economy and Finances: Jorge Camet
   Energy and Mines: Amado Yataco Medina
   Fisheries: Jaime Sobero Taira
   Industry, Tourism, Integration, and Trade Negotiations: Liliana Canale

Interior: Gen. Juan Briones Davila

Presidency: Jaime Yoshiyama

Transportation, Communications, Housing, and Construction: Adm. Juan Castilla

Other Officials:

Pres. of the Constituent Congress: Martha Chavez

Ambassador to U.S.: Ricardo Luna

Perm. Rep. to U.N.: Fernando Guillen

Political Parties:

New Majority/Change 90 Party, Christian Popular Party, Renovation Mov., Leftist Democratic Mov., American Popular Revolutionary Alliance, Popular Action, United Left, Liberty Party

 Political Influences on Business

Peru is a republic with a dominant executive branch headed by President Alberto Fujimori, who was first elected in 1990 and won reelection by a landslide in 1995. The President appoints a number of ministers to carry out and oversee the work of the executive branch. The legislative branch is a unicameral congress with 120 members elected at large. Like the president, they serve five-year terms.

Major political parties include President Fujimori's rather loosely organized "Cambio 90/Nueva Mayoria," which holds a majority in the new congress; the equally loosely organized "Union por el Peru" whose leader is former U.N. Secretary General and presidential runner-up Javier Perez de Cuellar; and the quasisocialist "American Popular Revolutionary Alliance" (APRA). There are a number of smaller parties with seats in the congress, including the socialist/Marxist "United Left," centrist "Accion Popular," center-right "Partido Popular Cristiano," and the "Frente Independiente Moralizador." APRA and Accion Popular currently control most of the country's municipal governments.

U.S. policy in Peru reflects varied goals: the strengthening of democracy, fostering respect for human rights, the curtailment of illegal narcotics trafficking, supporting U.S. businesses and citizens, and encouraging sustainable Development. The United States development and humanitarian assistance program is currently the largest in South America.

There has been considerable progress in Peru's human rights record during the last few years as the level of political violence has declined. The numbers of political disappearances and extrajudicial killings have dropped dramatically since 1992. Nonetheless, the U.S. government remains concerned about continued arbitrary detentions, lack of due process, reports of torture of detainees and limited prosecution of those government and military officials accused of abuses.

Armed conflict broke out between Peru and Ecuador in January 1995 over a portion of the undemarcated border. Casualties for both sides were about 100 to 150 killed. A cease-fire was agreed to in February 1995, and is still respected. The U.S., along with Argentina, Brazil, and Chile, are guarantors of the Peru-Ecuador 1942 border treaty and are supporting Peruvian and Ecuadorian efforts to end the border conflict.

The security situation has improved considerably since the September 1992 capture of terrorist leader Abimael Guzman. However, Peru's two terrorist groups, Sendero Luminoso and the Tupac Amaru Revolutionary Movement, although seriously debilitated by the capture of their top leaders, have not been defeated. Both groups continue to carry out terrorist activities, including attacks on foreign businesses and diplomatic missions.

For up-to-date information regarding the security situation, contact the U.S. Department of State or U.S. Embassy in Lima.

Contacts in the U.S.A. & in Peru

Contacts in the United States:

EMBASSY OF PERU
1700 Massachusetts Avenue, N.W.
Washington, D.C. 20036
Tel: (202) 833-9860
Fax: (202) 659-8124

U.S. DEPARTMENT OF STATE
Bureau of Consular Affairs
Tel: (202) 647-5225
Country Desk Officer, Peru
Tel: (202) 647-3360

Contacts in Peru:

U.S. EMBASSY
Corners of Avenidas Inca Garcilaso de la Vega and España
Lima, Peru or
P.O. Box 1995
Lima 1, Peru
APO AA 34031
Tel: [51] (14) 338-000
Telex: 25212 PE (USEMBGSO)
Fax: [51] (14) 316-682

U.S. DEPARTMENT OF COMMERCE
Andean Division
Tel: (202) 482-2521
Fax: (202) 482-2218

THE FOREIGN COMMERCIAL SERVICE
Larrabure y Unanue 110
Piso 6
Lima, Peru
Tel: [51] (14) 330-555
Telex: 25028 PE USCOMATT
Fax: [51] (14) 334-687

AMERICAN CHAMBER OF COMMERCE
Av. Ricardo Palma 836 Miraflores
Lima 18, Peru
Tel: [51] (14) 47-9349
Telex: (394) 21165 BANKAMER
Fax: [51] (14) 47-9352

DUN & BRADSTREET S.A.
Postal Address: Apartado 3571
Lima 100
Peru
Street Address: Republica de Chile 388
Piso 2, Edificio Sarmiento
Lima 11
Peru
Tel: [51] (1)433-5533
Fax: [51] (1)433-2897

PRESIDENT ALBERTO FUJIMORI
Office of the President
Palacio de Gobierno
Plaza de Armas S/N
Lima 1, Republic of Peru

PRESIDENT OF THE COUNCIL OF MINISTERS
EFRAIN GOLDENBERG
Jr. Landa 535
Lima 1, Republic of Peru

 Passport/Visa Requirements

Visa Information   Tel: (202) 663-1225

Entry Requirements: A passport is required. U.S. citizens do not need a visa for a 90-day stay. A fully paid onward or return ticket is required.

Entering Peru on business matters (on a temporary basis, for soliciting business, and so on), travelers require a valid passport to obtain a business visa. This business visa is given by a Peruvian Consular official after presentation of the following: a letter of guaranty from the applicant's business firm, and copy of an onward or return trip ticket. Visa fee is $27.00 payable by cash or money order. All business transactions done in Peru must be reported, and the corresponding tax paid before leaving the country (if applicable).

An airport tax of $17.50 is applied to Peruvians, foreign tourists, and foreign residents when leaving the country.

The importation of merchandise as baggage is prohibited.

For current information concerning entry and customs requirements for Peru, travelers can contact the Peruvian Embassy.

Faux Pas: In Lima, a recreation center for the national police requested a large number of Coca-Cola signs, which they placed on every outdoor wall surface. The local Coca-Cola representative was enthusiastic at this free advertising, until he discovered that the police were using the red Coca-Cola signs to obscure the graffiti on the walls! The Communist Shining Path always painted their revolutionary slogans in red, which the red-and-white Coca-Cola signs disguised nicely.

The Philippines

Official Name:	Republic of the Philippines (Republika ng Pilipinas)
Official Language:	English, Pilipino (based on Tagalog, national language)
Government System:	Unitary republic
Population:	73.2 million
Population Growth:	2.2%
Area:	300,000 sq. km. (117,187 sq. mi.); slightly larger than Arizona
Natural Resources:	timber, crude oil, nickel, cobalt, silver, gold, salt, copper
Major Cities:	Manila (capital), Quezon City, Davao, Cebu

Cultural Note: After years of foreign domination, by the Spanish, Japanese, and the United States, most Filipinos are highly nationalistic. Slights against their country, even in jest, are the quickest way to poison a relationship. Avoid even backhanded comments, such as comparing how efficiently something is done in the U. S. A. compared to the Philippines.

Age Breakdown

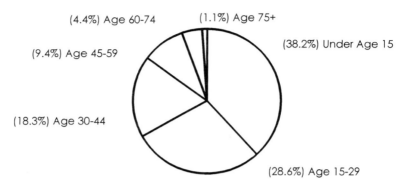

(4.4%) Age 60-74   (1.1%) Age 75+

(9.4%) Age 45-59   (38.2%) Under Age 15

(18.3%) Age 30-44

(28.6%) Age 15-29

Life Expectancy: 65 years male; 68 years female (1994)

 ## Time

Time is malleable in the Philippines. Foreign executives are expected to be on time to business meetings, but many Filipinos will not be punctual.

Everyone, even foreigners, are expected to be late for social events. But the exact amount of lateness depends upon the status of each person. (The highest-ranking person should arrive last.) Rather than try to decipher the ranking of each party guest, foreigners should just ask their host (in private) what time they should actually arrive.

The Philippines are eight hours ahead of Greenwich Mean Time (G.M.T. + 8), which is thirteen hours ahead of U.S. Eastern Standard Time (E.S.T. + 13).

 ## Holidays

(Update: Getting Through Customs *http://www.getcustoms.com*)

This list is a working guide. Dates should be corroborated before final travel plans are made. In cases where holidays fall on Saturday or Sunday, commercial establishments may be closed the preceding Friday or following Monday.

New Year's Day	1 January
Bataan & Corregidor Day and Heroism Day	9 April
Labor Day	1 May
Independence Day	12 June
National Heroes' Day	27 August

| Bonifacio Day | 30 November |
| Rizal Day | 30 December |

In addition, each town and region has annual fiestas, during which normal business is suspended. Two of the most important regional holidays are:

| Manila Day | 24 June |
| Quezon Day | 19 August |

Work Week

- Midmornings or mid-to-late afternoons are usually best for appointments.
- Business hours are generally from 8 A.M. to 5 P.M., Monday through Friday. Most offices close during the lunch break, which is usually from 12 noon to 1 P.M. but can easily stretch for two hours. Some offices may open from 8 A.M. to 12 noon on Saturdays.
- Government offices keep an 8 A.M. to 5 P.M. schedule, Monday through Friday. Many senior government officials work late, and some accept phone calls after hours—but only at their offices, never at home. (By contrast, many businesspeople can frequently be reached at home.)
- Banking hours are usually much shorter: from 9 A.M. to 2:30 or 3 P.M., Monday through Friday.

Religious/Societal Influences on Business

The Philippines have no official religion. The bulk of the population is (at least nominally) Roman Catholic, but various Protestant sects have experienced rapid growth. There are also breakaway sects of the Roman Catholic Church, such as the Philippine Independent Church. Islam is found in the south. Many of the Filipinos who have engaged in armed rebellion are both Muslim and Communist.

Social scientists have found that most Filipinos have a fairly low Uncertainty Avoidance Index. Societies which score high on this scale feel the need for creating rigid rules of behavior and extensive sets of laws to enforce them. At the opposite end of the scale, Philippine society and behavior exhibits flexibility and adaptability. The letter of the law is not observed strictly, nor are there regulations to cover every situation. This situation is probably ideal for a sprawling, geographically divided, multicultural society, with technology levels which range from stone age to cutting edge. (Some 70 different languages and dialects are spoken within the Philippines.) But it has disadvantages for foreigners who assume that laws exist and are complied with. For example, one cannot assume that comprehensive building codes exist in all areas of the Philippines, and where they are extant, one cannot assume that they are adhered to or enforced strictly.

In fact, regulation enforcement is often used as a weapon among competitors. One party with government connections is allowed to flout regulations, while competitors are strictly held to the letter of the law. It is summed up in this Philippine expression: "For my friends, everything; for my enemies, the law."

Curiously, this does not prevent companies from adopting extensive in-house regulations for their employees. This reflects the difficulty that a boss has in disciplining an employee who is probably related to several company employees (or even related to the boss). By detailing punishments for various infractions, the boss gains a face-saving distance from any necessary disciplinary action.

Great inequalities exist in the Philippines. The majority of the population is poor. But mobility (or the hope of mobility) exists.

The most important influence on Filipinos is the family. Nepotism is common and is not considered to be detrimental.

 5 Cultural Tips

1. Titles are important to the Filipinos, so important that many employees are rewarded with impressive-sounding titles (and little else). Address an executive by his or her title and surname, but do not expect to be able to tell much about a person's importance from the title.

2. Kinship is everything in the Philippines. You will be accepted more rapidly if you can explain your relationship to someone the Filipinos already know. Even if the relationship is distant (i.e., you are the friend of the brother of someone they know), that relationship helps establish you as a real person in Philippine eyes.

3. Philippine business operates at its own pace, and it cannot be speeded up by outsiders. Most Philippine executives will not consider doing business with you until they feel that they know you and like you. Extensive socializing will be necessary, both inside and outside the office. An extensive government bureaucracy slows down action even further. Be patient.

4. Perceiving face and the avoidance of shame are vital in the Philippines. Unfortunately, bad news is often interpreted as a loss of face, so many Filipinos will tell you only good news (or what they think you want to hear). Filipinos will often smile and say *yes* when they really mean *no*. They do not intend to deceive; they are trying to save the feelings of everyone involved.

5. Groups of Filipinos do not arrange themselves in neat lines. Instead, they form a pushing, shoving crowd, with each person out for him- or herself. The only times that Filipinos have queued in neat lines was under the gun of armed soldiers, such as under the Japanese occupation army in World War II, so queues may have bad associations for Filipinos.

Economic Overview

In the past few years the Philippines has undergone a remarkable transformation. In the late 1980s and early 1990s, the Philippines was saddled with political instability and unrest, weak economic growth, a badly neglected infrastructure and a slow pace of economic liberalization. Today, it is increasingly recognized by analysts that the Philippines has turned the corner economically, overcome several of its most pressing problems, and is on a heading for sustained economic growth and increased prosperity. GNP growth rates are up from near zero in the early 1990s to between 5 and 6%. Other economic indicators such as inflation and export growth are also positive.

Under the Ramos administration, confidence at home and abroad is up and political instability has disappeared as an issue. Democracy is secure in the Philippines. The Ramos Administration and the Philippine Congress have taken important, concrete steps toward economic liberalization, including import duty reductions, opening up of banking and telecommunications sectors, and liberalization of investment laws. These moves toward liberalization will create a climate more attractive than ever to U.S. business, and will strengthen an already strong commercial relationship. Historically, close bilateral ties and extensive people-to-people contacts have helped solidify the U.S. position as the Philippines' number one trading partner and foreign investor. Philippine-U.S. trade in 1995 totaled more than $12 billion, and placed the Philippines among America's top 25 trading partners worldwide.

Trade with the U.S. accounts for almost a third of the Philippines' total trade turnover, and about one-fifth of Philippine imports come from the U.S., consisting chiefly of electronic components, telecommunications equipment, data processing machines, and wheat.

U.S. direct investment in the Philippines is valued at about $2 billion, largely concentrated in manufacturing and banking. Gradual liberalization of Philippine foreign investment regulations have encouraged a growing number of U.S. companies to consider the country seriously as a new investment location. Relatively low costs of doing business, geographical location, and quality of the labor force have caused many companies to select the Philippines as a regional headquarters in Asia.

Deterrents to foreign trade and investment continue to exist including inadequate enforcement and slow adjudication of intellectual property rights, limitations on land ownership and on foreign investment in certain industries, and activities and customs barriers. The Ramos Administration is committed to improving the overall trade and investment climate to open the Philippine economy to greater foreign participation.

Cultural Note: Filipinos grow up in extended families and are rarely alone. Indeed, solitude makes most Filipinos uncomfortable. A foreigner's desire for privacy is not understood. If you are sitting alone on a bus or in a cinema, a Filipino is likely to ignore all the empty seats and sit next to you. Such action is not about you; it is simply a cultural trait.

Comparative Data

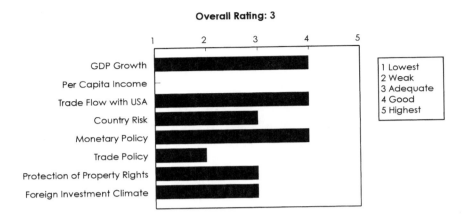

Overall Rating: 3

	1	2	3	4	5
GDP Growth					
Per Capita Income					
Trade Flow with USA					
Country Risk					
Monetary Policy					
Trade Policy					
Protection of Property Rights					
Foreign Investment Climate					

1 Lowest
2 Weak
3 Adequate
4 Good
5 Highest

Country Risk Rating

Gross Domestic Product: $74 billion
GDP Growth: 5.2%
Per Capita Income: $1,055

Trade Flows with the U.S.A.

Rank as Export Market for U.S.A. Goods & Services: 23rd
U.S.A. Exports to Philippines: $5.3 billion
Growth Rate of Exports: 36%
U.S.A. Imports from the Philippines: $7.0 billion
Growth Rate of Imports: 23%
Rank as a Supplier of Imports into the U.S.A.:   20th

Top U.S.A. Exports to the Philippines: Electrical components; machinery; cereals; plastics and resins; paper and paperboard; medical and optical equipment; organic chemicals; animal feed; cotton/yarn/fabric; tobacco.

Top U.S.A. Prospects for Export the Philippines: Telecommunications equipment; electrical power systems; building products; industrial chemicals; aircraft and parts; computers and peripherals; architectural; construction/engineering services; pumps/valves/compressors; food processing/packaging equipment; water and wastewater treatment equipment.

Country Risk

Dun & Bradstreet rates the Philippines as having sufficient capacity to meet outstanding payment liabilities.

Most business is conducted on letters of credit, although more liberal terms, including open account, are generally sufficient for repeat business. Credit terms of 30 to 60 days normally apply.

Monetary Policy

Average year-to-year consumer price inflation has been kept at single-digits since 1992.

Dun & Bradstreet forecasts inflation to range between 7% and 10% in 1996 and 1997. *Monetary Unit:* Philippine peso.

Trade Policy

TARIFFS: The Philippines' average nominal tariff is 20%. Tariffs are grouped into four tiers of 3%, 10%, 20% and 30%. Approximately 185 "strategic" product lines remain subject to a 50% tariff. This group, which includes rice, sugar, coconut oil, and luxury goods such as liquor, tobacco, candy, and leather goods, represents about 3% of tariff lines.

IMPORT LICENSING: Generally, all merchandise imports are allowed without a license. Several restricted and controlled items remain subject to quota restrictions for reasons of public health, morals, and national security.

Before any importation into the Philippines can be made, an importer must identify the product in the Philippine Standard Commodity Classification Manual. The Philippine government requires import permits for meat and meat products, fresh produce, planting seeds/plants, and all agricultural commodities which are officially prohibited for import. Until implementation of the new market access rules established under GATT, several agricultural commodities will continue to be prohibited from import.

IMPORT TAXES: A value-added tax of 10% is imposed on imports for resale or reuse. Firms located in export-processing zones and free ports are exempted from VAT.

Protection of Intellectual Property Rights

The Philippines was moved from the U.S. Trade Representative's special 301 priority watch list to the regular watch list following an agreement signed in April 1993 between the two governments which significantly strengthens intellectual property rights (IPR) protection in the Philippines. The Philippine government is a party to the Paris Convention for the Protection of Industrial Property, the Patent Cooperation Treaty, and is a member of the World Trade Organization and the World Intellectual Property Organization.

The life of a patent ranges from five to 17 years, depending on the type of patent registered. Inventions are protected for 17 years. Utility model patents and industrial design patents are protected for five years, extendable for another two terms. Licensing is required if, after two years from registration, the patented item is not being utilized in the Philippines on a commercial scale or if the domestic demand for the patented article is not being met to an adequate extent and on reasonable terms.

Trademark protection is granted for 20 years, extendable indefinitely for succeeding 25-year terms. Every five years, the trademark owner must file an affidavit of use or nonuse to avoid cancellation of registration. Trademark protection is limited to the manufacturing or marketing of the specific class of goods applied for, and to products with a logical linkage to the protected mark (i.e., trademark protection for a watch would extend to watch straps).

Philippine law is overly broad in allowing the reproduction, adaptation, or translation of published works without the authorization of the copyright owner. Video piracy is a problem as is computer software piracy.

Foreign Investment Climate

The Philippine government has taken important steps since 1990 to welcome foreign investment, despite occasional resistance by vested interests and nationalist groups. The 1991 Foreign Investment Act (FIA) lifted the 40% foreign ownership ceiling previously imposed on domestic enterprises, provided no incentives are sought and the activity does not appear on a foreign investment negative list. In 1994, amendments to the country's banking law allowed up to 10 foreign banks to establish branches in the Philippines. After decades of protection, the government is allowing additional foreign-owned companies to enter the insurance industry. While investment liberalization has been substantial, barriers to foreign entry remain for a variety of reasons. Depending on the industry or activity, the FIA's foreign investment negative list fully or partially restricts foreign ownership under three broad categories:

- *List A* restricts foreign investment in certain sectors because of constitutional or legal constraints. For example, industries such as mass media, retail trade, small scale mining, private security agencies, and the practice of licensed professions are fully reserved for Philippine citizens. Land ownership is also constitutionally restricted to Filipino citizens or to corporations with at least 60% Filipino ownership.
- *List B* restricts foreign ownership (generally to 40%) for reasons of national security, defense, public health, safety, and morals. This list also seeks to protect local small and medium-sized firms by restricting foreign ownership to no more than 40% in nonexport firms capitalized at less than $500,000.
- *List C* restricts foreign ownership (generally to 40%) in activities deemed adequately served by existing Philippine enterprises. This list has included sectors such as insurance, travel agencies, tourist lodging establishments, conference/convention

organizers, and import and wholesale activities not integrated with production. At present, this list is vacant. Over the next two years, domestic firms which believe their activity is adequately served may petition for inclusion in the C list. However, the inclusion criteria established are strict, and involve public hearings. Pending legislation, supported by the government, seeks to abolish the C list altogether.

Current Leaders & Political Parties

(Update: International Academy at Santa Barbara *http://www.iasb.org/cwl*)

State, Government, and Political Party Leaders:
  Pres.: Fidel V. Ramos
  Vice Pres.: Joseph Estrada

Cabinet Secretaries:
  Exec. Sec.: Ruben Torres
  Foreign Affairs: Domingo L. Siazon
  Finance: Roberto De Ocampo
  Agriculture: Roberto Sebastian
  Labor and Employment: José Brillantes
  Interior and Local Govt.: Rafael Alunan
  Environment and Natural Resources: Victor O. Ramos
  Trade and Industry: Rizalino Navarro
  Transportation and Communications: Jesus Garcia
  Tourism: Eduardo Pilapil
  Public Works and Highways: Gregorio Vigilar
  Science and Technology: William Padolina
  Budget and Management: Salvador Enriquez
  Press Sec.: Hector Ronaldo Romero Villanueva
  Economic Planning and Dir. Gen. of the Natl. Economic Dev. Authority: Cielito Habito
  Natl. Security Adviser: José Almonte

Other Officials:
  Pres. of the Senate: Edgardo Angara
  Speaker of the House of Representatives: José De Venecia
  Chmn. of the Presidential Comn. on Good Govt.: Magtanggol C. Gunigundo
  Gov. of the Central Bank of the Philippines: Gabriel Singson

Commisioner of the Comn. on Immigration and Deportation: Leandro Verceles
Ambassador to U.S.: Raul C. Rabe
Perm. Rep. to U.N.: Felipe Mabilangan

Political Parties:

Lakas Edsa-Natl. Union of Christian Democrats, Nationalist Party, Filipino
Democratic Party, Liberal Party, People's Reform Party, New Society Mov.

 Political Influences on Business

U.S.-Philippine relations have improved substantially since the Philippine Senate's 1991 rejection of a treaty which would have permitted the continuation of U.S. bases at Clark and Subic Bay. During President Ramos' visit to the United States in November 1993, he and President Clinton agreed on a new, postbases partnership centering on expanded trade and investment ties as well as continued security cooperation under a Mutual Defense Treaty.

Although U.S. economic and assistance security levels to the Philippines have declined steeply in recent years, a modest aid program continues. The bilateral relationship is buttressed by longstanding historical and cultural links and extensive people-to-people interaction. Since taking office in June 1992, President Ramos has largely restored democratic stability to the Philippines. Making national reconciliation a major goal of his administration, he initiated a domestic peace process which has as its goal a negotiated settlement with Muslim, communist, and military rebels. Although this peace process is still ongoing, the threat from communist insurgents and military rebels who destabilized his predecessor's government has receded greatly. Armed Muslim separatists still threaten public order in the southern part of the country, but the government has concluded a ceasefire agreement with the largest group and talks on a political settlement are continuing.

The Philippines has a presidential form of government patterned after that of the United States with a separation of powers among the Executive, Legislative, and Judicial branches. The Philippine Congress functions much like its U.S. counterpart and is the main arena for competition among the four principal political parties, all of which espouse moderate policies and appeal to similar constituencies. The House of Representatives is currently controlled by the administration-backed Lakas party, in alliance with other parties. The Laban party, which is in coalition with the Lakas party, dominates the Senate. The midterm elections in May 1995 returned proadministration majorities to the House and Senate, and provided President Ramos with a mandate to pursue policies aimed at spurring economic growth and fostering political stability.

Expatriates and foreign-owned businesses in the Philippines have been the target of a rising crime rate. Filipinos are also fed up with crime, but they are wary about giving the police increased powers. Memories of police abuse and martial law under former President Ferdinand Marcos still haunt the Philippines.

Contacts in the U.S.A. & in the Philippines

Contacts in the United States:

EMBASSY OF THE REPUBLIC OF THE PHILIPPINES
1600 Massachusetts Ave., N.W.
Washington, D.C. 20036
Tel: (202) 467-9300
Fax: (202) 328-7614

U.S. DEPARTMENT OF STATE
Visa Information
Tel: (202) 663-1225

U.S. DEPARTMENT OF COMMERCE
Philippines Desk
Int'l Trade Admin.
Office of the Pacific Basin
Tel: (202) 482-4958

PACRIM FAX INFO
Faxed Information
(Explanations for use online)
Tel: (202) 482-3875

TOURISM OFFICE
Philippine Center
556 Fifth Avenue
New York, N.Y. 10036
Tel: (212) 575-7915
Fax: (212) 302-6759

Contacts in the Philipines:

U.S. EMBASSY
1201 Roxas Blvd.
Ermita Manila 1000
APO AP 96440
Tel: [63] (2) 521-7116
Telex: 722-27366 AME PH
Fax: [63] (2) 522-4361

PRESIDENT FIDEL V. RAMOS
Office of the President
Malacanang Palace Compound
J.P. Laurel Sr. Street
San Miguel
Manila 1005, Republic of the Philippines

Passport/Visa Requirements

Visa Information   Tel: (202) 663-1225

Entry Requirements: A passport is required. A visa is not required for tourists from the U.S.A. for a stay not exceeding 21 days. However, such travelers must have a valid passport and onward or return booking by sea or air.

Businesspersons require a visa no matter what the length of their stay.

Faux Pas: Hosting visitors is an important tradition in the Philippines. Families have been known to impoverish themselves to provide an appropriate feast for a guest.

An American scientist was commissioned to improve poultry production in the Philippines. He imported several carefully selected roosters and distributed one each to poor local farmers. When the time came to inspect the program's progress, the scientist arranged to visit one of the farmers. Arriving at the farm, the scientist was escorted to a feast table. The centerpiece of the feast was the imported rooster, fried! (The farmer felt that the only bird he owned which was good enough to serve to the distinguished scientist was the imported rooster.)

Poland

Official Name:	Republic of Poland (Rzeczpospolita Polska)
Official Language:	Polish
Government System:	Multiparty republic
Population:	38.5 million
Population Growth:	.35%
Area:	312,680 sq. km. (120,725 sq. mi.); about the size of New Mexico
Natural Resources:	coal, sulfur, copper, natural gas, silver, zinc, iron ore, lead, salt
Major Cities:	Warsaw (capital), Lodz, Krakow, Wroclaw, Poznan, Gdansk

Cultural Note: Emigration has often been a solution to hard times in Poland. Thousands of Poles came to the U.S.A. in the past century. Today Poles are again emigrating, but this time it is the most educated Poles who are seeking opportunity abroad. In the 1990s one in five doctors and one in three mathematicians left Poland. This "brain drain" constitutes a serious problem for Poland.

Age Breakdown

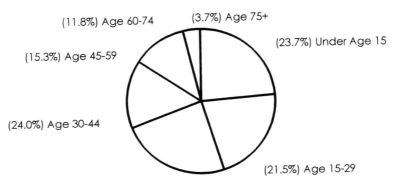

(11.8%) Age 60-74   (3.7%) Age 75+

(15.3%) Age 45-59   (23.7%) Under Age 15

(24.0%) Age 30-44

(21.5%) Age 15-29

Life Expectancy: 68 years male; 77 years female (1991)

 Time

Under Soviet domination, punctuality was not expected. The Communist government guaranteed everyone a job, and no one was fired for tardiness. This attitude is slowly changing.

As a foreign businessperson you are expected to arrive on time to all business appointments.

Poland is one hour ahead of Greenwich Mean Time (G.M.T. + 1), which is six hours ahead of U.S. Eastern Standard Time (E.S.T. + 6).

 Holidays

(Update: Getting Through Customs *http://www.getcustoms.com*)

This list is a working guide. Dates should be corroborated before final travel plans are made. In cases where holidays fall on Saturday or Sunday, commercial establishments may be closed the preceding Friday or following Monday.

New Year's Day	1 January
Constitution Day	3 May
National Independence Day	11 November
Boxing Day	26 December

Work Week

- The Polish work day starts early. Appointments at 8:00 A.M. are not unusual.
- Business lunches are often held quite late, around 4:00 or 5:00 P.M.
- Requests for appointments should be made in writing when possible. Translating the request into Polish will make a good impression.
- Most businesses have a 5 1/2 day work week: 8:00 or 9:00 A.M. to 2:00 or 3:00 P.M., Monday through Friday; 8:00 A.M. to 1:30 P.M., Saturdays.

Religious/Societal Influences on Business

Is the Pope Polish? Yes, and Catholicism is essentially the only religion in Poland. Only 1.5% of the population is identified as belonging to another religion, although almost 10% of Poles are nonreligious (an atheist legacy of Soviet-dominated Poland).

During centuries of foreign domination, the national aspirations of the Polish people were sublimated into the Catholic Church. Almost singlehandedly, the Church helped stave off Poland's cultural absorption by Lutheran Prussia and Orthodox Russia. For preserving their cultural identity, the Polish people owe their Church a debt they can never repay.

With Poland free and independent at last, it is not surprising that the Catholic Church should want to collect on that debt, by having a say in how Poland is run. Poland is now challenging Ireland for the honor of being "the most Catholic country in the world." As in Ireland, the major friction arises over the Church's prohibition of contraception and abortion. But unlike Ireland, Poland had abortion on demand during the decades of Soviet domination. New restrictions on abortion have been passed, but are opposed by many Polish citizens. Businesses (including medical insurers) whose products or services touch on birth control issues should be prepared for further changes in Poland.

Despite the fact that virtually all of Poland's Jews were exterminated by the Nazis in World War II, antisemitism is still extant in Poland. Former President Lech Walesa frequently came under foreign criticism for failing to repudiate the anti-semitic statements of his supporters.

5 Cultural Tips

1. Poland and Russia are locked into a complex historical relationship which colors all cross-border interactions. In brief: Poland was a civilized and sophisticated nation when the Russian city-states were still beating off Asiatic hordes. As Russia grew in stature, Poland's fortunes sank. To many Russians, Russia only became a great Western power after it humbled the proud Poles. And many Poles see Russia as the architect of Poland's misfortunes. Any interaction which involves Poles and Russians may involve these beliefs.

2. Poland suffered greatly in the Second World War, and most of its cities were devastated. The Polish love of history is evident in the way historic districts have been restored, using old photographs and prints as guides. Poles have a reverence for their past that is without equal in Europe.

3. The Polish people have a tradition of hospitality and gracious living inherited from the Polish nobility. This bears some similarity to the American tradition of "Southern hospitality," wherein the positive aspects of Southern planters are appreciated while the institution of slavery (which made such a lifestyle possible) is ignored. The Poles choose to honor their nobility's beneficence while ignoring the nobility's incompetence as rulers, which led to the foreign domination of Poland.

4. In common with other Slavic groups, Poles give the appearance of being rather dour. Smiles are reserved for friends; they are rarely used in public. (When U.S. game shows were adapted to Polish television, the biggest problem was getting the serious Polish contestants to look happy and excited on camera!)

5. Poland is still a male-dominated society. Despite the equality of the sexes mandated under Soviet domination, traditional attitudes about women remain. International businesswomen report that Poland is one of the more difficult places in Europe to be taken seriously.

 Economic Overview

Opportunities for trade and investment exist across virtually all industrial and consumer sectors in Poland. U.S. firms lead investment in Poland, accounting for approximately one-third of all foreign investment. The prospect for real economic growth, the size of the Polish market and political stability are the top reasons U.S. firms should consider the Polish market.

The U.S. Department of Commerce has designated Poland as one of the top 10 "Big Emerging Markets" in the world for U.S. exports.

The Polish economy has experienced tremendous growth over the last three years. A growth rate of 5 to 6% is expected in 1996. Other economic indicators, including balance of payments and unemployment, continue to improve.

U.S. exports to Poland increased in 1995 by 24%. The U.S. ranked as the sixth largest supplier of imports to Poland in 1995, representing a 4% share of the total import market. Poland's government changed in 1995 for the sixth time in six years. The transition was peaceful and democratic and Poland is essentially a stable country. Although the successive postcommunist governments have contributed greatly to Poland's economic recovery with their devotion to sound fiscal and monetary policies, frequent political changes limit consistency and momentum. U.S. exports are faced with significantly higher customs duties than competitors from the European Union. This can also affect investors, as it adds costs to imported capital goods used in production.

Comparative Data

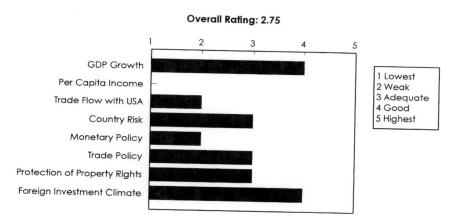

Overall Rating: 2.75

Country Risk Rating

Gross Domestic Product: $86 billion
GDP Growth: 5%
Per Capita Income: $2,500

Trade Flows with the U.S.A.

Rank as Export Market for U.S.A. Goods & Services: 56th
U.S.A. Exports to Poland: $776 million
Growth Rate of Exports: 24%
U.S.A. Imports from Poland: $663 million

Growth Rate of Imports: 2%

Rank as a Supplier of Imports into the U.S.A.:   59th

Top U.S.A. Exports to Poland: Machinery; electronic components; aircraft; meat; motor vehicles; medical and optical equipment; plastics; tobacco; cereals; pharmaceuticals.

Top U.S.A. Prospects for Export to Poland: Computers and peripherals; computer software; medical equipment; pollution control equipment; telecommunications; building products; broadcasting equipment; sporting goods; poultry and meat; wheat.

Country Risk

Dun & Bradstreet considers Poland to have sufficient capacity to meet outstanding payment liabilities. More than 60% of sales are now on open account terms according to Dun & Bradstreet with sight drafts widely used and cash-in-advance becoming less popular. Letters of credit are now used in approximately 10% of transactions, but are still recommended when dealing with new accounts.

Monetary Policy

Poland's government has won support from the international community in recognition of its commitment to disciplined financial policies. One important negative factor is inflation which has hovered around 30% annually. Inflation in 1995 was 22%, down from 32% in 1994 and 35% in 1993. In February 1995, the National Bank of Poland took action against inflation by partially floating the Polish zloty. *Monetary Unit:* zloty.

Trade Policy

TARIFFS: Tariff rates are subject to frequent change as Poland adjusts to becoming a market economy. Customs duties apply to all products imported into Poland. Tariffs range from 0 to 90%, with the average rate between 8 and 12%. Refund of duty paid on raw materials, semifinished goods and products used in the manufacture of goods for export within 30 days are possible, contingent on documentation certifying customs duty was paid on the goods when they were imported.

Many categories of U.S. products face tariff disadvantages compared to European competitors.

IMPORT LICENSING: There are few formal trade barriers, that is, import quotas or import bans in Poland. In some areas, including imports of strategic goods (such as police and military products, radioactive elements, weapons, transportation equipment, chemicals) a license or concession is required. Imports of beer and wine, gas, and certain agricultural and food products are also licensed.

Certain goods are subject to import quotas. These include gasoline, diesel fuel and heating oils, wine and other alcohols, and cigars and cigarettes.

Imports of all live plants require a phytosanitary import permit. The list of products requiring import certification in Poland is always subject to change and appears to be growing. There are lengthy testing procedures required for import permits of certain products. U.S. exporters should ascertain whether their product requires import certification before shipping.

IMPORT TAXES: In addition to customs tariffs, all commodities imported into Poland are subject to an obligatory 5% import tax. For some luxury and strategic products (including alcohol, cosmetics, cigarettes, sugar confectionery, video cameras, satellite antennas, cars, gasoline and oil), excise tax is also applied.

A value-added tax is also assessed. There are three VAT rates: 0%, 7%, and 22% depending on the product.

Protection of Intellectual Property Rights

Foreigners, both resident and nonresident in Poland, benefit from intellectual property ownership rights, whether as a result of Polish law or bilateral agreements. Poland is a signatory to a number of international intellectual property rights conventions, including the Berne and Paris conventions as well as the World Institute for Protection of Intellectual Property.

Patents are valid for 20 years from the filing date. A registered trademark is valid for 10 years from the date of filing, unless the mark is not used for three consecutive years. The registration may be renewed for 10-year periods. A new copyright law which became effective in June 1994 extends copyright protection from 25 to 50 years and protects not only authors, but also producers, artists, and performers.

Foreign Investment Climate

The Foreign Investment Act of 1991, and subsequent amendments to the Act, opened the Polish economy to foreign investment and established a level playing field between foreign and domestic investors. Under the law, any level of foreign ownership, up to 100%, is allowed. There is no screening of foreign investments.

The acquisition of real estate by a foreign entity requires a permit from the Ministry of Interior. Nonfarm real estate may be purchased outright.

Polish privatization efforts have been open to foreign investors and most of the largest transactions have involved sales to foreign firms. The exception to this openness to foreign investment is the Mass Privatization Program which will give control of over 400 state-owned enterprises to a group of national investment funds (NIF). Shares in the NIFs will initially be sold only to Polish citizens, and only over time will sale on a secondary market be permitted, at which time foreign investors may be able to buy shares

 # Current Leaders & Political Parties

(Update: International Academy at Santa Barbara *http://www.iasb.org/cwl*)

State, Government, and Political Party Leaders:

Pres.: Aleksander Kwasniewski

Council of Ministers:

Prime Min.: Wlodzimierz Cimoszewicz

Dep. Prime Min. and Min. of Finance: Grzegorz Kolodko

Dep. Prime Min. and Min. of Agriculture and Food: Roman Jagielinski

Dep. Prime Min. and Head of the Scientific Research Com.: Aleksander Luczak

Head of the Office of the Council of Ministers: Leszek Miller

Culture and Art: Zdzislaw Podkanski

Country Planning and Construction: Barbara Blida

Environmental Protection, Natural Resources, and Forestry: Stanislaw Zelichowski

Foreign Affairs: Dariusz Rosati

Foreign Economic Relations: Jacek Buchacz

Industry and Commerce: Klemens Scierski

Internal Affairs: Zbigniew Siemiatkowski

Labor and Social Policy: Andrzej Baczkowski

Natl. Defense: Stanislaw Dobrzanski

Natl. Education: Jerzy Wiatr

Privatization: Wieslaw Kaczmarek

Telecommunications: Andrzej Zielinski

Transport and Navigation: Boguslaw Liberadzki

Head of the Central Planning Office: Miroslaw Pietrewicz

Chmn. of the Scientific Research Com.: Aleksander Luczak

Other Officials:

Speaker of the Sejm (Parliament): Józef Zych
Speaker of the Senate: Adam Krzysztof Struzik
Pres. of the Natl. Bank: Hanna Gronkiewicz-Waltz
Ambassador to U.S.: Jerzy Kozminski
Perm. Rep. to U.N.: Zbigniew M. Wlosowicz

Political Parties:

Social Democratic Party, Polish Peasant Party, Labor Union, Confederation for an Independent Poland, Union for Freedom, Solidarity, Non-partisan Bloc in Support of Reform, Christian Natl. Union, Center Alliance, and several others.

Political Influences on Business

Poland's political leaders have repeatedly given strong public encouragement to western and specifically U.S. investment. There are nevertheless domestic political factors at play which can impinge on Poland's hospitality to foreign investment. Former Prime Minister Oleksy's Democratic Left Alliance encourages foreign investment, but seeks to regulate it to protect emerging Polish capital. Former Prime Minister Pawlak's Polish Peasant Party (PSL) contains fiercely protectionist elements which occasionally prompt hostility toward foreign investors. In one recent case, a significant portion of the PSL parliamentary caucus demanded the dismissal of the Minister of Privatization for his plan to open up the Polish tobacco industry to foreign investors. Former Prime Minister Pawlak attempted to slow the mass privatization program to allow more time for the Polish government to assess the economic impact of the program, but under Prime Minister Oleksy the program has moved forward. The Polish government has also imposed variable tariff levies on food imports to protect Polish domestic products.

Trade union politics are also an element for foreign business to consider. The Polish trade union movement, the engine of communism's collapse in the 1980s, has occasionally been problematic for foreign investors, particularly when managers of newly privatized state enterprises have instituted management changes. Strike activity at Polish coal mines in early 1994 briefly threatened power supplies in some localities, but generally strikes have not threatened or noticeably compromised Poland's industrial infrastructure.

Poland is organized as a parliamentary democracy according to the so-called "Little Constitution" adopted by the Polish parliament in 1992, pending the passage of a permanent constitution. Poland's parliamentary leaders are now at work on drafting a new constitution which they expect to submit to the Polish electorate in the spring of 1996. Since 1989, Poles have enjoyed largely unfettered rights to free speech, press, and assembly as well as other commonly accepted Western human rights.

Poland has a bicameral parliament, comprised of a lower house (Sejm) and upper house (Senate). Within the legislative branch of the government, the Sejm has most of the power; the Senate may only suggest amendments to legislation passed by the Sejm or delay it. Both bodies are elected democratically. Poland's last parliamentary elections were in September 1993 when the Democratic Left Alliance (SLD) and PSL won nearly two-thirds of the 460 seats in the Sejm and formed a coalition government. The parliament and government were elected to a four-year term which expires in September 1997. The president may dissolve the parliament and call new elections before then, if the government fails a vote of confidence or is unable to pass a budget.

The Polish Prime Minister, whom the president nominates to constitute a government and win a vote of confidence in the Sejm, chairs the Council of Ministers and serves as Poland's chief of government. There are 18 cabinet ministers, three of whom serve as deputy prime ministers, mostly drawn from the governing coalition parties. There are a few ministers without any party affiliation.

Poland's president, who serves as the country's head of state, has a five-year term. If no candidate wins an absolute majority, the top two vote-getters must compete in a run-off election. The Polish president is the commander of the armed forces and may veto legislation passed by the parliament. Presidential vetoes can be overturned by a two-thirds vote in each parliamentary house.

Provincial and local government can play an important role in facilitating or hindering trade and investment in Poland. Poland is divided into 49 provinces or *voivodships* each of which is headed by a provincial governor (*voivode*) appointed by the central government. There are also independent locally elected city and village governments. Party affiliations play an increasingly important role in local Polish politics, particularly in larger cities, but are not yet as significant as in the United States.

Contacts in the U.S.A. & in Poland

Contacts in the United States:

EMBASSY OF THE REPUBLIC OF POLAND
2640 16th St., N.W.
Washington, D.C. 20009
Tel: (202) 234-3800
Fax: (202) 328-6271

U.S. DEPARTMENT OF STATE
Bureau of Consular Affairs
Tel: (202) 647-5225
Country Desk Officer, Poland
Tel: (202) 647-1070

U.S. DEPARTMENT OF COMMERCE
Poland Desk
Internatl. Trade Admin.
Tel: (202) 482-4915
Fax: (202) 482-4505

EASTERN EUROPE BUSINESS INFORMATION CENTER
Int'l Trade Admin.
DOC
Room 7412
Washington, D.C. 20230
Tel: (202) 482-2645
Fax: (202) 482-4473

TOURISM OFFICE
Polish National Tourist Ofice
275 Madison Avenue
New York, N.Y. 10016
Tel: (212) 338-9412
Fax: (212) 338-9283

Contacts in Poland:

EMBASSY OF THE UNITED STATES
AmEmbassy Warsaw
Aleje Ujazdowskie 29/31
Box 5010, Unit 1340 or
APO AE 09213-1340
Tel: [48] (2) 628-3041
Telex: 817771 EMUSA PL
Fax: [48] (2) 628-8298

AMERICAN CHAMBER OF COMMERCE IN
POLAND
Plac Powstancow Warszawy 1
00-950 Warsaw
Tel: [48-22] 26-39-60
Fax: [48-22] 26-51-31

MINISTRY OF PRIVATIZATION INFORMATION
CENTER
36 Krucza/6 Wspolna Street
00-522 Warsaw
Tel: [48-22] 628-1190
Fax: [48-22] 625-1114

DUN & BRADSTREET POLAND SP. ZO. O.
Postal Address: Ul. Krzywickiego 34
02-078 Warsaw
Poland
Street Address: IMM Building
Ul. Krzywickiego 34
02-078 Warsaw
Poland
Tel: [48] (2)625-7202
Fax: [48] (2) 625-7200

PRESIDENT ALEKSANDER KWASNIEWSKI
Wiejska 10
00–902 Warszawa, Republic of Poland

PRIME MINISTER JOZEF OLEKSY
Office of the Council of Ministers
Aleje Ujazdowskie 1/3
00-950 Warszawa, Republic of Poland

Passport/Visa Requirements

Visa Information   Tel: (202) 663-1225

Entry Requirements: A passport is required. A visa is not required for stays of up to 90 days, depending upon the citizenship of the visitor. Visitors must register at a hotel or with local authorities within three days after crossing the Polish border. This requirement does not apply while the visitor is in transit. There is also a requirement to report the visitors location, to be completed within 48 hours of arrival. An AIDS test is required for student visas; U.S. test results are accepted.

Further information on entry requirements may be obtained from the Embassy of the Republic of Poland, Consular Section.

Cultural Note: If Western observers are dismayed by the resurgence of former Communists in Poland's political life, it should not be forgotten that the current Republic of Poland is the most democratic in the country's long history. Since its inception in 963 A.D., Poland has been plagued by bad leadership. Polish kings were selected (by Poland's powerful nobility) from various royal houses of Europe; many of these foreign-born kings had little interest in the Polish people. Even among feudal nations, the Polish nobility (the *szlachta*) was noteworthy for its fractiousness and shortsightedness. Poland's nobility was unable to cooperate in the face of foreign invasion, resulting in the partition of Poland by Prussia, Austria, and Russia.

The first Polish Republic came into being after World War I, and did not do much better. Political gridlock and infighting led to Marshal Pilsudski seizing power in 1926. Yet despite a dictatorship by military men, Poland vastly overestimated its military strength. Poland remained a dictatorship until it was overrun at the start of World War II, its antiquated armed forces proving no match for the Nazi war machine.

Russia

Official Name:	Russian Federation (Rossiyskaya Federatsiya)
Official Language:	Russian
Government System:	Multiparty federal republic
Population:	150 million
Population Growth:	0.2%
Area:	17,075,400 sq. km. (6,592,800 sq. mi.)
Natural Resources:	gold, crude oil, natural gas, coal, iron ore, hydropower, timber, coal, diamonds, bauxite, copper, nickel, lead, tin, uranium
Major Cities:	Moscow (capital), St. Petersburg, Nizhny Novgorod, Voronezh, Volgograd, Vladivostok, Ekaterinburg, Saratov

Cultural Note:

Russian Names and Titles

- Russian names are listed in the same order as in the West, but the Russian middle name is a patronymic (a name derived from the first name of one's father). For example, Fyodor Ivanovich Kuznetsov's first name is Fyodor (a Russian version of Theodore), his last name is Kuznetsov, and his middle name means "son of Ivan."
- Most Russian women add the letter "a" on the end of their surnames; Kuznetsov's wife would be Mrs. Kuznetsova. A woman's patronymic is also different, ending in "a." "Daughter of Ivan" would be "Ivanova," not "Ivanovich."

- Unless you are invited to do so, do not use first names. If a Russian has a professional title, use the title followed by the surname. If he or she does not have a title, just use Mr., Miss, Mrs., or Ms., plus the surname.
- Russians use a bewildering variety of diminutives and nicknames. Somewhat more formally, someone can be addressed by first name and patronymic, which can be quite a mouthful. As you establish a relationship with a Russian, you will be invited to use one of these. This is the time to invite them to use your first name.
- Despite the length of their names, there are relatively few variations of first names and surnames in Russia. In fact, some names (i.e., Ivan Ivanovich Ivanov) are so common that additional information is needed to identify the correct person. A date of birth may be needed to differentiate between identically named persons.

Age Breakdown

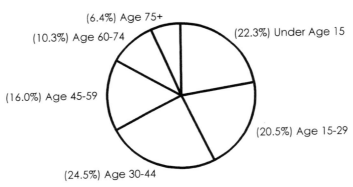

(6.4%) Age 75+

(10.3%) Age 60-74

(22.3%) Under Age 15

(16.0%) Age 45-59

(20.5%) Age 15-29

(24.5%) Age 30-44

Life Expectancy: 64 years male; 73 years female (1987)

 Time

As a foreigner, you are expected to be on time to all business appointments. However, your Russian counterpart may be late, or not show up at all. Do not expect an apology from a tardy Russian.

For social events, even foreigners are expected to be from 15 to 30 minutes late.

Holidays

(Update: Getting Through Customs *http://www.getcustoms.com*)

This list is a working guide. Dates should be corroborated before final travel plans are made. In cases where holidays fall on Saturday or Sunday, commercial establishments may be closed the preceding Friday or following Monday.

For many countries, such as those in the Moslem world, holiday dates are approximations since they depend upon actual lunar observations. Moslem holidays also vary in spelling. Many businesses in Moslem countries are closed on Fridays. (Some CIS countries are Moslem.)

New Year	1–2 January
Orthodox Christmas	7 January
International Women's Day	8 March
Labor Day	1 May
Spring Day	2 May
Victory Day, 1945	9 May
Independence Day	12 June
Anniversary of Great October Socialist Revolution, 1917	7 November

Work Week

- Business hours are generally from 9:00 A.M. to 5:00 P.M., Monday through Friday.
- Banks and currency exchanges are usually open from 9:00 A.M. to 5:00 P.M., Monday through Friday, and recently, some opened on Saturday. Some bank branches in tourist areas are open for currency exchanges until 7:50 P.M.
- Major stores are open from 9:00 or 10:00 A.M. to 8:00 or 9:00 P.M., Monday through Saturday. Smaller shops usually close by 7:00 P.M. Most close for an hour at lunchtime (usually between 1:00 and 2:00 P.M. for food stores, and from 2:00 to 3:00 P.M. for others). Food stores are also open on Sunday.

Religious/Societal Influences on Business

Due to the constant shortages under the Communist system, Russians grew accustomed to spending hours in lines. There were lines for virtually every product or service. Customers often had to stand in one line for goods and another line to pay for their purchases. The revered Soviet-era writer Anna Akhmatova actually wrote a poem about standing in line (although she was waiting outside a KGB prison for news about her imprisoned son).

People who wait endlessly are not prompt. Under Communism it was almost impossible to fire employees for tardiness. Many Russians arrived to work late, left early, or took overlong lunch breaks (during which they stood in line); after 70 years of this, it will take awhile to change Russian attitudes.

Now, Western attitudes toward punctuality and prompt customer service are taught from scratch to the Russian employees of foreign-owned companies. Managers find most Russians (especially younger ones) to be receptive.

 5 Cultural Tips

1. Patience is a traditional virtue among Russians; punctuality is not. Only the trains and theater performances begin on time in Russia. Do not be surprised if your business appointment begins one or even two hours late.

2. Russians have a reputation as great "sitters" during negotiations, able to wait out their opponents. In addition to their patience, many Russians regard compromise as a sign of weakness. To them compromise is, in and of itself, morally incorrect. Many Russians would rather out-sit the other negotiator, and gain more concessions from the other side.

3. Be aware that "Final Offers" are never final during initial negotiations. Be prepared to wait. The offer will usually be made more attractive if you can hold out.

4. Get emotional. If you (or your negotiators) have not walked out of the negotiating room in high dudgeon at least twice during the negotiations, you're being too easy. Russians *expect* walkouts and dire proclamations that the deal is off. Remember how often the Soviet delegation to the United Nations walked out in a huff? They always came back, sooner or later. Play hardball; they will.

5. Very little gets done in Russia without using *blat* which is Russian for "connections" or "influence." Blat involves an exchange of favors; when you do something for someone, they now owe you a favor. Gifts, monetary or otherwise, are often part of this exchange.

 Economic Overview

A country with 150 million people with tremendous natural and human resources is not a market which U.S. business can afford to neglect for long. Demand exists in Russia across the board, from consumer goods to capital equipment. Foreign-made products are now common in Russia today, a sharp contrast to just a few years ago.

The Russian Federation is currently a country in economic, political, and social transition. Uncertainty, risk, and great opportunity characterize the commercial environment in Russia today. Doing business in Russia is not for the timid, but for the bold.

Russian firms and customers admire U.S. technology and know-how and generally want to do business with U.S. companies. There are few products or services which are not in demand in Russia. Numerous U.S. consumer goods manufacturers have already made Russia a major expansion market for their companies. In fact, consumer products is the second largest foreign investment sector in Russia, trailing only gas and oil exploration. The United States is the largest foreign investor in Russia with more than 850 establishments there.

Russia's middle class is estimated at 20% of the total population. Conversely, one in every three Russians claims they have difficulty getting by on their incomes. Real income among Russians surged 11% and consumer spending 14% in 1994. Employment grew 13% in finance and insurance sectors in 1994 while the industrial workforce declined 13.5%. The private sector now accounts for a 55 to 60% share of Russia's GDP.

Of late, the rise in violent crime has also become a problem for foreign, as well as Russian, businesses and travelers.

Cultural Note: Don't overlook how large Russia is when you travel. (It's easy to forget after dealing with other European countries, most of which can be driven across in a day.) But the Russian Federation is so huge that it spans 11 time zones! Also, most of Russia's transportation systems are far below Western European standards, making transport even more time-consuming.

Comparative Data

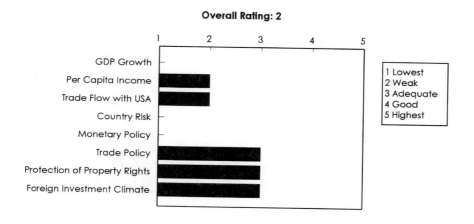

Overall Rating: 2

	1	2	3	4	5
GDP Growth					
Per Capita Income					
Trade Flow with USA					
Country Risk					
Monetary Policy					
Trade Policy					
Protection of Property Rights					
Foreign Investment Climate					

1 Lowest
2 Weak
3 Adequate
4 Good
5 Highest

Country Risk Rating

Gross Domestic Product: $900 billion

GDP Growth: −14%

Per Capita Income: $5,190

Trade Flows with the U.S.A.

Rank as Export Market for U.S.A. Goods & Services: 34th

U.S.A. Exports to Russia: $2.8 billion

Growth Rate of Exports: 8%

U.S.A. Imports from Russia: $4.0 billion

Growth Rate of Imports: 25%

Rank as a Supplier of Imports into the U.S.A.:   28th

Top U.S.A. Exports to Russia: Machinery (Computers/Office Equipment); Aircraft; Tobacco; Vehicles (Autos/Tractors); Electrical Products (TVs, Radios, Telephones); Medical/Optical Equipment; Cereals; Misc. Food; Animal Feed.

Top U.S.A. Prospects for Export to Country: Telecommunications; Computers and Peripherals; Pollution Control Equipment; Oil and Gas Field Machinery; Building Products; Medical Equipment; Electric Power Systems Equipment; Consumer Goods; Food Processing and Packaging; Forestry and Woodworking Equipment.

Credit Terms

Western businesses often request cash-in-advance terms when doing business with Russia. Dun & Bradstreet estimates that prepayment terms are requested in 75% of business transactions.

When cash-in-advance is not an option, Dun & Bradstreet recommends using an irrevocable letter of credit. Open-account terms should be reserved for only strong business relationships.

The payments climate remains poor in Russia with some remittances sometimes taking in excess of six months or more.

Monetary Policy

Russia has done a commendable job of reducing the astronomical level of inflation due to the government's commitment to noninflationary financing of the federal deficit.

Annual inflation has fallen since 1993 when it registered nearly 850%. Dun & Bradstreet estimates 1996 annual inflation at 25%.

U.S. currency is currently prized in Russia, more so than any other foreign currency. The U.S. $100 bill is hoarded widely. Due to fears of counterfeiting, many Russians will accept only new, pristine bills. Even a faint bank stamp may cause Russians to reject a bill. *Monetary Unit:* ruble.

Trade Policy

TARIFFS: Russia's tariffs range from 5 to 30% with the average tariff 12.5%, up significantly from the 7 to 8% level in 1994.

IMPORT LICENSING: Russia employs a liberal import licensing regime, generally free from quotas and licenses. Licenses are required for imports of medicines and chemical raw materials used for production of medicines, pesticides, and industrial waste.

Centralized importing has virtually been eliminated as most government-controlled firms have been privatized.

Many imports are subject to arbitrary certification requirements. However, Russia is establishing reciprocal standardization procedures with the U.S. and is reciprocally accepting foreign certification by accredited institutions.

IMPORT TAXES: Taxes are continually in flux and are often applied not just to profits but also to revenue, making business operations at times uneconomical. Because taxes are so high and arbitrary, tax evasion is widespread.

Russia imposes a 24% value-added tax (VAT) and excise taxes range from 35% to 250% on alcohol, tobacco, automobiles, and some luxury goods.

Protection of Intellectual Property Rights

In 1992/93 Russia enacted laws strengthening protection of patents, trademarks, and copyrights of semiconductors, computer programs, literary, artistic and scientific works, and audio/visual recordings.

Patents are protected for 20 years; industrial designs for 10 years.

The Law on Copyright and Neighboring Rights of 1993 protects all forms of artistic creation, including audio/visual recordings and computer programs as literary works for the lifetime of the author plus 50 years.

Enforcement has been a low priority to date. There is widespread marketing of pirated videocassettes, recordings, books, computer software, clothes, and toys.

Foreign Investment Climate

Few legal restrictions exist on foreign investment. The 1991 Investment Code guarantees foreign investors the same rights as those of Russian investors. Foreigners are not allowed to own land, but can take majority ownership in enterprises that own land. There are no restrictions on profit repatriation.

Joint-venture agreements should include a clause requiring partners to submit to arbitration in a neutral country when they can't come to an agreement. Sweden is currently the most popular choice for third-country arbitration.

The absence of sufficiently developed civil, commercial, and criminal codes is a major constraint.

Current Leaders & Political Parties

(Update: International Academy at Santa Barbara *http://www.iasb.org/cwl*)

State, Government, and Political Party Leaders:

 Pres. and Chmn. of the Security Cncl.: Boris N. Yeltsin
 Vice Pres.: vacant

Ministers:

 Prime Min.: Viktor S. Chernomyrdin
 First Dep. Prime Min. and Min. of the Press: vacant
 Dep. Prime Min. and Min. of Privitization: vacant
 Finance: Vladimir G. Panskov
 Dep. Prime Min.: Yuri F. Yarov
 Defense: Gen. Igor N. Rodionov
 Economics: Yevgeny Yasin
 Foreign Affairs: Yevgeny M. Primakov
 Nationalities: Vyacheslav A. Mikhailov
 Interior: Col. Gen. Anatoly Kulikov
 Foreign Trade: Oleg Davydon
 Social Welfare: vacant

Other Officials:

 Head of the Presidential Secretariat: Viktor V. Ilyushin
 Head of the Presidential Admin.: Sergei Filatov
 Head of Natl. Security: (vacant)
 Speaker of the Duma (Parliament): Ivan P. Rybkin
 Speaker of the Federation Cncl.: Vladimir F. Shumeiko
 Ambassador to U.S.: Yuli Vorontsov

Perm. Rep. to U.N.: Sergei Lavrov

Political Parties:

Liberal Democratic Party, Democratic Party of Russia, Russia's Choice,
Communist Party of the Russian Federation, Our Home is Russia, Agrarian
Party, Russian Movement of Democratic Reforms, Party of Russian Unity and
Accord, Yavlinsky-Boldyrev-Lukin Bloc, Women of Russia Party, Future of
Russia Party, Constructive Ecology Movement of Russia, Dignity and Charity
Party

Political Influences on Business

With the end of the Cold War and the reemergence of a Russian State, U.S. relations
with Moscow have evolved rapidly over the last few years. At meetings in Vancouver,
Tokyo and Moscow, Presidents Clinton and Yeltsin secured the basis for a U.S.-Russian
partnership. Great strides have been made in a number of important fields, particularly arms control. While disagreements persist on individual issues, the U.S. and
Russia now consult closely on major issues of mutual and international interest.

The United States firmly supports Russia's development into a democratic/market
society, and Russia's further integration into the international community. The United
States has made available substantial bilateral assistance, and has led international aid
efforts. The United States has also taken steps to clear from the books Cold War era
legislation limiting contacts with Russia.

One of the most pressing issues which defines the business climate in Russia is the
lack of legislation in most areas of economic activity. This is due primarily to the fact
that there is no political consensus in the State Duma and the government on how
business activities should be regulated, whether private business should be promoted,
and the role of foreign investment in Russian society. Not only does this make taxation
and business regulation an unpredictable prospect at best, there is no judicial basis for
resolution of disputes between individuals and/or companies. In the absence of legislation, many government decisions affecting business have been taken by executive
fiat, diminishing the prospects for their legitimacy and effectiveness, and often leading
to inconsistent policy.

Russia has a bicameral legislative system. The Upper House is called the Federation
Council, and consists of two representatives from each subject of the Russian
Federation. The Federation Council passes decrees on federation disputes and reviews
legislation passed by the Lower House, including the federal budget. The Lower House,
or State Duma, is made up of 450 deputies, one-half selected on the basis of geographic
districts and one-half on the basis of party lists. The Duma passes most federal laws.
Duma members are elected to four-year terms (after an initial two-year term which
began in 1994).

Contacts in the U.S.A. & in Russia

Contacts in the United States:

EMBASSY OF THE RUSSIAN FEDERATION
250 Wisconsin Ave., N.W.
Washington, D.C. 20007
Tel: (202) 628-7551
Fax: (202) 298-5735

U.S. DEPARTMENT OF STATE
Bureau of Consular Affairs
Tel: (202) 647-5225
Country Desk Officer
Tel: (202) 647-8671

U.S. DEPARTMENT OF COMMERCE
BISNIS (Business Information Service for
the Newly Independent States)
Tel: (202) 482-4655
Fax: (202) 482-2293
Flashfax BISNIS Bank (a 24-hour auto-
mated fax delivery system)
Fax: (202) 482-3145

RUSSIA AND INDEPENDENT STATES
Country Desk Officers
Tel: (202) 482-4655
Fax: (202) 482-8042

TOURISM OFFICE
Intourist
650 Fifth Avenue #868
New York, N.Y. 10111
Tel: (212) 757-3884
Fax: (212) 459-0031

Contacts in Russia

U.S. EMBASSY
Novinskiy Bulvar
19/23
Moscow
Mailing Address:
APO AE 09721
Moscow
Tel: [7] (095) 252-2451
Telex: 413160 USGSO SU
Fax: [7] (095) 956-4261

DUN & BRADSTREET CIS
Postal and Street Address:
3D Khoreshevski Proezd, Building 1/1
4th Floor
126007 Moscow
Russia
Tel: [7] (095)940-1816
Fax: [7] (095)940-1702

PRESIDENT BORIS N. YELTSIN
Government Offices
Moscow, Russian Federation

Passport/Visa Requirements

Visa Information　Tel: (202) 663-1225

Note: The Department of State notes that travel to the Caucasus Region of Russia is considered dangerous. U.S. citizens requiring further information should contact the U.S. Embassy in Moscow.

Entry Requirements: A passport and visa are required.

U.S. citizens may apply for the following visas: tourist, business, or, for a private visit to friends or relatives, a visitor or homestay visa.

The following procedures must be complied with in order to register different kinds of documents in the Consular Division. All documents must be: 1) acknowledged before a Notary Public; 2) certified by the Central Authority in the traveler's state capable of issuing the Hague Convention *Apostille* on documents intended for use in another convention country; 3) registered by Consular Division of the Russian Embassy. Consular fee for registration is $25 per document. Only money orders, payable to the Embassy of the Russian Federation are accepted.

All documents must be accompanied by a professional translation into Russian language, also notarized by a Notary Public. The translation must be attached properly to the original document. Documents and translations must be printed.

Visa processing fee is not refundable.

Papers must be submitted to the Consulate not earlier than three months before the date of the entry into Russia.

Faux Pas: The Russian word *nyekulturny* (literally, "uncultured" or "bad mannered") signifies the wrong way to do something. The following behaviors are considered unacceptable in Russia:

- Speaking or laughing loudly in public; Russians are generally reserved and somber.
- Entering a row of seats at the theater, cinema, or arena, while facing the stage (which is standard behavior in the U.S.A.). It is impolite to squeeze past seated people with your back to them.
- Standing with your hands in your pockets.

- Wearing your coat (and heavy boots) when you enter a public building, particularly the theater! You are expected to leave your coat in the *garderob* (cloakroom). One does not sit on one's coat at a concert or restaurant. Stadiums and cinemas generally do not have a garderob, but many office buildings do. Hint: To avoid the after-show waiting line at the theater, rent some opera glasses. Persons returning opera glasses to the garderob go to the front of the line.

Saudi Arabia*

Official Name:	Kingdom of Saudi Arabia (al-Mamlakah al-'Arabahīyah as-Sa'ūdīyah)
Official Language:	Arabic
Government System:	Monarchy with council of ministers and consultative council
Population:	18 million
Population Growth:	3.5%
Area:	1,960,582 sq. km. (1,176,349 sq. mi.); about one-fourth the size of the continental U.S.
Natural Resources:	crude oil, natural gas, iron ore, bauxite, coal, zinc, gold, copper
Major Cities:	Riyadh (capital), Jeddah, Makkah, Madinah, Taif, Dammam, Tabuk

*What's wrong with this picture? Alone among the 40 national flags in this book, the above flag is **not** depicted with the name of the country emblazoned upon it. This is because the flag of Saudi Arabia incorporates the name of Allah (in Arabic script). The name of Allah is considered sacrosanct by many Muslims; to obscure or trivialize it is considered blasphemy. Even disposing of anything adorned with the name of Allah is sensitive—hence the protests from Saudi officials when the Saudi Arabian flag has been printed (along with other flags) on such disposable items as paper bags.

Cultural Note: Westerners seem to have a particularly difficult time adapting to Saudi customs and traditions. Expats recommend these techniques: learn the rules before you go to Saudi Arabia, follow them as best you can, and resign yourself to the fact that you aren't going to change the Saudis. Also, remember that foreigners are fully subject to draconian Saudi law. A Westerner caught with a prohibited substance (such as alcohol or pornography) can expect imprisonment and deportation.

Age Breakdown

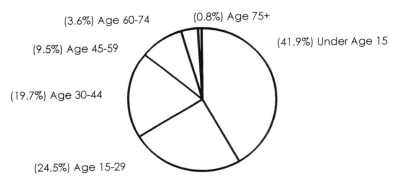

(3.6%) Age 60-74

(0.8%) Age 75+

(9.5%) Age 45-59

(41.9%) Under Age 15

(19.7%) Age 30-44

(24.5%) Age 15-29

Life Expectancy: 65 years male; 68 years female (1990)

 Time

As a foreigner, you are expected to be on time to all business appointments. However, Saudis view time very differently than Westerners. Saudis are not generally concerned with the clock, and they may or may not choose to be prompt. Often they will be very late; your appointment may start one or two hours late.

Muslims pray five times per day, and these provide convenient ways of dividing the daylight hours. Saudis may make an appointment referring to a prayertime (i.e., "after the noon prayer"), even though this does not specify an exact time.

Saudi Arabia is three hours ahead of Greenwich Mean Time (G.M.T. + 3), which is eight hours ahead of U.S. Eastern Standard Time (E.S.T. + 8)

Holidays

(Update: Getting Through Customs *http://www.getcustoms.com*)

- The dates for many Arabic holidays do not fall on the same day in the Western (Gregorian) calendar each year. This may be because Arabic holidays are dated using a calendar which does not correspond to the Western calendar (for example, the Arabic (Hijrah) calendar is only 354 days long). Or, it may happen because the date of the holiday is computed from a variable occurrence, such as sightings of the phases of the moon.

  In cases where holidays fall on Saturday or Sunday, commercial establishments may be closed the preceding Friday or following Monday. Also, remember that in the Muslim world, the Sabbath is celebrated on Friday. Many Islamic nations have their "weekend" on Thursday and Friday, with Saturday as the start of the work week.

- Check with your Saudi sponsor as to which holidays will be observed by the persons you intend to meet.

- Remember that the Islamic calendar uses lunar months of 28 days; an Islamic year of 12 months is 354 days long. Paperwork should carry two dates, the Gregorian (Western) date and the Hijrah (Arabic) date.

Ramazan (also called Ramadan):

- Observers fast from dawn until dusk; dusk is announced by a cannon shot. The faithful are awakened before sunrise by drummers who roam the streets, reminding them to eat before dawn. It is impolite for nonbelievers to eat, drink, or even smoke in the presence of those who are fasting. Be discreet. Office hours may be curtailed. Not surprisingly, fasting people may be short-tempered, especially when Ramazan falls during the days of summer. This is called Ramazan *kafasi* and means Ramazan irritability (literally, "Ramazan head").

Business travel to the Kingdom during the holy month of Ramadan is best avoided. Office hours are shortened and shifted to the evening, and people may be affected by the fasting and customary late night social gatherings. Hotels offer special daytime food services for their non-Muslim guests.

Sheker Bayram (or 'Aid-al-Fitr or Eid al Fitr): The Festival of Breaking Fast. Eid al-Fitr occurs at the end of the holy month of Ramadan. The Eid al-Fitr holiday generally begins in February.

- A three-day festival celebrating the end of the fasting of the month of Ramazan. Children go door-to-door asking for sweets; Muslims exchange greeting cards, feast, and visit one another. Banks and offices are closed for all three days.

Kurban Bayram (or 'Aid-al-Adha or Eid al Adha): The Feast of the Sacrifice. Eid al Adha celebrates the time of year when pilgrims arrive from around the world to perform the Hajj. Their timing is governed by the Islamic lunar calendar. The Eid al-Adha holiday begins in April.

- Celebrates the traditional story of Abraham's near-sacrifice of his son Isaac. This is the most important religious and secular holiday of the year. The holiday normally lasts for four days, but many businesses close for an entire week. Pilgrimages to Mecca are done during this time; resorts and transportation will be booked solid.

Government entities observe these holidays assiduously, and are generally closed for longer periods than the above dates.

The Saudi national day is celebrated September 23 (unification of the Kingdom). Almost all businesses and government offices remain open, with the notable exception of Saudi Aramco.

Work Week

- Saudi officials are prohibited by tradition from working more than six hours per day. Mornings are usually best for appointments.
- Friday is the Muslim holy day; no business is conducted. Most people do not work on Thursdays, either. The work week runs from Saturday through Wednesday.
- Government hours are 7:30 A.M. to 2:30 P.M., Saturday through Wednesday.
- Banking hours tend to be 8:30 A.M. to 12 noon and 5:00 P.M. to 7:00 P.M., Saturday through Wednesday Some banks keep Thursday morning hours as well.
- Business hours vary widely, but most close for much of the afternoon and reopen for a few hours in late afternoon.
- Because of the summer heat, some Saudi business people work after dark. They may request an evening appointment at any time up to midnight.

Religious/Societal Influences on Business

Saudi Arabia is the home and point of origin for Islam, which is the country's official religion. The Saudi branch of Islam is a Sunni fundamentalist variant called Wahabi Islam. (There are a small number of Shiite Muslims, who tend to be discriminated against.)

Wahabi Islam is even stricter and more fundamentalist than the Shiite Islam practiced in Iran. It is enforced in public by the religious police, the Matawain. They claim the right to enforce their religious precepts on everyone, including foreigners.

Westerners who dress immodestly (by Wahabi standards) have often felt the sting of the Matawain's camel-tail whips.

Saudi Arabia has changed enormously since the Second World War. The majority of its inhabitants went from a near-medieval existence to a modern technological society. It is useful to remember that Saudi values and traditions are still those of a non-technological society. For example, the renowned Saudi hospitality was vital in nomadic Bedouin society; travelers in the desert would die unless offered food and water by every household. No matter how many generations separate a town-dwelling Saudi from the nomadic life, he still considers himself a Bedouin at heart.

Bedouins are divided into tribes. Even today, a Saudi's loyalty belongs first to the family, then to the tribe, and only then to the state. When considering competing business offers, where one comes from a foreigner and the other from a fellow tribe member, the Saudi will generally chose the latter, even if the deal is less advantageous.

The Saudi King is both head of state and chief of the government. The kingdom of Saudi Arabia is very much a creation of the House of Saud. Tribal and religious differences still exist, and unity is provided only by allegiance to the king.

In some ways Saudi Arabia can be considered the ultimate male-dominated society. Women in Saudi Arabia do not have the right to interact with men (except relatives), drive a car, work outside the home except in a few occupations, or wear revealing or tight-fitting outfits.

Patience is the most important attribute for conducting business in Saudi Arabia. It takes a while for Saudis to get to know you, and a Saudi must like you before he will do business with you. At the beginning of their oil boom, Saudis were often duped by unscrupulous Westerners, so they are all the more determined to judge you before doing business.

5 Cultural Tips

1. Saudis speak at much closer quarters than do North Americans. Foreigners have sometimes claimed that a Saudi doesn't feel close enough until he (or she) can feel your breath on his (her) face. This is only a slight exaggeration. Saudis feel uncomfortable being far away from others, even if they are among strangers. For example, in an empty elevator, a Saudi may elect to stand next to you rather than in an opposite corner (as a Westerner would). Eye contact is intense and constant (unlike the intermittent eye contact of North Americans).

2. Learning to decipher Saudi hyperbole is a major challenge for foreigners. This includes the pleasant *"yes "* which really means *"maybe "* or even *"probably not."* It also is encountered when guests wish to leave but the host insists that they stay (generally, stay a few extra minutes, then leave).

3. Saudis generally keep their private life off-limits to foreigners. For example, a Saudi man might never mention his wife. On the other hand, many things which Westerners would keep private are entirely public in Saudi Arabia. Business often

falls in this category. A salesperson will be asked to give a pitch in a room full of extraneous people, including family members, friends, and unidentified strangers. Information which would be confidential or proprietary in the West may be discussed among a Saudi's entire circle of friends.

4. Be prepared to remove your shoes before entering a Saudi home. (This may or may not be done at an office.) When ushered into a Saudi's office or home, expect to greet everyone of your sex in the room, while any persons of the opposite sex will probably be ignored. As mentioned previously, you will have to make your presentation in front of everyone. Some of these people will pay attention, some will not. Be aware that the true decision maker may not be your host; it may be an old man sitting quietly, observing you but never speaking.

5. Saudis usually greet foreigners with a brief but firm hand-clasp; there is no actual shaking of the hands. Sit where and when your host indicates, and stay there even when your host goes to talk to others. An office will have chairs to sit on, but in a home you may be sitting on the floor (there may be a cushion to sit on or simply a low armrest called a *masnad*). Do not wander around, looking at the decorations. (Nor should you express your admiration for any object; your host may feel obliged to give it to you). As you sit, be sure you do not expose the soles of your feet to any person, which is highly insulting. If your host stands when someone new enters the room, you should stand as well.

 Economic Overview

The Saudi economy is the largest in the Near East/North Africa region and one of the top among non-OECD countries, with output topping $120 billion in 1994. In fact, Saudi per capita gross national product surpasses every African and Latin American state.

The Saudi private sector is assuming a larger role in the economy. Diversification of the Saudi economy remains a strategic goal in the government to counter abrupt fluctuations in world oil prices which, in turn, have dictated the upturns and downturns in the economy. Private sector contribution to GDP reached 37% in 1994 and was expected to increase further in 1995. Exporters will find that the Saudi market is similar to that of most intermediate developing nations. Saudi law requires a local sponsor to conduct business in the kingdom, and generally the sponsor is the exporter's agent, representative or distributor. Despite rapid economic development, Saudi society remains strongly conservative and religious. The king supports modernization as long as it does not undermine the country's stability and Islamic heritage. The United States remains Saudi Arabia's leading trading and joint-venture partner. Imports from the United States accounted for more than 20% of total Saudi imports in 1994. Price competitiveness, ongoing daily quality, and service should maintain the

United States' leading position in this competitive market. Saudi Arabia was America's 20th largest trading partner in 1995, consuming $6 billion of nonmilitary U.S. goods.

The U.S. also topped the list of foreign countries investing in the Kingdom of Saudi Arabia. Direct investment from the U.S. in both industrial and nonindustrial joint ventures was estimated at $4.9 billion in 1994, more than 40% of total foreign investment in Saudi Arabia. The U.S. and Saudi Arabia have enjoyed a strong, close relationship since the establishment of diplomatic relations in 1933. Saudi Arabia's huge oil reserve, one quarter of the world's known supply, provides an important basis for the close relationship. U.S. geostrategic interests in Saudi Arabia are equally important. Both countries share a common concern about regional security and stable development. Military cooperation during the 1991 Gulf War was extensive.

Comparative Data

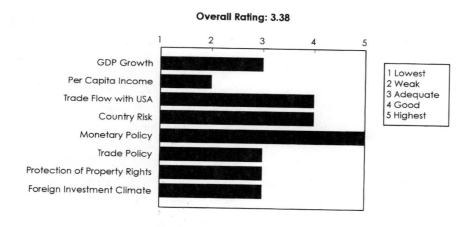

Overall Rating: 3.38

Country Risk Rating

Gross Domestic Product: $123 billion

GDP Growth: 2.0%

Per Capita Income: $6,800

Trade Flows with the U.S.A.

Rank as Export Market for U.S.A. Goods & Services: 20th

U.S.A. Exports to Saudi Arabia: $6 billion

Growth Rate of Exports: 1%

U.S.A. Imports from Saudi Arabia: $8.2 billion

Growth Rate of Imports: 8%

Rank as a Supplier of Imports into the U.S.A.: 17th

Top U.S.A. Exports to Saudi Arabia: Motor vehicles; machinery; electrical components; aircraft and parts; tobacco; arms and ammunition; cereals; medical and optical equipment; furniture and bedding; plastics and resins.

Top U.S.A. Prospects for Export to Saudi Arabia: Air conditioning and refrigeration equipment; oil and gas equipment and services; automotive parts and services equipment; pumps; valves and compressors; computers and peripherals; computer software; mining industry equipment; chemical production machinery; franchising.

Country Risk

Dun & Bradstreet rates Saudi Arabia as having good capacity to meet outstanding payment liabilities.

Sight drafts remain the most frequent method of payment, although letters of credit are also commonly used. When open account terms are extended, 30 to 90 days is the norm.

Monetary Policy

Inflation remains low in Saudi Arabia. Inflation in 1995 was slightly below 5.0% and was forecast to be about 1.0% in 1996. *Monetary Unit*: Saudi riyal.

Trade Policy

TARIFFS: Saudi tariff protection is generally moderate, but has increased over the years. A number of Saudi industries, primarily new ones, now enjoy 20% tariff protection as opposed to the general rate of 12%.

IMPORT LICENSING: Only Saudi nationals are permitted to engage in trading activities. Non-Saudis are not permitted to register as commercial agents. The importation of certain articles is either prohibited or requires special approval from competent authorities. In addition, import of the following products requires special approval by Saudi authorities: agricultural seeds, live animals, and fresh and frozen meat; books, periodicals, movies, and tapes; religious books and tapes; chemicals and harmful materials; pharmaceutical products; wireless equipment; horses; products containing alcohol (e.g., perfume); and natural asphalt.

Importation of the following products is prohibited by law: weapons; narcotics; pork; pornographic materials; alcohol and alcohol distillery equipment; and certain sculptures.

IMPORT TAXES: Saudi Arabia has a liberal tax system and as a result, no import taxes are levied beyond import tariffs.

Protection of Intellectual Property Rights

The Saudi legal system protects and facilitates acquisition and disposition of all property rights, including intellectual property. The Saudi Arabian government has acceded to the Universal Copyright Convention and implementation began July 13, 1994. Saudi Arabia has had a Patent Law since 1989 and the Patent Office accepts applications, but as of mid 1996, it had yet to issue a patent. Protection is available for product and product-by-process. Product-by-process protection is extended to pharmaceuticals. The term of protection is 15 years. The patent holder may apply for a five-year extension after the initial protection period is up.

Saudi Arabia's copyright law does not extend protection to works that were first displayed outside of Saudi Arabia, unless the author is a Saudi citizen. However, Saudi Arabia has acceded to the Universal Copyright Convention (UCC) and the Saudi government maintains that this is sufficient to extend protection to foreign works. The Saudi government has taken action to enforce copyrights of U.S. firms, and pirated material has been seized or forced off the shelves of a number of stores.

Trademarks are protected under the Trademark Law. Trade secrets are not specifically protected under any area of Saudi law, however they are often protected by contract. While there is no specific protection for semiconductor chip layout design, it would nevertheless be protected under the Patent Law and the Copyright Law.

Foreign Investment Climate

The Saudi government generally encourages direct foreign investment. This is particularly true of foreign investment in joint ventures with Saudi partners, though Saudi Arabia allows wholly foreign-owned firms to operate. The government and the private sector actively promote investment opportunities in Saudi Arabia. The government hopes to attract investment in infrastructure, but has yet to make such investments financially attractive. The foreign capital investment code specifies three conditions for foreign investments:

- The undertaking must be a development project.
- The investment must generate technology transfer.
- Saudi partner should own a minimum of 25% equity (though this can be waived).

Foreign investors are denied national treatment in the following sectors: catering, cleaning, maintenance and operations of facilities, power generation, trading, transportation, and businesses that affect national security.

Wholly foreign-owned firms are guaranteed the same protection accorded Saudi nationals in the Foreign Capital Investment Code. They are also eligible for a wide range of investment incentives, including advantageous utility rates, land in industrial estates at nominal rents, treatment as domestic producers for government procurement contracts, and custom duty exemptions on capital goods and raw materials. One of the leading obstacles for foreign investors are restrictive Saudi visa requirements. Investors or potential investors wishing to visit Saudi Arabia must have a Saudi sponsor to obtain the necessary business visa.

 # Current Leaders & Political Parties

(Update: International Academy at Santa Barbara *http://www.iasb.org/cwl*)

Head of State, Prime Min., and Custodian of the Two Holy Mosques:
  King Fahd bin Abdulaziz Al-Saud
  Crown Prince, First Dep. Prime Min., and Cdr. of the Natl. Guard:
  Prince Abdullah Bin Abdulaziz Al-Saud

Ministers:
  Second Dep. Prime Min., Min. of Defense and Aviation, and Inspector Gen.: Prince Sultan Bin Abdulaziz Al-Saud
  Public Works and Housing: Prince Mut'eb Bin Abdulaziz
  Interior: Prince Naif Bin Abdulaziz Al-Saud
  Foreign Affairs: Prince Saud Al-Faisal
  Agriculture and Water: Dr. Abdullah Bin Abdulaziz Bin Muammar
  Commerce: Dr. Osama Bin Jaafer Faqih
  Communications: Dr. Nasser Bin Muhammad Al-Salloum
  Finance and Natl. Economy: Ibrahim Al-Asaf
  Higher Education: Dr. Khalid Bin Muhammad Al-Angary
  Industry and Electricity: Dr. Hashim Bin Abdullah Bin Hashim Yamani
  Information: Dr. Fuad Bin Abdulsalam Farsi
  Islamic Affairs and Endowments: Dr. Abdullah Bin Abdulmohsen Al-Turki
  Municipal and Rural Affairs: Dr. Muhammad Bin Ibrahim Al-Jarallah
  Petroleum and Mineral Resources: Ali Bin Ibrahim Al-Naimi
  Pilgrimage: Dr. Mahmoud Bin Muhammad Safar
  Planning: Dr. Abdul Wahab Bin Abdul Salam Attar

Other Officials:
  Head of the Consultative Cncl.: Muhammad Bin Ibrahim Bin Jubeir
  Head of the Supreme Cncl. of Justice: Saleh bin Muhammad Al-Luhaidan
  Head of the Court of Grievances: Nasser bin Hamad Al-Rashid
  Ambassador to U.S.: Prince Bandar Bin Sultan

Perm. Rep. to U.N.: Gaafar Allagany

Political Parties:

 ## Political Influences on Business

The United States and Saudi Arabia have enjoyed a strong, close relationship since the establishment of diplomatic relations in November 1933. Saudi Arabia's huge oil reserves, one quarter of the world's known supply, form one important basis for our close relationship. But U.S. geostrategic interests in Saudi Arabia are equally important. Saudi Arabia is situated between the Red Sea and the Arabian Gulf (don't call it the Persian Gulf in front of a Saudi!), which are two of the world's most critical waterways. Because of its location, Saudi Arabia is the key to controlling the movement of a major part of the world oil trade plus a large amount of commercial and military traffic, both on the water and in the air. Saudi Arabia also represents a growing market for U.S. goods and services.

The Saudi Government has relied heavily on the U.S. Government and private U.S. organizations for technical expertise and assistance in developing its human and mineral resources. In addition to the U.S. Embassy in Riyadh, the U.S. has Consulates General in Jeddah and Dhahran.

The United States has a large foreign military sales program in Saudi Arabia, including the F-15, AWACS, missiles, air defense weaponry, military vehicles, and other equipment. A U.S. military training mission provides training and support for these weapons and other security-related services to the Saudi armed forces. A similar program assists the Saudi Arabian National Guard.

The United States benefits in the promotion of its interests from the leadership role Saudi Arabia plays in the Arab and Islamic communities. The Saudi government acts as a behind-the-scenes arbiter and partner in encouraging negotiating parties to move forward in the Middle East Peace Process. Saudi and American interests also coincide in support of moderate regimes and disapproval of destabilizing elements.

The United States and Saudi Arabia share a common concern about regional security and stable development. Military cooperation during the 1991 Gulf War was extensive. While supporting the Middle East Peace Process, the Saudi Government has chosen to let the parties negotiating bilateral peace agreements with Israel take the lead in normalizing relations with Israel.

Despite rapid economic development, Saudi society remains strongly conservative and religious. The King supports modernization as long as it does not undermine the country's stability and Islamic heritage.

Saudi Arabia is a traditional monarchy. It is ruled by descendants of its founder, King Abdul Aziz al Saud, who unified the country in the early 1920s. The concept of separation of religion and state is foreign to Saudi society. The legitimacy of the royal regime depends to a large degree on its perceived adherence to Wahabism, a conservative form of Islam.

Saudi Arabia's legal system, Shari'a law, is based on the body of Islamic jurisprudence derived from the Koran and traditional sayings (hadiths) of the Prophet Mohammed, and interpreted by the Ulema, a body of religious experts. Shari'a law governs both civil and criminal law. In cases not covered by Shari'a law, civil officials make administrative decisions.

Judicial appeals are reviewed by the Justice Ministry, the Court of Cassation, or the Supreme Judicial Council to ensure that court procedures were correct and that judges applied the appropriate legal principles and punishments. In capital cases, the King acts as the highest court of appeal and has the power to pardon. There is no written constitution. There are no elected assemblies and political parties are not permitted.

In 1993, the king appointed a 60-member consultative council and 13 provincial councils. A 35-member Council of Ministers performs executive and legislative functions. The Council of Ministers advises and makes recommendations to the King, examines proposed royal decrees, and directs the government bureaucracy. The King promulgates his decisions by issuing royal decrees.

Political consensus is formed through traditional means of consultation and petition on an individual basis. Every citizen has the right to petition high officials and the King during public audiences. Political expression unfavorable to the government is not allowed.

Saudi Arabia is divided into 13 administrative provinces. The governors are appointed by the King, and are generally princes or close relatives of the royal family. The governors report to the Minister of Interior and often directly to the king.

Three independent bodies are charged with security duties. The Ministry of Defense and Aviation uses four uniformed services to protect against external military threats. The Saudi Arabian National Guard is responsible for defending vital internal resources (oilfields and refineries), internal security, and supporting the Ministry of Defense and Aviation as required. The Ministry of Interior is charged with internal security, police functions, and border protection.

 Contacts in the U.S.A. & in Saudi Arabia

Contact in the United States:

THE EMBASSY OF THE KINGDOM OF SAUDI ARABIA
601 New Hampshire Ave., N.W.
Washington, D.C. 20037
Tel: (202) 342-3800

U.S. DEPARTMENT OF STATE
Bureau of Consular Affairs
Tel: (202) 647-5225
Saudi Arabia Desk
Tel: (202) 647-7550

U.S. Department of Commerce
Int'l Trade Admin.
Country Desk Officer, Saudi Arabia
Tel: (202) 482-1860

Office of the Near East
Tel: (202) 377-5767

Contacts in Saudi Arabia:

U.S. Embassy
Collector Road M
Riyadh Diplomatic Quarter
Saudi Mailing Address:
P.O. Box 94309
Riyadh, 11693
Tel: [966] (01) 488-3800
Telex: 406866 AMEMB SJ
Fax: [966] (01) 488-7364
U.S. Mailing Address:
APO AE 09803-1307

King Fahd bin Abdulaziz Al-Saud
Head of State, Prime Minister, and
Custodian of the Two Holy Mosques
Royal Court
Riyadh 11111
Kingdom of Saudi Arabia

Passport/Visa Requirements

Visa Information   Tel: (202) 663-1225

Entry Requirements: Passports and visas are required. Tourist visas are not available for travel to Saudi Arabia.

Visitors to Saudi Arabia should obtain meningitis and cholera vaccinations, prior to arrival. A medical report is required to obtain a work and residence permit. This includes a medical certificate stating that the individual is free of AIDS. Temporary visitors need not present an AIDS-free certification.

Exit visas are required for all foreigners with work visas who wish to leave Saudi Arabia. Latest details and regulations should be obtained from Saudi officials.

For further information on entry requirements, travelers may contact the Royal Embassy of Saudi Arabia.

Cultural Note: The left hand is considered unclean in Saudi Arabia. People eat with the right hand only. If you must use your left hand in public for some reason, you may wish to say the phrase *shimaalin ma tishnaak*, which means "the left hand does not injure."

Singapore

Official Name:	Republic of Singapore [English]
	Hsin-chia-p'o [Chinese]
	Republik Singapura [Malay]
	Singapore Kudiyarasu [Tamil]
Official Languages:	English, Mandarin Chinese, Bahasa Malaysia, and Tamil
Government System:	Parliamentary democracy
Population:	3.3 million
Population Growth:	2.4% (1994)
Area:	621 sq. km. (239 sq. mi.); about one-fifth the size of Rhode Island
Natural Resources:	fish, deepwater ports
Major Cities:	Singapore (capital)

Cultural Note: Since World War II, Singapore has remade itself from a minor trading center to a booming entrepot of capitalism in Southeast Asia. For visitors, Singapore is considered very safe (even antiseptic). But be warned that Singapore's myriad laws apply to natives and foreigners alike. Before arrival, travelers should become familiar with these laws, e.g.: no littering, no chewing gum, no illegal drugs, no pornographic materials, no weapons, no jaywalking, no spitting, no smoking in most public places—and the fine for failing to flush a public toilet after use is $150!

Age Breakdown

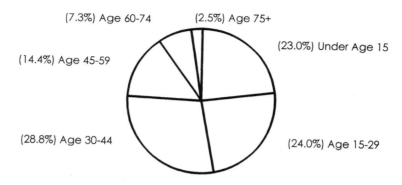

(7.3%) Age 60-74   (2.5%) Age 75+

(14.4%) Age 45-59   (23.0%) Under Age 15

(28.8%) Age 30-44   (24.0%) Age 15-29

Life Expectancy: 74 years male; 78 years female (1990)

 Time

The different cultures of Singapore have different attitudes about time. Be on time for all business appointments; making a Singaporean executive wait can be taken as an insult. For social events, most Singaporeans arrive on time or slightly late. Some cultural traditions maintain that arriving on time to a dinner makes them appear greedy and impatient. Singapore is eight hours ahead of Greenwich Mean Time (G.M.T. + 8), or add thirteen hours to U.S. Eastern Standard Time (E.S.T. + 13).

 Holidays

(Update: Getting Through Customs *http://www.getcustoms.com*)

This list is a working guide. In cases where holidays fall on Saturday or Sunday, commercial establishments may be closed the preceding Friday or following Monday.

Singapore has no official religion. This is a wise policy, since Singapore's varied ethnic population observes widely different religious tenants, from the indigenous Malays (who are mostly Muslim), to the majority Chinese (who may profess to follow Buddhism, Confucianism, Taoism, none of these, or several simultaneously).

In many faiths, religious holidays are set via lunar calendars. Thus, the scheduled dates for the following religious holidays are approximations since they depend upon actual lunar observations.

New Year's Day	1 January
Chinese New Year	varies
Hari Raya Puasa [Muslim: Feast of Fast-Breaking]	varies
Good Friday	varies
Hari Raya Haji [Muslim: Feast of Sacrifice]	varies
Labor Day	1 May
Vesak Day [Buddhist: Birthday of Buddha]	varies
Singapore National Day	9 August
Deepavali [Hindu: Festival of Lights]	varies
Christmas	25 December

Work Week

- Business hours are generally 9:00 A.M. to 5:00 P.M., Monday through Friday. However, many offices stagger their work hours, with workers arriving any time from 7:30 A.M. to 9:30 A.M. Some offices will be open for a half-day on Saturdays, generally in the morning.

- Many Singapore banks keep traditional banking hours: 9:30 A.M. to 3:00 P.M., Monday through Friday, and 9:30 A.M. to 11:30 A.M. on Saturdays.

- Shop hours vary, with some shops staying open until 9:00 or 10:00 P.M., Monday through Saturday. Some have Sunday hours as well.

- The traditional lunchtime was from 12:00 noon to 2:00 P.M. Efforts have been made to reduce this to a single hour, from 1:00 P.M. to 2:00 P.M.; nevertheless, many people will take longer than an hour for lunch. Friday is the Muslim Holy Day, and Muslims who work on Fridays will take a two-hour break at lunchtime.

Religious/Societal Influences on Business

Singapore has no official religion, since its varied ethnic population observes widely different religious tenants: the indigenous Malays are mostly Muslim, the Indian community may be Hindu or Muslim, and the majority Chinese may follow Buddhism, Confucianism, Taoism, Christianity, or several of these simultaneously. (For specifics on the influence of Islam, see the chapter on Malaysia. For the ethics of Overseas Chinese, see Hong Kong. For Hinduism, see India.)

The government of Singapore is known for its efforts at social engineering. In the name of its citizens' best interests, the government's actions have ranged from banning chewing gum to acting as a dating service (to encourage ethnic Chinese citizens to produce more children). The government also maintains an active propaganda department. The main thrust of this propaganda involves Singaporean unity. The disparate ethnic groups of Singapore have little in common, and, before Singaporean independence, violence sometimes broke out between them. To establish a sense of nationhood among these groups, Singapore's government produces slick television commercials (some of them using the skills of the best jingle writers in the United States).

As in neighboring Indonesia, the Singaporean government has established a national ethic of patriotism, hard work, thrift, and obedience to the law. (The latter has made Singapore one of most graft-free places in Asia.) Since these largely reflect traditional Confucian values, they have been relatively easy to impose. Concomitantly, the civil liberties of the West are seen as excessive and corrupting. As long as Singapore's economy continues to rise, its citizens are likely to accept their intrusive government's guiding hand.

5 Cultural Tips

1. English is widely spoken in Singapore. It is one of the country's four official languages, and it is used in most business transactions and virtually all business or government correspondence. But be aware that the English spoken in Singapore often has native inflections, syntax and grammar, which can easily lead to misunderstandings. For example, in Chinese, it is polite to offer both the positive and negative options in virtually every question. Even when speaking in English, they are likely to add a "Yes/No" pattern to a question. Rather than asking "Would you like to have dinner?" they are likely to ask "You want dinner or not?" The phrases involved ("Want or not want?" "Good or not?" "Can or cannot?") are direct translations of Chinese phrases into English. They can sound oddly aggressive to Western ears.

2. Business cards are very important in Singapore. Since most Singaporean businesspeople are Chinese, have one side of your card printed in English, the other in Chinese. The exchange of cards is quite formal: after being introduced, the visiting executive should offer his or her card to each person present. With both hands on your card, present it to the recipient with the print facing him or her (so that he or she can read it). The recipient will receive the card with both hands and study it for a few moments before carefully putting it away in a pocket. You should do the same when a card is presented to you. Never put a card in your back pocket (where many men carry their wallets), and don't write on someone's business card.

3. Successful business relationships in Singapore require politeness. Keep your voice calm and quiet. Never display anger; a person who expresses anger in public has lost their self-control and will not be trusted or respected. Avoid causing anyone to lose face, which means do not openly disagree with anyone! Politeness demands that you find a more subtle way of expressing your disagreement.

4. The word "No" is rarely heard in Singapore. The polite but evasive "Yes" is considered a valid technique to avoid giving offense. In Singapore, "Yes" can mean anything from "I agree" to "Maybe" to "I hope you can tell from my lack of enthusiasm that I really mean 'No.' " A clear way to indicate "No" is to suck in air through the teeth. This sound always indicates a problem, no matter what words are said. A true "Yes" will be followed by paperwork and documentation.

5. Show respect for age and seniority. In a group, the most important persons will be introduced first. If you are introducing two people, state the name of the most important person first (e.g., "President Smith, this is Engineer Wong.").

Economic Overview

Singapore has one of the most developed industrial, commercial, financial, and consumer economies in the world and is an excellent market for U.S. products and services. Its role as the "Gateway to Southeast Asia" means that almost any American product can find an interested buyer here.

Singapore buys a diverse variety of goods from the U.S. for both internal consumption within the country, and for reexports to other markets throughout Southeast Asia. Many U.S. companies use Singapore as a distribution center for Asia. Almost 40% of Singapore's imports are reexported to other destinations.

Comparative Data

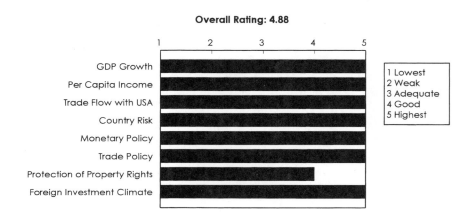

Overall Rating: 4.88

	1	2	3	4	5
GDP Growth					
Per Capita Income					
Trade Flow with USA					
Country Risk					
Monetary Policy					
Trade Policy					
Protection of Property Rights					
Foreign Investment Climate					

1 Lowest
2 Weak
3 Adequate
4 Good
5 Highest

Country Risk Rating

Gross Domestic Product: $51.6 billion
GDP Growth: 10%
Per Capita Income: $16,700

Trade Flows with the U.S.A.

Rank as Export Market for U.S.A. Goods & Services: 9th
U.S.A. Exports to Singapore: $15.3 billion
Growth Rate of Exports: 18%
U.S.A. Imports from Singapore: $18.5 billion
Growth Rate of Imports: −9%
Rank as a Supplier of Imports into the U.S.A.:   9th

Top U.S.A. Exports to Singapore: Electrical equipment, machinery (computers, office machines, and so on), aircraft, optical and medical equipment, mineral fuel, plastics, organic chemicals, miscellaneous chemical products, photography equipment and supplies, motor vehicles.

Top U.S.A. Prospects for Export to Singapore: Electronic components, aircraft parts, industrial process controls, oil/gas field machinery, construction equipment, laboratory and scientific instruments, computer hardware and peripherals, medical equipment, telecommunications equipment, and pumps/valves/compressors.

Credit Terms

Dun & Bradstreet rates Singapore as having the highest creditworthiness with excellent capacity to meet outstanding payment liabilities. It carries the lowest degree of risk when compared with other countries.

The business environment in Singapore remains sound and liberal credit terms are used on most transactions. Open account 30- to 60-day terms are usually granted. More secure terms such as letter of credit or sight draft are advised for new or small and private accounts along with credit checks where available.

Monetary Policy

There is free movement of capital and profits in Singapore. Inflation is under control. The inflation rate in 1994 was 3.6% and at 2.2% in 1995. *Monetary Unit:* Singapore dollar.

Trade Policy

TARIFFS: Tariffs are minimal with 96% of goods entering Singapore duty-free. Significant tariffs remain on cigarettes, alcoholic beverages, automobiles, and gasoline. The average tariff in Singapore is well under 1%.

IMPORT LICENSING: Singapore maintains very few trade barriers. Most goods can be imported freely without import licenses. Generally, the import of goods which pose a threat to health, security, safety, and social decency is controlled. Import licenses are required for pharmaceuticals, hazardous chemicals, films, arms and ammunition. Companies wanting to import controlled items into Singapore must apply for licenses from appropriate government agencies. Companies must make an inward declaration for all goods imported into Singapore. Singapore prohibits the import of chewing gum, firecrackers, horns, sirens, silencers, toy coins, and currencies. A complete list of prohibited products can be obtained from the Trade Development Board.

IMPORT TAXES: A Goods and Services Tax (GST) of 3% is levied on all imports into Singapore. The GST is not levied on goods stored in free trade zones.

Protection of Intellectual Property Rights

Singapore enacted strict copyright protection legislation in 1987, strengthened its trademark law in 1991, and passed a new patent law in 1994 which was scheduled to be amended by January 1, 1996. Although piracy rates are down according to industry sources, the illegal copying, use, and distribution of computer software continues to pose problems for U.S. industry. Singapore is a signatory to the Paris Convention for the Protection of Industrial Property as well as to the Patent Cooperation Treaty, but it is not a signatory to the Berne Convention for the Protection of Literary and Artistic Works.

Foreign Investment Climate

Singapore has one of the world's most open investment regimes. Singapore encourages foreign investment, especially in leading-edge industries. Foreign investment accounted for approximately 75% of total investment in 1994. U.S. investment accounted for 55% of total foreign investment in 1994, concentrated in the petroleum, chemical, and electronics industries. Investment policies are transparent and the bureaucracy is not oppressive. There are no taxes on capital gains and no restrictions on foreign ownership of businesses. Foreign investors are not required to take on private or official joint ventures or cede management control to local interests.

Some restrictions apply to a limited number of sectors including news media, telecommunications, broadcasting, property ownership, and domestic banks. Armament manufacturing is closed to foreign investment.

Foreign law firms may only set up offices in Singapore to advise clients on U.S. or international law. They cannot hire or form partnerships with Singaporean lawyers to practice local law in Singapore.

Singapore law requires that two-thirds ownership of an engineering firm be in the hands of Singapore-registered professionals.

Current Leaders & Political Parties

(Update: International Academy at Santa Barbara *http://www.iasb.org/cwl*)

State, Government, and Political Party Leaders:

Pres.: Ong Teng Cheong

Cabinet Ministers:

Prime Min.: Goh Chok Tong

Senior Min. in the Prime Minister's Office: Lee Kuan Yew

Dep. Prime Min. (Trade and Industry): Brig. Gen. Lee Hsien Loong

Dep. Prime Min. and Min. of Defense: Dr. Keng Yam Tony Tan

Trade and Industry: Yeo Cheow Tong

Finance: Dr. Richard Hu Tsu Tau

Law and Foreign Affairs: S. Jayakumar

Home Affairs: Wong Kan Seng

Health and Comm. Dev.: Brig. Gen. George Yong-Boon Yeo

Muslim Affairs: Abdullah Tarmugi

Natl. Dev.: Lim Hng Kiang

Communications: Mah Bow Tan

Environment: Teo Chee Hean

Other Officials:

Ambassador to U.S.: Prof. Chan Heng Chee

Perm. Rep. to U.N.: Bilahari Kausikan

Political Parties:

People's Action Party, Workers' Party, Singapore Democratic Party, Natl.
Solidarity Party

Political Influences on Business

Singapore is a parliamentary republic that prides itself on political stability and the predictability this offers to foreign investors and traders. Following independence in 1965, the country's basic economic strategy was molded by former Prime Minister Lee Kuan Yew, who stepped aside in November 1990 after twenty-four years on the job. The political succession was achieved with what some observers called "clockwork-like" precision.

Mr. Lee's policies have changed little under his successor, 54-year-old Goh Chok Tong. Moreover, Lee Kuan Yew continues to exercise considerable influence as head of the dominant People's Action Party (PAP) and as Senior Minister, a Cabinet position created expressly for him. Thus, Singapore's political leadership remains dedicated to free-market principles and to maintaining a first-rate infrastructure and labor force.

The PAP's dominance was confirmed by results of the most recent General Election, held in August 1991, in which it secured 77 out of 81 seats in Singapore's single chamber Parliament. However, the opposition emerged with an unprecedented net gain of three parliamentary seats, which jolted the country's leadership out of its complacency. A by-election held December 29, 1992, and a presidential election in August 1993 confirmed the popular support for the PAP establishment. The opposition is not expected to upset the PAP's dominance at any time in the foreseeable future.

Contacts in the U.S.A. & in Singapore

Contacts in the United States:

EMBASSY OF THE REPUBLIC OF SINGAPORE
3501 International Place, N.W.
Washington, D.C. 20008
Tel: (202) 537-3100
Fax: (202) 537-0876

U.S. DEPARTMENT OF STATE
Bureau of Consular Affairs
Tel: (202) 647-5225
Country Desk Officer,
Singapore Desk
Tel: (202) 647-3278

U.S. DEPARTMENT OF COMMERCE
Singapore Desk
Int'l Trade Admin.
Tel: (202) 482-3647

TOURISM OFFICE
Singapore Tourist Promotion Board
590 Fifth Avenue
12th Floor
New York, N.Y. 10036
Tel: (212) 302-4861
Fax: (212) 302-4801

Contacts in Singapore:

U.S. EMBASSY
30 Hill Street
Singapore 0617
Tel: [65] 338-0251
Fax: [65] 338-4550
FPO AP 96534-0006

AMERICAN BUSINESS COUNCIL OF SINGAPORE
1 Scotts Road
#16-07 Shaw Center
Singapore 0922
Tel: [65] 235-0077
Fax: [65] 732-5917

DUN & BRADSTREET (SINGAPORE) PTE. LTD.
Postal and Street Address: 9 Penang
Road
#09-20 Park Mall
Singapore 0923
Tel: [65] 334-3336
Fax: [65] 334-2465, [65] 334-2469

PRESIDENT ONG TENG CHEONG
Office of the President
Orchard Road
Istana, Republic of Singapore 0922

PRIME MINISTER GOH CHOK TONG
Prime Minister's Office
Istana Annexe
Istana, Republic of Singapore 0923

 ## Passport/Visa Requirements

Visa Information   Tel: (202) 663-1225

Entry Requirements: U.S. citizens need a valid passport (valid for six months or longer beyond the last day of stay) and return/onward tickets. A visa is not required for tourist/business stays of up to two weeks.

A visa is required to establish residence in Singapore either as a private citizen or in a business capacity.

Cultural Note: The Republic of Singapore is a meritocracy. To get ahead, in business or government, one has to work hard and put in long hours. Executives often work late into the night and on weekends. Many executives travel frequently, so appointments must be made with them at least two weeks in advance.

South Africa

Official Name:	Republic of South Africa
Official Languages:	English, Afrikaans, & nine African languages
Government System:	Multiparty republic with bicameral parliament
Population:	41 million
Population Growth:	2.5%
Area:	1,233,404 sq. km. (472,359 sq. mi.); about twice the size of Texas
Natural Resources:	gold, chromium, antimony, coal, iron ore, manganese, nickel, lead, phosphates, tin, uranium, gen diamonds, platinum, copper, vanadium, salt, natural gas, titanium, zinc, asbestos, zirconium
Major Cities:	Pretoria (administrative capital), Cape Town (legislative capital), Bloemfontein (judicial capital), Johannesburg, Durban

Cultural Note: South Africans are big sports fans, and sports are always a good topic of conversation. Rugby is the most popular team sport among white South Africans. After rugby, the most popular sports in South Africa are football (soccer), squash, tennis, and golf. Jogging and bicycling are also very popular, as is swimming (many homes have swimming pools). The Afrikaners have an indigenous sport called *jukskei*, which is analogous to throwing horseshoes.

Age Breakdown

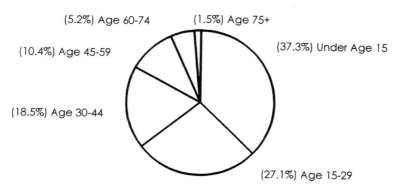

(5.2%) Age 60-74

(1.5%) Age 75+

(10.4%) Age 45-59

(37.3%) Under Age 15

(18.5%) Age 30-44

(27.1%) Age 15-29

Life Expectancy: 61 years male; 67 years female (1990)

Time

Each of South Africa's cultural groups has different attitudes toward time. Punctuality is highly emphasized among white South Africans. Be on time for all business appointments. Punctuality is not enforced for social events, but do not be more than a half-hour late.

When working with native Africans, take your cues for the concept of time from them. They may consider time from a "polychronic" view: Many activities going on concurrently, a flexible attitude toward schedule changes, and a constant information flow from many sources demanding many interruptions.

Due to the hot temperatures, the South African morning is often the most comfortable part of the day. As a result, most South Africans are early risers. It is not unusual for businesspeople to be in their offices by 8:00 A.M., or to schedule their first appointment for 9 A.M.

Holidays

(Update: Getting Through Customs *http://www.getcustoms.com*)

New Year's Day	1 January
Human Rights Day	21 March
Good Friday	varies
Family Day	8 April
Workers' Day	1 May
Youth Day	16 June
National Women's Day	9 August

Heritage Day	24 September
Day of Reconciliation	16 December
Christmas Day	25 December
Day of Goodwill	26 December

Work Week

- Official business hours are generally from 8:30 or 9 A.M. to 4:30 or 5 P.M., Monday through Friday.
- Government offices keep earlier hours, starting at 7:15 or 7:30 A.M., Monday through Friday. They may close anytime after 3:30 P.M.
- Banks hours vary, but most are open from 9 A.M. to 3:30 P.M., Monday through Friday. Some banks open for a few hours on Saturday mornings.
- Store hours also vary, but most are open from 8:30 A.M. to 5 P.M., Monday through Friday. Many shops are open for at least a half-day on Saturdays. Until recently, most establishments were closed on Sundays due to Calvinist blue laws.
- In South Africa, a "cafe" is not a European-style bistro; a "cafe" is a local convenience store. They are open for long hours, 7 days a week.

Religious/Societal Influences on Business

South Africa's diverse population follows many religious beliefs. Most of the world's faiths are represented in South Africa. Christians constitute the largest group at 67.8%, followed by followers of traditional African beliefs, Hindus, Muslims, and Jews. Of the Christian groups, the black independent churches form the largest group (22%). The influence of such churches on the majority black population cannot be underestimated. Without the influence of black clergy and their followers, it is doubtful if South Africa could have undergone a peaceful transition from white minority to black majority rule.

The second largest Christian sect is the Afrikaans Reformed Church (formerly known as the Dutch Reformed Church), which makes up 11.8% of Christians. This Church supported the Afrikaners during their years of domination by the British. Scattered by the Great Trek, defeated during the Boer War, the Afrikaners were united and supported by their Church. The Church's Calvinist teachings encouraged hard work and thrift while shunning ostentation and conspicuous consumption. The Dutch Reformed Church also provided a theological basis for Apartheid through its belief that each culture had a distinct and separate place in God's plan. This concept was extended by some whites (English as well as Afrikaner) to the belief that God made the black races inferior, and it was God's will that blacks were to be ruled by whites. The Dutch Reformed Church also established itself as the moral arbiter of South African society, establishing a highly puritanical tone.

As for more recent arrivals to South Africa, since the discovery of mineral wealth, most immigrants have considered South Africa to be a place to become rich. Consequently, South Africa is a place where drive and ambition are considered positive traits. In this respect, white South Africans are unlike their relatives in Britain or the Netherlands. As in the U.S.A., South Africans love a good rags-to-riches story.

5 Cultural Tips

1. White South Africans usually begin talking about business after a very brief exchange of small talk, whether in the office or at a restaurant. South Africans of other races may spend more time on small talk. African tradition requires long inquiries about your health and your family. Indian and Chinese businesspeople also may take more time getting to know you.

2. Most (but not all) South African businesspeople have business cards. There is no formality involved in exchanging cards. Your card will not be refused, but you might not be given one in exchange. Don't be offended by this.

3. While businesspeople are respected in South Africa, they are not expected to be cutthroat. A businessperson who gloats over crushing his or her competitors is not liked. The ideal business deal (to white South Africans) will be a "win-win situation." Both parties should be seen to gain from the deal. On the other hand, the Indian and Chinese populations came to South Africa as merchants; they have generations of trading experience and are considered shrewd businesspeople. Their business dealings may be more aggressive than those of white South Africans.

4. White South Africans are very concerned that they might be taken advantage of by foreigners. The two-decade boycott left them out of many international business dealings. High-pressure tactics or emotion have little place in dealings with white South Africans. Most would rather let a deal fall through than be rushed.

5. Business deals with white South Africans often involve invitations to a barbecue, which is called a *braaivleis* (Afrikaans for "roasted meat"), often shortened to *braai*. While business is not discussed at a braai, it is considered an important part of the business process. Guests usually bring something to a braai. Residents often bring one course of the meal, but foreign visitors need only bring something to drink or a dessert. Even if your host says you don't need to bring anything, it is good form to bring a bottle of wine or candy. (Large amounts of alcohol are often consumed at a braai.)

Economic Overview

South Africa is the largest export market for U.S. goods and services in Sub-Saharan Africa. It offers immediate and long-term opportunities for many U.S. exporters and investors with the right products, resources, and ideas. U.S. companies now employ 45,000 workers in South Africa, a 36% increase over the previous year.

While South Africa's profound political change and the lifting of international sanctions ushered in a new climate in which to build a stronger bilateral trade agenda, the attraction of South Africa for American companies to a large degree lies in the country's fundamentals. South Africa is the most advanced, broadly based, and productive economy in Africa, with a gross domestic product (GDP) nearly four times that of Egypt, its nearest competitor on the African continent. It possesses a modern infrastructure supporting an efficient distribution of goods to major urban centers throughout the region, and well-developed financial, legal, communications, energy, and transport sectors. South Africa boasts a stock exchange which ranks among the top 10 in the world. Additionally, South Africa offers excellent potential in its long-term reconstruction and development efforts required to distribute economic benefits, traditionally enjoyed by only five or six million South Africans, to the 35 million people disenfranchised by Apartheid.

Most economists have forecasted 3% to 4% growth for 1996 and expect the upturn to continue for the next few years. All economic sectors, with the exception of mining, have shared in South Africa's economic recovery. Nonetheless, even the 3% to 4% growth would not be enough to make major dents in unemployment and poverty in South Africa. The new government has inherited an economy whose structures were built in an era of isolation and which are not always congruent with those needed in today's intensely competitive world economy.

Cultural Note: Each of the many cultures of South Africa has its own traditions. However, the vast majority of businesspeople in South Africa will be from either the English or the Afrikaans ethnic groups. Businesspeople from other ethnic groups are usually familiar with Western customs, but differences do exist. For example, among most black ethnic groups, men precede women when entering or exiting.

Comparative Data

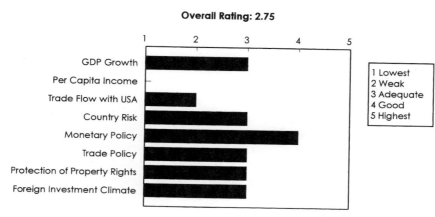

Overall Rating: 2.75

Country Risk Rating

Gross Domestic Product: $122 billion

GDP Growth: 2.3%

Per Capita Income: $3,000

Trade Flows with the U.S.A.

Rank as Export Market for U.S.A. Goods & Services: 35th

U.S.A. Exports to South Africa: $2.7 billion

Growth Rate of Exports: 23%

U.S.A. Imports from South Africa: $2.2 billion

Growth Rate of Imports: 10%

Rank as a Supplier of Imports into the U.S.A.:   36th

Top U.S.A. Exports to South Africa: Machinery (computers, office machines, and so on), electrical goods, organic chemicals, aircraft, medical and optical equipment, motor vehicles, cereals, plastics, paper/paperboard, miscellaneous chemical products.

Top U.S.A. Prospects for Export to South Africa: Healthcare equipment, avionics, telecommunications equipment, franchising, textile machinery and equipment, industrial chemicals, drugs and pharmaceuticals, security and safety equipment, computer software, computers and peripherals.

Credit Terms

According to Dun & Bradstreet, South Africa is considered to have sufficient capacity to meet outstanding payment liabilities. Letters of credit are used for an estimated 20% of total trade transactions. Settlement by open account is common, with usual terms of 60 to 120 days.

Monetary Policy

South Africa's restrictive monetary policy has succeeded in reducing consumer inflation to its lowest level in more than 20 years. Inflation in 1994 dipped to 9% in 1994 from more than 11% in 1993. Inflation has continued its recent downtrend, with the annual rate falling to 7.5% in August 1995. Continuing fiscal and monetary prudence have set the stage for sustained noninflationary growth. *Monetary Unit:* South African rand.

Trade Policy

TARIFFS: While many goods enter South Africa duty-free, those subject to duty generally pay a rate between 5 and 25%. However, rates of tariff protection can reach over 60%, with luxury goods tariffs as high as 60% and automobiles at 100%. The South African government is now in the process of simplifying the tariff system by consolidating categories of similar goods, and lowering many tariff levels.

IMPORT LICENSING: Most goods may be imported into South Africa without restrictions. Import permits are required only for specific categories of goods and are obtainable from the Director of Import and Export. Importers must possess an import permit.

IMPORT TAXES: Import surcharges on luxury goods were abolished in March 1995. A value-added tax of 14% is payable on nearly all imports. However, goods used in manufacturing or resale by registered importers may be exempt. Specific excise duties are levied on alcoholic and nonalcoholic beverages, tobacco and tobacco products, mineral waters, some petroleum products, and motor vehicles. Ad valorem excise duties are levied on office machinery, photographic film, and luxury consumer goods such as cosmetics, home entertainment products, and motorcycles.

Protection of Intellectual Property Rights

Property rights, including intellectual property, are protected under a variety of laws and regulations. Patents may be registered under the Patents Act of 1978 and are granted for 20 years. Trademarks can be registered under the Trademarks Act of 1993. They are granted for 10 years and may be renewed for an additional 10 years. New designs may be registered under the Designs Act of 1967 which grants copyrights for five years. Literary, musical, and artistic works are eligible for copyrights under the Copyright Act of 1978.

South Africa is a member of the Paris Union and acceded to the Stockholm text of the Paris Convention for the Protection of Industrial Property. It is also a member of the World Intellectual Property Organization. There are a number of cases where trademarks have been violated and software piracy occurs frequently in South Africa, according to the U.S. Department of Commerce.

Foreign Investment Climate

Foreign investors are permitted 100% ownership. The government encourages investments that strengthen, expand, and/or update various industries but does not require that new investments comply with specific requirements. Foreign firms are treated the same as domestic companies for various investment incentives such as export incentive programs and tariffs, and other trade regulations. Foreign investors do face differences regarding access to domestic financing, and local borrowing restrictions imposed by exchange control authorities. Companies that are 25% or more owned or controlled by nonresidents face limits on local borrowing. Foreign-owned firms do not have unlimited access to local credit. It is estimated that between 500 and 600 U.S. companies are located within South Africa, with more than 200 having direct investments.

Current Leaders & Political Parties

(Update: International Academy at Santa Barbara *http://www.iasb.org/cwl*)

State, Government, and Political Party Leaders:
   Pres.: Nelson Mandela
   First Vice Pres.: Thabo Mbeki

Cabinet Ministers:
   Justice: Dullah Omar
   Defense: Joe Modise
   Safety and Security: Sidney Mufamadi
   Education: Sibusiso Bhengu
   Trade, Industry, and Tourism: Trevor Manuel
   Foreign Affairs: Alfred Nzo
   Labor: Tito Mboweni
   Posts, Telecommunications, and Broadcasting: Jay Naidoo
   Health: Nkosazana Zuma
   Transport: Mac Maharaj
   Provincial Affairs and Constitutional Dev.: Valli Moosa
   Land Affairs: Derek Hanekom
   Public Enterprises: Stella Sigcau

Public Service and Admin.: Zola Skweyiya
Housing: Sankie Mthembi-Nkondo
Public Works: Jeff Radebe
Home Affairs: Chief Mangosuthu G. Buthelezi
Water and Forestry: Kader Asmal
Environmental Affairs: Dr. Z. Pallo Jordan
Minerals and Energy: Penuell Maduna
Arts, Culture, Science, and Technology: Ben Ngubane

Other Officials:
Ambassador to U.S.: Franklin Sonn
Perm. Rep. to U.N.: Khiphusizi J. Jele

Political Parties
African Natl. Congress (ANC), Natl. Party (NP), Conservative Party (CP),
Democratic Party (DP), Labor Party (LP), South African Communist Party
(SACP), Inkatha Freedom Party (IFP), Pan-Africanist Congress (PAC), Freedom
Front

 Political Influences on Business

Just as South Africa underwent an historic transformation in 1994, from white minority rule to democratic nonracial government, so has its bilateral relationship with the United States changed. Under the Comprehensive Anti-Apartheid Act (CAAA) of 1986, the U.S. Congress enacted some of the most stringent economic sanctions imposed on South Africa during the apartheid years. Most CAAA economic and trade sanctions were lifted by Executive Order in July 1991. The removal of sanctions in all but two instances was accomplished by the South Africa Transition to Democracy Act which was signed on November 23, 1992. The reestablishment of trading links was given a substantial boost with the November 1993 trade and investment mission to South Africa which was led by the late Secretary of Commerce Ron Brown.

The U.S./South Africa relationship was strengthened even further in October 1994 when Presidents Clinton and Mandela signed an agreement in Washington D.C., which created the U.S./South Africa Binational Commission to be cochaired by Vice-President Al Gore and Deputy President Thabo Mbeki. Only the second one of its kind (the U.S./Russia Binational Commission was the first), the U.S./South Africa Binational Commission will oversee, coordinate, and promote the development of relations between our two countries across the broadest possible spectrum of activities: trade and business development, energy, environment, human resource development, and science and technology.

Following the election of April 26–29, 1994, the international community normalized both its diplomatic and economic relations. Since the election, South Africa has not only resumed its full membership of the United Nations and rejoined the Commonwealth but has also become a member of the Organization of African Unity and the Nonaligned Movement.

South Africa's aApartheid-era government, while preaching free-market economics, was essentially statist. The African National Congress, on the other hand, many of whose leaders were exiled for years in the Soviet Union and its satellite states, returned to South Africa firmly believing in centralized economic planning and nationalization of the means of production. However, as South Africa's Interim Constitution took shape at the multiparty negotiations, the African National Congress began to see the merits of open and unfettered competition. For all practical purposes, the ANC has dropped its traditional nationalization plank from its policy framework.

Another major factor which could continue to affect the business climate in South Africa is the extent of violence prevailing in the country. Political violence alone claimed 4,364 lives in 1993, and continued to disrupt the life of the nation until the Inkatha Freedom Party decided to participate in the election, shortly before the April 26–29, 1994, poll. Since then political violence has declined dramatically throughout much of the country and is now largely restricted to certain areas of KwaZulu/Natal where the conflict between the African National Congress, which favors a strong central-government hand at the nation's helm, and the Inkatha Freedom Party, which favors greater autonomy for the country's regions and provinces, is at its most intensive. Political violence will likely remain at a low ebb, nevertheless, as the nation applies itself to the task of implementing the government's ambitious Reconstruction and Development Program. Criminally motivated violence, on the other hand, can be expected to persist throughout the country's period of transition to political maturity and social stability.

As stipulated in South Africa's Interim Constitution, the country's parliamant has two chambers: the National Assembly and the Senate. The 400 seats in the National Assembly are allocated to political parties on the basis of proportional representation in accordance with their share of the national vote. As a result of the April, 1994, election, the African National Congress, which won 62.8% of the vote, now holds 252 Assembly seats. The National Party holds 82 seats, the Inkatha Freedom Party holds 43 seats, and the remaining 23 seats are held by four smaller parties. The 90-member Senate consists of ten Senators elected from each of South Africa's nine provinces, selected by the provincial legislatures. The parties in the provincial legislature are awarded a number of Senate seats based on their share of the provincial vote. The African National Congress holds 60 Senate seats, the National Party holds 17, the Inkatha Freedom Party and the conservative Freedom Front hold five each, and the Democratic Party holds three. The 490 members of the National Assembly and Senate sitting in joint session also comprise the Constitutional Assembly, a body whose principal responsibility is to formulate a permanent constitution for South Africa.

Once elected, the members of the National Assembly elect the President who is vested with broad executive powers, including the power to appoint a 27-member cabinet. All parties which receive at least 20% of the national vote are guaranteed representation by a Deputy President, while all parties which receive at least 5% of the national vote are entitled to representation in the Cabinet proportional to their electoral strength. Under South Africa's current Government of National Unity, State President Nelson Mandela has two Deputy Presidents, Thabo Mbeki, representing the African National Congress, and F.W. De Klerk representing the National Party. Of the 27 ministers in the cabinet, 18 belong to the African National Congress, 6 to the National Party, and 3 to the Inkatha Freedom Party. A 28th member of the cabinet, Minister of Finance Chris Liebenberg, is politically unaffiliated but was allowed to join the cabinet as a result of a constitutional amendment.

Local government in the country is based not on a proportional system of elections but on voting by constituency. Step by step, this system is being put in place.

Some 22 million voters participated in South Africa's first democratic, nonracial election. When South Africans went to the polls, they had 19 parties to choose from in the election for the National Assembly. An additional seven parties participated in one or more of the provincial elections only. The African National Congress won 62.6 percent of the national vote, and in addition, won controlling majorities in seven out of the nine provincial legislatures. The National Party won control of Western Cape province, and the Inkatha Freedom Party won control of Kwazulu/Natal province.

Seven parties are represented in the National Assembly. By far the largest, the African National Congress, has a broadly based, predominantly black membership, although it enjoys growing support within the liberal white community. Representing the preelection national liberation movement, the African National Congress is now overwhelmingly preoccupied with the critical need to provide adequate healthcare, housing, education and employment to the millions of black and "colored" South Africans whose standard of living was depressed under the old racist regime.

Second in size, the National Party ruled South Africa for 46 years prior to the recent election. It was responsible for creating the Apartheid policy, but later, under F.W. de Klerk's leadership, abandoned it and entered into negotiations with the African National Congress. It has a right-of-center, still largely white membership, although it also enjoys majority support within the "colored" and Asian communities. In preparation for the election, the National Party worked hard to attract middle-class black voters, though with only limited success.

The third largest party is the mainly Zulu Inkatha Freedom Party whose support is heavily concentrated in KwaZulu/Natal province (though, even there, the party won only 50.3% of the vote). Inkatha made a strong appeal to Zulu ethnic pride, which proved effective especially in rural areas of the province. The party's policies have long favored federalism as a check on the powers of the central government; its economic policy is generally characterized as free-market oriented.

There are four other smaller parties in the National Assembly.

Contacts in the U.S.A. & in South Africa

Contacts in the United States:

EMBASSY OF THE REPUBLIC OF SOUTH AFRICA
3051 Massachusetts Avenue, N.W.
Washington, D.C. 20008
Tel: (202) 232-4400
Fax: (202) 265-1607

U.S. DEPARTMENT OF STATE
Bureau of Consular Affairs
Tel: (202) 647-5225
Country Desk Officer,
South Africa Desk
Tel: (202) 647-8432

U.S. DEPARTMENT OF COMMERCE
South Africa Desk
Int'l Trade Admin.
Tel: (202) 482-5148

Contacts in South Africa:

U.S. EMBASSY
225 Pretorius Street
Arcadia 0083
P.O. Box 9536
Pretoria, S.A.
Tel: [21] (12) 342-2244

AMERICAN CHAMBER OF COMMERCE IN SOUTH AFRICA
P.O. Box 62280, 2107
Marshalltown, S.A.
Tel: [27] (11) 788-0265
Fax: [27] (11) 880-1632

TOURISM OFFICE
South African Tourism Board
747 Third Avenue, 20th Floor
New York, N.Y. 10017
Tel: (212) 838-8841
Fax: (212) 826-6928

INFORMATION TRUST CORPORATION (PTY.) LTD.
(A Joint Venture with Dun & Bradstreet International and Trans Union Corporation)
Postal Address: P.O. Box 4522
Johannesburg 2000
South Africa
Street Address: Information Trust House
8 Junction Avenue
Parktown 2193
South Africa
Tel: [27] 11-488-2911 (General)
Fax: [27] 11-499-2282

PRESIDENT NELSON MANDELA
Office of the President
Private Bag X83
Pretoria 0001
Republic of South Africa

Passport/Visa Requirements

Visa Information   Tel: (202) 663-1225

Entry Requirements: For U.S. and Canadian citizens, and all EU countries, a valid passport is required; a visa is not required for passport holders on vacation, business, or in transit. Visas are required for extended stays for employment, study, diplomatic, and official passport holders. Evidence of a yellow fever vaccination is necessary, if arriving from an infected area.

Business Visa Requirements: Letter from applicant's firm guaranteeing the applicant's expenses in South Africa, giving the names of South African businesses which will be approached, and stating the nature of the business to be conducted in South Africa. Visa application form on which all questions must be answered. No photographs for any visas are necessary.

Those applicants wishing to have visaed passports returned by mail should submit a stamped, self-addressed envelope with application. Metered postage is not acceptable. All passports are returned by certified mail; therefore, sufficient postage to cover this type of mail service must be placed on envelope.

For more information, the traveler may contact the Embassy of South Africa

---

Faux Pas: While the boycott of South Africa during the Apartheid era may have been successful, most white South Africans resented what they saw as outside interference in their domestic affairs. It is important for a foreigner not to take any credit for changing South Africa's political system.

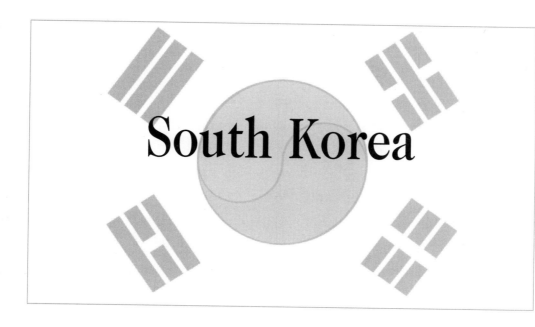

South Korea

Official Name:	Republic of Korea (South) (Taehan Min'guk)
Official Language:	Korean
Government System:	Unitary multiparty republic
Population:	44.5 million
Population Growth:	0.9%
Area:	99,173 sq. km. (38,031 sq. mi.); about the size of Indiana
Natural Resources:	coal, tungsten, graphite, limestone, molybdenum, lead
Major Cities:	Seoul (capital), Pusan, Taegu, Inchon, Kwangju, Taejon

Cultural Note: If there is one classic Korean characteristic, it would be resiliency. Koreans seem to be able to survive almost any hardship. Sacrifice has been demanded of one generation after another of Koreans. The results of this sacrifice in South Korea are evident to any visitor: a poor, war-torn, agricultural country with few resources has transformed itself into the world's eleventh-richest economy.

Age Breakdown

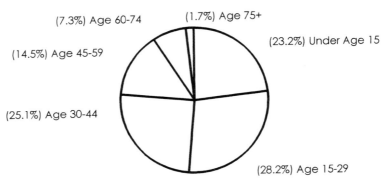

(7.3%) Age 60-74

(1.7%) Age 75+

(14.5%) Age 45-59

(23.2%) Under Age 15

(25.1%) Age 30-44

(28.2%) Age 15-29

Life Expectancy: 67 years male; 73 years female (1992)

 Time

Just a generation ago, Korea was primarily an agricultural country, and there was no call for punctuality. Now that Korea has industrialized, promptness has more value. However, most Koreans consider themselves to be essentially on time if they are within half an hour of the scheduled meeting time (either before or after). A Korean will not usually apologize for being 30 minutes late, nor would he or she understand why a foreigner might be upset at the delay.

Since it is possible that a Korean will arrive 30 minutes early, a host needs to be ready early.

Of course, Koreans who deal with foreigners on a regular basis understand punctuality. These Koreans endeavor to be prompt, and they expect punctuality from foreigners.

South Korea is nine hours ahead of Greenwich Mean Time (G.M.T. + 9), which is fourteen hours ahead of U.S. Eastern Standard Time (E.S.T. + 14).

 Holidays

(Update: Getting Through Customs *http://www.getcustoms.com*)

This list is a working guide. Dates should be corroborated before final travel plans are made. In cases where holidays fall on Saturday or Sunday, commercial establishments may be closed the preceding Friday or following Monday.

New Year's	1–2 January
Lunar New Year	January or February
Independence Movement Day (Independence from Japan)	1 March
Arbor Day	5 April
Children's Day	5 May
Buddha's Birthday	varies; usually in May
Memorial Day	6 June
Constitution Day	17 July
Independence Day	15 August
Chusok-Korean Thanksgiving Holidays	late September–early October
National Foundation Day	3 October
Christmas	25 December

Work Week

- Business hours are generally 9:00 A.M. to 5:00 P.M., Monday through Friday, and 9:00 A.M. to 1:00 P.M. on Saturday.
- Banking hours are 9:00 A.M. to 4:30 P.M., Monday through Friday, and 9:00 A.M. to 1:00 P.M. on Saturday. (During December through February, banks open and close 1/2 hour earlier.)
- Government offices are open 9:00 A.M. to 5:00 P.M., Monday through Friday, and 9:00 A.M. to noon on Saturday.
- The best time for business meetings are 10:00 to 11:00 A.M. and 2:00 to 3:00 P.M. Prior appointments are necessary. Business dinners are common, and meetings may take place in a local coffee shop, but business breakfasts are rare.

Religious/Societal Influences on Business

South Korea is a society run along Confucian precepts. In fact, Confucianism may have had a more profound effect on Korea than it has had even in China, where Confucianism originated. (Remember that Confucianism is not a religion in the classic sense of the word. Rather, it is a philosophy and guide for living.)

Every person has a place and status in Korean society. This place is determined by Confucianism. Thus, the son must defer to his father, the wife must defer to her husband, the younger sibling must defer to the older siblings, the employee must defer to the boss, and so on. This ranking in society is all-important in Korea; it even dictates how people address each other. Even identical twins have rankings: the younger twin must defer to the older one!

The only relationships of equality in Korea are between members of the same class. One's closest friends are drawn from this group.

Confucianism dictates an inferior position for women. Korea is a male-dominated society, where women are not expected to pursue lifelong careers in business. Only a few generations ago, women were completely isolated from society, kept in seclusion in a manner similar to Middle Eastern cultures.

Korea has no official religion. Buddhism has traditionally been the major Korean religion, but Buddhism has gone through periods where it has been repressed by Korea's Confucian rulers. Buddhism is Korea's most popular religion, although only 27.6% of Koreans identify themselves as Buddhist. (Over half of Koreans follow no formal religion at all.)

The Koreans are proud that Christianity did not reach Korea through missionaries. Instead, a Korean scholar studying in Beijing was baptized a Catholic in 1777. It was this scholar, on his return, who introduced Catholicism to Korea. Protestantism gained a foothold in 1884, via a Protestant doctor who became the royal physician. About 18.6% of Koreans identify themselves as Protestant; 5.7% are Catholic.

Whatever their formal religion, most Koreans also follow traditional Shamanistic beliefs. These include a belief in spirits, the veneration of ancestors, and the usefulness of fortune telling.

 5 Cultural Tips

1. Fortune tellers are consulted by Koreans in all walks of life. Even executives consult them about business transactions. A negative report from a fortune teller could ruin an entire deal. A fortune teller is called a *mudang* in Korean.

2. The Korean boss is king of his (or, rarely, her) company. His employees defer to him and treat him with great respect. Bad news is never given to the boss at the start of the day; no one would want to start the day by upsetting the boss. Foreigners should attempt to show proper respect to Korean supervisors. This includes not putting anything on the boss' desk (not even sales literature) during a presentation. Korean executives are very territorial about their desks.

3. Koreans do not maintain as much eye contact as North Americans. As a general rule, Koreans of equal status will look at each other only half the time during their conversation. When persons are of unequal status, the lower-ranking person will often avert his or her eyes during much of the conversation. Extended or intense eye contact is associated with anger. North Americans who try to maintain continuous eye contact with a Korean may appear hostile or aggressive.

4. South Korea is one of the most crowded nations on Earth, even more densely populated than India or Japan. In such a crowded country, personal space is limited. Koreans are accustomed to standing or sitting close together. On the street, they compete aggressively, bumping each other and treading on feet without apology. Since such contact is unintentional, Koreans do not feel the need to apologize for such behavior.

5. Never write a Korean's name in red ink. Korean Buddhists only write a dead person's name in red ink (either at the time of their death or at the anniversary of a death).

Economic Overview

The Korea of the 1990s is modern, cosmopolitan, fast-paced, and dynamic with abundant business opportunities for savvy American businesses. Since the devastation left behind from the Korean War in the early 1950s, the Republic of Korea (ROK) has matured and expanded into a bustling and thriving economy buttressed by political and macroeconomic stability. Consumption spending, which accounts for more than half of Korea's total GDP, is growing along with optimism about the economy. The U.S. Embassy in Seoul estimated that GDP growth was 8.7% in 1995 and forecast 6.5% growth in 1996.

The World Bank estimates that Korea's economy is ranked number 11 in the world. As an indicator of Korea's industrialized status, Korean GNP in 1995 was expected to surpass that of Russia and is already larger than the GNPs of Australia and Mexico. Korea is the fifth largest market for U.S. exports, and the eighth largest partner in two-way trade.

Overall, U.S. exports to Korea in 1995 totaled $25.4 billion. The fact that U.S. exports to Korea are twice that to China (even though China has a population 22 times larger) illustrates the importance of the Korean market.

The domestic political situation in South Korea has been stable enough to permit remarkable growth over the last generation. While Americans planning to do business in Korea should continue to follow developments involving North Korea closely, they should also realize that the North Korean threat has yet to serve as a brake on South Korea's economic growth. U.S. manufactured goods related to infrastructure, consumables, and high-tech goods are expected to do well in the coming years. Korea was the fourth largest market for U.S. agricultural, fishery, and forestry products, importing $3.2 billion from the U.S. in 1994.

The U.S. Department of Commerce has designated Korea as one of the 10 Big Emerging Markets (BEMs). The potential for businesses is immense, especially in the major projects area. The Korean government estimates it will invest $100 billion over the next three years to improve its infrastructure systems.

Cultural Note: Separated by the language barrier, foreigners are often unaware of the scope of Korean humor. The Korean sense of humor has helped the Korean people survive centuries of hardship. Yet their humor is so untranslatable that Westerners often don't know it exists.

However, foreigners should know that not all smiles in Korea are happy ones. Embarrassment, even serious loss of face, is often responded to with a smile and a nervous giggle. The attentive foreigner can learn to distinguish between amused smiles and embarrassed ones.

Comparative Data

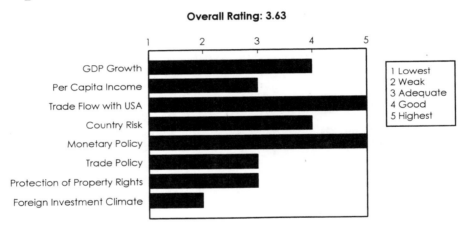

Overall Rating: 3.63

	1	2	3	4	5
GDP Growth					
Per Capita Income					
Trade Flow with USA					
Country Risk					
Monetary Policy					
Trade Policy					
Protection of Property Rights					
Foreign Investment Climate					

1 Lowest
2 Weak
3 Adequate
4 Good
5 Highest

Country Risk Rating

Gross Domestic Product: $380 billion
GDP Growth: 8.4%
Per Capita Income: $8,528

Trade Flows with the U.S.A.

Rank as Export Market for U.S.A. Goods & Services: 5th
U.S.A. Exports to South Korea: $25.4 billion
Growth Rate of Exports: 41%
U.S.A. Imports from South Korea: $24.1 billion
Growth Rate of Imports: 23%
Rank as a Supplier of Imports into the U.S.A.:   8th

Top U.S.A. Exports to South Korea: Electrical components; machinery; aircraft and parts; medical and optical equipment; organic chemicals; hides and skins; mineral fuel and oil; motor vehicles; cereals; plastics and resins.

Top U.S.A. Prospects for Export to South Korea: Electrical power systems; aircraft and parts; transportation services; computers and peripherals; telecommunications equipment; pollution control equipment; security and safety equipment; medical equipment; computer software; building products.

Country Risk

Dun & Bradstreet rates South Korea as having good capacity to meet outstanding payment liabilities.

Unconfirmed letters of credit predominate on sales to South Korea, although more liberal terms are increasingly used. When open account terms are extended, 60 to 90 days is the norm.

Monetary Policy

Despite annual average growth in excess of 8% in both 1994 and 1995, inflation remained steady at around 5 to 6%. The forecast soft landing for the economy in 1996, combined with continued monetary stability, will ensure that inflation is maintained below 5% in 1996. *Monetary Unit:* won.

Trade Policy

TARIFFS: The average tariff rate on manufactured goods imported into South Korea is about 8%. However, tariffs on agricultural products range from 30% to 100%. Adjustment tariffs also exist which are used for balance of payment purposes.

Import duties are not assessed on capital goods and raw materials imported in connection with foreign investment projects. Additionally, certain raw materials used in the production of export goods are often exempt from duty, and certain machinery, materials, and parts used in design industries may enter South Korea either duty-free or at reduced rates. Tariffs and taxes are payable in South Korean *won* before goods are permitted to clear customs.

IMPORT LICENSING: An import license is required for every transaction and before a letter of credit may be opened. The license is valid for up to 12 months. All applications for import licenses must be accompanied by firm offers issued by the foreign supplier. Only firms that are registered as foreign traders are eligible to receive import licenses. Under the system of licensing, all commodities may be freely imported unless included on a negative list, which includes commodities that are either prohibited or restricted. The negative list, known as the *Export and Import Notice*, is published by the Ministry of Trade, Industry, and Energy, and remains effective until revised to meet changing economic conditions. Restricted items include firearms, illicit drugs, endangered species, and so forth.

IMPORT TAXES: South Korea has a flat 10% value-added Tax (VAT) on all imports. A special excise tax of 15% to 100% is also levied on the import of certain luxury items and durable consumer goods.

Protection of Intellectual Property Rights

South Korea is a signatory to the World Intellectual Property Organization, the Universal Copyright Convention, the Paris Convention for the Protection of Industrial Property, and the Patent Cooperation Treaty.

South Korean patent law is fairly comprehensive on paper, extensively protecting most products and technology. A patent may be granted to the first applicant to file in South Korea, notwithstanding proof of development or international ownership. However, at just 15 years calculated from the date of publication, patent life falls short of the international standard of 20 years from the date of application. Patent applicants must request an examination of their application within five years of filing.

The Universal Copyright Convention, to which South Korea acceded in 1987, obliges South Korea to treat works from participating countries as it does its own. Copyright protection is generally provided for under the Copyright Law. Copyrights expire 50 years after the author's death and are derived from the work itself; no registration is required.

In 1989, the *Computer Program Protection Act* was enacted to extend copyright protection to computer software. Protection is afforded for 50 years, dating from authorship, and applies only to computer programs written after the law went into effect in 1989.

The Trademark Law extends protection if registration has taken place in South Korea. This provision has worked to disadvantage U.S. rights holders who attempt to enter the market relatively late but discover that their marks have already been registered by South Korean firms.

The U.S.-Korea 1986 bilateral agreement obligates the South Korean Industrial Property Office to protect under administrative practice U.S. trademarks not registered in South Korea, whether or not they are considered well known. However, the South Korean government historically has not enforced this provision.

Trademark registration is good for 10 years and renewable in subsequent 10-year periods. To retain validity, trademarks must be used. The period of nonuse is three years.

Foreign Investment Climate

South Korea has a poor reputation for attracting foreign direct investment. Foreign direct investment flows as a share of GNP rank only ninth among Asian economies, behind poorer countries such as Malaysia, Indonesia, and the Philippines.

In an effort to reverse South Korea's reputation as a difficult environment for foreign investment, the South Korean government under President Kim Young Sam has announced an ambitious program of economic reforms designed to remove unnecessary regulations and give more scope for decision making to the private sector. The government announced in June 1994 a new program to attract foreign direct investment which offers a one-stop approval service for prospective investors, expanded land availability for factory sites, financing incentives for high-technology firms, and tax holidays.

Currently, South Korea restricts foreign investment in approximately 150 categories, including 24 in the agricultural sector, 12 in the manufacturing sector, and 114 in the services sector. Among the sectors in which foreign investment is restricted, 43 are partially open to foreign investors who satisfy certain specified conditions. In June 1993, the Ministry of Finance announced a schedule by which all but 91 categories will open by 1997, and only seven categories will limit foreign participation to joint venture investment.

A host of laws, regulations, and changing policies make for a challenging business environment. For example, the South Korean government's procurement law generally favors domestic over foreign suppliers. In addition, a variety of industry-specific laws in construction, insurance, combine and tractor manufacture, and vegetable and alcoholic beverage products restrict foreign investment.

Foreign equity ownership limitations exist for a number of sectors including petroleum product manufacturing, fishing, seafood processing, game trapping, animal oils and fats, air transport and air freight, ship brokerage and leasing of water transport equipment, as well as wireless telephone and telegraph.

South Korean law does not permit direct investment through merger with or acquisition of an existing domestic firm. In general, foreign and domestic investors are not permitted to acquire more than 10% in aggregate of the shares in a South Korean firm listed on the South Korea Stock Exchange.

Current Leaders & Political Parties

(Update: International Academy at Santa Barbara *http://www.iasb.org/cwl*)

State, Government, and Political Party Leaders:

    Pres.: Kim Young Sam

Cabinet ministers:

    Prime Min.: Lee Soo Sung
    Dep. Prime Min. and Min. of Finance and Economics: Rha Woong-bae
    Dep. Prime Min. and Min. of Natl. Unification: Kwon O-Kie
    Construction and Transportation: Choo Kyung Suk
    Information and Communications: Lee Suk-chae

Natl. Defense: Lee Yang-ho
Environment: Chung Chong Teck
Govt. Admin.: Kim Ki-jae
Information and Communications: Lee Suk-chae
Internatl. Trade and Industry: Park Jae-yoon
Science and Technology: Chung Kun-mo

Other Officials:
Speaker of the Natl. Assembly: Kim Soohan
Gov. of the Bank of Korea: Lee Kyong-Shik
Ambassador to U.S.: Park Kun Woo
Perm. Rep. U.N.: Park Soo Ail

Political Parties:
Democratic Liberal Party (DLP), Democratic Party, United People's Party

 # Political Influences on Business

South Korea's democratization, which began with free presidential elections in 1987, has led to a mature, bilateral relationship between South Korea and the U.S. The two countries consider themselves friends, partners, and allies. South Korea and the U.S. share common democratic values and practices and are working together, both in the region and in the rest of the world, to advance democratization and human rights.

The U.S. has a strong security relationship with South Korea and is committed to maintaining peace and stability on the Korean peninsula. The U.S. is obligated under the 1954 U.S.-Korea Mutual Defense Treaty to help South Korea defend itself from external aggression. In support of that commitment, the U.S. maintains about 37,000 uniformed men and women in the country, commanded by a U.S. four-star general who is also commander of the United Nations forces, including the Second Infantry Division and air force squadrons.

The major political issue affecting the business climate is President Kim's push to globalize South Korea in order to improve the country's international economic competitiveness. The policy of globalization includes some market liberalization, but there are parts of the government bureaucracy that continue to significantly impede foreign imports. In addition, there is a nationalistic sentiment that colors popular attitudes against imports and foreign companies in South Korea.

Despite the country's amazing economic success, the prevailing attitude is that South Korea remains a poor country. For this reason, the South Koreans feel they should be exempt from the "level playing field" demanded by United States trade negotiators. Even though South Korea now has the world's 11th largest economy, in the minds of its citizens its success is still tenuous. The perception exists that South Korea still needs assistance and protectionist trade policies to survive.

South Korea is governed by a directly elected president and a unicameral National Assembly that is selected by both direct and proportional elections. The president serves five years and can serve only one term. National Assembly legislators are elected in a single election every four years.

In February 1993, Kim Young Sam of the ruling Democratic Liberal Party (DLP) was inaugurated as the country's first chief executive who did not come from the military ranks in over three decades. In his first year in office, President Kim, a former opposition leader, implemented sweeping political and economic reforms, including an anti-corruption drive, which represented a fundamental policy-break from the previous administration and ended the political careers of a number of key officials from that administration.

Local elections were held in 1995 for the first time in over 30 years. Elections for the National Assembly's 299 seats will be held in 1996, followed in the next year by a presidential election. Since 1990, following the three-party merger which produced the ruling Democratic Liberal party (DLP), Korea has essentially had a two-party political system, although smaller parties are also represented in the National Assembly. The 1990 three-party merger combined the conservative ruling party with the party of the then-opposition leader Kim, and a third minor party. The Democratic Party (DP) has been in the opposition since it was formed.

Contacts in the U.S.A. & in South Korea

Contacts in the United States:

EMBASSY OF THE REPUBLIC OF KOREA
(SOUTH)
2450 Massachusetts Ave., N.W.
Washington, D.C. 20008
Tel: (202) 939-5600

U.S. DEPARTMENT OF STATE
Bureau of Consular Affairs
Tel: (202) 647-5225
Country Desk Officer, Korea
Tel: (202) 647-7717

U.S. DEPARTMENT OF COMMERCE
Korea Desk
Int'l Trade Admin.
Tel: (202) 482-4957

TOURISM OFFICE
Korea National Tourism Corp.
Two Executive Dr.
7th Floor
Fort Lee, N.J. 07024
Tel: (201) 585-0909
Fax: (201) 585-9041

Contacts in Korea:

U.S. EMBASSY
82 Sejong-Ro
Chongro-Ku
Seoul
Mailing Address:
AMEMB, Unit 15550
APO AP 96205-0001
Tel: [82] (2) 397-4114
Fax: [82] (2) 738-8845

THE AMERICAN CHAMBER OF COMMERCE IN
KOREA
Room 307
Chosun Hotel
Seoul
Tel: [82] (2) 753-6471
Telex: 23745 Chosun

PRESIDENT KIM YOUNG SAM
Office of the President
Chong Wa Dae
1 Sejong-no
Chongno-gu
Seoul, Republic of Kore

PRIME MINISTER LEE SOO SUNG
Office of the Prime Minister
77 Sejong-no
Chongno-gu
Seoul, Republic of Korea

 Passport/Visa Requirements

Visa Information   Tel: (202) 663-1225

Entry Requirements: A passport is required. A visa is not required for tourist stays of up to 15 days. For longer stays and other types of travel, visas must be obtained in advance.

Faux Pas: A foreign manufacturer of dog food experienced delay after delay in his efforts to put dog food commercials on South Korean television. Only after months of fruitless effort did he discover the reason for the opposition: too many South Koreans still remember hunger and poverty. When people do not have enough food, South Koreans consider it shameful to promote a special food for dogs. Although there has been no famine in South Korea in decades, the memory of it is still present.

Spain

Official Name:	Kingdom of Spain (Reino de España)
Official Language:	Spanish
Government System:	Constitutional monarchy
Population:	39.2 million
Population Growth:	0.4%
Area:	505,992 sq. km. (194,884 sq. mi.), including the Balearic and Canary Islands; about the size of Arizona and Utah combined
Natural Resources:	coal, lignite, iron ore, uranium, mercury, pyrites, fluorspar, gypsum, zinc, lead, tungsten, copper, kaolin, potash, hydropower
Major Cities:	Madrid (capital), Barcelona, Valencia, Seville, Zaragoza, Malaga, Bilbao

Cultural Note: The family always comes first in Spain. Nepotism is the rule rather than the exception. Given a choice between a bad offer from a relative, and a good offer from a stranger, many Spaniards would chose the relative's offer.

Age Breakdown

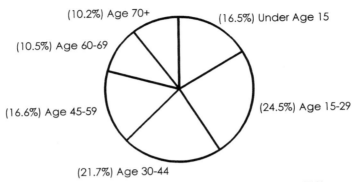

(10.2%) Age 70+   (16.5%) Under Age 15

(10.5%) Age 60-69

(16.6%) Age 45-59   (24.5%) Age 15-29

(21.7%) Age 30-44

Life Expectancy: 74 years male; 80 years female (1990)

 ## Time

Time seems to run slower in Spain. While foreigners are expected to be punctual, Spaniards do not consider themselves ruled by the clock. They generally consider deadlines an objective to be achieved if possible, but do not become overly concerned with delays.

Spain is one hour ahead of Greenwich Mean Time (G.M.T. + 1), or add six hours to U.S. Eastern Standard Time (E.S.T. + 6).

 ## Holidays

(Update: Getting Through Customs *http://www.getcustoms.com*)

This list is a working guide. Dates should be corroborated before final travel plans are made. In cases where holidays fall on Saturday or Sunday, commercial establishments may be closed the preceding Friday or following Monday.

New Year's Day	1 January
Labor Day	1 May
San Isidro (Madrid)	16 May
Our Lady of Mercy (Barcelona)	24 September
National Day and Hispanic Day	12 October

Our Lady of Almudena (Madrid)	9 November
Constitution Day	6 December
St. Stephen's Day (Barcelona)	26 December

Additional holidays are celebrated in different regions of Spain.

Work Week

- The work week is 40 hours in Spain, but hours of operation may vary.
- In Madrid, businesses are open from 9:00 A.M. to 1:30 P.M. and again from 3:00 P.M.to 6:00 P.M., Monday to Friday. In July and August, when most people take their vacations, hours may change to 8:30 A.M. to 2:30 P.M. Monday through Thursday and 8:30 A.M. to 2:00 P.M. on Friday.
- Government offices are usually open to the public from 9:00 A.M. to 1:00 P.M. Monday through Friday.
- Banks are generally open from 9:00 A.M. to 1:00 or 2:00 P.M., although on Saturday they stay open from 9:00 A.M. to 3:00 P.M.

Religious/Societal Influences on Business

Although Spain has no official religion, the vast majority of Spaniards are raised in the Roman Catholic Church. The Church still wields great influence in Spain. The large size of Spanish families was attributed to the Church's opposition to contraception and divorce.

Children are still pampered in Spain, but the birth rate has been falling since the 1970s. Small children are taken everywhere. Foreigners are often disconcerted by the presence of noisy children at expensive restaurants, where the staff is more likely to indulge them than remonstrate them.

Despite the Church, Spanish men were never expected to observe fidelity. As a result of the sexual revolution which followed the puritan Franco era, Spanish women have demanded equal freedom. Machismo still defines the expected code of conduct for men, and insults to their honor must be responded to. An ill-conceived joke can easily provoke a hostile response, or, in a business context, subvert a business deal.

Related to machismo is the "*yo primero*" (me first) attitude, evident in the Spanish reluctance to form queues. If you are doing business with multiple customers at a single site (such as a single sales counter) in Spain, provide a method of crowd control. Serving customers by number is a common technique. *Yo primero* can also be seen in the aggressive Spanish driving style, which endangers motorists and pedestrians alike.

Since the supremacy of the Catholic Church has never been challenged in Spain, it is Catholicism itself which has split into different factions. The best known of these organizations is called *"Opus Dei"*("The Work of God"). A right-wing organization which uses Freemason-like rituals, its encouragement of hard work and achievement means that you may encounter members among successful business executives.

Catholics must be baptized under the same given name as a Catholic saint, and that saint's yearly Feast Day is celebrated by the saint's namesakes, rather like a second birthday.

5 Cultural Tips

1. While many Spanish businesspeople speak English, you should have all of your materials printed in Spanish. Your business cards should have English on one side and Spanish on the other. Present your business card with the Spanish side facing your Spanish colleague.

2. Business in Spain is conducted via personal relationships. It takes time to establish such relationships. Take great care when selecting your Spanish representative, since once you have chosen him or her, it is difficult to switch to another person.

3. Get used to chaotic business discussions. It may seem like everyone is talking at once. Negotiations are an extended, laborious affair in Spain.

4. Eating is part of establishing business relationships in Spain. Your business associates may join you at all four meals: breakfast, lunch, the afternoon snack, and dinner. A business breakfast should be scheduled late, no earlier than 8:30 A.M. Lunch is the main meal of the day, and doesn't start until 2 P.M. But many businesspeople go home for lunch every day. Around 5 or 6 P.M., many Spaniards go out for a drink and hors d'oevres, which are called *tapas.* Tapas are often eaten at more than one establishment; Spaniards will walk from one bar to another, eating salted almonds in one place, potato omelettes in another. Dinner is never served before 9 P.M.

5. Although the Spaniards have become more relaxed in recent years, they still dress more formally than many other Europeans. In Spain, it is important to project an image of good taste and propriety. Wear well-made, conservative attire. Name brands are noticed in Spain!

Economic Overview

Although still faced with serious structural problems, Spain's economy has begun a slow but steady recovery. The government is moving ahead with major infrastructure projects and privatization in a number of key sectors. U.S. firms are responding to these changes and stepping up their activities in Spain.

The Spanish economy is catching up along with the rest of Western Europe with moderate economic growth following the recession of 1993 and slow recovery in 1994. The recovery has shifted from export-led to investment-led growth. The Spanish government forecasts GDP growth of nearly 4% in 1996. The economic recovery is being fueled by increased industrial production, which rose 7.1% in 1994, the largest increase in 20 years. U.S. exporters face stiff competition from the European Union. The market leaders are France, Germany, and Italy, followed by the U.S. (7%) and the U.K.

Although Spain maintains an open and transparent trading system and U.S. products and technologies are in demand, U.S. companies are disadvantaged vis-à-vis their competitors by duties imposed on products from outside the EU, higher transportation costs, and the entrenched presence of EU firms in the Spanish markets. U.S. firms should find increased opportunities for trade and investment as the Spanish government moves ahead with privatization in the telecommunications, power, and oil and gas sectors.

Cultural Note: Although Spanish is the official language of Spain, there are several regional variants of Spanish. Catalan is spoken in the east, and Gallego in the northwest. Each has different pronunciations and spellings (such as using an "X" instead of a "J"). The native language of the Basque region, Euskera, is not Spanish at all, and linguistically unrelated to any known language.

Comparative Data

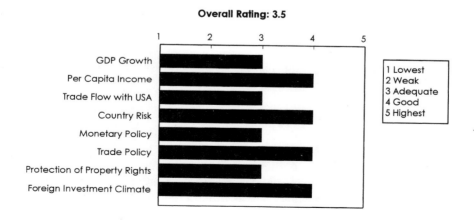

Overall Rating: 3.5

	1	2	3	4	5
GDP Growth					
Per Capita Income					
Trade Flow with USA					
Country Risk					
Monetary Policy					
Trade Policy					
Protection of Property Rights					
Foreign Investment Climate					

1 Lowest
2 Weak
3 Adequate
4 Good
5 Highest

Country Risk Rating

Gross Domestic Product: $483 billion
GDP Growth: 2%
Per Capita Income: $12,323

Trade Flows with the U.S.A.

Rank as Export Market for U.S.A. Goods & Services: 22nd
U.S.A. Exports to Spain: $5.5 billion
Growth Rate of Exports: 19%
U.S.A. Imports from Spain: $3.9 billion
Growth Rate of Imports: 8%
Rank as a Supplier of Imports into the U.S.A.:   27th

Top U.S.A. Exports to Spain: Machinery (office machines, computers, and so on); aircraft; electrical goods; miscellaneous grains, seeds, fruit; medical and optical equipment; mineral fuel; motor vehicles; organic chemicals; cereals; animal feed.

Top U.S.A. Prospects for Export to Spain: Pollution control and water resources equipment; computers and peripherals; aircraft and parts; telecommunications services; franchising; electric power systems; medical equipment; building products; architectural/construction/engineering services; telecommunications equipment; chemical machinery and equipment.

Credit Terms

Dun & Bradstreet rates Spain as a good creditworthy country with good capacity to meet outstanding payment liabilities. Credit terms vary according to sector and size of transaction, but are usually open accounts with terms of 60 to 120 days. Letter of credit is advised with new customers. Credit checks are advised especially for small or newly established businesses.

Monetary Policy

Inflation was running at between 4% and 5% in 1995. The inflationary outlook still appears somewhat suspect. Fiscally induced inflationary pressure continues to be exerted as the government expands the domestic money supply to finance its fiscal deficit. The Spanish *peseta* has experienced strong fluctuations over the last several years, having been devalued five times between September 1992 and March 1995.

Restraining inflation may be the most difficult challenge facing the Spanish economy. *Monetary Unit:* peseta.

Trade Policy

TARIFFS: For U.S. products, the tariff rate averages 5%. Spanish tariffs for European countries have been zero since January 1, 1993, while those from third-country goods, including those from the U.S., receive the EU's Common External Tariff. U.S. goods are taxed according to the standard EU duty rate. While a few agricultural commodities are duty-free or subject to minimal duties, the great majority of agricultural products (those covered by the Common Agricultural Policy) and food products are subject to high duties or variable import levies which significantly restrict access into the Spanish market.

IMPORT LICENSING: An Import Authorization form is used to control imports which are subject to quotas. While Spain does not enforce any quotas on U.S.-origin manufactured products, this document may still be required if part of the shipment contains products or goods produced or manufactured in a third country.

Importers apply for import licenses at the Spanish General Register of Spain's Department of Commerce or any of its regional offices. The license application must be accompanied by a commercial invoice. Spanish customs accepts commercial invoices via fax. Import licenses when granted are usually valid for six months.

Spanish regulations ban the import of illicit narcotics and drugs. They also set up very restrictive regulations for imports of explosives, fire weapons, defense equipment and material in general, tobacco, and gambling material. U.S. exporters should ensure, prior to making shipment, that the necessary licenses have been obtained by their importing party. Additionally, they should have their importer confirm with Spanish customs whether any product approvals or other special certificates are required for the shipment to pass customs.

IMPORT TAXES: Spain has a 15% value-added tax.

Protection of Intellectual Property Rights

Spain is a signatory to the Paris Convention for the Protection of Industrial Property. Spain is also a party to the Madrid Agreement on Trademarks.

Public and private sector enforcement actions using Spain's new patent, copyright, and trademark legal framework have increased sharply the number of criminal and civil actions taken against intellectual property pirates. Despite overall improvement, software piracy remains a serious problem in Spain.

A nonrenewable 20-year period for working patents is available, and the patent must be worked within three years of patenting. Spain is revising its patent laws pertaining to chemicals, pharmaceuticals and biotechnology to conform with EU standards. The Industrial Property Registry provides protection of trademark for a 10-year period from the date of application, although such protection may be renewed. Trademarks must be registered to be protected. Copyright protection is extended for all literary, artistic, or scientific creations, including computer software. Spain and the U.S. are members of the Universal Copyright Convention.

Foreign Investment Climate

The Spanish government is interested in attracting new foreign investment to modernize the economy. Spanish law permits foreign investment up to 100% of equity, except in a small number of strategic sectors. Capital movements have been liberalized completely.

More than 550 U.S. firms have established subsidiaries in Spain. The U.S. ranks third among investor nations after the Netherlands and France.

The Spanish central, regional, and local governments all actively encourage foreign investment.

 Current Leaders & Political Parties

(Update: International Academy at Santa Barbara *http://www.iasb.org/cwl*)

Chief of State: King Juan Carlos I

Cabinet:
Prime Min.: José María Aznar
Foreign Affairs: Javier Solana Madariaga
Justice and Interior: Juan Alberto Belloch Julbe
Defense: Gustavo Suárez Pertierra
Economy and Finance: Pedro Solbes Mira
Public Works, Transportation, and the Environment: José Borrell Fontelles
Education and Science: Jerónimo Saavedra Acevedo
Industry: Juan Manuel Eguiagaray Ucelay
Agriculture, Food, and Fisheries: Luis Atienza Serna
Presidency: Alfredo Pérez Rubalcaba
Public Admin.: Joan Lerma Blasco
Culture: Carmen Alborch Bataller
Commerce and Tourism: Javier Gómez-Navarro Navarrete

Other Officials:
Ambassador to U.S.: Jaime De Ojeda
Perm. Rep. to U.N.: Juan Antonia Yáñez

Political Parties:

Socialist Workers' Party (PSOE), Popular Party (PP), United Left (IU), Basque Nationalist Party (PNV)

Political Influences on Business

Based on its constitution of December 1978, Spain is a parliamentary democracy.

The last Prime Minister (a position technically known as President of the Government) was Felipe Gonzalez Marquez, the Secretary General of the PSOE. He was first elected to his position in 1982; his party governed with absolute parliamentary majorities from 1982–1993. After the June 1993 general election, Prime Minister Gonzalez won an unprecedented fourth consecutive term, although his Socialist Party presided over a minority government. The PSOE's chief allies in the coalition were the Catalan nationalist party, CiU (which itself is a coalition). Continued party factionalism, high unemployment, a series of corruption scandals, and the GAL case involving extra legal security force operations against ETA terrorists in the early '80s, led to a significant decline in Gonzalez's popularity. Also damaging was a scandal involving the phone-tapping (by the Spanish intelligence unit, CESID) of leading politicians, prominent businessmen and even the king of Spain! But the CiU publicly committed itself to supporting Gonzalez through 1995, allowing Gonzalez to remain in office through the Spanish EU presidency (July–December 1995).

During the Gonzalez administration, the principal opposition party was the center-right Popular Party (PP). As a result of the continuing scandals of the Gonzalez administration, the Popular Party emerged the winner in the elections of March 1996. However, continued political infighting kept the Popular Party's choice for Prime Minister, José María Aznar, from taking office until May. Mr. Aznar's accession was supported by both the Catalan and the Basques regional parties. It is hoped that this support by the moderate Basque Nationalist Party will eventually result in an end to the bombing campaign waged against Spain by the Basque terrorist group ETA.

The electoral term for national government is a maximum of four years, but elections can be called before that term expires.

Contacts in the U.S.A. & in Spain

Contacts in the United States:

EMBASSY OF THE KINGDOM OF SPAIN
2375 Pennsylvania Ave., N.W.
Washington, D.C. 20037
Tel: (202) 452-0100
Fax: (202) 728-2317

U.S. DEPARTMENT OF STATE
Overseas Travel Advisories
Tel: (202) 647-5225
Country Desk Officer, Spain
(202) 647-1412

U.S. DEPARTMENT OF COMMERCE
Spain Desk
Int'l. Trade Admin.
Tel: (202) 482-4508

Contacts in Spain:

U.S. EMBASSY
Serrano 75
28006 Madrid
Spain
Mailing address:
APO AE 09642
Tel: [34] (1) 577-4000
Telex: 27763
Fax: [34] (1) 577-5735

AMERICAN CHAMBER OF COMMERCE IN SPAIN
Avda. Diagonal 477
8th Floor
08036 Barcelona, Spain
Tel: [34] (3) 405-1266
Fax: [34] (3) 405-3124

TOURIST INFORMATION
(Main Office in Madrid)
Plaza Mayor 3
Tel: [34] (1) 266 54 77

TOURIST OFFICE OF SPAIN
665 Third Avenue
New York, N.Y. 10022
Tel: (212) 759-8822

DUN & BRADSTREET, S.A.
Postal Address: Apartado de Correos 209
28080 Madrid
Spain
Street Address: Salvador de Madariaga,
1,-20
28027 Madrid
Spain
Tel: [34] (1) 377-9100
Fax: [34] (1) 377-9101

KING JUAN CARLOS I
Palacio de la Zarzuela
28071 Madrid, Kingdom of Spain

PRIME MINISTER JOSÉ MARÍA AZNAR
Presidencia del Gobierno
Complejo de la Moncloa
28071 Madrid, Kingdom of Spain

Passport/Visa Requirements

Visa Information   Tel: (202) 663-1225

Entry Requirements: A passport is necessary, but a visa is not required for tourist stays of up to three months; visitors may subsequently apply for an extension of stay at a Spanish immigration office.

For further information concerning entry requirements, travelers may contact the Embassy of Spain.

Faux Pas: Foreigners who buy or lease homes or offices in Spain sometimes fall afoul of Spain's "Ley de Propriedad Horizontal" (Law of Horizontal Property). This applies to anything buildings share in common: electric or telephone lines, sewers, road frontages, and so on. The law holds all the tenants equally responsible for the shared item. You may find yourself paying a recalcitrant neighbor's share of a fee, just so you can have electric or sewer service!

Spanish Names and Titles

- First names are appropriate among close friends and young people only. Always wait for your Spanish counterpart to initiate the use of first names, or the use of the familiar form of address (*tú*) as opposed to the formal form (*Usted*).

- In Spain, the use of the familiar (*tú*) and formal (*Usted*) forms of address are different from their usage in Latin America. For example, Spaniards always speak to domestic servants in the formal (*Usted*) manner; they feel this confers dignity and shows respect for the servant as a person. Also, the informal (*tú*) form is more likely to be used by colleagues in a Spanish office than in a Latin American office. Sometimes employees even speak to their bosses using the *tú* (informal) form. This would border on insubordination in other Spanish-speaking countries.

- Most people you meet should be addressed with a title and their surname. Only children, family members, and close friends address each other by their first names.

- Persons who do not have professional titles should be addressed as Mr./Mrs./Miss + their surname. In Spanish, these are: Mr. for Señor, Mrs. for Señora, and Miss for Señorita.

- Most Spaniards have two surnames: one from their father, which is listed first, followed by one from their mother. Only the father's surname is commonly used when addressing someone verbally, i.e., Señor Juan Antonio Martinez de Garcia for Señor Martinez, and Señorita Pilar María Nuñez de Cela for Señorita Nuñez.

  When a woman marries, she usually adds her husband's surname and goes by that surname. If the two people in the above example married, she would be known as: Señora Pilar María Nuñez Cela de Martinez. Most people would refer to her as: Señora de Martinez, or, less formally, Señora Martinez.

- As a general rule, use only one surname when speaking to a person, but use both surnames when writing.

- It is important to address individuals with any titles they may have, followed by their surnames. For example, teachers prefer the title "*Profesor*" while engineers go by "*Ingeniero*."

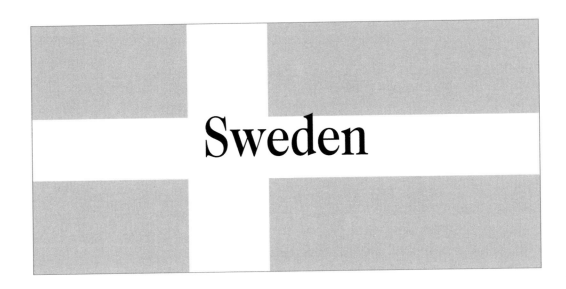

Sweden

Official Name:	Kingdom of Sweden (Konungariket Sverige)
Official Language:	Swedish
Government System:	Parliamentary state under constitutional monarchy
Population:	8.8 million
Population Growth:	0.5%
Area:	449,964 sq. km. (173,731 sq. mi.); about the size of California
Natural Resources:	zinc, iron ore, lead, copper, silver, timber, uranium, gold, hydropower potential
Major Cities:	Stockholm (capital), Goteborg, Malmo, Orebro, Norrkoping, Uppsala

---

Cultural Note: The Swedish language has three letters which do not appear in English, two versions of "a" and one of "o," all with diacritical marks. In Swedish telephone books, they are listed at the end of the alphabet, after the letter "z."

Age Breakdown

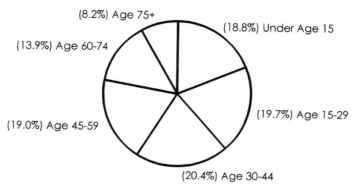

(8.2%) Age 75+

(13.9%) Age 60-74

(18.8%) Under Age 15

(19.0%) Age 45-59

(19.7%) Age 15-29

(20.4%) Age 30-44

Life Expectancy: 75 years male; 81 years female (1990)

 Time

Swedes expect punctuality. Be on time for both business and social events. It is not appropriate to be "fashionably late" to social engagements. Swedes take most things seriously, including meals and recreational time. Many people go home for lunch every day between 11:30 and 1:30 P.M. The minimum vacation time for Swedish workers is five weeks per year. Most people take their vacations in July, so it can be difficult to conduct business in midsummer. There is also a long Christmas holiday, extending from December 22 to January 6.

 Holidays

(Update: Getting Through Customs *http://www.getcustoms.com*)

This list is a working guide. Dates should be corroborated before final travel plans are made. In cases where holidays fall on Saturday or Sunday, commercial establishments may be closed the preceding Friday or following Monday.

New Year's Day	1 January
Epiphany and the 13th day of Christmas	6 January
Good Friday	varies
Easter Monday	varies
Labor Day	1 May

Ascension	varies
Whit Monday	varies
Midsummer Eve	late June
All Saints' Day	1 November
Christmas Eve	24 December
Christmas	25 December
Boxing Day	26 December
New Year's Eve	31 December

Offices usually close at 1:00 P.M. on the day preceding a holiday. On January 6 and December 31, banks and stores stay open for half a day, but other businesses are closed. Check with your local contact to review regional holidays, as well as those listed above.

Work Week

- The work week is 8:30 or 9:00 A.M. to 5:00 P.M., Monday through Friday. There is one hour for lunch, and many people go to lunch between noon and 1 P.M.
- Banks are open Monday through to Friday, 9:30 A.M. to 3:00 P.M. In large towns, many banks open one or more evenings from 4:30 to 6:00 P.M.

Religious & Societal Influences on Business

For hundreds of years, the Lutheran Church of Sweden has been the official church. A portion of every Swedish citizen's taxes was donated to the Church of Sweden. However, with only a small percentage of Swedes going to church, the connection between church and state is being dissolved.

5 Cultural Tips

1. Rather than begin with small talk, Swedes often get right down to business. Be prepared to start your pitch right away.
2. Swedes generally avoid confrontation. They must reach a consensus with all parties before agreeing to a deal. You may find management in favor of your proposal, but opposed by a labor representative.
3. Keep your presentation precise and factual. Have data to back up all your claims. Avoid hyperbole, but do not leave anything to the imagination.
4. Business lunches and dinners are popular in Sweden. Make reservations in advance at a formal restaurant. Spouses should be invited to dinner, but not to lunch.

5. Women are accepted as equals to men in Sweden. It is not unusual for a business-woman to pick up the check in Sweden, especially if she has an expense account.

Economic Overview

Sweden, which joined the European Union in January 1995, is an advanced, industrialized country with a high standard of living. Sweden is an excellent market for U.S. products and services. U.S. exports to Sweden will continue to grow as Sweden's economy and foreign trade expand. While Sweden imports a wide range of manufactured and agricultural products from the U.S., high-technology products are experiencing the fastest growth.

U.S. products are highly regarded in the Swedish market. The U.S. is Sweden's third largest foreign supplier after Germany and the U.K. The U.S. has a 9% share of the Swedish import market. Sweden's economy is experiencing an export-led recovery. Sweden recently pulled out of the deepest and most protracted recessionary period experienced since the depression years of the early 1930s.

Foreign trade is vital to Sweden's economy. About 35% of Sweden's manufactured goods are exported. Because trade is so important to the economy, Sweden has traditionally maintained a policy favoring trade liberalization. With stable political conditions, a skilled workforce, educated population, well-developed infrastructure, and relatively low corporate tax rates, Sweden is an attractive location for foreign investment.

Cultural Note: Be serious. Avoid jokes. Many Americans find the Swedish sense of humor to be incomprehensible, and vice versa. If you approach a sensitive topic, a Swede may abruptly change the topic of the conversation. Do not display excessive emotion in public.

Comparative Data

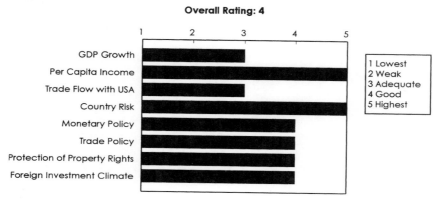

Overall Rating: 4

	1	2	3	4	5
GDP Growth					
Per Capita Income					
Trade Flow with USA					
Country Risk					
Monetary Policy					
Trade Policy					
Protection of Property Rights					
Foreign Investment Climate					

1 Lowest
2 Weak
3 Adequate
4 Good
5 Highest

Country Risk Rating

Gross Domestic Product: $196 billion
GDP Growth: 2.2%
Per Capita Income: $22,400

Trade Flows with the U.S.A.

Rank as Export Market for U.S.A. Goods & Services: 31st
U.S.A. Exports to Sweden: $3.0 billion
Growth Rate of Exports: 20%
U.S.A. Imports from Sweden: $6.2 billion
Growth Rate of Imports: 24%
Rank as a Supplier of Imports into the U.S.A.:   22nd

Top U.S.A. Exports to Sweden: Machinery (office machines, computers, and so on), electrical goods (telecommunications equipment, semiconductors/integrated circuits, and so on), medical and optical equipment, motor vehicles, aircraft, plastics, pharmaceutical products, mineral fuel, edible fruit and nuts, miscellaneous chemical products.

Top U.S.A. Prospects for Export to Sweden: Computers and peripherals, computer software, electronic components, aircraft and parts, telecommunication services, telecommunications equipment, pollution control equipment, medical equipment, drugs and pharmaceuticals, analytical and scientific instruments.

Credit Terms

Dun & Bradstreet rates Sweden as having the highest creditworthiness with an excellent capacity to meet outstanding payment liabilities. Compared with other countries, Sweden carries the lowest degree of risk. All normal methods of payment may be used, but Swedish buyers are not always willing to accept bills of exchange and suppliers are often forced to deal on open account terms, usually 30 to 90 days.

Monetary Policy

Inflationary pressures in the economy are forecast to remain relatively subdued. Inflation was 2.2% in 1994 and estimated at between 3.0 and 3.5% in 1995. The Swedish krona has depreciated more than 20% since November 1992. This has pushed up the price of imports. Foreign exchange restrictions in Sweden were removed in 1991. *Monetary Unit:* krona.

Trade Policy

TARIFFS: Sweden now applies external European Union tariffs to imports from the United States. Most industrial products are charged between 5% and 14% duty. Certain agricultural products are subject to import duties and/or fees, which are imposed in accordance with EU rules and regulations. Among the products subject to these duties and fees are cereals, flour, certain fats and oils, fishery products, butter, cheese, eggs, poultry, meat, and some cattle and hogs.

IMPORT LICENSING: Import licenses are required for only a few goods, including live animals. Certain goods, such as weapons, explosives, drugs, and poisons may be imported by authorized persons and institutions only.

IMPORT TAXES: Goods imported into Sweden are subject to a value-added tax (VAT) of 25%. Certain goods such as food and some services are subject to a lower 12% VAT rate effective 1996.

Protection of Intellectual Property Rights

The Swedish legal system provides adequate protection to all property rights including intellectual property. Sweden is a member of the Paris Union International Convention for the Protection of Intellectual Property. American inventors are thus entitled to receive national treatment in Sweden under laws regarding the protection of patents and trademarks. Sweden is also a member of the Universal Copyright Convention and the Berne Union Copyright Convention. Patent protection in all areas of technology may be obtained for 20 years. Protection of copyrights is governed by Law No. 729 of 1960 as amended. The term copyright protection of a work is for the author's life plus 50 years after the author's death. Sweden protects trademarks under the Trademark Act, effective January 1, 1961. Trademark registrations are valid for 10 years from the date of registration and are renewable for like periods.

Foreign Investment Climate

Until the mid-1980s, Sweden's approach to direct investment from abroad was quite restrictive and governed by a complex system of laws and regulations. Foreigners were restricted from acquiring shares of Swedish firms and laws required foreigners to obtain permission to transact business in Sweden. Today, Swedish authorities have implemented reforms to improve the business regulatory environment that will benefit investment inflows. Foreign exchange transactions have been decontrolled; the law requiring foreigners to obtain permission to acquire shares or holdings in Swedish firms has been abolished, and real estate regulations have been changed so that foreigners can now acquire commercial real estate and land for mining in Sweden. The estimated book value of direct U.S. investment in Sweden at the end of 1994 stood at $2.7 billion.

Current Leaders & Political Parties

(Update: International Academy at Santa Barbara *http://www.iasb.org/cwl*)

Head of State: King Carl XVI Gustaf

Ministers:

Prime Min.: Göran Persson
Justice: Laila Freivalds
Foreign Affairs: Hjelm-Wallén
Defense: Thage G. Peterson
Transportation and Communication: Ines Uusmann
Finance: Erik Åsbrink
Culture: Marita Ulvskog
Industry and Commerce: Anders Sundström

Other Officials:

Speaker of Riksdag (parliament): Birgitta Dahl
Ambassador to U.S.: Carl Henrik Liljegren
Perm. Rep. to U.N.: Peter Osvald

Political Parties

Social Democratic Party, Center Party, Christian Democratic Party, Moderate
Party, Left Party, Liberal Party, Green Party, New Democracy

Political Influences on Business

Parliamentary elections were held in September, 1994, and the Social Democrats now
form the ruling party of the parliament under the leadership of Prime Minister Ingvar
Carlsson. The referendum on European Union Membership was voted yes on
November 13, 1994 and Sweden became a member of the EU on January 1, 1995.

Sweden is a constitutional monarchy and a multiparty, parliamentary democracy.
The king is the head of state. All executive authority is vested in the Cabinet, which
is formed through direct parliamentary elections every four years (until the 1994 elections this was only three years) and consists of the Prime Minister (head of government) and some 20 ministers. The present government is a Social Democratic gov-

ernment, with strong influence from the Left party and the Environment party, the Greens. The present PM is a Social Democrat.

The next election is scheduled for the third Sunday of September 1998.

The Social Democratic Party regained power after the 1994 elections. The party has strong ties to the trade union movement and has made combatting unemployment its top priority. It has its strongest support among blue-collar workers and public-sector employees. The party has abolished many of its former socialist ideas but resists all attempts to concentrate power in the hands of the few.

Contacts in the U.S.A. & in Sweden

Contacts in the United States:

EMBASSY OF THE KINGDOM OF SWEDEN
1501 M Street, N.W.
Washington, D.C. 20005
Tel.: (202) 467-2600
Fax: (202) 467-2699

U.S. DEPARTMENT OF STATE
Country Desk Officer, Sweden
Tel.: (202) 647-6071

U.S. DEPARTMENT OF COMMERCE
International Trade Administration
Sweden Desk Officer
Tel.: (202) 482-4414

SWEDISH TOURIST OFFICE
655 Third Ave.
New York, N.Y. 10017
Tel.: (212) 949-2333
Telex: 620681 SCANDIA NY
Fax: (212) 983-5260

SCANDINAVIAN TOURIST BOARDS (STB)
655 Third Ave.
New York, N.Y. 10017
Tel.: (212) 949-2331

SWEDISH INFORMATION SERVICE
1 Dag Hammarskjold Plaza,
45th Floor
New York, N.Y. 10017
Tel.: (212) 751-5900
Telex: 125385 INFOR SWED NYK
Fax: (212) 752-4789

Contacts in Sweden:

U.S. EMBASSY
Strandvagen 101
S-115 89 Stockholm
Tel.: [46] (8) 783-5300
Fax : [46] (8) 661-1964

STOCKHOLM CHAMBER OF COMMERCE
Vastra Tradgardsgatan 9
Box 16050
S-103 22 Stockholm
Tel.: [46] (8) 23 12 00
Telex: 15638 CHAMBER S
Fax: [46] (8) 11 24 32

ASSOCIATION OF SWEDISH CHAMBERS OF
COMMERCE AND INDUSTRY
Box 16050
S-103 22 Stockholm
Tel.: [46] (8) 23 12 00
Telex: 15638 CHAMBER S

DUN & BRADSTREET SOLIDITET AB
Postal Address: Box 1506
S-171 29 Solna/Stockholm, Sweden
Street Address: Sundbybergsvagen 1
Solna/Stockholm, Sweden
Tel: [46] (8) 705-1000
Fax: [46] (8) 735-4263

KING CARL XVI GUSTAF
Office of the King
Kungliga Slottet
S-111 30 Stockholm, Kingdom of
Sweden

PRIME MINISTER INGVAR CARLSSON
Office of the Prime Minister
Rosenbad 4
S-103 33 Stockholm, Kingdom of
Sweden

 Passport/Visa Requirements

Visa Information   Tel: (202) 663-1225

Entry Requirements: A passport is required. A tourist or business visa is not required for U.S. citizens for stays up to three months (the 90-day period begins when entering the Nordic area: Sweden, Norway, Denmark, Iceland, or Finland). A visit longer than three months requires a special residence permit which is granted by the National Immigration and Naturalization Board and applied for at the nearest Consulate General or Embassy of Sweden. A foreigner who wishes to accept employment must first obtain a work permit.

For further information concerning entry requirements, travelers can contact the Embassy of Sweden.

Faux Pas: Swedish drinking customs have come a long way since the Vikings quaffed ale, wine, and mead around a roaring fire. Toasting could be a painful process among the Normans, Saxons, and Danes, and not just because of hangovers. In order to prove the sincerity of their toast, some drinkers would cut their foreheads and allow drops of their own blood to drip into their cups!

Nowadays, one major rule for toasting is to look the person you are toasting in the eye. Once the toast is given, everyone says "Skål" ("Cheers") and drinks. The host gives the first toast, then others may toast in order of seniority. The other major rule is to take a taxi if you've had too many toasts. Sweden has strict rules prohibiting drinking and driving.

Switzerland

Official Name:	Swiss Confederation (Confederation Suisse, French) (Schweizerische Eidgenossenschaft, German) (Confederazione Svizzera, Italian)
Official Languages:	French, German, Italian (A fourth language, Romansch, is protected but not official)
Government System:	Federal state
Population:	7.0 million
Population Growth:	0.57%
Area:	41,288 sq. km. (15,941 sq. mi.); about twice the size of New Jersey
Natural Resources:	hydropower potential, timber, salt
Major Cities:	Berne (capital), Zurich, Basel, Geneva, Lausanne

---

Cultural Note: Switzerland has four distinct cultures, which are usually identified by their native languages: French, Italian, German, and Romansch. (Romansch is spoken by less than 1% of the Swiss, but it is accorded protected status as Switzerland's only indigenous language. Romansch may be ignored by foreigners.) German-speakers are in the majority with about 70% of the population. French account for approximately 19% and Italian for 10%. Most Swiss are multilingual, and the majority of businesspeople include English as one of their languages.

391

Age Breakdown

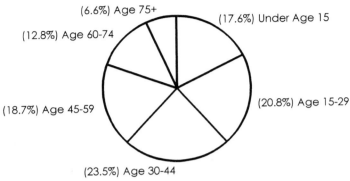

(6.6%) Age 75+
(12.8%) Age 60-74
(17.6%) Under Age 15
(18.7%) Age 45-59
(20.8%) Age 15-29
(23.5%) Age 30-44

Life Expectancy: 74 years male; 80 years female (1990)

 Time

Punctuality is very important in Switzerland. Everyone and everything is expected to be on time: people, deadlines, and transportation. Be on time for all business and social events.

Switzerland is one hour ahead of Greenwich Mean Time (G.M.T. + 1), which is six hours ahead of U.S. Eastern Standard Time (E.S.T. + 6).

 Holidays

(Update: Getting Through Customs *http://www.getcustoms.com*)

This list is a working guide. Dates should be corroborated before final travel plans are made. In cases where holidays fall on Saturday or Sunday, commercial establishments may be closed the preceding Friday or following Monday.

New Year's Day	1 January
Baerzelistag Day (observed in some Cantons)	2 January
Whit Monday	varies
Swiss National Day	1 August
Christmas	25 December
St. Stephen's Day and Boxing Day	26 December

Work Week

- The work week is generally Monday through Friday from 7:30 A.M. to 5:30 P.M., with a one- or two-hour lunch break.
- Banks are open from 8:30 A.M. to 4:30 or 5:00 P.M., Monday through Saturday.
- Stores are open from 8:00 A.M. to noon, and from 1:30 to 6:30 P.M., Monday through Saturday. Some close on Saturday or Monday mornings. The bigger stores do not close for lunch.

Religious/Societal Influences on Business

Switzerland's four cultures, German, French, Italian, and Romansch, encompass a variety of religious traditions. Roman Catholics, at 46%, constitute the majority, with various Protestant denominations making up 40%. But most religions are represented in Switzerland, including Islam, Judaism, Buddhism, and Mormon.

Switzerland was at the center of the Protestant Reformation. Reformer Ulrich Zwingli (1484–1531) lived in Zurich; Jean Calvin (1509–1564) was French but was exiled to Geneva. Years of warfare between Protestants and Catholics devastated Switzerland. As a result, the Swiss today consider religion to be a private concern. Religion is rarely discussed in public.

The doomsday cult known as the Order of the Solar Temple came to international prominence when 53 members were found dead in October of 1994, the victims of murder and mass suicide. The Swiss were aghast at these events, which served to drive religion even further out of public discourse. Nevertheless, the Swiss consider themselves privately devoted to religious principals.

The Swiss believe that they have developed a fair and beneficent society, and exert strong social pressures on their citizens to conform to Swiss patterns of behavior.

Divided by language and religion, the Swiss find unity in their devotion to their families, their work, and their country. The Swiss are patriotic and deeply involved in their country's politics. Their political system, which involves strong local government, allows each citizen's vote to have great effect on their everyday lives. Referendums are frequent. Even the Swiss constitution can be challenged by a system called the People's Initiatives. Basic institutions such as the Swiss Army can be challenged by a People's Initiative. (At the last such vote, in 1989, the Swiss decided to keep their military.)

The Swiss are intensely concerned about the environment. They recycle most consumer products, and are second only to Germany in environmental restrictions.

5 Cultural Tips

1. Since Switzerland has four native cultures, try to find out the primary language of the people you will do business with. German cultural traditions are quite different from those of the French or Italians. Fortunately, since most Swiss executives speak English, it is not necessary to translate your business cards or promotional literature.

2. Age and seniority are important in Switzerland. Avoid sending a young executive alone to Switzerland; he or she will not be taken seriously. Expect to defer to the elderly. Also, if your company has a long lineage, the year it was established should appear on your business card and/or letterhead.

3. Bring plenty of business cards. You will need at least two for each appointment. You will give your business card to the secretary when you arrive, and she will keep that card for her file. When you meet the executive, you will need a second card to give to him or her.

4. Business in Switzerland is serious business, especially among the German-speaking populace. Humor is out of place in business negotiations. Keep your posture erect and your body language formal. Slouching back in a chair or propping one's feet up would convey the wrong image in Switzerland.

5. Swiss executives dress conservatively, but they are often quite fashionable. Exclusive brand names are recognized and respected. Dress as well as you can afford. (Remember that Switzerland has the highest standard of living in Europe, so it is an expensive country in which to do business.)

Economic Overview

Switzerland is a small, highly developed, multilingual market located at the crossroads of Europe. Its population of seven million people is diversified, well-educated, and affluent. It has a strong and stable economy, low inflation, relatively low unemployment, and a highly qualified workforce, all of which contribute to make the Swiss Confederation a desirable market environment. Per capita income is the highest in Europe and spending power for foreign goods and services is thus extremely high.

Trade and prosperity are synonymous in Switzerland. The country is dependent upon export markets to absorb its production and sustain its wealth, but is also equally dependent upon imports for raw materials and to expand the range of goods and services available in-country. The U.S. ranks fourth as a source of Swiss imports, and third as a destination for Swiss exports.

Switzerland is known for liberal trade and investment policies. Fiscal policy is moderate and cautious. The Swiss franc is one of the world's soundest and most stable currencies. The country is famous for its high standard of banking, ensuring rapid and reliable processing of business transactions.

After several years of stagnation and recession, the Swiss economy showed recovery in the last quarter of 1993 and has been expanding continuously since then. Real GDP increased by a modest 2.1% in 1994, and the pace of expansion was expected to slow in 1995 and 1996. U.S. relations with Switzerland are excellent. The Swiss feel comfortable doing business with Americans. U.S. promotional themes are popular at stores, shopping centers, and restaurants, and many social groups feature American activities. American products have a favorable reputation, particularly high technology and labor-saving capital goods and consumer products.

Cultural Note: The Swiss attribute much of their success to their work ethic. They work hard (and play hard). Punctuality is required and planning is done in advance. Everything is kept clean (this also applies to the country as a whole). Perhaps the only negative is that the Swiss are not usually good at improvising. But if everything follows the plan, they don't need to improvise.

Comparative Data

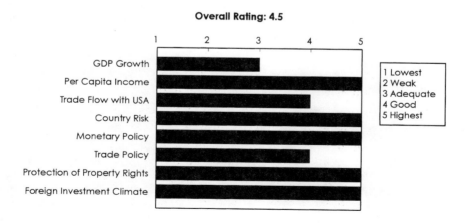

Overall Rating: 4.5

	1	2	3	4	5

GDP Growth
Per Capita Income
Trade Flow with USA
Country Risk
Monetary Policy
Trade Policy
Protection of Property Rights
Foreign Investment Climate

1 Lowest
2 Weak
3 Adequate
4 Good
5 Highest

Country Risk Rating

Gross Domestic Product: $260 billion (1994)
GDP Growth: 2.1% (1994)
Per Capita Income: $37,677

Trade Flows with the U.S.A.

Rank as Export Market for U.S.A. Goods & Services: 19th

U.S.A. Exports to Switzerland: $6.2 billion

Growth Rate of Exports: 11%

U.S.A. Imports from Switzerland: $7.6 billion

Growth Rate of Imports: 19%

Rank as a Supplier of Imports into the U.S.A.:   19

Top U.S.A. Exports to Switzerland: Precious stones; machinery; art and antiques; medical and optical equipment; electrical components; organic chemicals; pharmaceutical products; aircraft and parts; motor vehicles; clocks and watches.

Top U.S.A. Prospects for Export to Switzerland: Computer software, computers and peripherals; telecommunications equipment; aircraft and parts; medical equipment; pollution control equipment; laboratory scientific equipment; industrial process controls; security and safety equipment; sporting goods and recreational equipment.

Credit Terms

Dun & Bradstreet rates Switzerland as having excellent capacity to meet outstanding payment liabilities. It carries the lowest degree of risk.

Credit terms vary according to sector and size of transaction, but are usually between 60 and 90 days. Open account terms are most common and letters of credit are rarely used.

Monetary Policy

Swiss inflation remains low and is forecast to remain below 2.0% through 1996 and 1997. *Monetary Unit:* Swiss Franc.

Trade Policy

TARIFFS: Import duties are generally low, averaging about 3.2% in the industrial goods sectors. Switzerland's tariff policy favors the development of trade. Imports of virtually all agricultural products are subject to import and supplementary duties and to variable import quotas.

IMPORT LICENSING: Import licenses are required only for a limited number of products, and generally fall into two categories: measures for the protection of the country's agriculture, and measures of state control.

The system of import licensing for agricultural products was expected to be significantly modified in 1995, following implementation of the GATT Uruguay Round reforms for agriculture.

Products subject to quota may not be imported without an import license, and licenses are granted only to importers established in Switzerland. Most quotas vary from year to year according to the size of harvests, volume of stocks, and market requirements.

IMPORT TAXES: In addition to customs duties, the Swiss customs administration levies a 3% statistical tax on the total customs duty payable.

A value-added tax (VAT) is levied on all imports of goods and services. The standard VAT rate is 6.5%, although there is a reduced rate of 2% for certain goods and services such as food and drinks (excluding alcoholic beverages and prepared meals), meats of all kinds, cereals, plants, seeds and flowers, some basic farming supplies, medicine and drugs, newspapers, magazines and books.

Protection of Intellectual Property Rights

Switzerland has one of the best regimes in the world for the protection of intellectual property, and protection is afforded equally to foreign and domestic rightsholders. Switzerland is a member of all major international intellectual property rights conventions.

Patent protection is very broad, and Swiss law provides rights to inventors comparable to those in the United States. Switzerland is a member of both the European Patent Convention and the Patent Cooperation Treaty, making it possible for inventors to file a single patent application in the U.S. and receive protection in Switzerland. The duration of a patent is 20 years. Patents are not renewable beyond the original 20-year term.

Trademarks are also well protected. Switzerland recognizes well-known trademarks and has established simple procedures to register and renew all marks. The initial period of protection is 20 years. Trademark infringement is very rare in Switzerland.

A new copyright law in 1993 improved a regime that was already quite good. The new law explicitly recognizes computer software as literary work and establishes a remuneration scheme for private copying of audio and video works which distributes proceeds on the basis of national treatment. Copyright protection lasts the life of the author plus 70 years.

Foreign Investment Climate

The Swiss welcome foreign investment and accord it national treatment. Foreign investment is neither actively encouraged nor unduly hampered by barriers. The federal government adopts a relaxed attitude of benevolent noninterference toward foreign investment, confining itself to creating and maintaining the general conditions that are favorable both to Swiss and foreign investors. Such factors include economic and political stability, a firmly established legal system, a reliable infrastructure, and efficient capital markets. The government does not offer large-scale incentives to prospective investors, and those that exist are open to foreign and domestic investors alike.

With the exception of national security areas (such as hydroelectric and nuclear power, operation of oil pipelines, transportation of explosive materials, operation of airlines and marine navigation) national treatment is granted to foreign investors. A major law affecting foreign investments is the 1993 Federal Law on Authorization of Acquisition of Real Estate by Persons with Residence or Headquarters Abroad. This law limits the freedom of foreigners to purchase real estate in Switzerland and makes such purchases subject to local government approval. A modified law that would have removed the necessity for foreigners to have an authorization to acquire property for residential and commercial activity purposes was rejected by the Swiss electorate in June 1995.

 Current Leaders & Political Parties

(Update: International Academy at Santa Barbara *http://www.iasb.org/cwl*)

Pres. of the Confederation and Head of the Fed. Dept. of Economy:
Jean-Pascal Delamuraz
Vice Pres. and Head of the Fed. Dept. of Justice and Police: Arnold Koller

Federal Council and Allocation of Departments:
Chancellor: François Couchepin
Finance: Kaspar Villiger
Transport, Communications, and Energy: Moritz Leuenberger
Interior: Ruth Dreifuss
Foreign Affairs: Flavio Cotti
Military: Adolf Ogi

Other Officials:
Pres. of the Natl. Cncl. (House of Representatives): Jean-François Leuba
Pres. of the Cncl. of States: Otto Schoch
Ambassador to U.S.: Carlo Jagmetti
Observer to U.N.: Johannes Manz

Political Parties:
Radical Democrats, Social Democrats, Christian Democrats, Volkspartei (People's Party), Liberal Party, Independent Party, Green Party, Coalition of Progressive Organisations and Greens, Swiss Democrats, Evangelical People's Party

Political Influences on Business

In the wake of the Swiss voters' rejection of the European Economic Area (EEA) Agreement in 1992, the Swiss federal government is attempting to negotiate bilateral sectoral agreements with the European Union. To what extent the government will succeed, and on what terms, is a major political issue that will affect the domestic business climate. The Swiss federal government is committed to achieve EU membership as a long-term goal, although this course is opposed by a significant number of Swiss.

U.S. companies already doing business in and with Switzerland have not to date indicated any direct problems associated with the EEA rejection on their business; any negative repercussions to trade are more likely to impact domestic companies' relations with the EU. U.S. companies already acclimated to EU business practices and regulations should experience no difficulties in Switzerland, as the underlying Swiss goal is not to reject EU trade, but rather to make its trading environment as compatible as possible with that of the EU while still maintaining Swiss political and economic integrity.

Switzerland has a relatively weak federal government and no recent tradition of executive leadership wielded by one individual. Many executive and administrative powers are vested in the 26 cantonal governments rather than in the federal government in Berne. Federal executive decision making is undertaken by the seven-member Federal Council (cabinet). Its members head the various federal ministries: Treasury, Foreign Affairs, Justice, Economics, Interior, Transportation and Energy, and Defense. The entirely ceremonial position of President of the Federal Council (head of government) is rotated annually among the councilors according to seniority. Some councilors may exchange ministerial portfolios as new members are added. The Federal Council strives to present a collegial image and to govern by consensus. Its deliberations are private. Contentious issues that cannot be decided by consensus are determined by majority vote, results of which are not released.

The composition of the Federal Council reflects the so-called "magic formula" coalition that has governed Switzerland since 1959. Under this informal arrangement, the four largest political parties, which generally receive 70–75% of the popular vote in federal parliamentary elections held every four years, fill the seven positions on the Federal Council. The three bourgeois parties in the coalition (Free Democrats, Christian Peoples' Party, and Swiss Peoples' Party) reflect center-right constituencies. The left-of-center Social Democrats are the fourth coalition party. The three largest parties in terms of popular vote (Free Democrats, Christian Peoples' Party, and Social Democrats) each receive two Federal Council seats; the Swiss Peoples' Party receives one. In addition, it is understood that there will always be at least two members from French-speaking cantons on the Federal Council. According to the Constitution, no canton may have more than one representative on the Federal Council. Federal Councilors are elected by Parliament for life, but political tradition dictates that they retire in their sixties.

Treaties, agreements, and legislation approved by the Parliament are subject to challenge by popular vote in Switzerland's unique system of initiative and referendum procedures. These votes allow unusually intense popular involvement in the legislative process and keep the federal government under pressure and scrutiny. Most of the interesting moments in Swiss politics occur during these initiative and referendum campaigns.

Contacts in the U.S.A. & in Switzerland

Contacts in the United States:

THE EMBASSY OF SWITZERLAND*
2900 Cathedral Ave., N.W.
Washington, DC 20008-3499
Tel. (202) 745-7900
Fax: (202) 387-2564

* Note that the Swiss Embassy in Washington also hosts the "Cuban Interests Section," the de facto Cuban Embassy to the U.S.

U.S. DEPARTMENT OF STATE
Bureau of Consular Affairs
Tel: (202) 647-5225
Country Desk Officer, Switzerland
Tel: (202) 647-1484

U.S. DEPARTMENT OF COMMERCE
Switzerland Desk
Washington, D.C. 20230
Tel. (202) 482-2920

TOURISM OFFICE
Switzerland Tourism
608 Fifth Avenue
New York, N.Y. 10020
Tel: (212) 757-5944
Fax: (212) 262-6116

Contacts in Switzerland:

U.S. EMBASSY
Jubilaeumstrasse 93
3005 Berne, Switzerland
Tel. [41] (31) 437-011
Telex: 845-912603
Fax: [41] (31) 437-344

SWISS-AMERICAN CHAMBER OF COMMERCE
Talacker 41
CH-8001 Zurich
Tel.: [41] (1) 211-24-54
Telex: 813448 IPCO CH
Fax: [41] (1) 211-9572

DUN & BRADSTREET NOVINFORM AG
Postal Address: P.O Box
CH-8010 Zurich, Switzerland
Street Address: In der Luberzen 1
CH-8902 Urdorf
Switzerland
Tel: [41] (1)735 61 11
Fax: [41] (1)735 61 61

PRESIDENT JEAN PASCAL DELAMURAZ
Office of the President
Federal Chancellery
Bundeshaus Nord
3003 Berne, Switzerland

Passport/Visa Requirements

Visa Information   Tel: (202) 663-1225

Entry Requirements: A passport is required. A visa is not required for tourist or business stays up to three months. For further information on entry requirements, travelers can contact the Embassy of Switzerland.

Faux Pas: Avoid comments on the Second World War. Although Switzerland remained neutral, it was still affected by the war. Many Swiss had friends or relative in the neighboring countries, all of which were at war. Few Swiss families escaped tragedy during World War II.

Taiwan

Official Name:	Republic of China (Chung-hua Min-kuo)
Official Language:	Mandarin Chinese
Government System:	Unitary Republic
Population:	21.2 million (1995)
Population Growth:	1.1% (1994)
Area:	35,981 sq. km. (14,000 sq. mi.); about the size of West Virginia
Natural Resources:	some coal, natural gas, limestone, marble, asbestos
Major Cities:	Taipei (capital), Kaohsiung, Taichung, Tainan, Keelung

---

Cultural Note: The Chinese phrase that describes so much of Taiwanese life is *re nau*, which means hot and raucous. This describes not just Taiwan's lively nightlife, but the aggressive nature of daytime Taiwan as well. The streets are jammed and the noise is overwhelming; everyone has something to do and is in a hurry to get there. It is this energy that developed Taiwan into a major industrial power in half a century. Foreigners may find it unbearably noisy. But the Taiwanese know that death is the ultimate silence: as long as they can make noise, they're still alive.

Age Breakdown

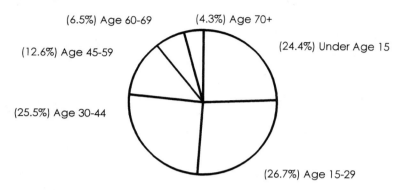

(6.5%) Age 60-69   (4.3%) Age 70+

(12.6%) Age 45-59   (24.4%) Under Age 15

(25.5%) Age 30-44

(26.7%) Age 15-29

Life Expectancy: 71 years male; 76 years female (1994)

 ## Time

Far more important than punctuality is the protection of face. When you make a higher-ranking person wait for you, both of you have lost face.

As a general rule, foreigners should try to be on time to all business appointments. This is not easy in Taiwan's congested traffic. However, do not get upset if your Taiwanese counterpart is late.

Taiwan is eight hours ahead of Greenwich Mean Time (G.S.T. + 8), which is thirteen hours ahead of U.S. Eastern Standard Time (E.S.T. + 13).

 ## Holidays

(Update: Getting Through Customs *http://www.getcustoms.com*)

There are 10 holidays and three festivals in Taiwan. Dates for the three festivals, which include Chinese Lunar New Year day, Dragon Boat Festival, and Mid-Autumn (Moon) Festival, change with the lunar calendar.

Founding Day	1 January
Spring Festival (Chinese New Year)	Late Jan.–Mid-Feb.
Youth Day	29 March
Women and Children's Day	4 April

Tomb Sweeping Day and President Chiang Kai-Shek Day	5 April
Dragon Boat Festival	Late May–Mid-June
Mid-Autumn Festival	September
Confucius' Birthday	28 September
Double Ten National Day	10 October
Taiwan Retrocession Day	25 October
President Chiang Kai-Shek's Birthday	31 October
Dr. Sun Yat-Sen's Birthday	12 November
Constitution Day	25 December

Work Week

- Business hours are generally 8:30 A.M. to noon and 1:00 to 5:00 P.M., Monday through Friday, and 8:30 A.M. to noon on Saturday.
- Banking hours are 8:30 A.M. to 3:30 P.M., Monday through Friday, and 8:30 A.M. to noon on Saturday.
- Government offices are open 8:30 A.M. to 12:30 P.M. and 1:30 to 5:30 P.M., Monday through Friday, and 8:30 A.M. to noon on Saturday.
- Many business people nap after lunch (between 1:00 P.M. and 1:30 P.M.). They may not be fully awake for a 2:00 P.M. appointment.
- Plan a visit to Taiwan between April and September. Many people vacation from January through March.

Religious/Societal Influences on Business

A Taiwanese citizen does not have to wonder about the meaning of life. The Mandarin term, *shengyi* translates as "meaning of life." It also means "business." There could be no greater work ethic than this: the purpose of life in Taiwan is to work hard, be successful in business, and accumulate wealth for one's family.

Confucian ethics form the backbone of Taiwan society. Confucianism is not a religion in the Western sense, but it does provide guides for living. Unlike the People's Republic of China (where the Communists preached loyalty to one's work group) in Taiwan the family remains the central unit of society.

Taiwan has no official religion, reflecting the ability of the Taiwanese to simultaneously follow more than one religion. Aside from Confucianism and traditional folk beliefs, Taiwanese are likely to be Buddhist, Taoist, or Christian. (To make matters more complicated, many Taiwanese follow Taoist philosophy while ignoring the Taoist priesthood.)

5 Cultural Tips

1. If you wander into a traditional Taiwanese office between 1 and 1:30 P.M., you may think you've stumbled into a roomful of headless corpses! Taiwanese workers generally take a short nap after lunch, and many pull their jackets over their heads to help them sleep. The office management cooperates by dimming the lights and keeping activity to a minimum. Obviously, this is not a good time for an appointment.

2. The Taiwanese are a fairly small and slender people. The larger size of the average Westerner can be intimidating to many Taiwanese. If you can find a way to compensate for this difference (such as standing on a lower level, so you and your Taiwanese counterpart are at eye level), do so. Also, large Westerners should expect to be uncomfortable in Taiwan, where everything from furniture to clothing is made to a smaller scale.

3. Western men who wear beards can be at a disadvantage in Taiwan. Taiwanese men are usually clean-shaven except after the death of their father or brother (they stay unshaven during the traditional seven-week mourning period). In fact, one of the Taiwanese terms for foreigners is *ang mo*, meaning "red beard." The term can be used for bearded or clean-shaven foreigners of any hair color, and it is not complimentary. It plays into the stereotype of Westerners as hairy, unkempt barbarians. Westerners can fight this characterization by being beardless and well-groomed.

4. Executives in the healthcare and medical supply industries must face the Taiwanese reluctance to discuss illness. People in Taiwan do not even like to give health warnings, nor do they comment on illness to a sick person. The insurance industry has gotten around this reluctance by speaking of insurance as if it were a bet (most Taiwanese love gambling). A life insurance salesperson will explain a policy by saying, "We will bet that you will live to age sixty, and if we lose, we will pay your beneficiaries."

5. While nepotism is a fact of life in Taiwan, foreign companies are advised to avoid hiring multiple members of the same family. Since loyalty to the family is one of the basic tenets of Taiwanese life, when you have several family members working in an office they may begin to work for their family's interest rather than the company's. Furthermore, if they learn how to run your business, they may all quit and form their own competing firm.

Economic Overview

Through 40 years of hard work and sound economic management, the people of Taiwan have built the island into the world's nineteenth largest economy. Taiwan is an economic powerhouse with more than $175 billion in two-way trade. The economy continues to expand at almost 7% a year with full employment and low inflation. An expanding democratic government, strong economic performance, and economic liberalization shape the Taiwan market.

The island's ambition to transform itself from an export platform to a high-tech production center is proceeding on schedule. In 1994, the percentage of Taiwan's exports accounted for by high-tech and capital-intensive products for the first time exceeded labor-intensive exports. As in other developed economies, services is the sector growing most rapidly. Services accounted for 47% of GDP in 1986, 59% in 1994, and more than 60% in the first quarter of 1995. Many new private banks, insurance companies, and securities firms have emerged. New financial services, such as automatic tellers machines and credit cards, have become common.

Taiwan is an excellent market for U.S. firms. Taiwan firms and consumers are receptive to foreign products, have money, and are not afraid to spend.

Comparative Data

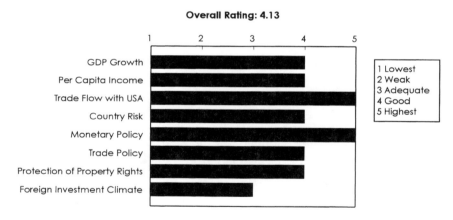

Overall Rating: 4.13

1	Lowest
2	Weak
3	Adequate
4	Good
5	Highest

Country Risk Rating

Gross Domestic Product: $261 billion
GDP Growth: 6.5%
Per Capita Income: $12,342

Trade Flows with the U.S.A.

Rank as Export Market for U.S.A. Goods & Services: 7th
U.S.A. Exports to Taiwan: $19.3 billion

Growth Rate of Exports: 12%

U.S.A. Imports from Taiwan: $28.9 billion

Growth Rate of Imports: 8%

Rank as a Supplier of Imports into the U.S.A.:   6th

Top U.S.A. Exports to Taiwan: Electrical components; machinery; aircraft and parts; motor vehicles; organic chemicals, cereals; medical and optical equipment; plastics; miscellaneous grain, seeds, and fruit.

Top U.S.A. Prospects for Export to Taiwan: Electronic components; aircraft and parts, insurance services; computer software; electronics industrial production/ testing equipment; electric power systems; analytical and scientific instruments; plastic materials and resins; household consumer goods; pollution control equipment.

Credit Terms

Dun & Bradstreet rates Taiwan as having good capacity to meet outstanding payment liabilities. Most transactions are undertaken on open account terms, although more secure letters of credit are still used widely. Credit terms of 60 to 90 days are common, although longer terms may be requested. A letter of credit is still recommended until good business relations have been established.

Monetary Policy

Despite robust economic growth, Taiwan's inflationary pressures remain subdued. Inflation in 1994 was 3.9%, and finished 1995 at under 3.6%; it is forecast at 3.5% for 1996. *Monetary Unit:* New Taiwan dollar.

Trade Policy

TARIFFS: Taiwan has made significant progress in reducing its tariff level on products of interest to the U.S. New legislation in 1995 resulted in the reduction of import duties on 758 industrial and agricultural products, by an average of 2.8%.

Thirty import categories will be exempted from import duties. This is the first time Taiwan authorities have cut tariffs on fresh fruits and vegetables which are grown on the island.

IMPORT LICENSING: The number of items requiring import licenses is being reduced gradually. The import licensing system was replaced in 1993 with a "negative list," thus reducing the number of items subject to licensing. As of June 1995, 93% of the 9,350 items in Taiwan's tariff schedule could be imported without an import license.

Approximately 240 items, including arms, munitions, and several important agricultural products including rice, are banned from import.

IMPORT TAXES: Importers must pay a 0.5% harbor construction fee and a 5% value-added tax. Air shipments are exempt from the harbor fees. A commodity tax ranging from 2% to 60% is charged on imported products that fall into any of the following seven categories: rubber tires, cement, beverages, oil and gas, electric appliances, flat glass, and automotive products.

Protection of Intellectual Property Rights

Taiwan's copyright, patent, and trademark laws already provide a level of protection for rights holders that meet most international standards.

Foreign Investment Climate

Taiwan has long encouraged and facilitated direct foreign investment. Regulations affecting foreign-invested enterprises are thus generally transparent and nondiscriminatory. In its negotiations to enter the World Trade Organization as a developed economy, Taiwan has committed to bring its trade and investment regimes into full compliance with all international standards. Most ownership restrictions in the securities, trading, insurance, and banking industries have been removed. The vast majority of industrial categories are open to foreign investment. A "negative list" adopted in 1990 specifies industries closed to foreign investment. These include agriculture, cigarette manufacturing, liquor distilling, petroleum refining, basic telecommunications, broadcasting, and electricity distribution. Foreign ownership is restricted in such industries as general construction, shipping, mining, and legal and accounting services.

Taiwan has a comprehensive legal system to protect foreign investments and property rights and ensure fair competition.

Current Leaders & Political Parties

(Update: International Academy at Santa Barbara *http://www/iasb.org/cwl*)

President: Lee Teng-hui
Prime Min. & Vice President: Lien Chan

Cabinet Ministers:
Vice Prime Min.: Hsu Li-teh
Interior: Lin Fong-cheng
Foreign Affairs: John Chang
Natl. Defense: Chiang Chung-ling
Finance: Paul Chiu

Economic Affairs: Wang Chih-kang

Transportation and Communications: Tsay Jaw-yang

Chmn. of the Cncl. for Economic Planning and Dev.: Chiang Pin-lung

Chmn. of the Overseas Chinese Affairs Comn.: James Chu

Chmn. of the Research, Dev., and Evaluation Comn.: Huang Ta-chou

Sec. Gen. of the Cabinet: Chao Shou-po

Other Officials:

Chmn. of the Natl. Science Cncl.: Liu Chao-shiuan

Chmn. of the Environmental Protection Admin.: Tsai Hsung-hsiung

Pres. of the Legislative Yuan: Liu Sung-fan

Pres. of the Judicial Yuan: Shih Chi-yang

Speaker of the Taiwan Provincial Assembly: Liu Ping-wei

Gov. of the Central Bank of China: Y. D. Sheu

Dir. Gen. of Budget, Accounting, and Statistics: Wei Duan

Head of the Taipei Economic and Cultural Office in the U.S.: Jason C. Hu

Gov. of Taiwan: James Soong

Perm. Rep. to U.N.: none, not a member

Political Parties:

Kuomintang (KMT), Democratic Progressive Party (DPP), New Party, Young China Party (YCP), China Democratic Socialist Party (CDSP), Labor Party

Political Influences on Business

Over the past few years Taiwan has made significant progress in its transition from a single-party, authoritarian policy to a democratic, multiparty political system. Martial law, which had been in force since the 1940s, was lifted in 1987. Taiwan's first democratically elected legislature was chosen in December 1992. The democratization process continued with the first direct elections of the Mayors of Taiwan's two largest cities (Taipei and Kaohsiung) and the Governor of Taiwan Province in December 1994. These officials were previously appointed by the central authorities.

Taiwan's constitutional system divides the government into five branches, or Yuans. The five branches are the Executive Yuan, the Legislative Yuan, the Judicial Yuan, the Control Yuan and the Examination Yuan. At the top of this structure is the President; Taiwan held its first popular election for president in March 1996.

Although Taiwan has progressed rapidly toward full democracy, the Kuomintang (KMT, or Nationalist Party), which ran the previous authoritarian government on Taiwan, still holds most of the key political posts on the island. The KMT continues to hold a majority in the law-making Legislative Yuan (LY). Factional fighting and weak party discipline within the KMT limits the Party's ability to take full advantage of its numerical superiority in the legislature, but when push comes to shove the KMT has been able to muster the votes to achieve its most important goals.

Now that martial law has been lifted, the main opposition party is the Democratic Progressive Party (DPP). The Party's most salient policy difference with the KMT has been the controversial issue of Taiwan independence. The DPP has also staked out generally populist positions of concern for the environment and for working people.

The KMT, which brought its political power and two million people over from Mainland China in 1949, was historically associated with the Mainlanders (i.e., people who fled to Taiwan with the KMT and the descendants of those people). The DPP has sought to identify itself with the Taiwanese (ethnic Chinese who immigrated to Taiwan during the past 300 years, mostly from Fujian Province). Yet a majority of the officials and members in the KMT, including the president, are now ethnic Taiwanese. A new opposition party, the Chinese New Party consisting mainly of second generation "mainlanders" who have grown up in Taiwan, broke off from the KMT in 1993.

The defining characteristic of Taiwan's international relationships is its lack of diplomatic ties with most nations of the world. The ruling authorities of Taiwan call their administration the "Republic of China," and for many years claimed to be the legitimate government of all China. Foreign nations wishing to establish diplomatic relations with a government of China had two choices: to recognize the "Republic of China" or to recognize the People's Republic of China (PRC). Most chose to recognize the PRC. The PRC was admitted to the United Nations and most related organizations in the early seventies, while Taiwan left. The U.S. switched diplomatic recognition to the PRC in 1979.

The Taiwan authorities several years ago backed away from their stance of insisting that they are the legitimate rulers of all China. While still admitting that Taiwan is part of China, they now seek recognition as one of two "legitimate political entities" in China, the other being the PRC. Under this policy, the Taiwan authorities are seeking to join various international organizations, including the United Nations. Taiwan has been able to join the Asia-Pacific Cooperation (APEC) dialogue and is applying to join the World Trade Organization (WTO) as a "customs territory."

Although the United States does not have diplomatic relations with Taiwan, the U.S.-Taiwan relationship is generally excellent. The American Institute in Taiwan (AIT), a private, nonprofit institution, was established in 1979 to maintain the unofficial relations between the peoples of the United States and Taiwan.

Contacts in the U.S.A. & in Taiwan

Contacts in the United States:

In an effort to strenghten economic and commercial ties, U.S. President Clinton approved the first adjustment in U.S. policy toward Taiwan in 15 years (September 1994). Taipei's de facto embassy in the United States, the Coordination Council for

North American Affairs, had been upgraded to a representative office and will now be known as the Taipei Economic and Cultural Representative Office. Its U.S. office is located at 4201 Wisconsin Avenue, N.W., 20016, Washington, D.C., Tel: (202) 895-1800.

AMERICAN INSTITUTE IN TAIWAN/
WASHINGTON
Trade and Commercial Programs
1700 N. Moore Street
Suite 1700
Arlington, VA 22209
Tel: 703-525-8474
Fax: 703-841-1385

U.S. DEPARTMENT OF COMMERCE
Taiwan Desk Officers
14th and Constitution Ave., N.W.
Room 2327
Washington, D.C. 20230
Tel: 202-482-4681
Fax: 202-482-4098

U.S. DEPARTMENT OF COMMERCE
U.S. & F.C.S. East Asia Pacific

14th and Constitution Ave., N.W.
Room 1229
Washington, D.C. 20230
Tel: 202-482-2429
Fax: 202-482-5179

U.S. DEPARTMENT OF COMMERCE
Trade Information Center
14th and Constitution Ave., N.W.
Room 7424
Washington, D.C. 20230
Tel: 1-800-USA-TRADE

REPUBLIC OF CHINA
Information Division
Taipei Economic and Cultural Office
6300 Wilshire Blvd.
Suite 1510
Los Angeles, CA 90048

Contacts in Taiwan:

AMERICAN INSTITUTE IN TAIWAN (AIT)
Commercial Section
Chief: William Brekke
Deputy Chief: Alan Turley
333 Keelung Rd.
Suite 3207
Sec. 1, Taipei, Taiwan
Tel: [886] (2) 720-1550
Fax: [886] (2) 757-7162

AMERICAN CHAMBER OF COMMERCE
96 Chungshan N. Rd.
Rm. 1012
Sec. 2, Taipei, Taiwan
Tel: [886] (2) 581-7089
Fax: [886](2) 542-3376

CHINA EXTERNAL TRADE DEVELOPMENT
COUNCIL
Secretary-General: Ronie H.K. Huang
4-8F, 333 Keelung Rd.
Sec. 1
Taipei, Taiwan
Tel: [886] (2) 725-5200
Fax: [886] (2) 757-6653

DUN & BRADSTREET INTERNATIONAL, LTD.
TAIWAN BRANCH
Postal Address: 12/F, National
Enterprises Centre
No. 188 Nanking E. Road
Sec. 5
Taipei, Taiwan, R.O.C.
Tel: [886] (2) 756-2922
Fax: [886] (2) 749-1936

President Lee Teng-hui
Office of the President
Chieh-Shou Hall
Chung-King South Rd.
Taipei, Republic of China

 Passport/Visa Requirements

Visa Information   Tel: (202) 663-1225

Entry Requirements: A passport and visa are required. (*Note*: Taiwan eased its visa regulations in early 1994, allowing citizens from 12 countries, including the United States, to enter Taiwan without a visa for a stay of up 14 days.) Visas for stays of up to two months are issued without charge.

U.S. citizens who plan to visit Taiwan (ROC) for less then 180 days may apply for a visitor visa. (Initial duration of stay is 60 days; however, this can be extended twice to the maximum of 120 days subject to the approval of authorities).

Applicants may apply for a resident visa, if duration of stay in ROC is more than 180 days.

Cultural Note: The founders of the Republic of China considered themselves to be the legitimate rulers of all China. After the Communist victory on the mainland, the Nationalists retreated to Taiwan, where they have remained ever since.

To underscore its claim as true ruler of all China, the Taiwanese government chose traditional Mandarin Chinese as its official language. Initially, Taiwan used the old forms of written Chinese, rejecting the improved, simplified Chinese characters developed by the Communists. Over the years, though, Taiwan adopted some (but not all) of the Communists' most successful reforms to written Chinese. Business executives having materials translated into Chinese should make sure the Taiwanese variant is used in Taiwan.

Westerners who wish to speak Chinese should be thankful that Mandarin was chosen as Taiwan's official language. Mandarin, with four different tones, is difficult enough to learn. The native Taiwanese language (imported from southern Fukien province) has six tones, which change depending upon the position of a word in the sentence!

Thailand

Official Name:	Kingdom of Thailand (Muang Thai)
Official Language:	Thai
Government System:	Constitutional monarchy
Population:	60 million
Population Growth:	1.2%
Area:	513,115 sq. km. (198,114 sq. mi.); about the size of Texas
Natural Resources:	tin, rubber, natural gas, tungsten, tantalum, lead, fish, gypsum, ignite, fluorite, gemstones, crude oil, iron ore
Major Cities:	Bangkok (capital), Chiang Mai, Hat Yai, Nakon Ratchasima

Cultural Note: The royal family of Thailand is seen as a strong unifying influence. Faced with a fractious parliament and a strong military, the Thai people turn to their constitutional monarch for leadership. Never make fun of the royal family.

The high standing of the Thai royal family stems in part from history: Thailand was the only nation in Southeast Asia which never became a European colony. By playing France and England off each other, the Thai kings kept their country free.

413

Age Breakdown

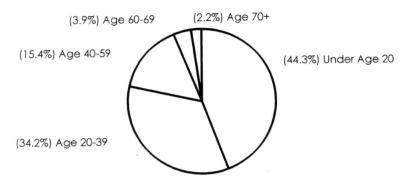

(3.9%) Age 60-69   (2.2%) Age 70+

(15.4%) Age 40-59   (44.3%) Under Age 20

(34.2%) Age 20-39

Life Expectancy: 65 years male; 72 years female (1993)

 Time

Punctuality is expected from foreigners for business appointments. However, promptness is not a universal habit in Thailand.

Thailand is seven hours ahead of Greenwich Mean Time (G.M.T. + 7), which is twelve hours ahead of U.S. Eastern Standard Time (E.S.T. + 12)

 Holidays

(Update: Getting Through Customs *http://www.getcustoms.com*)

This list is a working guide. Dates should be corroborated before final travel plans are made. In cases where holidays fall on Saturday or Sunday, commercial establishments may be closed the preceding Friday or following Monday.

New Year's Day	3 January
Chinese New Year (date varies)	late January - mid February
Magha Puja Day	February
King Rama I Memorial Day and Chakri Day	6 April
Songkran Days–traditional New Year's Days	12–14 April

Coronation Day	5 May
Visakha Puja Day	May–June
Buddhist Lent	12 July
Queen's Birthday	12 August
Chulalongkorn Memorial Day	23 October
Birthday of King of	5 December
Thailand and National Day	
Constitution Day	10 December

- Be certain to confirm your appointments with local representatives to avoid conflicts with regional festivities.
- The best time to schedule a visit to Thailand is between November and March. Most business people vacation during April and May. Avoid the weeks before and after Christmas, and the month of April. Thailand's Water Festival is held in April, and businesses close for an entire week.

Work Week

- Business hours: 8:30 A.M. to 5:00 P.M., Mon.-Fri. ; bank hours: 8:30 A.M. to 3:30 P.M., Mon.-Fri.; government hours: 8:30 A.M. to 4:30 P.M., Mon.-Fri.; Shops: 10:00 A.M. to 6:30 or 7:00 P.M., Mon.-Sat. Smaller shops open earlier and close later.

Religious/Societal Influences on Business

Thailand's official religion is Buddhism. Almost 95% of Thais follow the Theravada form of Buddhism. Other religions are also represented, including Islam and Christianity.

Adherents to the Theravada school consider themselves followers of the form closest to Buddhism as it was practiced originally. The spiritual liberation of the individual is a main focus of the Theravada school. Each individual is considered responsible for his or her own actions and destiny.

Each person in Thai society has a specific place. It is every person's job to fulfill his or her role with a minimum of fuss. Failure to do so involves loss of face. The Thai phrase *mai pen rai* (meaning "never mind," or "no worries") is frequently invoked as a reminder not to risk face on opposing the unopposable.

5 Cultural Tips

1. Thailand advertises itself as "The Land of Smiles," and the Thai people are genuinely friendly and polite. But their extreme politeness vanishes as soon as they get behind the wheel of a car. Driving is aggressive, and pedestrians seem to be fair game. Be very cautious every time you cross a street; use an overhead walkway if possible.

2. Because of travel difficulties in large Thai cities, many foreign executives plan on making only two meetings per day. The gridlock in Bangkok is so bad that many Thai businesspeople conduct business from their cars, with cell phones and mobile fax machines. (Remember that Bangkok and other Thai cities have passenger service on canals. When the street traffic is stalled, consider commuting by boat.)

3. English is often spoken by Thai executives. For those who do not speak English, a translator is usually close at hand. Note that taxi drivers do not usually speak English. To arrive at your destination, have the street address written down in Thai, plus the name of the nearest major cross street.

4. Business entertaining is part of developing business relationships. Thais place great value on enjoyment (*kwam sanuk*). Laughter comes easily to Thais, and a foreigner can minimize his or her inevitable errors by laughing at them. Laughter can also be used to cover embarrassment.

5. Giving gifts will help create a good first impression. A bottle of imported liquor (especially scotch) is a good gift for an executive. Have the gift wrapped locally, and do not be dismayed if the gift is immediately set aside; Thais do not open gifts in the presence of the giver. Some executives recommend giving a small gift to the office receptionist or secretary as well. In this case, food that can be shared with the rest of the office staff is recommended, such as cookies or candy.

Economic Overview

Thailand is one of Asia's fastest growing, most attractive markets for U.S. exporters and investors. It has succeeded in developing an open market economy based on a free enterprise system. Thai leaders have pursued consistently conservative fiscal and monetary policies that have benefited the private sector.

Thailand's economy recovered rapidly from the political unrest in May 1992 to post an impressive 7.5% growth rate for the year, 7.8% in 1993, and 8% in 1994. One of the more advanced developing countries in Asia, Thailand depends on exports of manufactures and the development of the service sector to fuel the country's rapid growth.

Comparative Data

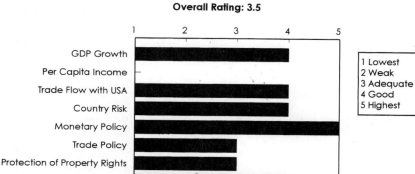

Overall Rating: 3.5

	1	2	3	4	5
GDP Growth					
Per Capita Income					
Trade Flow with USA					
Country Risk					
Monetary Policy					
Trade Policy					
Protection of Property Rights					
Foreign Investment Climate					

1 Lowest
2 Weak
3 Adequate
4 Good
5 Highest

Country Risk Rating

Gross Domestic Product: $143 billion
GDP Growth: 8.5%
Per Capita Income: $2,423

Trade Flows with the U.S.A.

Rank as Export Market for U.S.A. Goods & Services: 18th
U.S.A. Exports to Thailand: $6.4 billion
Growth Rate of Exports: 30%
U.S.A. Imports from Thailand: $11.3 billion
Growth Rate of Imports: 10%
Rank as a Supplier of Imports into the U.S.A.:   13th

Top U.S.A. Exports to Thailand: Electrical components; machinery; aircraft and parts; iron and steel products; medical and optical equipment; plastics; organic chemicals; cotton/yarn/fabrics; tobacco; miscellaneous chemical products.

Top U.S.A. Prospects for Export to Thailand: Computer software; telecommunications equipment; electric power systems; airport/ground support equipment; pumps/valves/compressors; computers and peripherals; pollution control equipment; food processing/packaging equipment; medical equipment; franchising.

Credit Terms

Dun & Bradstreet rates Thailand as having good capacity to meet outstanding payment liabilities. Less than 50% of sales to Thailand are conducted on letter of credit while about 25% of goods are shipped on open account. Confirmed irrevocable letter of credit is still advised for new and/or small accounts. Credit terms are usually 90 to 180 days.

Monetary Policy

Inflation has risen since 1993 from 3% to 5% in 1995 on an annualized basis. Adoption of a tighter monetary line by the government should negate further credit expansion and money supply growth in 1996 and limit inflation to 5% for the year. *Monetary Unit:* baht.

Trade Policy

TARIFFS: The Thai government has undertaken to reduce import duties as part of its obligations as a founding member of the World Trade Organization. There will be a phased implementation of the new tariffs. The full tariff reduction will not become effective until January 1, 1997. There will be a special tariff rate of 30% maximum, down from 100%, for locally produced goods in need of special protection.

Tariff categories will be reduced from 39 to six. While tariff reductions began in 1995, they will not be complete until 1997, perhaps later for agricultural products. The average trade-weighted tariff for items with tariffs was 30% in 1994. Tariff reductions enacted at the end of 1994 along with tariff reductions made in early 1995, will decrease the average tariff rate on 20 categories of imports by 1997 to 17%. Duty exemptions are routinely granted to firms with investment promotion privileges, and rebates of import duties on raw materials are granted upon export of the finished product.

IMPORT LICENSING: In 1995 Thailand began the process of converting import licensing restrictions for many items to tariff rate quotas and tariffs under its World Trade Organization obligations. Import licenses are still required on industrial products.

IMPORT TAXES: Imported alcoholic beverages are assessed a separate excise duty with rates varying from 10 to 48%. Separate excise duties are also assessed on a number of other products such as tobacco and some electrical and petroleum products.

Protection of Intellectual Property Rights

Although protection for copyrights, patents, and trademarks in Thailand is improving, intellectual property protection remains a key bilateral trade issue with the United States.

The Thai Parliament passed a new copyright law in late 1994, which became effective on March 21, 1995. This new law resolved many concerns of American holders of intellectual property and resulted in Thailand being removed from the Priority Watch List under Section 301 of the U.S. Trade Act. Other significant steps include creation of an Intellectual Property Department within the Ministry of Commerce, increased legal expertise in intellectual property matters within the police and the Justice Ministry and Cabinet approval of an International Trade and Intellectual Property Court.

Foreign Investment Climate

The Thai government maintains an open, market-oriented economy and encourages foreign direct investment as a means of promoting economic development, employment, and technology transfer.

The U.S.-Thai Treaty of Amity and Economic Relations of 1966 allows U.S. citizens and businesses incorporated in the U.S. or in Thailand that are majority-owned by U.S. itizens to engage in business on the same basis as Thais, exempting them from most of the restrictions on foreign investment imposed by the Alien Business Law of 1972. Under the Treaty, Thailand restricts American investment only in the fields of communications, transport, banking, the exploitation of land or other natural resources and domestic trade in agricultural products.

Current Leaders & Political Parties

(Update: International Academy at Santa Barbara *http://www.iasb.org/cwl*)

Head of State: King Bhumibol Adulyadej

Ministers:

Prime Min. and Min. of Interior: Banharn Silapa-archa

Dep. Prime Ministers:

Air Chief Mar. Somboon Rahong, Gen. Chavalit Youngchaiyudh, Lt. Col. Thaksin Shinawatra, Boonphan Kaewatana, Samak Sundaravej, Amnuay Viraven

Attached to the Prime Minister's Office: Pongpol Adireksarn, Ruangwit Lik, Prasong Buranapong, Charas Puachuay, Rakkiat Sukthana, Phokin Palakul

Finance: Surakiat Sathirathal

Foreign Affairs: Kasem S. Kasemsri

Transport and Communications: Wan Muhammad Nor Matha

Commerce: Shucheep Harnsawat

Defense: Gen. Chavalit Yongchalyudh

Science, Technology, and Environment: Yingphan Manasikarn

Industry: Chaiwat Sinsuwong

Other Officials:

Pres. of the Natl. Assembly: Marut Bunng

Speaker of the Senate: Meechai Ruchupaan

Ambassador to U.S.: Manaspas Xuto

Perm. Rep. to U.N.: Nitya Pibulsonggram

Political Parties:

Chart Thai Party, Solidarity Party, Prachakorn Party, Social Action Party, Democratic Party, New Aspiration Party, Siam Democratic Party, Puangchon Chaothai, Samakkhi Tham Party, Palang Dharma, Chart Pattana Party

 Political Influences on Business

The recent government of Chuan Leekpai devoted much effort to nurturing democratic institutions, including working with the military (long a force in Thai politics) to identify an appropriate role in the post-Cold War world. Policy priorities of the Chuan government included meeting basic economic needs and developing rural areas. While the Chuan government was criticized for the slowness of its decision making, it was generally regarded as honest and friendly to business. The succeeding government of Banharn Silapa-archa has adopted this approach as well.

The U.S. government has been pressing for improvements in Thai protection of intellectual property rights, particularly protection of computer software, and enforcement against violators. The goal is to encourage Thailand to raise protection of intellectual property up to international levels. A new copyright law was enacted in March 1995. Enforcement of existing laws and regulations has generally improved. Progress on IPR issues was sufficient for Thailand to be removed from the USTR's Priority Watch List. However, this issue is likely to be an area of continued discussion between the Thai and U.S. governments.

The United States has also sought improvements in Thailand's protection of internationally recognized worker rights. Other concerns are child labor abuse, workplace safety, and restrictions on public sector employees' freedom of association and collective bargaining rights.

Thailand is a constitutional monarchy with a Westminster-style Parliament. Elections must be held every four years, but may be called more frequently. The Prime Minister must be an elected member of Parliament. Political parties are not usually oriented ideologically. In nearly every case, they are formed around a key figure, usually the party leader. Thailand's political orientation is moderate to conservative, and all political parties support a free market system.

On May 19, 1995, Prime Minister Chuan Leekpai dissolved Parliament after one of the parties in his five-party coalition withdrew from the government. During its two and one-half years in office, the Chuan government restored domestic and foreign economic confidence in Thailand through its prodemocracy and promarket stances. General elections that were held on July 2, 1995, resulted in continuity for Thailand's economy and its investment climate.

Contacts in the U.S.A. & in Thailand

Contacts in the United States:

EMBASSY OF THE KINGDOM OF THAILAND
1024 Wisconsin Avenue, N.W.
Suite 103
Washington, D.C. 20007
Tel: (202) 944-3625
Fax: (202) 944-3627

U.S. DEPARTMENT OF STATE
Bureau of Consular Affairs
Tel: (202) 647-5225
Country Desk Officer
Tel: (202) 647-7108

U.S. DEPARTMENT OF COMMERCE
Thailand Desk
Int'l Trade Admin.
Tel: (202) 482-3647

TOURISM OFFICE
Tourism Authority of Thailand
5 World Trade Center #3443
New York, N.Y. 10048
Tel: (212) 432-0433
Fax: (212) 912-0920

Contacts in Thailand:

U.S. EMBASSY
95 Wireless Rd.
Bangkok
Mailing Address:
APO AP 96546
Tel: [66] (2)252-5040
Fax: [66] (2)254-2990

THE AMERICAN CHAMBER OF COMMERCE IN
THAILAND
Kian Gwan Bldg.
140 Wireless Rd.
7th floor
P.O. Box 11–1095
Bangkok
Tel: [66] (2) 251-9266
Telex: 82827 KGCOM TH
Fax: [66] (2) 255-2454

KING BHUMIBOL ADULYADEJ
Office of the King
Bangkok, Kingdom of Thailand

PRIME MINISTER BANHARN SILAPA-ARCHA
Office of the Prime Minister
Government House
Nakhon Pathom Road
Bangkok 10300, Kingdom of Thailand

Passport/Visa Requirements

Visa Information   Tel: (202) 663-1225

Entry Requirements: Passport and onward/return tickets are required. Visas are not needed for stays of up to 30 days. However, without a visa, entry is permitted only when arriving at international airports in Bangkok, Phuket, or Chiang Mai.

For more current information, travelers may contact the Royal Thai Embassy.

Cultural Note: Thai is a complex language with five different tones. While this makes it difficult for Westerners to speak, Thais will appreciate a foreigner who takes the time to learn even a few phrases in Thai.

There are only eight possible consonants that a word in Thai may end with. The sound "s" is not one of them. Consequently, when Thais speak English, they tend to leave the "s" sound off words.

Turkey

Official Name:	Republic of Turkey (Turkiye Cumhuriyeti)
Official Language:	Turkish
Government System:	Multiparty republic
Population:	63 million
Population Growth:	2%
Area:	779,452 sq. km. (301,382 sq. mi.); slightly larger than Texas
Natural Resources:	antimony, coal, chromium, mercury, copper, borate, sulpher, iron ore
Major Cities:	Ankara (capital), Istanbul, Izmir, Adana, Konya, Bursa

---

Cultural Note: Tenacity is one of the most notable of Turkish traits. In a country as old as Turkey, inertia is always a problem. Tenacity and single-mindedness are necessary to get anything done. This characteristic is exemplified by the founder of the modern Turkish State, Kemal Atatürk. The venerated Atatürk, whose stern picture is everywhere in Turkey, is to Turkey what Chairman Mao Tse-Tung was to China. Atatürk's many accomplishments include:

- Forging a new Turkish state out of the ruins of the old Ottoman Empire.
- Replacing Arabic script with the easier-to-master Roman alphabet.
- Suppressing the influence of Islam and making Turkey a secular nation.
- Changing age-old patterns of dress; he outlawed the fez on men and denounced the head scarf on women.

Age Breakdown

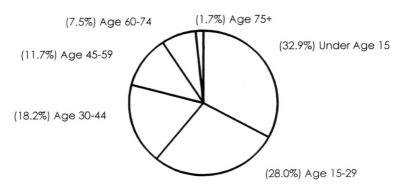

(7.5%) Age 60-74   (1.7%) Age 75+

(11.7%) Age 45-59   (32.9%) Under Age 15

(18.2%) Age 30-44

(28.0%) Age 15-29

Life Expectancy: 64 years male; 67 years female (1990)

 Time

Foreigners are expected to be on time to appointments. However, promptness has never been a virtue in Turkey. Your Turkish counterpart could easily be an hour late.

The pace of everything in Turkey is much slower than in the United States. This goes for everything from meetings to decision making. Pressuring Turks to speed things up will probably be counterproductive. The only thing in Turkey which moves fast is rural traffic. Once outside of the gridlocked cities, Turkish drivers often zoom about at a lethal pace.

Turkey is two hours ahead of Greenwich Mean Time (G.M.T. + 2), which is seven hours ahead of U.S. Eastern Standard Time (E.S.T. + 7).

 Holidays

(Update: Getting Through Customs *http://www.getcustoms.com*)

This list is a working guide. Dates should be corroborated before final travel plans are made. In cases where holidays fall on Saturday or Sunday, commercial establishments may be closed the preceding Friday or following Monday.

For many countries, such as those in the Moslem world, holiday dates are approximations since they depend upon actual lunar observations. Moslem holidays also vary in spelling. Many businesses in Moslem countries are closed on Fridays.

New Year's Day   1 January
National Sovereignty Day   23 April

(celebrating the first meeting of
the republican Parliament in
Ankara in 1920); this date is also
Children's Day

Youth and Sports Day (which also celebrates Atatürk's birthday in 1881)	19 May
Commemoration of the conquest of the city from the Byzantines in 1453 (Istanbul only)	19 May
Victory Day (celebrating the defeat of the invading Greek army in 1922)	30 August
Republic Day (commemorating Atatürk's proclamation of the Turkish Republic in 1923; Turkey's biggest civil holiday)	29 October
Remembrance of the death of Atatürk in 1938 (It is a serious insult not to observe the moment of silence at 9:05 A.M., the time of Atatürk's death.)	10 November

- Business appointments can rarely be made during the months of June, July, and August; most Turkish businesspeople take extended vacations during this time.

- Obviously, you cannot expect to conduct business on a Turkish holiday. But be aware that many people will begin the holiday around noon the day before.

- The Muslim holidays are computed on a 13-month lunar calendar. Like Easter, they will fall on different days every year. From a foreigner's point of view, the most important Muslim observances in Turkey are:

  Ramazan (called Ramadan in other Muslim countries): The Holy Month. Observers fast from dawn until dusk. Dusk is announced by a cannon shot. The faithful are awakened before sunrise by drummers who roam the streets, reminding them to eat before dawn. It is impolite for nonbelievers to eat, drink, or even smoke in the presence of those who are fasting; be discreet. Office hours may be curtailed. Not surprisingly, fasting people may be short-tempered, especially when Ramazan falls during the sweltering days of summer. This is called *Ramazan kafasi* (or irritability, literally "Ramazan head").

  Sheker Bayram: The three-day festival at the end of the Ramazan fast. Children go door-to-door asking for sweets; Muslims exchange greeting cards, feast, and visit one another. Banks and offices are closed for all three days.

  Kurban Bayram: The Feast of the Sacrifice. Celebrating the traditional story of Abraham's near-sacrifice of his son Isaac, this is the most important religious and secular holiday of the year. The holiday lasts for four days, but many banks and businesses close for an entire week. Resorts and transportation will be booked solid.

 ## Work Week

- Business and banking hours: 9:00 A.M. to 12 noon and 2:00 P.M. to 5:00 P.M., Mon.–Fri. Note that business executives generally arrive between 9:30 and 10:00 A.M. and return from lunch around 2:30 P.M.
- Store hours: 9:00 A.M. to 1:00 P.M. and 2:30 P.M. to 7:00 P.M., Mon.–Fri. 9:00 A.M. to 12 noon and 1:30 P.M. to 8:00 P.M. Saturday.
- The recently-created Istanbul Stock Exchange (one of the fastest-growing in the world) currently conducts business for only two hours per day, from 10:00 A.M. to 12 noon.
- Although Friday is the Muslim Holy Day, business is still conducted on that day. Sunday is the government mandated "day of rest."

 ## Religious/Societal Influences on Business

The majority of Turks (about 80%) are Sunni Muslims. Except for a few thousand Christians, the rest of the population are Shiite Muslims, mostly of a nonorthodox sect called Alevi. Since its founding in 1923, the Turkish Republic has been a secular state with no official religion. But there is great pressure to change this. Islam seems to grow stronger every year. In the general elections of December 1995, the Islamic Welfare Party took the largest number of seats in the Turkish Parliament. While Prime Minister Tansu Ciller had worked hard for Turkish acceptance into the European Union, the Welfare Party rejects Western influence, including the EU. This tug-of-war between Turkish secularists and Islamic fundamentalists is expected to continue.

Every Turkish citizen, religious or not, is familiar with the standard Islamic teachings. Islam teaches submission to Allah. Fortune and misfortune are attributed to the will of Allah. Destiny is not under the control of man.

Turkish children are trained to be self-reliant, to care for others, and to be satisfied with one's lot in life.

 ## 5 Cultural Tips

1. All meetings will begin with extensive small talk. Expect to be asked about your journey, your lodgings, and how you like Turkey. (Be sure to have good things to say about Turkey. Citizens can be negative about Turkey, but foreigners may not.)

Sports and family are good topics of conversation, but avoid asking a man about his wife or daughters unless he brings them up first. Only when a Turk has gotten to know you will he or she feel comfortable doing business with you.

2. Age is respected in Turkey. Defer to elders in all circumstances. Elders are served first, introduced first, and allowed to go through doors first. Since most Turkish businesses are family owned, the decision maker is probably an elder.

3. Politeness is very important in Turkey. To disagree openly with someone in public will cause them to lose face, so Turks rarely say no (except, of course, while bargaining). Foreigners often have difficulty recognizing when a *yes* is just a polite way of saying *no*. Turks will even let someone make an error rather than correct them, when the correction would result in loss of face.

4. *Yok* is a Turkish phoneme with several meanings, most of which are negative. The use of yok is analogous to the use of *nu* in Yiddish or *ayah* in Chinese. The exact meaning of yok depends upon the context and tone of voice, but generally, it is not good. If you hear yok, the ambiguity is over.

5. Historical enmities in the region remain strong. Try to avoid being associated with (or even discussing) Turkish minority groups, which include Greeks, Armenians, and Kurds. The Turkish government does not even wish to recognize Turkish Kurds as a culturally distinct people. Armed opposition to Ankara continues from the Kurdish Workers' Party (abbreviated as PKK).

Economic Overview

Turkey remains unexplored territory for most American companies outside the Fortune 500 and defense suppliers.

Until the early 1980s, Turkey was an insulated, state-directed economy. However, in the 1980s, the country began an economic turnaround based on increased reliance on market forces, export-led development, lower taxes, integration with the world economy, and privatization. A much-needed austerity and stabilization program in April 1994 cooled down the economy. GNP fell 6% in 1994, setting a post-war record. Unemployment jumped and real wages fell. The economy in 1995 began to show signs of recovery. Driven by a dynamic private sector and the prospect of a customs union with the European Union in 1996, Turkey's future now looks bright. The Turkish market now offers excellent growth prospects for U.S. exports. Increased spending on infrastructure projects and private sector investment will generate strong demand for a wide range of capital goods.

Turkey's young population of 63 million is growing rapidly, both in numbers and purchasing power. Turkey's outstanding growth prospects led to its designation by the U.S. Department of Commerce as one of the world's 10 Big Emerging Markets.

Cultural Note: Despite being a very male-oriented society, a few Turkish women achieve positions of great power, such as former Prime Minister Tansu Ciller. In general, however, women in Turkey take a backseat to men. There is strict segregation of the sexes, everywhere from schools to mosques. Outside of the cities, adult women are rarely seen except in groups, and are usually dressed in the black head-to-foot garment called the *chador*. The rural woman spends most of her life at home.

Comparative Data (from 1994; 1995 data not available)

Overall Rating: 2.13

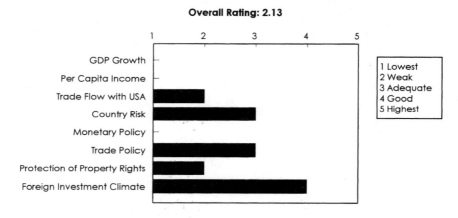

Country Risk Rating

Gross Domestic Product: $131 billion

GDP Growth: –6%

Per Capita Income: $2,192

Trade Flows with the U.S.A.

Rank as Export Market for U.S.A. Goods & Services: 36th

U.S.A. Exports to Turkey: $2.7 billion

Growth Rate of Exports: –4%

U.S.A. Imports from Turkey: $1.8 billion

Growth Rate of Imports: 12%

Rank as a Supplier of Imports into the U.S.A.:   **42nd**

Top U.S.A. Exports to Turkey: Aircraft and parts; machinery; electrical components; iron and steel; tobacco; motor vehicles; organic chemicals; medical and optical equipment; fats and oils; mineral fuel.

> **Top U.S.A. Prospects for Export to Turkey:** Telecommunications equipment; electric power systems; textile machinery and equipment; medical equipment; building products; computer software; automotive parts; airport/ground support equipment services; electronic industry production and test equipment; pollution control equipment.

Country Risk

Dun & Bradstreet rates Turkey as having sufficient capacity to meet outstanding payment liabilities. Irrevocable confirmed letters of credit are traditional import instruments for private sector transactions.

Monetary Policy

In spite of efforts undertaken under the April 1994 reform program, Turkey's principal economic problem remains inflation, fueled by large public sector deficits. Annual consumer price inflation has averaged 74% since prices began to escalate in 1988. Inflation in 1994 soared to record levels, due mainly to huge one-time increases in state-administered prices as part of the April 1994 reform program. For 1994, consumer prices rose 126% compared with a 71% rise recorded in 1993. Dun & Bradstreet estimated that 1995 inflation rates would be about 70%, and predicts 1996 inflation at 80 to 90%. *Monetary Unit:* Turkish lira.

Trade Policy

TARIFFS: Turkey began to align its tariff system with the European Union's in 1994. Turkey was scheduled to completely align its tariffs with the EU's common external tariffs by January 1, 1996. Alignment with the EU rates will reduce the overall rate of protection against imports from the U.S. The EU tariff system also simplifies the calculation of duties of U.S. goods.

IMPORT LICENSING: All importers must obtain a general import license valid for one year from the Undersecretaries of Foreign Trade. Importers are also required to obtain an import permission certificate for each type of item to be imported. Without this certificate, a bank cannot issue foreign exchange for payment.

Cigarettes and alcohol can be imported only by state-operated monopolies. Weapons and narcotics are prohibited import.

IMPORT TAXES: Imports are subject to a value-added tax. Most industrial products are charged a rate of 15%, however some products can incur a rate as high as 23%. Capital goods, some raw materials, and imports by government agencies and enterprises are exempt from import fees.

Protection of Intellectual Property Rights

Turkey lacks adequate, modern laws concerning intellectual property protection. Since 1992, the United States has listed Turkey on the priority watch list of countries which fail to protect American firms' intellectual property rights.

There has been progress on the legislative front driven primarily by Turkey's desire to enter into a customs union with the European Union effective January 1, 1996. The agreement with the EU requires Turkey to meet EU standards for intellectual property protection.

Turkey amended its 1951 copyright law in June 1995. The amended law significantly improves protection for books, videos, sound recording, computer programs, and other copyright-protected media.

Turkey enacted a new patent law in June 1995. The agreement with the EU allows Turkey to postpone introduction of patent protection for pharmaceuticals until 1999. Turkey is a member of the Paris Convention for the Protection of Industrial Property. Patent terms are for 15 years from date of filing.

A trademark law has been drafted but not yet enacted. Counterfeiting of foreign trademarked products is currently widespread.

Foreign Investment Climate

Turkey has a liberal investment regime in which foreign investments receive national treatment. Almost all areas open to the Turkish private sector are also open to foreign participation and investment.

Screening mechanisms are routine and nondiscriminatory. Foreign companies established in Turkey are considered Turkish businesses. Apart from aviation, maritime transportation, insurance, and broadcasting, where equity participation by foreign shareholders is limited to 49%, there are no major sectors in which foreign investors do not receive national treatment. Foreign investors receive national treatment in privatization programs, too.

The stock of U.S. foreign investment in Turkey was $1 billion in 1993, or 52% greater than in 1992. U.S. direct investment in Turkey is largely concentrated in manufacturing, petroleum, and banking.

 # Current Leaders & Political Parties

(Update: International Academy at Santa Barbara *http://www.iasb.org/cwl*)

Pres.: Suleyman Demirel

Council of Ministers:

Prime Min.: Necmettin Erbakan

Natl. Defense: Tarhan Tayan

Interior: Mehmet Ağar
Finance: Abdullatif Sener
Public Works and Resettlement: Cevat Ayhan
Transportation and Communications: Omer Barutçu
Industry and Commerce: Yalim Erez
Energy and Natural Resources: Recai Kutan
Tourism: Bahattin Yücel
Forestry: Halit Dağli
Environmental Affairs: Ziyaettin Tokar

Other Officials:

Pres. of the Constitutional Court: Yekta Güngör Özden
Pres. of the Grand Natl. Assembly: Mustafa Kalemli
Chief of the Armed Services Staff: Ismail Hakki Karadayi
Gov. of the Central Bank: Gazi Erçel
Ambassador to U.S.: Nüzhet Kandemir
Perm. Rep. to U.N.: Hüseyin Çelim

Political Parties:

Truth Path Party, Motherland Party, People's Republican Party, Social Democratic
   Populist Party, Democratic Left Party, Welfare Party, Nationalist Democracy
   Party, Reformist Democracy Party

 Political Influences on Business

The 1991 Gulf War brought Turkey in closer contact with the West. By supporting the
Alliance, Turkey lost millions of dollars in trade with neighboring Iraq. Turkey also
found itself in the ironic position of supporting Iraqi Kurds (by allowing Allied aircraft
to use Turkish air bases) while simultaneously fighting a guerrilla movement among
Turkish Kurds. In return for these sacrifices, Turkey expected to gain increased aid
and trade with the West.

As often happens, such expectations were only realized partially. Turkey has long
sought entry into the European Union. Former Prime Minister Tansu Ciller and the
late President Turgut Ozal did much to bring Turkey closer to this goal. This has
included improving Turkey's human-rights record, which the EU has maintained was
the primary obstacle toward membership for Turkey.

However, just as Turkey's human rights record began improving, Turkey itself may
have changed its mind about entering the EU. The parliamentary elections of
December 1995 resulted in major gains for the Islamist Welfare Party. The Welfare
Party ran against Turkish secularism—the very secularism which has been official government policy since the founding of the Turkish Republic in 1923. Welfare Party

leader Necmettin Erbakan became Turkey's new Prime Minister, and he wants to reduce Turkish contacts with the West in favor of closer relations with Islamic states. Prime Minister Erbakan has stated that Turkey must shrug off "the yoke of the West."

Although the Welfare Party now holds the largest bloc of seats (158 out of a total of 550) in the Parliament, Ms. Ciller's center-right True Path Party (DYP) remains powerful. The DYP and the Welfare Party now rule in a shaky coalition.

 Contacts in the U.S.A. & in Turkey

Contacts in the United States:

EMBASSY OF THE REPUBLIC OF TURKEY
1714 Massachusetts Avenue, N.W.
Washington, D.C. 20036
Tel: (202) 659-8200

U.S. DEPARTMENT OF STATE
Bureau of Consular Affairs
Tel: (202) 647-5225
Country Desk Officer, Turkey
Tel: (202) 647-6114

U.S. DEPARTMENT OF COMMERCE
Turkey Desk
Int'l Trade Admin.
Tel: (202) 482-5373

OFFICE OF THE TOURISM COUNSELOR OF THE TURKISH EMBASSY
1717 Massachusetts Avenue N.W.
Washington, D.C. 20036
Tel: (202) 429-9944
Fax: (202) 429-5649

TURKEY TOURISM AND INFORMATION OFFICE
821 United Nation Plaza
New York, N.Y. 10017
Tel: (212) 687-2194
Fax: (212) 599-7568

Contacts in Turkey:

U.S. EMBASSY
110 Atatürk Blvd.
Ankara
PSC 93, Box 5000
Mailing Address:
APO AE 09823
Tel: [90] (4) 468-6110
Fax: [90] (4) 467-0019

PRESIDENT SULEYMAN DEMIREL
Office of the President
Cumhurbaskanligi Kosku
Cankaya
Ankara, Republic of Turkey

PRIME MINISTER TANSU CILLER
Office of the Prime Minister
Basbakanlik
Bakanliklar
Ankara, Republic of Turkey

Passport/Visa Requirements

Visa Information   Tel: (202) 663-1225

Entry Requirements: Valid passport and visa required. U.S. citizens with regular passports may obtain visas at Turkish border crossing points for tourist/business visits up to three months or through overseas Turkish consular offices (one application form is required).

For further information on entry requirements to Turkey, travelers can contact the Embassy of the Republic of Turkey, or the nearest Turkish Consulate.

Faux Pas: Two foreigners traveling about Turkey on their motorbike decided to spend the night at a small hotel. They brought their motorcycle through a narrow door into the hotel courtyard for safekeeping. The next morning, they were surprised to find that they couldn't get their motorcycle out of the courtyard; it wouldn't fit through the door. A crowd gathered, giving fruitless advice. Finally, the travelers dismantled the motorcycle and took it through the doorway, piece by piece. One of the travelers angrily observed that the motorcycle fit through the door last night, and it should've fit in the morning. Only then did one of the crowd point out that they were using the wrong door; last night they had used an almost identical (but slightly larger) door across the courtyard!

The Turks had been constrained by their standards of politeness. If the foreign travelers wanted to get their motorbike through a too-small door, they were entitled to. (Foreigners do many strange things.) To publicly point out the existence of a larger door might have embarrassed the travelers. Only when one of the foreigners articulated their error could someone politely correct them.

United Kingdom

Official Name:	United Kingdom of Great Britain and Northern Ireland
Official Language:	English (additionally, Welsh and Gaelic)
Government System:	Constitutional monarchy
Population:	58 million
Population Growth:	0.3%
Area:	244,820 sq. km. (97,928 sq. mi.); slightly smaller than Oregon
Natural Resources:	coal, crude oil, natural gas, tin, limestone, iron ore, salt, clay, chalk, gypsum, lead, silica
Major Cities:	London (capital), Birmingham, Glasgow, Leeds, Sheffield, Liverpool, Bradford, Manchester, Edinburgh, Bristol

---

Cultural Note: The United Kingdom consists of four distinct regions: England, Wales, Scotland, and Northern Ireland. The Scots, Welsh, and Irish are not English and are offended when referred to as such. Use the correct terminology. Furthermore, the citizens of the United Kingdom do not consider themselves European, even though their nation is a member of the European Union.

Age Breakdown

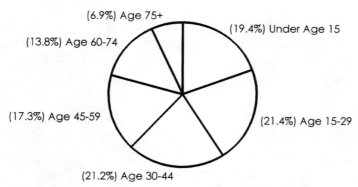

(6.9%) Age 75+

(13.8%) Age 60-74

(19.4%) Under Age 15

(17.3%) Age 45-59

(21.4%) Age 15-29

(21.2%) Age 30-44

Life Expectancy: 73 years male; 79 years female (1991)

Time

Punctuality is expected for both business appointments and social events.

The U.K. is in Greenwich Mean Time, which is five hours ahead of U.S. Eastern Standard Time (E.S.T. + 5).

Holidays

(Update: Getting Through Customs *http://www.getcustoms.com*)

New Year's Day	1 January
May Day	6 May
Spring Holiday	27 May
Queen's Birthday	11 June
Summer Bank Holiday	26 August
Christmas	25 December
Boxing Day	26 December

It is advisable to check with your local representatives for additional regional holidays and vacations during July, August, and September.

Work Week

- The work week is 9:00 A.M. to 5:00 P.M., Monday through Friday, although government offices close from 1:00 to 2:00 P.M. and stay open until 5:30 P.M.
- Executives leave their offices by about 5:30 P.M.

Religious/Societal Influences on Business

Technically, there are no official religions in the United Kingdom; instead, some parts of the U.K. have established churches. These are:

England: Church of England (Anglican Church)
Scotland: Church of Scotland (Presbyterian Church)
Wales: None
Northern Ireland: None

The majority (about 80%) of people in the U.K. are Christian. Roman Catholics have a slight numerical majority at 21% of the population, followed by Anglican (Church of England) 20%, Presbyterian (Church of Scotland) 14%, Methodist 5%, and Baptist 3%. Of non-Christian religions, Muslims form the largest group at 11% of the population, followed by Sikhs at 4%, Hindus at 2%, and Jews at 1%.

While most Britons would assert that they live in a Christian nation, religion plays a relatively small part in their day-to-day lives. Many people find age-old religious precepts to be ineffectual in the modern world. Secular activities and societal pressures exert more influence on behavior than do religious beliefs. Church attendance continues to fall, and many of Britain's great churches and cathedrals would have a hard time financially were it not for tourism.

The influence of the Royal Family has also lessened significantly, although the Queen Mother, Elizabeth II, is still held in respect. As the sovereign, she is Chief of State of the United Kingdom. Anti-Royalists (also called Republicans) desire the dissolution of the monarchy, partially based upon the expense of financing the royalty vs. their usefulness.

The British seem to apologize often, even over seemingly inconsequential events or for things over which they have no control. This is considered simple politeness, and should not be taken for a sign of weakness or insecurity.

The stiff-upper-lip stereotype of the British has some basis in fact. Most English are unemotional in public and downplay situations which would be cause for noisy outbursts in other cultures. There are considerable differences between the various people of the United Kingdom. But stereotypes are risky; not all Welsh are romantic and not all Scots are parsimonious. A self-deprecating sense of humor can be said to be common to most of the natives of the United Kingdom. As the butt of a joke, nothing is sacred, from the Royal Family to the Church.

One downside of British reserve is a hesitancy to complain about poor customer service. This can tend to aggravate problems; if more complaints were articulated, such situations might improve.

The British are enthusiastic gamblers, and buy more lottery tickets than any other people on the globe. An estimated 75% of British adults purchase at least one lottery ticket per week.

 5 Cultural Tips

1. The British are a private and traditional people. Violating conventions will not make you any friends. The standard U.S. conversation-starter *"What do you do?"* is considered too personal. Avoid other invasive questions as well, even *"What part of England are you from?"*

2. Introductions are important for conducting business. The best way to make contact with British businesspeople is via a third-party introduction. (Note that after the introduction, the third party's responsibilities are over. It would be inappropriate to ask this same third party to intervene later.)

3. Don't underestimate British wherewithal in entering new markets. The Gillette company developed a new stainless steel blade which lasted too long; it was so superior to other blades that it would need far fewer replacements. Gillette decided not to market razor blades using the new technology. Instead, they offered the technology to the British Wilkinson company, then a manufacturer of garden tools. Gillette never imagined that Wilkinson would enter the disposable razor blade business, so they placed no restrictions on Wilkinson's use of the technology. But Wilkinson did enter the razor blade market, and did so well that they nearly supplanted Gillette as the market leader.

4. British consumers look for different things than U.S. consumers. British advertisements for Goodyear tires proclaim the product's safety. (In contrast, the same tire is advertised for its mileage and durability in the U.S., and for its performance and agility in Germany.)

5. Provide as many objective facts as possible during presentations and negotiations. To the English, scientific evidence is the truth, and interjecting your opinions, feelings, or ideologies into a business transaction muddies up the waters.

 Economic Overview

The United Kingdom remains solidly entrenched as the United States' largest European market and fourth largest worldwide. In 1995, U.K. imports from the U.S. reached $28.8 billion, generating a $1.9 billion U.S. trade surplus. Given just its size and growth potential, the U.K. represents a uniquely important overseas market. Over the next few years, new and established U.S. exporters can expect to find exceptional trading opportunities.

The U.K. market is based on a commitment to the principles of free enterprise and open competition. International trade is vital to its economy. The absence of major trade barriers and the relative ease of doing business ensure that the U.K. remains an attractive market. Demand for U.S. goods and services is growing as the sustained recovery in the U.K.'s industrial sector strengthens and as corporate investment is stepped up to meet competitive challenges of an integrated European Union.

The U.K. shares a long cultural heritage with the U.S., and the great sense of affinity which the British generally feel toward Americans translates into a high level of receptivity to U.S. goods, services, and investment.

Comparative Data

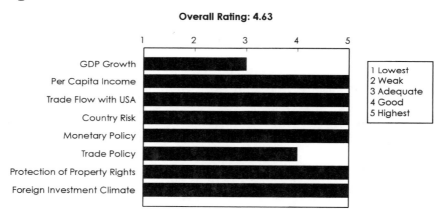

Overall Rating: 4.63

	1	2	3	4	5
GDP Growth					
Per Capita Income					
Trade Flow with USA					
Country Risk					
Monetary Policy					
Trade Policy					
Protection of Property Rights					
Foreign Investment Climate					

1 Lowest
2 Weak
3 Adequate
4 Good
5 Highest

Country Risk Rating

Gross Domestic Product: $1,024 trillion
GDP Growth: 3.8%
Per Capita Income: $17,572

Trade Flows with the U.S.A.

Rank as Export Market for U.S.A. Goods & Services: 4th
U.S.A. Exports to the U.K.: $28.8 billion
Growth Rate of Exports: 6.6%
U.S.A. Imports from the U.K.: $26.9 billion
Growth Rate of Imports: 8%
Rank as a Supplier of Imports into the U.S.A.:   7th

Top U.S.A. Exports to the U.K.: Machinery; electrical components; aircraft and parts; precious stones and metals; medical and optical equipment; motor vehicles; plastics and resins; organic chemicals; books and newspapers; pharmaceutical products.

Top U.S.A. Prospects for Export to the U.K.: Aircraft and parts; computer software; pollution control equipment; apparel; drugs and pharmaceuticals; building products; medical equipment; sporting goods; defense equipment; franchising.

Country Risk

Dun & Bradstreet rates the United Kingdom as having excellent capacity to meet outstanding payment liabilities. It carries the lowest degree of risk.

Open account terms are common. Normally terms are between 30 and 60 days, although they vary according to the sector and type of transaction.

Monetary Policy

From a high of 10.9% at the beginning of the recession in September 1990, the underlying rate of inflation dropped to 2.6% in April 1995. Steep declines in domestic demand early in the recession drove down inflation. High levels of unemployment and restrained wage growth should keep the underlying inflation rate from going over 3% in 1996. *Monetary Unit:* United Kingdom pound sterling.

Trade Policy

TARIFFS: The U.K. is a member of the European Union which provides for a common external tariff. Rates on most manufactured goods fall within a range of 5 to 7%, while most raw materials enter duty free or at low rates of duty. Duties on textiles can range up to 15% and some electronic products reach 14%.

IMPORT LICENSING: Only a very limited range of goods is subject to import licenses. These include firearms and explosives, controlled drugs, and controlled military equipment. There are monitoring measures that apply to certain sensitive products. The most important of these measures is the automatic import license for textiles. This is granted to U.K. importers when they provide the requisite forms.

IMPORT TAXES: The U.K. applies a value added tax on most goods and services. The standard current rate is 17.5%. Certain items such as most foods, medicines, children's clothing and shoes, and books are exempt from VAT.

Protection of Intellectual Property Rights

U.K. intellectual property rights laws are strict, comprehensive, enforced rigorously, and conform to the harmonized approach to intellectual property rights adopted by the European Union. The U.K. is a member of the Paris Union International Convention for the Protection of Industrial Property. Three kinds of patents are granted. These include basic patents, patents of addition, and secret patents. Basic patents are issued on new inventions and discoveries for a period of four years from the date of application and are renewable every year for up to 20 years.

The first user of a trademark is entitled to its registration. Trademarks are registered for seven years from the date of application and are renewable for periods of 14 years each.

Copyrights are granted for the life of the author and for 50 years after his death.

The U.K. is a signatory of the Universal Copyright Convention.

Foreign Investment Climate

The U.K. does not discriminate between nationals and foreigners in the formation and operation of British companies. There are no restrictions on the repatriation of earnings, and foreign companies are treated the same as companies for tax purposes. There are no requirements for joint ventures or local management participation or control. The Mergers and Industry Act of 1986 prohibits the takeover by nonresidents of certain manufacturing operations which might be deemed vital to national interests.

Foreign-owned companies provide 16% of the country's manufacturing jobs, 22% of its net output, and 27% of its net capital expenditure. The United States is by far the largest foreign investor in the U.K. There are 3,500 branches, subsidiaries, and affiliates of U.S. firms resident, compared to 1,000 from Germany and approximately 250 from Japan. In 1992, the U.K. economy attracted 40% of all U.S. investment into the EU. One in eight of the U.K.'s 500 largest companies is an affiliate of a U.S. company. The U.K. imposes no impediments to foreign ownership, nor restrictions to the free flow of capital.

Current Leader & Political Parties

(Update: International Academy at Santa Barbara *http://www.iasb.org/cwl*)

State, Government, and Political Party Leaders:
> Head of State: Queen Elizabeth II

Cabinet:
> Prime Min., First Lord of the Treasury, and Min. for Civil Service: John Major
> Dep. Prime Min. and First Sec. of State: Michael Heseltine
> Lord Chancellor: Lord Mackay

Chancellor of the Exchequer: Kenneth Clarke

Sec. of the Home Dept.: Michael Howard

Sec. of State for Foreign and Commonwealth Affairs: Malcolm Rifkind

Pres. of the Board of Trade: Ian Lang

Lord Pres. of the Cncl. and Leader of the House of Commons: Antony Newton

Sec. of State for the Environment: John Selwyn Gummer

Chief Sec. to the Treasury: William Waldegrave

Sec. of State for Northern Ireland: Sir Patrick Mayhew

Sec. of State for Education and Employment: Gillian Shephard

Sec. of State for Defense: Michael Portillo

Sec. of State for Health: Stephen Dorrell

Sec. of State for Transport: Sir George Young

Sec. of State for Scotland: Michael Forsyth

Sec. of State for Wales: William Hague

Other Officials:

Speaker of the House of Parliament: Betty Boothroyd

Ambassador to U.S.: Sir John Kerr

Perm. Rep. to U.N.: Sir John Weston

Political Parties:

Conservative Party, Labour Party, Social and Liberal Democrats, Social Democratic Party, Scottish Natl. Party, Plaid Cymru (Welsh Natl.), Ulster Unionist (Northern Ireland), Democratic Unionists (Northern Ireland), Social Democratic and Labour (Northern Ireland), Ulster Popular Unionist (Northern Ireland), Sinn Fein (Northern Ireland), Green Party, Communist Party

Political Influences on Business

The Anglo-American partnership is one of the most enduring of bilateral relationships. It remains securely anchored in historical traditions, common political systems and values, compatible security interests, and a shared cultural heritage. At the government level, the closeness of the relationship ensures a remarkable degree of cooperation on a very broad range of issues.

With the end of the Cold War and the diminished relative importance of security issues, and with the movement toward European integration, this bilateral relationship has evolved further. The United States now emphasizes to a greater extent than previously the value of our economic interests in Asia and Latin America. The United Kingdom, for its part, is working now more closely with its European partners on political, trade, and other economic matters.

The United Kingdom of Great Britain and Northern Ireland is comprised of four national entities: England, Scotland, Wales (together making Great Britain), and Northern Ireland. The United Kingdom is a constitutional monarchy.

The constitution is largely unwritten, and almost all political power is vested in one chamber of the bicameral Parliament, the House of Commons. The other chamber, the House of Lords, consisting of hereditary and life peers, as well as senior officials of the Church of England, has limited legislative powers. The House of Commons consists of 651 members: 524 from England, 72 from Scotland, 38 from Wales, and 17 from Northern Ireland. Members are elected from specific geographic constituencies, each representing about 60,000 voters.

Because of population shifts, constituencies in England vary considerably over time. General elections are held no more than five years apart, the last having been in April 1992. They are always held at a date of the government's choosing. The next election must be held by the spring of 1997.

The government, a cabinet headed by a Prime Minister, is formed by whichever party, or coalition of parties, can command a majority in the Commons. Legislation is passed by majority vote.

At present, the major parties are the ruling Conservatives (Tory Party) and the opposition Labour Party. The Liberal Democrats constitute the only other significant political force.

Administratively, the United Kingdom acts as a centralized state. The national government, consisting of some 17 cabinet-level departments, plus smaller entities, is staffed by career, nonpartisan civil servants. Only the three or four senior policy positions in each department (the Secretary of State, the Minister of State, and the junior ministers) are occupied by political appointees. They are drawn from the ranks of the ruling party in the House of Commons or the House of Lords.

The current Conservative government under Prime Minister John Major is probusiness in orientation and seeks to maximize the growth of private enterprise. While still coping with the economic and social effects of having "weathered" Britain's longest recession in decades, it remains enthusiastically committed to the philosophy and policies of the previous Thatcher administration.

Contacts in the U.S.A. & in the United Kingdom

Contacts in the United States:

EMBASSY OF THE UNITED KINGDOM OF GREAT BRITAIN AND NORTHERN IRELAND
3100 Massachusetts Avenue, N.W.
Washington, D.C. 20008
Tel: (202) 462-1340
Fax: (202) 898-4255

U.S. DEPARTMENT OF STATE
Bureau of Consular Affairs
Tel: (202) 647-5225
Country Desk Officer
United Kingdom
Tel: (202) 647-8027

U.S. Department of Commerce
United Kingdom Desk
Int'l Trade Admin.
Tel: (202) 482-3748

Tourism Office
British Tourist Authority
551 Fifth Avenue
New York, N.Y. 10176
Tel: (212) 986-2200 or
(800) 462-2748

Contacts in the United Kingdom:

U.S. Embassy
24/31 Grosvenor Sq.
W.1A 1AE
London, England
Mailing Address:
FPO AE 09498-4040
Tel: [44] (71) 499-9000
Telex: 266777
Fax: [44] (71) 499-4022

The American Chamber of Commerce
(United Kingdom)
75 Brook Street
London, England WIY 2EB
Tel: [44] (71) 493 03 81
Telex: 23675 AM CHAM
Fax: [44] (71) 493 23 94

Dun & Bradstreet Europe Ltd.
Postal and Street Address: Holmers Farm
Way
High Wycombe
Bucks HP12 4UL, England
Tel: [44] (1494)42-2000
Fax: [44] (1494)42-2260

Queen Elizabeth II
Buckingham Palace
London, SW1A 1AA
United Kingdom of Great Britain and
Northern Ireland

Prime Minister John Major
10 Downing Street
London, SW1A 2AA
United Kingdom of Great Britain and
Northern Ireland

Passport/Visa Requirements

Visa Information   Tel: (202) 663-1225

Entry Requirements: A passport is required. U.S. citizens are not required to obtain a visa for stays up to six months for business or tourism purposes provided the Immigration officer (at the point or place of entry) is satisfied that they do not intend to settle or to work there, can support themselves and any dependents without working, and are able to meet the cost of their journey.

A person given permission to enter should read carefully the endorsement placed in his passport by the Immigration Officer which may restrict the period allowed to stay and certain other conditions.

A person admitted as a visitor is normally prohibited from taking employment and may not remain longer than six months (maximum) on this basis. Special provisions apply to nationals of member states of the EU, Austria, Liechtenstein, Monaco, and Switzerland.

Cultural Note: Seemingly minor difference in nomenclature between U.K. and U.S. English can cause major business headaches. For example, what British mechanics refer to as a right-handed motor is considered a left-handed motor in the United States. To table a subject in England usually means to begin a discussion of it, while in the U.S.A. it means to postpone the discussion. And the term ground floor in England refers to what an American would call the first floor. The English first floor is the second floor in the U.S.A.

Venezuela

Official Name:	Republic of Venezuela (República de Venezuela)
Official Language:	Spanish
Government System:	Federal multiparty republic
Population:	21.3 million
Population Growth:	2.3%
Area:	916,445 sq. km. (353,841 sq. mi.); about the size of Texas and Oklahoma combined
Natural Resources:	crude oil, natural gas, coal, iron ore, gold, bauxite, other minerals, hydropower, diamonds, marble, timber
Major Cities:	Caracas (capital), Maracaibo, Valencia, Barquisimeto, Maracay, Menda

Cultural Note: Venezuela is a highly class- and status-conscious country. Power flows from the top down, and bosses expect compliance. Employees do not contradict their bosses in Venezuela. Teams of foreigners in Venezuela should be careful not to argue with each other in public, since Venezuelans will interpret this as demonstrating poor leadership.

Age Breakdown

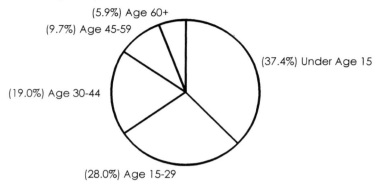

(5.9%) Age 60+

(9.7%) Age 45-59

(37.4%) Under Age 15

(19.0%) Age 30-44

(28.0%) Age 15-29

Life Expectancy: 71 years male; 78 years female (1991)

 Time

Unlike in many parts of Latin America, Venezuelans tend to be prompt. Foreigners are expected to be on time to all business appointments. Social engagements also tend to begin on time.

Venezuela is four hours behind Greenwich Mean Time (G.M.T. – 4), which is one hour ahead of U.S. Eastern Standard Time (E.S.T. + 1).

 Holidays

(Update: Getting Through Customs *http://www.getcustoms.com*)

This list is a working guide. Dates should be corroborated before final travel plans are made. In cases where holidays fall on Saturday or Sunday, commercial establishments may be closed the preceding Friday or following Monday.

New Year's Day	1 January
Declaration of Independence Day	19 April
Labor Day	1 May
Independence Day	5 July
Simon Bolivar's Birthday	24 July

Work Week

- The work week is Monday to Friday, 8:00 A.M. to 5:00 P.M. with at least an hour break for lunch (many executives take a two-hour lunch).
- Stores are open from 9:00 A.M. to noon and again from 2:00 or 3:00 P.M. to 6:00 P.M. or later. Shopping malls stay open later.
- Banks generally are open Monday to Friday, 8:30 to 11:30 and 2:00 P.M. to 4:30 P.M. Post offices stay open through lunch, except in small towns.
- Avoid scheduling appointments two or three days before a holiday.

Religious/Societal Influences on Business

There is no official religion in Venezuela, but over 92% of the population belongs to the Roman Catholic Church. While most Venezuelans derive a sense of stability from the Church, it does not have a great influence on their daily lives.

The family is the single most important institution in Venezuela. Extended families are the norm, and relatives often go into business with each other. When deciding between competing offers, a Venezuelan is likely to ignore the best offer in favor of an offer coming from a relative, even a distant relative.

Venezuela is also a male-dominated society. Sociologists who rank cultures along a Masculinity Index rank Venezuela as one of the "most masculine" in Latin America.

Another sociological finding puts Venezuela at the far end of the Individuality Index. This places the individual as the *least*-important person in a decision-making scenario. The best interests of one's family are considered first. Not surprisingly, the United States ranks at the other end of this scale, with the individual decision maker considering his or her self-interest above all. (Readers from the U.S.A. will see the contrast when they consider the last time they made a decision on the basis of "*Will this benefit or dishonor my family?*")

In politics as in business, Venezuelans tend to follow strong leaders. Leadership styles tend to be authoritarian rather than inclusive.

5 Cultural Tips

1. At a first meeting, a Venezuelan will shake hands and announce his or her full name. You should do the same.
2. Business dress in Venezuela is conservative, but quality and fashion are important. A poorly dressed or shabby person cannot command respect. Dark colored suits

are preferred in a business environment. Fashionable upper-class Venezuelans sometimes exchange clothes with their siblings or friends so that they never appear in the same outfit twice.

3. Business decisions in Venezuela involve far more than the bottom line. Decisions may depend upon what is perceived as best for one's family, one's company, even Venezuelan society as a whole. What is best for the individual decision maker may come last.

4. The decision-making process will probably involve emotional reactions. It is quite acceptable for a Venezuelan decision maker to "go with his (or her) instincts." Even if all the paperwork would indicate a favorable decision, he or she may decline on the basis of "gut instinct."

5. Venezuelan executives establish business relationships with individuals, not with companies. Changing your company's representative in Venezuela may have serious consequences. At the very least, the old representative should personally introduce the new representative. Ideally, your new representative would be a blood-relation to your old one, since nepotism is respected in Venezuela as "good for the family."

 ## Economic Overview

The government of Venezuela faces continued economic policy challenges. There has been a return to government intervention throughout the economy, reversing the 1989–1993 trend toward loosening of government controls. The current government's measures originated in response to the economic and financial crisis which came to a head in early 1994. According to the Venezuelan government, Venezuela's total imports dropped 31% in 1994 due in part to the recession and currency restrictions enacted in June of that year.

The effects of the economic crisis that struck Venezuela in 1993 and 1994 continue to be felt. A recession began in 1993 and deepened with the failure of many banks. In mid-1994, the government instituted tight exchange controls to stop capital flight and fixed the exchange rate. Price controls were decreed on a basket of basic commodities. Additional government measures, including utility rate controls, new checks on government spending, an anti-inflation pact, and delays in exchange approvals for private debt and dividend remittances, have cut into free market advances of the past decade.

Over the long term, however, Venezuela's strong fundamentals should assure a return to robust growth. It is rich in natural resources, enjoys relatively cheap skilled labor, has extraordinary advantageous energy costs, and is geographically located to take advantage of several major markets, including the United States. The United States has traditionally been Venezuela's most important trading partner. It exported $4.6 billion worth of merchandise to Venezuela in 1995, representing more than 50%

of the country's total imports. The short-term outlook for U.S. exports is mixed. In the aggregate, private sector demand is expected to remain somewhat depressed.

The investment climate has been depressed due to a range of unfavorable factors. Recent memory of 1992-93 instability, debt service concerns, the reintroduction of exchange controls and skepticism over the government's ability to manage the economy together translate into falling international investor confidence.

The key sector for foreign investment is petroleum. In July 1995, the Venezuelan Congress approved foreign participation in light and medium oil exploration and development. Some government-owned aluminum companies may also be opened to private investment. In other sectors, privatization efforts have been stalled since 1992.

Comparative Data

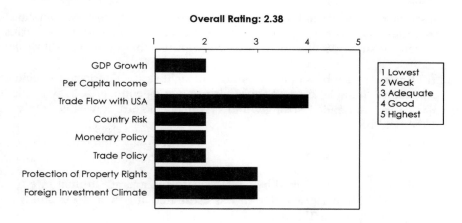

Overall Rating: 2.38

	1 Lowest
	2 Weak
	3 Adequate
	4 Good
	5 Highest

GDP Growth
Per Capita Income
Trade Flow with USA
Country Risk
Monetary Policy
Trade Policy
Protection of Property Rights
Foreign Investment Climate

Country Risk Rating

Gross Domestic Product: $56 billion
GDP Growth: 2.2%
Per Capita Income: $2,624

Trade Flows with the U.S.A.

Rank as Export Market for U.S.A. Goods & Services: 24th
U.S.A. Exports to Venezuela: $4.6 billion
Growth Rate of Exports: 15%
U.S.A. Imports from Venezuela: $9.7 billion
Growth Rate of Imports: 15%
Rank as a Supplier of Imports into the U.S.A.:   16th

Top U.S.A. Exports to Venezuela: Machinery; electrical components; motor vehicles; ships and boats; cereals; organic chemicals; medical and optical equipment; plastics and resins; mineral fuel; iron and steel products.

Top U.S.A. Prospects for Export to Venezuela: Telecommunications services; telecommunications equipment; oil and gas field machinery and service; automobiles and light trucks; automobile parts and services equipment; computers and peripherals; medical equipment; electrical power systems; computer software and services; pumps/valves/compressors.

Country Risk

Dun & Bradstreet rates Venezuela as having necessary capacity to meet outstanding payment liabilities, however, caution is advised. Venezuela has endured a series of political challenges since 1989 which have contributed to worsening political-risk assessments.

Liberal trading terms such as open account and sight drafts continue to decline in usage in response to financial crisis. Secure terms such as confirmed irrevocable letter of credit are recommended strongly and credit checks are advisable. Only reputable banks should be used.

Monetary Policy

Since 1993 inflation has not dropped below 40%, with the average annual rate reaching 46% in 1993 and 71% in 1994. Inflation was estimated at 55% in 1995 and is forecast to be in the 90% range in 1996. *Monetary Unit:* bolivar.

Trade Policy

TARIFFS: Venezuela generally adheres to the Andean Pact's Common External Tariff, which has four tariff levels: 5, 10, 15, and 20%. Automobiles carry a duty of 35%.

Venezuela's average tariff is about 10%. Import duties remain at a maximum of 20% in almost all categories.

IMPORT LICENSING: Import licenses are required rarely, but there are a number of products which still require permits. These include arms and explosives, which require an import permit from the Ministry of the Interior.

Import certificates are required for certain products subject to special supervision. Almost all foods and agricultural imports must have sanitary or phytosanitary import certificates issued by the Ministry of Agriculture.

Medicines, foods, and cosmetics require registration with the Ministry of Health.

Imports of used autos, used clothing, and used tires are prohibited. Pork from most countries and poultry from the United States is also banned.

Some products can only be imported by the government such as cigarette paper, bank notes, weapons of war, and certain explosives. Weapons for private use, such as shotguns, sporting rifles, air rifles, nonmilitary pistols, and commercial explosives can only be imported with authorization of the Interior Ministry's National Office of Arms and Explosives.

IMPORT TAXES: All imports are assessed a 1% customs handling charge. A 12.5% tax on the value of imports is also applied. A luxury tax, on a sliding scale of up to 20%, will also apply to some goods, including certain alcoholic beverages and luxury cars.

Protection of Intellectual Property Rights

Although intellectual property protection in Venezuela has improved over the last year or two, U.S. companies continue to express concern about inadequacies in enforcement of patent, trademark, and copyright protection, particularly as applied to pharmaceuticals, computer software, and motion pictures. Venezuela remained on the United States Trade Representative's Special 301 Watch List for the review completed in spring 1995.

Venezuela is an active member of the World Intellectual Property Organization (WIPO) and a signatory to the Berne Convention for the Protection of Literary and Artistic Works, the Geneva Phonograms Convention, the Universal Copyright Convention, and has ratified its membership in the Paris Convention for the Protection of Industrial Property.

Venezuela's legal framework for patent and trademark protection is currently provided by Andean Pact Decision 344, superseding Venezuela's national Patent and Trademark Law which dates from 1955. Decision 344 provides for patentability of pharmaceutical products, except those listed on the World Health Organization's list of essential medicines.

Venezuela's 1993 Copyright Law is modern and comprehensive and extends copyright protection to all creative works, including computer software. Andean Pact Decision 351 is complimentary to Venezuela's national law for copyrights. The Venezuelan government announced in June 1995 that it was in the process of establishing a national Copyright Office for the registration and protection of copyrights.

Since Venezuela does not automatically recognize foreign patents, trademarks, or logos, foreign investors should be sure to register patents and trademarks appropriately. It is necessary to register with the Autonomous Service of the Industrial Property Registry of the Ministry of Development.

Care should be taken to use the registered trademark. Venezuelan regulations allow for cancellation of the registration if the trademark is not used in at least one of the Andean Pact countries for three consecutive years.

Foreign Investment Climate

The Venezuelan government has eliminated legal barriers to foreign investment in most sectors. Presently, disincentives to invest in Venezuela stem principally from government economic policies, including its management at the macroeconomics level and the imposition of price and foreign exchange controls.

Venezuela's main legal framework for foreign investment is provided in Presidential Decree 2095 of 1992. Decree 2095 expanded foreign investment opportunities in Venezuela by lifting most restrictions on foreign participation. All sectors of Venezuela's economy, except those noted specifically, are open to 100% foreign participation. Since 1992, foreign companies have been able to operate in certain sectors formerly reserved to companies with a Venezuelan majority interest, including retail sales, export services, telephone and telecommunication services, electrical services, and water and sewage services. Decree 2095 does not cover investments in the petroleum, petrochemical, coal, mining, banking, and insurance sectors, which are regulated by special laws. The process for making a foreign investment in Venezuela was also simplified. Decree 2095 eliminated the requirement to obtain prior government authorization for foreign investments in sectors covered by Decree 2095. The decree only requires that investors register with the Superintendent of Foreign Investment within 60 days of the date the new investment is realized.

Decree 2095 guarantees foreign investors the right to repatriate 100% of profits and capital, including proceeds from the sale of shares or liquidation of the company, and allows for unrestricted reinvestment of profits. However, Venezuela's current exchange control system does establish certain procedures and documentary requirements for investors wishing to remit dividends, capital, and royalty payments.

Foreign investment is restricted to a maximum of 19.9% in enterprises engaged in radio, television, the Spanish language press, and professional services subject to licensing legislation.

Venezuela achieved initial success in its privatization program with partial sales of the state telephone company, CANTV, and the state airline, VIASA, in 1991. The program has stalled as the country has struggled with banking and economic crises. In 1993 and 1994, only six minor privatizations were completed generating revenues of $22 million and $3 million respectively.

Current Leaders & Political Parties

(Update: International Academy at Santa Barbara *http://www.iasb.org/cwl*)

President: Dr. Rafael Caldera

Cabinet Ministers:
Sec. of the Presidency: Asdrubal Aquiar
Interior: José Guillermo Andueza
Foreign Affairs: Miguel Angel Burelli Rivas

Defense: Gen. Pedro Nicolás Valencia Vivas

Dev.: Freddy Parra

Agriculture and Livestock: Raul Alegrett

Labor: Dr. Juan Nepumuceno Garrido

Communications and Transport: Ciro Caá

Energy and Mines: Edwin José Arrieta Valera

Environment and Natural Resources: Roberto Pérez Lecuna

Urban Dev.: Francisco González

Other Officials:

Pres. of the Central Bank: Antonio Casas

Pres. of the Senate: Eduardo Gomez Tamayo

Pres. of the Chamber of Deputies: Cristobal Fernandez Dalo

Ambassador to U.S.: Pedro Luís Echeverria

Perm. Rep. to U.N.: Enrique Tejera Paris

Political Parties:

Democratic Action Party, Social Christian Party, Radical Cause Party, Mov.
Toward Socialism, Venezuelan Communist Party, Democratic Republic Union
Party

 Political Influences on business

Venezuela is a republic with an active multiparty democratic system and a longstanding commitment to democracy.

Since 1958, Venezuelan politics has been mostly dominated by two large parties: the Democratic Action party (AD), associated with the Socialist International, and the Social Christian Party (COPEI) which is affiliated with the Christian Democratic movement. In recent years, other political parties have challenged the political dominance of AD and COPEI. These parties include: the Movement Toward Socialism (MAS), consisting of democratic-leftists allied with Caldera; the Radical Cause Party (Causa R), a working-class oriented group; and the Convergence Party (Convergencia), a new party established in 1993 by Rafael Caldera.

Venezuela held presidential and congressional elections in December of 1993 and President Caldera began his current five-year term in February 1994. President Caldera represents a coalition of political factions, incorporating most of the political spectrum from left to right, distinct from the two parties, AD and COPEI, that have dominated Venezuela's 40-year democratic history. Caldera emerged as the victor in the 1993 four-way race with little more than a 30 percent plurality. As a result of the 1993 national elections, the congress has evolved from a bi-party system dominated by AD and COPEI to a more diverse five-party system. This has complicated the legislative process. Nonetheless, Caldera has had repeated success in securing from Congress the major pieces of economic legislation which his administration has proposed.

The election of mayors and governors took place for the first time in 1989. The direct election of state and local officials represents an important development in the ongoing process of political decentralization and transformation in Venezuela. State and municipal elections to choose 22 state governors, over 320 mayors, state legislators, and city councilmen were held in December 1995.

The next round of national elections are scheduled for 1998.

Contacts in the U.S.A. & in Venezuela

Contacts in the United States:

EMBASSY OF THE REPUBLIC OF VENEZUELA
1099 30th Street, N.W.
Washington, DC 20007
Tel: (202) 342-2214
Fax: (202) 342-6820

U.S. DEPARTMENT OF STATE
Bureau of Consular Affairs
Tel: (202) 647-5225
Venezuela Desk
Tel.: (202) 647-3338

U.S. DEPARTMENT OF COMMERCE
Venezuela Desk
Int'l Trade Admin.
Tel: (202) 482-4303

TOURISM OFFICE
Venezuelan Tourism Association
Box 3010
Sausalito, CA 94966
Tel: (415) 331-0100 or
(800) 331-0100

Contacts in Venezuela:

THE AMERICAN EMBASSY
Avenida Francisco de Miranda and
Avenida Principal de la Floresta
P.O. Box 62291, Caracas 1060A or
APO AA 34037
Tel: [58] (2) 285-2222
Telex: 25501 AMEMB VE
Fax: [58] (2) 285-0366

VENEZUELAN-AMERICAN CHAMBER OF
COMMERCE AND INDUSTRY
Torre Credival, Piso 10
2da Avenida de Campo Alegre

Apartado 5181
Caracas 1010-A
Tel.: [58] (2) 263-0833
Telex: (395) 23627 CAVEA VC
Fax: [58] (2) 263-1829

PRESIDENT RAFAEL CALDERA
Office of the President
Palacio de Miraflores
Caracas 1010, Republic of Venezuela

Passport/Visa Requirements

Visa Information   Tel: (202) 663-1225

Entry Requirements: A passport and a visa or tourist card are required. Tourist cards can be obtained from airlines serving Venezuela.

Note: When visas are submitted and need to be returned by mail, a self-addressed, stamped envelope is required.

All visitors must pay a departure tax in bolivares at the Venezuelan airport or port.

All persons holding a business or transient visa must obtain an income declaration (Declaracion de Rentas) at the office of the Ministry of Finance (Ministerio de Hacienda), 8 A.M. to 4 P.M., Monday through Friday, required at time of departure.

Visas and current information concerning entry, tax, and customs requirements for Venezuela can be obtained from the Venezuelan Embassy, or their nearest consulate.

Cultural Note: In general, Venezuelans display much of the easygoing informality of their Caribbean neighbors. Venezuelans tend to be outgoing and friendly. But their honor must be defended against any slight, and a single ill-chosen comment can quickly anger most Venezuelan men. Sensitive topics include the family, women (especially mothers), honesty, and politics.

Appendix 1:
Documents Used in International Trade

Proper documentation is vital for success in international trade. Inaccurate or incomplete paperwork can result in delays and fines. The fines for false or incorrect declarations of weight and measure, as well as simple description of the merchandise itself, can be severe. When in doubt, contact an international trade expert. Aside from commercial firms like Dun & Bradstreet, such experts can be found at the U. S. Department of Commerce and at the commercial offices of U.S. Embassies abroad.

Bill of Lading

One of the most important shipping documents, the *Bill of Lading* has several functions:

1. It represents a contract between the shipper and the ocean carrier.
2. It serves as a receipt.
3. It conveys title to the merchandise.

A Bill of Lading may be *straight* (meaning nonnegotiable) or a *Shipper's Order* Bill of Lading (meaning negotiable). Some countries permit a third type, called a *To Order* Bill of Lading, which is made out to the order of a consignee or a foreign bank. But even in those countries which permit the use of the To Order Bill of Lading, it does not always offer the legal protection of the other types of Bills of Lading.

The Bill of Lading is filled out by the shipper on forms provided by the ocean carrier. Styles of forms vary. A typical straight Bill of Lading follows.

Air Waybill

When the shipper is an air carrier instead of an ocean carrier, an *Air Waybill* (also called an Air Consignment Notice) is used. However, unlike a Bill of Lading, an Air Waybill does not convey title.

456

As with Bills of Lading, the shipper fills out an Air Waybill form provided by the air carrier. Remember that air carriers (of necessity) have stricter shipping regulations for merchandise than do ocean carriers. Some items which safely go aboard a ship may not withstand the sudden changes in temperature and air pressure in an airplane's cargo hold.

An Air Waybill can also be used between a shipper and a freight consolidator (or freight forwarder). In this case the Air Waybill will be issued by the consolidator/forwarder rather than the airline.

Air Waybills are, by design, nonnegotiable.

Certificate of Origin

Trade treaties have made the *Certificate of Origin* increasingly more important. The same item imported from one country may be subject to a tariff; from another country, there may be no tariff at all. Sometimes a Certificate of Origin is required, and sometimes not. In some countries, a *Statement of Origin* will suffice. At times, a Certificate of Origin contains the same information as the Commercial Invoice.

Certificates of Origin vary from destination to destination. A few countries require a special form (which, in some cases, is only available through that nation's Consulate). Two Certificates of Origin, which would be by a U.S. exporter are on following pages. The first would be used for shipment within the North American Free Trade Agreement (thus, from the U.S. to Canada or Mexico), the second is for a shipment from the U.S.A. to Israel.

Commercial Invoice

With or without a Certificate of Origin, each shipment generally needs a *Commercial Invoice*. This document is used for clearance through customs at the shipment's destination.

This form requires the listing of the sale price of each item in the shipment. Follow each country's regulations carefully, especially with regard to the prices you list on the forms.

Three Commercial Invoices follow. The first is a generic form.

In most British Commonwealth Countries, the Commercial Invoice is called a Customs Invoice. The following is a Canadian Customs Invoice, in English and French is included.

The final form is a Mexican Commercial Invoice, in English and Spanish.

Dock Receipt

Depending upon the agreement, the shipper's responsibility may end when the merchandise arrives at the port in the country of destination. In this case, it becomes someone else's responsibility to get the goods from port to distributor or destination.

The *Dock Receipt* is a document which attests that the merchandise has arrived at a pier or warehouse. It is issued by the carrier or a carrier's agent after delivery. Dock Receipts are non-negotiable.

If the merchandise does not arrive complete in one shipment, a temporary receipt is issued for each partial shipment. Upon completion of the full shipment, the temporary receipts are exchanged for a Dock Receipt:

Shipper's Export Declaration

The United States Commerce Department requires this form to be filled out when an export shipment is valued at more than U.S. $2,500 (or more than U.S. $500 for a postal shipment).

Packing List

A *Packing List* has several uses:

1. It allows an exporter (or forwarder) to know the total shipping weight and volume of the shipment; information required to reserve shipping space.
2. It is used as a check-off list at the port of export.
3. It is also used as a check-off list at the port of import.
4. It is used by the buyer to inventory the merchandise upon receipt.
5. Finally, it is used if an insurance claim is filed.

However, for small shipments, the data on the Packing List can be incorporated into the Commercial Invoice, provided that no party has requested a Packing List. Some countries require the use of a Packing List.

Packing lists are available from commercial stationers. A sample Packing List follows.

Proforma Invoice

The *Proforma* Invoice is a form of preliminary, provisional invoice. It notifies an importer (and, if needed, an importer's government) of the main details of a planned shipment.

Some countries require a Proforma Invoice to be filled out before they will issue a Foreign Exchange Permit or an Import License.

Because a Proforma Invoice is prepared long before the merchandise is actually ready to ship, all parties understand that it will not be completely accurate. Data such as shipping charges, weight, and values are subject to change.

DELIVERING CARRIER TO STEAMER:	CAR NUMBER—REFERENCE
FORWARDING AGENT—REFERENCES	EXPORT DEC. No.

BILL OF LADING
(Conditions Continued from Reverse Side Hereof)

SHIPPER ....

CONSIGNEE: ORDER OF ....

ADDRESS ARRIVAL NOTICE TO	ALSO NOTIFY

SHIP	VOYAGE NO.	FLAG	PIER	PORT OF LOADING

FOR. PORT OF DISCHARGE *(Where goods are to be delivered to consignee or on-carrier)* | For TRANSSHIPMENT to *(If goods are to be transshipped or forwarded at port of discharge)*

PARTICULARS FURNISHED BY SHIPPER OF GOODS

MARKS AND NUMBERS	No. of PKGS.	DESCRIPTION OF PACKAGES AND GOODS	MEASURE-MENT	GROSS WEIGHT

FREIGHT PAYABLE IN

...................................@............PER 2240 LBS...... $................		(CONDITIONS CONTINUED FROM REVERSE SIDE HEREOF)
...................................@............PER 100 LB.......... $................		IN WITNESS WHEREOF, THERE HAVE BEEN EXECUTED........
.......FT.........IN. @............PER 40 CU. FT...... $................		BILLS OF LADING, ALL OF THE SAME TENOR AND DATE, ONE OF WHICH BEING ACCOMPLISHED, THE OTHERS TO STAND VOID.
.......FT.........IN. @............PER CU. FT......... $................		
.... $................		
.... $................		BY..
.... $................		FOR THE MASTER
.... $................		ISSUED AT...
		(DATE)
TOTAL.......... $................		B/L No....................................

Form 35-084 ©, 1986 *UNZ&CO* 190 Baldwin Ave., Jersey City, NJ 07306 • (800) 631-3098 • (201) 795-5400

	House Air Waybill Number	

Shippers Name and Address	Shippers account Number	Not negotiable **Air Waybill** (Air Consignment note) Issued by
		Copies 1, 2 and 3 of this Air Waybill are originals and have the same validity
Consignee's Name and Address	Consignee's account Number	It is agreed that the goods described herein are accepted in apparent good order and condition (except as noted) for carriage SUBJECT TO THE CONDITIONS OF CONTRACT ON THE REVERSE HEREOF. THE SHIPPER'S ATTENTION IS DRAWN TO THE NOTICE CONCERNING CARRIERS' LIMITATION OF LIABILITY. Shipper may increase such limitation of liability by declaring a higher value for carriage and paying a supplemental charge if required.

These commodities licensed by the United States for ultimate destination

Diversion contrary to

United States law prohibited.

Airport of Departure (Addr. of first Carrier) and requested Routing						

to	By first Carrier Routing and Destination	Air Waybill Number	Currency	CHGS Code	WT/VAL PPD COLL	Other PPD COLL	Declared Value for Carriage	Declared Value for Customs
Airport of Destination	Flight/Date For Carrier Use only Flight/Date		Amount of Insurance		INSURANCE: If Carrier offers insurance and such insurance is requested in accordance with conditions on reverse hereof, indicate amount to be insured in figures in box marked "amount of insurance".			

Handling Information

No. of Pieces RCP	Gross Weight	kg lb	Rate Class / Commodity Item No.	Chargeable Weight	Rate / Charge	Total	Nature and Quantity of Goods (incl. Dimensions or Volume)

Prepaid	Weight Charge	**Collect**	Other Charges
	Valuation Charge		
	Tax		
Total other Charges Due Agent			Shipper certifies that the particulars on the face hereof are correct and that insofar as any part of the consignment contains dangerous goods, such part is properly described by name and is in proper condition for carriage by air according to the applicable Dangerous Goods Regulations.
Total other Charges Due Carrier			
Total prepaid	Total collect		Signature of Shipper or his Agent
Currency Conversion Rates	cc charges in Dest. Currency		Executed on (Date) at (Place) Signature of Issuing Carrier or its Agent

Form 16-810 ©, 1986 *UNSCO* 190 Baldwin Ave., Jersey City, NJ 07306 • (800) 631-3098

	House Air Waybill Number

EXTRA COPY

DEPARTMENT OF THE TREASURY
UNITED STATES CUSTOMS SERVICE

NORTH AMERICAN FREE TRADE AGREEMENT

CERTIFICATE OF ORIGIN

19 CFR 181.11, 181.22

Approved through 12/31/96
OMB No. 1515-0204
See back of form for Paper-
work Reduction Act Notice.

1. Exporter Name and Address	2. Blanket Period *(DD/MM/YY)*
Tax I.D. Number	FROM TO
3. Producer Name and Address Tax I.D. Number	4. Importer Name and Address Tax I.D. Number

5. Description of Good(s)	6. HS Tariff Classifi- cation Number	7. Prefer- ence Criterion	8. Producer	9. Net Cost	10. Country of Origin

I Certify that:

- The information on this document is true and accurate and I assume the responsibility for proving such representations. I understand that I am liable for any false statements or material omissions made on or in connection with this document;

- I agree to maintain, and present upon request, documentation necessary to support this certificate, and to inform, in writing, all persons to whom the certificate was given of any changes that would affect the accuracy or validity of this certificate;

- The goods originated in the territory of one or more of the parties, and comply with the origin requirements specified for those goods in the North American Free Trade Agreement, and unless specifically exempted in Article 411 or Annex 401, there has been no further production or any other operation outside the territories of the Parties;

- This certificate consists of [   ] pages, including all attachments.

11a. AUTHORIZED SIGNATURE	11b. Company:
11c. NAME	11d. Title:
11e. DATE *(DD/MM/YY)*	11f. TELEPHONE ▷ NUMBER	*(Voice)*	*(Facsimile)*

Form No. 16-765 Printed and Sold by *UNZCO* 700 Central Ave., New Providence, NJ 07974 ● 800-631-3098

Customs Form CF434 (121793)

This is a Certificate of Origin for a shipment from the U.S. to Israel:

U.S. CERTIFICATE OF ORIGIN
FOR EXPORTS TO ISRAEL

1. Goods consigned from exporter's business (name, address):	Reference No.
	U.S.—ISRAEL FREE TRADE AREA
	CERTIFICATE OF ORIGIN
	(Combined declaration and certificate)
2. Goods consigned to (consignee's name, address)	
	(See notes over leaf)
3. Means of transport and route (as far as known)	**4. For official use**

5. Item number	6. Marks and numbers of packages	7. Number and kind of packages, description of goods	8. Origin criterion (see notes over leaf)	9. Gross Weight or other quantity	10. Number and date of invoices

11. CERTIFICATION

The _____ a recognized chamber of commerce, board of trade, or _____ _____ under the laws of the State of _____ _____ has examined the manufacturer's invoice or shipper's affidavit concerning the origin of the merchandise and, according to the best of its knowledge and belief, finds that the products named originated in the United States of America.

_____
Certifying Official

EXPORTER AS PRODUCER:

The undersigned hereby declares that he/she is the producer of the goods listed in this invoice and that they comply with the origin requirements specified for those goods in the U.S.—Israel Free Trade Area Agreement for goods exported to Israel.

_____
Signature of Exporter

12. DECLARATION BY THE EXPORTER

The undersigned hereby declares that the above details and statements are correct; that all the goods were produced in the United States of America and that they comply with the origin requirements specified for those goods in the U.S.—Israel Free Trade Area Agreement for goods exported to Israel.

_____
Signature of Exporter

Sworn to before me this _____ day of _____ 19_____

_____
Signature of Notary Public

COMMERCIAL INVOICE

SELLER (Name, Full Address, Country)	INVOICE DATE AND NO.	CUSTOMER'S ORDER NO.
	OTHER REFERENCES	
CONSIGNEE (Name, Full Address, Country)	BUYER (If Other Than Consignee)	
	PRESENTING BANK	
	COUNTRY OF ORIGIN OF GOODS	
PORT OF LADING	TERMS AND CONDITIONS OF DELIVERY AND PAYMENT	
COUNTRY OF FINAL DESTINATION / SHIP / AIR / ETC.		
OTHER TRANSPORT INFORMATION	CURRENCY OF SALE	

MARK AND NUMBERS DESCRIPTION OF GOODS	GROSS WEIGHT (Kg.)	CUBIC METRES

NO. AND KIND OF PACKAGES	SPECIFICATION OF COMMODITIES (IN CODE AND/OR IN FULL)	NET WEIGHT (Kg.)	QUANTITY	UNIT PRICE	AMOUNT
		PACKING			
		FREIGHT			
		OTHER COSTS (Specify)			
IT IS HEREBY CERTIFIED THAT THIS INVOICE SHOWS THE ACTUAL PRICE OF THE GOODS DESCRIBED, THAT NO OTHER INVOICE HAS BEEN OR WILL BE ISSUED AND THAT ALL PARTICULARS ARE TRUE AND CORRECT.		INSURANCE			
SIGNATURE AND STATUS OF AUTHORIZED PERSON DATE PLACE		TOTAL INVOICE AMOUNT			

Revenue Canada Customs and Excise	Revenu Canada Douanes et Accise	**CANADA CUSTOMS INVOICE** *FACTURE DES DOUANES CANADIENNES*	Page of de

1. Vendor (Name and Address)/*Vendeur (Nom et adresse)*	2. Date of Direct Shipment to Canada/*Date d'expédition directe vers le Canada*
	3. Other References (Include Purchaser's Order No.) *Autres références (Inclure le n° de commande de l'acheteur)*

4. Consignee (Name and Address)/*Destinataire (Nom et adresse)*	5. Purchaser's Name and Address (If other than Consignee) *Nom et adresse de l'acheteur (S'il diffère du destinataire)*
	6. Country of Transhipment/*Pays de transbordement*
	7. Country of Origin of Goods *Pays d'origine des marchandises* — IF SHIPMENT INCLUDES GOODS OF DIFFERENT ORIGINS ENTER ORIGINS AGAINST ITEMS IN 12 *SI L'EXPÉDITION COMPREND DES MARCHANDISES D'ORIGINES DIFFÉRENTES, PRÉCISER LEUR PROVENANCE EN 12*

8. Transportation: Give Mode and Place of Direct Shipment to Canada *Transport: Préciser mode et point d'expédition directe vers le Canada*	9. Conditions of Sale and Terms of Payment (i.e. Sale, Consignment Shipment, Leased Goods, etc.) *Conditions de vente et modalités de paiement* *(p. ex. vente, expédition en consignation, location de marchandises, etc.)*
	10. Currency of Settlement/*Devises du paiement*

11. No. of Pkgs *N^{bre} de colis*	12. Specification of Commodities (Kind of Packages, Marks and Numbers, General Description and Characteristics, i.e. Grade, Quality) *Désignation des articles (Nature des colis, marques et numéros, description générale et caractéristiques, p. ex. classe, qualité)*	13. Quantity (State Unit) *Quantité* *(Préciser l'unité)*	Selling Price/*Prix de vente*	
			14. Unit Price *Prix unitaire*	15. Total

18. If any of fields 1 to 17 are included on an attached commercial invoice, check this box *Si les renseignements des zones 1 à 17 figurent sur la facture commerciale, cocher cette boîte* ☐ Commercial Invoice No. */N° de la facture commerciale* _____	16. Total Weight/*Poids Total*		17. Invoice Total *Total de la facture*
	Net	Gross/*Brut*	

19. Exporter's Name and Address (If other than Vendor) *Nom et adresse de l'exportateur (S'il diffère du vendeur)*	20. Originator (Name and Address)/*Expéditeur d'origine (Nom et adresse)*

21. Departmental Ruling (If applicable)/*Décision du Ministère (S'il y a lieu)*	22. If fields 23 to 25 are not applicable, check this box *Si les zones 23 à 25 sont sans objet, cocher cette boîte* ☐

23. If included in field 17 indicate amount: *Si compris dans le total à la zone 17, préciser:*	24. If not included in field 17 indicate amount: *Si non compris dans le total à la zone 17, préciser:*	25. Check (If applicable): *Cocher (S'il y a lieu):*
(i) Transportation charges, expenses and insurance from the place of direct shipment to Canada *Les frais de transport, dépenses et assurances à partir du point d'expédition directe vers le Canada* $ _____	(i) Transportation charges, expenses and insurance to the place of direct shipment to Canada *Les frais de transport, dépenses et assurances jusqu'au point d'expédition directe vers le Canada* $ _____	(i) Royalty payments or subsequent proceeds are paid or payable by the purchaser *Des redevances ou produits ont été ou seront versés par l'acheteur* ☐
(ii) Costs for construction, erection and assembly incurred after importation into Canada *Les coûts de construction, d'érection et d'assemblage après importation au Canada* $ _____	(ii) Amounts for commissions other than buying commissions *Les commissions autres que celles versées pour l'achat* $ _____	(ii) The purchaser has supplied goods or services for use in the production of these goods *L'acheteur a fourni des marchandises ou des services pour la production des marchandises* ☐
(iii) Export packing *Le coût de l'emballage d'exportation* $ _____	(iii) Export packing *Le coût de l'emballage d'exportation* $ _____	

DEPARTMENT OF NATIONAL REVENUE — CUSTOMS AND EXCISE   *MINISTÈRE DU REVENU NATIONAL — DOUANES ET ACCISE*

Printed and Sold by *UNZ&CO* 190 Baldwin Ave., Jersey City, NJ 07306

Factura Comercial Para México

Commercial Invoice for Mexico

Número de Factura *(Invoice No).*	Lugar y Fecha de Emisión de la Factura *(Place and Date of Issuance of Invoice)*	Orden de Compra Número *(Customer P.O. No.)*

Exportador/Vendedor *(Exporter/Vendor)*	Fabricante *(Producer)*	
Destinatario Final *(Ultimate Consignee)*	País de Origen de la Mercancia *(Country of Origin of mdse)*	¿Certificación NAFTA? ☐ Si *(yes)* ☐ No
	Términos de Pago *(Terms of Payment)*	
Destinatario Intermedio *(Intermediate Consignee)*		
Agente de Transporte de Carga *(Freight Forwarder)*	Términos de Venta *(Terms of Sale)*	
Transportista *(Carrier)*	Otras Referencias e Instrucciones para Consignación *(Other References, Consignment Instructions)*	
Puerto de Exportación *(U.S. Port of Export)*	Puerto de Descarga *(Port of Unloading)*	

Número y clase de Bultos *(Number & kinds of pkgs)*	Descripción Detallada de la Mercancia (incluyendo clase, tipo, número de serie, marcas, cantidades parciales/a granel); número de fracción arancelaria, primeros 6 dígitos. *(Detailed Commercial Description of Merchandise (include class, type, serial numbers, trademarks, partial/bulk quantities), 6-digit HS number.)*	Cantidad de Unidades *(Quantity, units)*	Peso Bruto, en kilos *(Gross weight in kg)*	Precio por Unidad *(price per unit)*	Valor Total en Dólares de los EUA *(Total Value, U.S. Dollars)*
	Nota: La Descripción Deberá Ser en Españöl *(Note: Description must be in Spanish!)*				

Dictamen Anticipado *(Advanced Ruling)* Fecha *(Date)*	Valor Comercial, LAB *(Commercial Value, FOB)*	
Identificación de Empaque *(Package Marks)*	Costos de Transporte, Seguro, Empaque, y Otros *(Transportation, Insurance, Packing, Other Costs)*	
	Valor Total de la Factura *(Total Invoice Value)*	

"Declaro bajo protesta de decir la verdad, que el valor y las declaraciones contenidas en esta factura son verdaderas y correctas." *("I declare under oath that the value and specifications contained in this Invoice are true and correct.")*

Firma del Declarante *(Signature of Preparer)*

© Copyright 1990 UNZ & CO.

(SPACES IMMEDIATELY BELOW ARE FOR SHIPPERS MEMORANDA—NOT PART OF DOCK RECEIPT)

DELIVERING CARRIER TO STEAMER:	CAR NUMBER—REFERENCE
FORWARDING AGENT—REFERENCES	EXPORT DEC. No.

DOCK RECEIPT
NON-NEGOTIABLE

SHIPPER- -

SHIP	VOYAGE NO.	FLAG	PIER	PORT OF LOADING
FOR. PORT OF DISCHARGE *(Where goods are to be delivered to consignee or on-carrier)*			For TRANSSHIPMENT TO *(If goods are to be transshipped or forwarded at port of discharge)*	

PARTICULARS FURNISHED BY SHIPPER OF GOODS

MARKS AND NUMBERS	No. of PKGS.	DESCRIPTION OF PACKAGES AND GOODS	MEASURE-MENT	GROSS WEIGHT

DIMENSIONS AND WEIGHTS OF PACKAGES TO BE SHOWN ON REVERSE SIDE

DELIVERED BY:

RECEIVED THE ABOVE DESCRIBED MERCHANDISE FOR SHIPMENT AS INDICATED HEREON, SUBJECT TO ALL CONDITIONS OF THE UNDERSIGNED'S USUAL FORM OF DOCK RECEIPT AND BILL OF LADING. COPIES OF THE UNDERSIGNED'S USUAL FORM OF DOCK RECEIPT AND BILL OF LADING MAY BE OBTAINED FROM THE MASTER OF THE VESSEL, OR THE VESSEL'S AGENT

LIGHTER }
TRUCK   } . . . .

ARRIVED—   DATE . . . . TIME . . . .

UNLOADED— DATE . . . . TIME . . . .

CHECKED BY . . . .

PLACED IN SHIP ON DOCK LOCATION . . . .

AGENT FOR MASTER

BY . . . .
RECEIVING CLERK

DATE . . . .

Form 35-585 Printed and Sold by *UNZCO* 190 Baldwin Ave., Jersey City, NJ 07306 • (800) 631-3098

U.S. DEPARTMENT OF COMMERCE—BUREAU OF THE CENSUS—INTERNATIONAL TRADE ADMINISTRATION

FORM **7525-V** (1-1-88)

SHIPPER'S EXPORT DECLARATION

OMB No. 0607-0018

1a. EXPORTER *(Name and address including ZIP code)*

ZIP CODE	**2. DATE OF EXPORTATION**	**3. BILL OF LADING/AIR WAYBILL NO.**

b. EXPORTER EIN (IRS) NO.

c. PARTIES TO TRANSACTION

☐ Related   ☐ Non-related

4a. ULTIMATE CONSIGNEE

b. INTERMEDIATE CONSIGNEE

5. FORWARDING AGENT

6. POINT (STATE) OF ORIGIN OR FTZ NO.	**7. COUNTRY OF ULTIMATE DESTINATION**

8. LOADING PIER *(Vessel only)*	**9. MODE OF TRANSPORT** *(Specify)*
10. EXPORTING CARRIER	**11. PORT OF EXPORT**
12. PORT OF UNLOADING *(Vessel and air only)*	**13. CONTAINERIZED** *(Vessel only)* ☐ Yes ☐ No

14. SCHEDULE B DESCRIPTION OF COMMODITIES,
15. MARKS, NOS., AND KINDS OF PACKAGES   } *(Use columns 17-19)*

D/F (16)	SCHEDULE B NUMBER (17)	CHECK DIGIT	QUANTITY—SCHEDULE B UNIT(S) (18)	SHIPPING WEIGHT (Kilos) (19)	VALUE (U.S. dollars, omit cents) (Selling price or cost if not sold) (20)

21. VALIDATED LICENSE NO./GENERAL LICENSE SYMBOL	**22. ECCN** *(When required)*

23. Duly authorized officer or employee

The exporter authorizes the forwarder named above to act as forwarding agent for export control and customs purposes.

24. I certify that all statements made and all information contained herein are true and correct and that I have read and understand the instructions for preparation of this document, set forth in the "Correct Way to Fill Out the Shipper's Export Declaration" (available Bureau of Census, Wash., DC 20233). I understand that civil and criminal penalties, including forfeiture and sale, may be imposed for making false or fraudulent statements herein, failing to provide the requested information or for violation of U.S. laws on exportation (13 U.S.C. Sec. 305; 22 U.S.C. Sec. 401; 18 U.S.C. Sec. 1001; 50 U.S.C. App. 2410).

Signature	Confidential—For use solely for official purposes authorized by the Secretary of Commerce (13 U.S.C. 301 (g)).
Title	Export shipments are subject to inspection by U.S. Customs Service and/or Office of Export Enforcement.
Date	**25. AUTHENTICATION** *(When required)*

Form No. 15-795 Printed and Sold by **UNACO** 700 Central Ave., New Providence, NJ 07974 • (800) 631-3098

UNZ & CO., 190 BALDWIN AVE., JERSEY CITY, N.J. 07306 N.J. (201) 795-5400. (800) 631-3098

PACKING LIST

© Copyright 1990 UNZ & CO.

_____ 19 _____
Place and Date of Shipment

To

Gentlemen:

Under your Order No. _____ the material listed below
was shipped   via
To

Shipment consists of:		Marks
_____ Cases	_____ Packages	
_____ Crates	_____ Cartons	
_____ Bbls.	_____ Drums	
_____ Reels	_____	

*LEGAL WEIGHT IS WEIGHT OF ARTICLE PLUS PAPER, BOX, BOTTLE, ETC., CONTAINING THE ARTICLE AS USUALLY CARRIED IN STOCK.

PACKAGE NUMBER	WEIGHTS IN LBS. or KILOS			DIMENSIONS			QUANTITY	CLEARLY STATE CONTENTS OF EACH PACKAGE
	GROSS WEIGHT EACH	*LEGAL WEIGHT EACH	NET WEIGHT EACH	HEIGHT	WIDTH	LENGTH		

Form 30-036 Printed and Sold by *UNZ&CO* 190 Baldwin Ave., Jersey City, NJ 07306 • (800) 631-3098 • (201) 795-5400

PROFORMA INVOICE

PRO FORMA INVOICE NO.	**DATE ISSUED**

S
H
I
P
P
E
R

S
O
L
D

T
O

S
H
I
P

T
O

TERMS AND CONDITIONS OF SALE

MODE OF TRANSPORT	**CARRIER**
AIR/OCEAN PORT OF EMBARKATION	**LOADING PIER**
AIR/OCEAN PORT OF UNLOADING	**CONTAINERIZED** ☐ Yes ☐ No

MARKS:

GROSS WEIGHT:

QUANTITY	U/M	DESCRIPTION OF MERCHANDISE	UNIT PRICE	AMOUNT
			FREIGHT	
			EXPORT PACKING	
			INSURANCE	
			MISC	
			TOTAL	

WE HEREBY CERTIFY This Invoice Is True and Correct and that the
merchandise described is origin of the United States of America.

Authorized Signature   Title

Appendix 2:
Websites

There are a multitude of information resources available on the Internet, and they seem to multiply each day. One of our goals for this book was to provide readers with options for updating the dynamic data online. The majority of our recommendations are for excellent government or government-related sites which are either free, or reasonably priced.

Dun & Bradstreet Corporation at http://www.dbisna.com. From individual entrepreneurs entering the global market for the first time, to major multinationals maneuvering to increase their market share—Dun & Bradstreet can provide the right data for your needs. One particular publication which has become an industry standard for U.S. exporters is Dun & Bradstreet *Exporters' Encyclopaedia*.

The International Academy at Santa Barbara at http://www.iasb.org/cwl. As you may have noticed, we culled information from one of the Academy's publications: *Current World Leaders* for this book. An excellent resource from an outstanding team. Tel: 1-800-530-2682 or (805) 965-5010 for subscription information.

The U.S. Department of State at http://www.stat-usa.gov is a comprehensive source of international trade information. It includes the National Trade Data Bank (available by subscription in CD-ROM also), access to market research reports, County Commercial Guides, Trade Opportunity Leads, the Export Yellow Pages, import and export statistics, and much more. There is a subscription fee.

U.S. Department of Commerce at http://www.ita.doc.gov is the Trade Information Center. They publish an Internet Resource Guide which lists more than 200 export-related Internet sites. Included are sources of export financing, country and industry specific information, federal export resources, and international law. Copies are also available by calling 1-800-872-8723.

The Bureau of Consular Affairs at http://travel.state.gov can give you detailed information on obtaining passports, visa requirements, and their consular affairs bulletins.

The Central Intelligence Agency at http://www.odci.gov/cia/publications/pubs.html is a great site to get the CIA's Publications and Handbook.

The U.S. Census Bureau at http://www.census.gov/ opens up a rich store of data from the U.S. Census Bureau . . . particularly the Foreign Trade Division information.

The Center for Disease Control at http://www.cdc.gov/ gets you valuable information on any outbreaks of virulent infections at your destination before you go. (Of course, always consult your physician for prophylactic precautions as well.)

The Library of Congress at http://www.loc.gov/ is the definitive repository of knowledge in Washington, D.C.

CompuServe has a variety of trade and culturally oriented databases and forums. Their web address is **www.compuserve.com**. Try **go Trade** to see their libraries, conferences, and message center on international trade; then hit **go GTC** to explore a smaller version of Getting Through Customs' database on business and social practices around the world.

Embassies and Consular Offices. Our first suggestion is to use a search engine, and enter the name of the country + embassy (i.e., Italy embassy). While some embassies are building their own websites, the search request may take you to www.embpage.org, or to www.embassy.org. Both are organizations that list various embassies, consulates, and related resources.

Like all websites, the preceding internet addresses are subject to change, and there is no guarantee that they will continue to provide the data we list here.

If you would like to contact us for updates on websites, we will be happy to try and "link" you in the right direction. Our website is **http://www.getcustoms.com**. It provides a variety of information, from current holidays, business and cultural data, to challenging and entertaining Cultural I.Q. Quizzes on topics from international greetings and gestures to great leaders and language tips in our global village.

Thanks—from all of us, to:

Our families and friends; next stop: the Villa in Spain!

Tom Power, a terrific editor who knows how to close, stays calm, and keeps us happy. We appreciate every step you took for us.

The late Dr. George Borden, co-author on our first book: *Kiss, Bow or Shake Hands: How to Do Business in Sixty Countries*. A dedicated teacher, Fulbright scholar, and communications theorist.

Jennifer Lickey, for being smart, patient, and intuitive. Your boss would quit if you did.

Joyce Haden, WebWizard. An efficient and effective player (albeit not by any of the rules <g>.)

Ron Rosenberry, for his expertise, support and friendship.

Hans H.B. Koehler, Director, Wharton Export Network. (215) 898-4189. . . The leader of legions of experts who personally guide firms through the global marketplace.

Renee Remington and Ellie Skehan of Dun & Bradstreet Information Services. Two people who deserve praise, but would probably settle for a real lunch break.

Bill Doescher, Senior Vice President, Corporate Communications, Dun & Bradstreet Corporation. For his vision and support on this project.

Bob Lee, whose sage counsel is always worth more than gold.

And, of course, Dun & Bradstreet Corporation, which today comprises three successful businesses with highly recognizable company names and outstanding reputations for quality, customer service, and a breadth of product offerings second to none. When combined, these three organizations—Dun & Bradstreet Information Services, Moody's Investors Service, and Reuben H. Donnelly—form a strong, independent public company that builds on Dun & Bradstreet's 155-year legacy of success. Today's D&B employs approximately 16,000 people in 40 countries and produces an estimated annual revenue of $2 billion.

For information on D&B's global capabilities, please contact the D&B International Solutions Center at 1-800-923-0025.

Final Note

The authors of this book wish to express their appreciation to Getting Through Customs of Newtown Square, Pennsylvania. Getting Through Customs is a software training and research firm for international business travelers. GTC produces the PASSPORT System, the leading online database of global business, religious, & social practices; cognitive styles & cultural overviews; medical & travel information; political data & contacts.

The authors augmented their own research and experience with Getting Through Customs' online PASSPORT database. A demo of the database is available on their website: **http://www.getcustoms.com**. The website also gives an overview of GTC Seminars in Intercultural Communications, and well as their *Spanish for the Business Traveler* Audiocassettes, and a previous highly regarded book by Morrison, Conaway and Borden called *Kiss, Bow or Shake Hands: How to Do Business In Sixty Countries* (which was serialized by American Airlines' inflight magazine, *American Way*).

CompuServe's version of the database is called Getting Through Customs. To access it, type Go GTC. For a free sign-up kit from CompuServe, call 1-800-848-8199 (or 614-529-1349) and ask for representative 730 for GTC, vendor code 3560.

The study of intercultural communications and trade represents a lifelong interest for the authors of *Dun & Bradstreet's Guide to Doing Business Around the World*. By way of continuing that research, the authors invite your comments. Whether your own experience confirms or diverges from the data in this book, they would like to hear from you. Your comments may be sent to the following.

email:	74774.1206@compuserve.com
tel:	(610) 353-9894 fax: (610) 353-6994
website:	http://www.getcustoms.com
	or

Dun & Bradstreet's Guide c/o Getting Through Customs
address: Box 136, Newtown Square, PA 19073

Audentis Fortuna Juvat
(Fortune favors the bold)
—Virgil

Index